INTRODUCTION

Welcome to the world of pressure cookers. Although you may have seen these devices before, you probably associate them with over-cooked vegetables and bland, tasteless food. Nothing could be further from the truth!

In fact, pressure cooking today is a combination of advanced technology and healthy, tasty food. Pressure cookers have become an essential part of the modern kitchen—in many cases replacing the ubiquitous microwave. In this book, you'll find 500+ great recipes to try at home. Don't be afraid to experiment—half the fun of this kind of cooking is adding new ingredients and tasting the results.

You'll see next to many of the recipes an icon:  . This means the recipe is vegetarian. Pressure cookers are great for preparing vegetarian food. In fact, in many ways they're the preferred method for this kind of cooking, since they allow you to use a wide variety of grains and beans, due to the shortened cooking times.

You'll also find a wide variety of pressure cooker recipes—everything from a healthy breakfast to start the day to mouth-watering desserts, including cakes, pies, and puddings.

Good luck. Have fun. And happy eating!

PART I

PRESSURE COOKERS 101

Pressure cookers cook food up to 70 percent faster than conventional methods. Steam trapped in the pot builds up pressure, which creates a hotter cooking temperature. The pressure bears down on the surface of the liquid, which isn't able to break down the molecules to create more steam; this produces more heat. The end result is that the pressure raises the boiling point. The tight seal on the cooker also helps seal in vitamins and minerals and prevents the cooker from boiling dry during the cooking process.

Today's improved pressure cookers usually feature a stationary pressure regulator that's either a fixed weight or a spring valve. The pressure regulator keeps the pressure even in the cooker by occasionally releasing a burst of steam. The pressure regulator also provides an easy way to quick-release the pressure at the end of the pressure cooking time; this is usually done by pressing a button or flipping a pressure-release switch.

New pressure cookers have backup pressure-release mechanisms that prevent the excess pressure accidents that were associated with older models. They also have safety features that cause the lid to remain locked into place until after all of the pressure has been released.

Equipment Considerations

Your cooking equipment can make a difference in how easy it is to prepare foods. Buy the best you can afford. Better pan construction equals more even heat distribution, which translates to reduced cooking time and more even cooking.

Food will burn more easily in an inexpensive pan with a thinner pan bottom. How well your cooking pan conducts the heat will make a difference in how high you set the burner temperature. With some practice, you'll soon learn the perfect heat settings for your pressure cooker: It might take a medium-high setting to sauté food in an inexpensive pressure cooker and a lot more stirring to prevent the food from burning, but you can accomplish the same task in a heavier pan when it's over medium heat, and with less frequent stirring.

On the flipside, a heavier pan will retain the heat longer once it's removed from the burner than will an inexpensive one, so to prevent it from overcooking, food cooked to perfection in a heavier pan must be moved to a serving dish more quickly. This is especially true of foods like gravy that tend to thicken the longer they sit; gravy can turn from a succulent liquid to one big lump if it stays on the heat too long.

Read the instruction manual that came with your pressure cooker. Never exceed the fill line for your pressure cooker; adjust the recipe or prepare it in two batches if you need to. Overfilling the pressure cooker can cause it to explode, so be careful!

Pressure Release Methods

The ways pressure is released from the pressure cooker are:

- The natural-release method, which refers to turning off the heat under the pressure cooker and either removing the pan from the heat or letting the pan remain on the burner, and then waiting until the pressure cooker has cooled sufficiently for all of the pressure to be released.
- The quick-release method, which refers to using the valve on the pressure cooker to release the pressure.
- The cold-water release method, which occurs when the pan is carried to the sink and cold water from the tap is run over the lid of the pressure cooker (but not over the valve!) until the pressure is released.

Explanation of Cooking Methods

Cooking terms that you'll encounter in this book are:

- Bain-marie, or water bath, is a method used to make custards and steamed dishes by surrounding the cooking vessel with water; this helps maintain a more even cooking temperature around the food.
- Baking involves putting the food in a preheated oven; the food cooks by being surrounded by the hot, dry air of your oven. In the pressure cooker, foods that are traditionally baked (like a cheesecake, for example) are baked in a covered container that's placed on a rack submerged in water. The water in the bottom of the pressure cooker creates the steam that builds the pressure and maintains the heat inside the pressure cooker. The cover over the pan holding the food maintains the dry environment inside.
- Braising usually starts by browning a less expensive cut of meat in a pan on top of the stove and then covering the meat with a small amount of liquid, adding a lid or covering to the pan, and slowly cooking it. Braising can take place on the stovetop, in the oven, or in a slow cooker or pressure cooker. The slow-cooking process tenderizes the meat. The cooking environment in the pressure cooker greatly reduces the braising time needed. For example, a roast that would normally take two and a half to three hours in the oven or on the stove only requires forty-five to sixty minutes in the pressure cooker.

- Deglazing refers to the process of ridding a pan of any excess remaining fat by putting it over a medium-high heat and then adding enough cooking liquid to let you scrape up any browned bits stuck to the bottom of the pan. Doing this step before you add the other ingredients for your sauce or gravy gives the end result more flavor and color.
- Poaching is accomplished by gently simmering ingredients in broth, juice, water, wine, or other flavorful liquids until they're cooked through and tender.
- Roasting, like baking, is usually done in the oven, but generally at a higher oven temperature. Roasting meat in the moist environment inside a pressure cooker requires some trial and error because you can't rely on a programmable meat thermometer to tell you when the meat has reached the desired internal temperature. The upside is that the meat will roast much quicker when browned and then placed on the rack in a pressure cooker, and, even if it's cooked beyond your preferred preference, the meat will still be more moist than it would be if you had cooked it to that point in the dry environment of an oven.
- Sautéing is the method of quickly cooking small or thin pieces of food in some oil or butter that has been brought to temperature in a sauté pan (or in the pressure cooker) over medium to medium-high heat.
- Steaming is the cooking method that uses the steam from the cooking liquid to cook the food.
- Stewing, like braising, involves slowly cooking the food in a liquid; however, stewing involves a larger liquid-to-food ratio. In other words, you use far more liquid when you're stewing food. Not surprisingly, this method is most often used to make stew.
- Stir-frying is a cooking process similar to sautéing that's used to cook larger, bite-sized pieces of meat or vegetables in oil.
- Tempering is the act of gradually increasing the temperature of one cooking ingredient by adding small amounts of a hotter ingredient to the first. For example, tempering beaten eggs by whisking small amounts of hot liquid into them before you add the eggs to the cooking pan lets them be mixed into the dish; tempering prevents them from scrambling instead.

Pressure Cooker Tips and Troubleshooting Pointers

There will be a learning curve with each pressure cooker that you use. You also need to keep in mind that the same pressure cooker will behave differently on different stovetops. For example, electric burners usually retain heat longer than do gas burners; therefore, if you need to reduce the pressure when cooking over an electric burner, after you adjust the burner setting, you may need to lift the cooker off of the heat.

Also, pressure cookers are like any other pan in your kitchen: There's less chance that foods will burn or stick to the bottom of better pans with thicker pan bottoms. If burning is a problem with your pressure cooker, you can try one of these solutions:

- Add more liquid the next time you make that recipe.
- Begin to heat or bring liquids to a boil before you lock on the lid.
- Bring the cooker up to pressure over a lower heat.
- Use a heat diffuser.

If liquid or foam is released from the vent, remove the pressure cooker from the heat and wait until the pressure is released naturally. This problem can occur when the pressure cooker is filled beyond capacity; in this case, remove some of the ingredients before proceeding. Another possibility is that you're cooking a food that foams. Adding additional oil and cleaning the area around the pressure regulator should alleviate the problem.

There will be times when the pressure cooker will come to pressure almost immediately and other times when it can take twenty minutes or more to do so. Keep in mind that it can delay the time it takes the cooker to reach the desired pressure when you are cooking a much higher ratio of food to liquid or if the food was very cold when you began the cooking process.

After you've worked with your pressure cooker, you'll come to recognize the signs that the cooker is about to reach pressure by the sounds it makes. (The cooker will usually release some steam before the pressure gasket finally settles into place.) If the pressure cooker fails to come to pressure, chances are:

- The gasket isn't allowing for a tight seal. Coating the gasket in vegetable oil will sometimes help solve this problem. If it doesn't, you'll need to replace the gasket.
- The lid isn't properly locked into place.
- Something is clogging the pressure regulator. You'll need to use the quick release method so you can remove the lid and then follow the manufacturer's direction for cleaning the gasket before you can proceed.
- There isn't sufficient liquid in the cooker. If you believe this to be the case, you'll need to test the pressure by using the quick-release method so that you can remove the lid, then add more liquid, lock the lid back into place, and try again.
- You have too much food in the pressure cooker. You'll need to remove some of the food and try again.

Tips for Using This Cookbook

Don't be afraid to experiment a little with the recipes in this cookbook. Swap your favorite ingredients for those you're not too fond of. Adjust cooking times and measurements to suit your preferences. Keep in mind that the browning and sautéing times given in the recipes are suggestions. Once you become familiar with your pressure cooker's quirks, you'll be able to gauge the correct burner temperature and the amount of time you will need to sauté or brown foods on your own.

As you get more comfortable with your pressure cooker, you can try adapting conventional recipes to use with the pressure cooker. Just remember to add the nonliquid ingredients first. For example, for a stew you'd add the meat and vegetables first and only add as much of the liquid called for in the recipe to cover the food and bring the liquid level up to the fill line. You can stir in more liquid later. Choose your cooking time based on what's required to cook the meat.

PART II
START THE DAY

CHAPTER 1

BREAKFAST

RECIPE LIST

APPLE STREUSEL OATMEAL **16**

BANANA NUT BREAD OATMEAL **16**

IRISH OATMEAL WITH FRUIT **17**

MAPLE-PECAN OATMEAL **18**

BREAKFAST BURRITO **19**

BREAKFAST CASSEROLE **20**

GRITS **20**

RED PEPPER GRITS **21**

HASH BROWNS **21**

HASH BROWNS WITH SMOKED SAUSAGE AND APPLES **22**

POBLANO HASH BROWNS **22**

APPLE STREUSEL OATMEAL

Get creative and turn any of your favorite desserts into a breakfast oatmeal.

INGREDIENTS

Serves 2

¾ cup water

1 cup milk or soymilk

1 cup quick-cooking oats

2 apples, peeled, cored, and diced

2 tablespoons brown sugar

2 teaspoons cinnamon

2 tablespoons chopped pecans

1. Place all of the ingredients in the pressure cooker.

2. Lock the lid into place. Bring to high pressure and maintain for 5 minutes. Remove from the heat and allow pressure to release naturally.

3. Remove the lid and stir the oatmeal, adding more milk if desired.

BANANA NUT BREAD OATMEAL

Skip instant oatmeal packets, which can be high in sugar, for a homemade version instead.

INGREDIENTS

Serves 2

¾ cup water

1 cup milk or soymilk

1 cup quick-cooking oats

2 bananas, sliced

2 tablespoons brown sugar

2 teaspoons cinnamon

2 tablespoons chopped walnuts

1. Place all of the ingredients in the pressure cooker.

2. Lock the lid into place. Bring to high pressure and maintain for 5 minutes. Remove from the heat and allow pressure to release naturally.

3. Remove the lid and stir the oatmeal, adding more milk if desired.

IRISH OATMEAL WITH FRUIT 🌿

You can substitute other dried fruit according to your tastes. Try prunes, dates, and cherries for different flavors.

INGREDIENTS

Serves 2

3 cups water

1 cup toasted steel-cut oats

2 teaspoons butter, or vegan margarine, such as Earth Balance

1 cup apple juice

1 tablespoon dried cranberries

1 tablespoon golden raisins

1 tablespoon snipped dried apricots

1 tablespoon maple syrup

¼ teaspoon ground cinnamon

Pinch salt

1. Place the rack in the pressure cooker; pour ½ cup water over the rack.

2. In a metal bowl that will fit inside the pressure cooker and rest on the rack, add the 2½ cups water, oats, butter, apple juice, cranberries, raisins, apricots, maple syrup, cinnamon, and salt; stir to combine.

3. Lock the lid into place. Bring to low pressure. For chewy oatmeal, maintain the pressure for 5 minutes. For creamy oatmeal, maintain pressure for 8 minutes.

4. Remove from the heat and allow pressure to release naturally. Use tongs to lift the metal bowl out of the pressure cooker.

Cooking Ahead

If you're not a morning person, you can make Irish Oatmeal with Fruit the night before. Once it's cooled, divide between two covered microwave-safe containers and refrigerate overnight. The next morning, cover each bowl with a paper towel to catch any splatters and then microwave on high for 1–2 minutes or until heated through.

MAPLE-PECAN OATMEAL

Rolled oats or quick-cooking oats will work in this recipe. Just be sure to adjust the cooking time accordingly.

INGREDIENTS

Serves 2

¾ cup water

1 cup milk or soymilk

1 cup quick-cooking oats

2 tablespoons maple syrup

2 tablespoons chopped pecans

1. Place all of the ingredients in the pressure cooker.

2. Lock the lid into place. Bring to high pressure and maintain for 5 minutes. Remove from the heat and allow pressure to release naturally.

3. Remove the lid and stir the oatmeal, adding more milk if desired.

Syrup Substitutions

Maple syrup can be expensive. If you don't have any in your cupboards, use plain pancake syrup instead. Agave nectar is another type of sweetener that will also work in this recipe.

BREAKFAST BURRITO 🌱

To make this burrito vegetarian instead of vegan, use cooked eggs instead of tofu.

INGREDIENTS
Serves 4

2 tablespoons olive oil

16 ounces firm tofu, drained and diced

¼ cup red onion, diced

½ cup tomato, diced

¼ cup cilantro, chopped

¼ cup water

1 teaspoon salt

4 large flour tortillas

1 cup cooked black beans, warmed

1 avocado, peeled and sliced

Optional: Sour cream or soy sour cream

Optional: Shredded Cheddar cheese, or vegan Cheddar, such as Daiya Cheddar Style Shreds

1. Heat the olive oil in the pressure cooker over medium-high heat. Add the tofu, stir until well coated, and sauté until it begins to brown, about 5 minutes. Add the onion, tomato, cilantro, water, and salt.

2. Lock the lid into place. Bring to high pressure and maintain for 6 minutes. Remove from the heat and quick-release the pressure.

3. Steam or microwave the tortillas until softened, then lay one tortilla on a flat surface to build the burrito. Place one fourth of the tofu mixture, one fourth of the drained beans, and ¼ of the avocado slices in a line in the center of the tortilla.

4. Roll your burrito by first folding the sides of the tortilla over the filling. Then, while still holding the sides closed, fold the bottom of the tortilla over the filling. Next, roll the burrito from the bottom up, while still holding the sides closed and pushing the filling down into the burrito if it tries to spill out. Repeat for remaining burritos.

5. Top with sour cream and/or cheese, if desired.

Steaming Tortillas

For best results, steam tortillas on the stovetop using a steamer basket. If you're in a hurry, throw the tortillas into the microwave one at a time and heat for about 30 seconds.

BREAKFAST CASSEROLE

Yes, even casseroles can be made in a pressure cooker!

INGREDIENTS
Serves 4

2 tablespoons vegetable oil

1 onion, diced

½ green bell pepper, chopped

1 8-ounce package Morningstar Farm Sausage Style Crumbles, or Gimme Lean Sausage

3 cups potatoes, peeled and shredded

6 eggs, beaten, or 16 ounces firm crumbled tofu

1 cup cottage cheese, or omit

2 cups Cheddar cheese, or 2 cups vegan Cheddar, such as Daiya Cheddar Style Shreds

Salt and pepper, to taste

1. Add the vegetable oil to the pressure cooker and sauté the onion and bell pepper until tender. Add the crumbles and cook for 2–3 minutes more. Add the rest of the ingredients to the pressure cooker.

2. Lock the lid into place; bring to high pressure and maintain for 5 minutes. Remove from the heat and allow pressure to release naturally.

GRITS

Slowly adding grits to boiling water, while gently stirring, will help prevent clumping.

INGREDIENTS
Serves 4

4 cups water

1 teaspoon salt

½ teaspoon black pepper

1 cup stone-ground grits

1 tablespoon butter, or vegan margarine, such as Earth Balance

1. Bring the water, salt, and pepper to a boil in the pressure cooker over high heat. Slowly stir in the grits.

2. Lock the lid into place. Bring to high pressure and maintain for 10 minutes. Remove from the heat and allow pressure to release naturally.

3. Remove the lid and stir in butter before serving.

Grits
Grits are a southern breakfast staple that are served topped with butter or margarine, salt, pepper, and sometimes cheese. It's very similar to polenta, especially when polenta is served creamy.

RED PEPPER GRITS 🌿

Cooking grits in vegetable stock instead of water adds more depth to the flavor and makes them more appropriate for dinner or lunch.

INGREDIENTS
Serves 4

4 cups vegetable stock

1 teaspoon salt

¼ teaspoon dried thyme

1 cup stone-ground grits

½ tablespoon dried red pepper flakes

1. Bring the stock, salt, and thyme to a boil in the pressure cooker over high heat. Slowly stir in the grits.

2. Lock the lid into place. Bring to high pressure and maintain for 10 minutes. Remove from the heat and allow pressure to release naturally.

3. Remove the lid and stir in the red pepper flakes before serving.

HASH BROWNS 🌿

Let Waffle House inspire you to serve these hash browns any way you'd like—scattered, covered, or smothered.

INGREDIENTS
Serves 4

4 cups russet potatoes, peeled and grated

2 tablespoons olive oil

2 tablespoons butter, or vegan margarine, such as Earth Balance

Salt and freshly ground pepper, to taste

1. Prepare the potatoes and set aside.

2. Add the oil and butter to the pressure cooker and bring to temperature over medium heat.

3. Add the hash brown potatoes; sauté for 5 minutes, stirring occasionally, until they are just beginning to brown. Season with the salt and pepper.

4. Use a wide metal spatula to press the potatoes down firmly in the pan.

5. Lock the lid in place and bring to low pressure; maintain pressure for 6 minutes. Remove from the heat and quick-release the pressure.

HASH BROWNS WITH SMOKED SAUSAGE AND APPLES

To make your own hash browns, peel and grate 1 pound baking potatoes, squeeze out any excess water with a potato ricer, and fry the potatoes in oil until they're golden brown. This dish is good topped with a fried or poached egg.

INGREDIENTS
Serves 4

2 tablespoons olive oil

2 tablespoons butter

1 12-ounce bag frozen hash brown potatoes

Salt and freshly ground pepper, to taste

6 ounces cooked smoked sausage, coarsely chopped

2 medium apples, such as Golden Delicious, cut into thin slices

Optional: 1 teaspoon cinnamon

Optional: 1–2 tablespoons toasted walnuts, chopped

Optional: 1–2 tablespoons maple syrup

1. Add the oil and butter to the pressure cooker and bring to temperature over medium heat.

2. Add the hash brown potatoes; sauté for 5 minutes, stirring occasionally, until they are thawed and just beginning to brown. Season with the salt and pepper.

3. Use a wide metal spatula to press the potatoes down firmly in the pan. Add the sausage and apple over the top of the potatoes.

4. Sprinkle the cinnamon over the apples, top with the toasted walnuts, and drizzle with the maple syrup if using.

5. Lock the lid in place and bring to low pressure; maintain pressure for 6 minutes. Remove from the heat and quick-release the pressure. Serve.

POBLANO HASH BROWNS

Any type of pepper will do, such as poblano, jalapeño, or bell pepper, in these spicy hash browns.

INGREDIENTS
Serves 4

4 cups russet potatoes, peeled and grated

2 tablespoons olive oil

2 tablespoons butter, or vegan margarine, such as Earth Balance

¼ cup onion, diced

1 poblano pepper, cored and diced

1 clove garlic, minced

Salt and freshly ground pepper, to taste

1 teaspoon cumin

1. Prepare the grated potatoes by rinsing in a colander, then air drying or using a towel to remove excess water.

2. Add the oil and butter to the pressure cooker and bring to temperature over medium heat. Add the onion and poblano pepper and sauté until just soft, about 5 minutes.

3. Add the garlic and hash brown potatoes; sauté for an additional 5 minutes, stirring occasionally, until they are just beginning to brown. Season with the salt, pepper, and cumin.

4. Use a wide metal spatula to press the potatoes down firmly in the pan.

5. Lock the lid in place and bring to low pressure; maintain pressure for 6 minutes. Remove from the heat and quick-release the pressure.

CHAPTER 2

BRUNCH

RECIPE LIST

COUNTRY HAM WITH RED-EYE GRAVY

Red-eye gravy is akin to au jus (a dipping sauce) rather than a traditional thickened gravy. Serve with biscuits.

INGREDIENTS
Serves 4

1 tablespoon lard or vegetable oil

4 4-ounce slices country ham

¾ cup coffee

1 teaspoon sugar

1. Heat the lard or oil in a pressure cooker. Add ham and fry on both sides for 2 minutes. Add coffee. Lock the lid into place, bring to low pressure, and maintain for 8 minutes.

2. Remove from heat and quick-release the pressure. Remove ham to a serving platter. Add the sugar to the pan and stir until it dissolves, scraping the bottom of the pan as you do so. Pour over the ham and serve immediately.

Cajun-Style Red-Eye Gravy
Following the directions for the Country Ham with Red-Eye Gravy recipe, substitute a pound of cooked roast beef for the country ham. When you add the coffee, add cayenne pepper or hot sauce, to taste. Serve over cooked rice and butter beans or peas.

COUNTRY SAUSAGE GRAVY

This type of gravy is referred to as sawmill gravy in some parts of the country and as milk gravy in others. Serve it over buttermilk biscuits and hash browns with eggs.

INGREDIENTS
Serves 8

2 pounds ground pork sausage

2 tablespoons butter

¼ cup all-purpose flour

2 cups half-and-half

Salt and freshly ground black pepper, to taste

1. Add the sausage to the pressure cooker. Breaking it apart as you do so, fry over medium-high heat for 5 minutes or until the sausage begins to brown.

2. Lock the lid into place and bring to low pressure; maintain for 8 minutes. Remove from the heat and quick-release the pressure. Drain and discard most of the fat.

3. Return the pressure cooker to medium-high heat. Add the butter and stir into the sausage until it's melted.

4. Sprinkle the flour over the meat and stir-fry into the meat for a minute, stirring continuously. Whisk in half-and-half a little at a time.

5. Bring to a boil and immediately reduce the heat; maintain a simmer for 3 minutes or until the gravy thickens. Taste for seasoning and add salt and pepper.

GARDEN TOFU SCRAMBLE 🌱

Go gourmet with this tofu scramble by substituting shiitake mushrooms and Japanese eggplant instead of the broccoli and button mushrooms.

INGREDIENTS
Serves 2–4

16 ounces firm tofu, drained and mashed

1 teaspoon fresh lemon juice

1 teaspoon salt

½ teaspoon black pepper

½ teaspoon turmeric

1 tablespoon olive oil

½ cup broccoli florets, blanched

½ cup button mushrooms, sliced

½ cup tomato, diced

1 clove garlic, minced

¼ cup water

2 tablespoons parsley, chopped

1. In a large bowl, mash the tofu with your hands or a fork, then stir in the lemon juice, salt, pepper, and turmeric.

2. Bring the olive oil to medium heat in the pressure cooker. Add the broccoli and mushrooms and sauté for 5 minutes. Add the tomato and garlic, and sauté for an additional 30 seconds.

3. Pour in the tofu mixture and water, stir, then lock the lid into place. Bring to medium pressure and maintain for 6 minutes. Remove from the heat and allow pressure to release naturally.

4. Remove the lid and stir in the parsley before serving.

HOME FRIES

Like hash browns, home fries can also be served with a variety of toppings or plain with a side of ketchup.

INGREDIENTS
Serves 4

2 tablespoons olive oil

4 cups red potatoes, diced

1½ teaspoons paprika

1 teaspoon chili powder

1½ teaspoons salt

1 teaspoon black pepper

1. Bring the olive oil to medium heat in the pressure cooker. Add the potatoes and sauté for about 3 minutes.

2. Add all remaining ingredients and stir. Lock the lid in place and bring to high pressure; maintain pressure for 7 minutes. Remove from the heat and quick-release the pressure.

SAUSAGE AND CHEESE SCRAMBLE

Serve with toasted whole grain bread or biscuits spread with some honey-butter. Experiment with different types of cheese to find your favorite.

INGREDIENTS
Serves 8

1 tablespoon olive oil or vegetable oil

1 large sweet onion, diced

1 green bell pepper, seeded and diced

1 red bell pepper, seeded and diced

1 yellow or orange bell pepper, seeded and diced

1 pound ground sausage

1 1-pound bag frozen hash browns, thawed

8 large eggs

¼ cup water or heavy cream

Optional: A few drops hot sauce

Salt and freshly ground pepper, to taste

½ pound Cheddar cheese, grated

1. Add the oil to the pressure cooker and bring it to temperature over medium-high heat.

2. Add the onion and diced bell peppers; sauté until the onion is transparent, about 5 minutes. Stir in the sausage and hash browns.

3. Bring to low pressure; maintain for 10 minutes. Remove from the heat and quick-release the pressure. Remove the lid. Drain and discard any excess fat.

4. Return the pan to medium heat. Whisk together the eggs, water or heavy cream, hot sauce (if using), and salt and pepper.

5. Pour the eggs over the sausage-potato mixture. Stir to combine and scramble the eggs until they begin to set.

6. Add the cheese and continue to scramble until the eggs finish cooking and the cheese melts.

7. If you prefer, instead of stirring the cheese into the mixture, you can top it with the cheese, then cover the pressure cooker and continue to cook for 1–2 minutes or until the cheese is melted. Serve immediately.

SAUSAGE BRUNCH GRAVY

This gravy substitutes aromatic vegetables for some of the sausage. Serve it over rice or buttermilk biscuits and hash browns with eggs.

INGREDIENTS
Serves 8

1 pound ground pork sausage

1 small sweet onion, peeled and diced

1 green bell pepper, seeded and diced

1 red bell pepper, seeded and diced

2 tablespoons butter

¼ cup all-purpose flour

2 cups half-and-half

Salt and freshly ground black pepper, to taste

1. Add the sausage, onion, and diced bell peppers to the pressure cooker. Fry over medium-high heat and break sausage apart for 5 minutes or until it begins to brown.

2. Lock the lid into place and bring to low pressure; maintain for 10 minutes. Remove from the heat and quick-release the pressure. Remove the lid. Drain and discard any excess fat.

3. Return the pressure cooker to medium-high heat. Add the butter and stir into the sausage mixture until it's melted.

4. Add the flour and stir-fry it into the meat for 1 minute, stirring continuously. Whisk in the half-and-half a little at a time.

5. Bring to a boil and then immediately reduce the heat; maintain a simmer for 3 minutes or until the gravy thickens. Taste for seasoning and add salt and pepper if needed.

SPICY TOFU SCRAMBLE

Serve this spicy scramble on its own, or rolled up in a flour tortilla to make a delicious breakfast burrito.

INGREDIENTS

Serves 2–4

16 ounces firm tofu, drained and mashed

1 teaspoon fresh lemon juice

1 teaspoon salt

½ teaspoon black pepper

½ teaspoon turmeric

1 tablespoon olive oil

¼ cup onion, diced

¼ cup red bell pepper, diced

¼ cup tomato

1 clove garlic, minced

1 teaspoon cumin

½ teaspoon chipotle powder

½ teaspoon chili powder

¼ cup water

2 tablespoons cilantro, chopped

1. In a large bowl, mash the tofu with your hands or a fork, then stir in the lemon juice, salt, pepper, and turmeric.

2. Bring the olive oil to medium heat in the pressure cooker. Add the onion and bell pepper and sauté for 3 minutes. Add the tomato, garlic, cumin, chipotle powder, and chili powder and sauté for an additional 30 seconds.

3. Pour in the tofu mixture and water, stir, then lock the lid into place. Bring to medium pressure and maintain for 6 minutes. Remove from the heat and allow pressure to release naturally.

4. Remove the lid and stir in the cilantro before serving.

SPINACH AND PORTOBELLO BENEDICT

If making this recipe vegan, read the label before purchasing your English muffins. Some brands are not vegan.

INGREDIENTS
Serves 2

½ cup silken tofu

1 tablespoon lemon juice

1 teaspoon Dijon mustard

⅛ teaspoon cayenne pepper

⅛ teaspoon turmeric

1 tablespoon vegetable oil

Salt, to taste

1 tablespoon olive oil

4 small portobello mushroom caps

2 cups fresh spinach

2 English muffins, toasted

1. Add the silken tofu to a food processor and purée until smooth. Add the lemon juice, mustard, cayenne, and turmeric. Blend until well combined. With the food processor still running, slowly add the vegetable oil and blend until combined. Season with salt, to taste, to complete the vegan hollandaise.

2. Pour the hollandaise into a small saucepan over low heat and cook until the sauce is warm. Keep warm until ready to serve.

3. Heat the olive oil in the pressure cooker over low heat. Add the mushroom caps and spinach and stir until coated with the oil.

4. Lock the lid into place. Bring to medium pressure and maintain for 3 minutes. Remove from the heat and quick-release the pressure.

5. Place two open-faced English muffins on each plate and top each half with one portobello cap and sautéd spinach. Drizzle with a spoonful of the warm vegan hollandaise to finish.

THREE-PEPPER VEGAN FRITTATA

Frittatas are traditionally made with eggs, but you can use tofu for a cholesterol-free breakfast dish instead.

INGREDIENTS
Serves 4

2 tablespoons olive oil

1 cup red potatoes, peeled and diced

½ cup onion, diced

½ cup red bell pepper, diced

½ cup green bell pepper, diced

1 teaspoon jalapeño, minced

1 clove garlic, minced

¼ cup chopped parsley

16 ounces firm tofu

½ cup unsweetened soymilk

4 teaspoons cornstarch

2 teaspoons nutritional yeast

1 teaspoon mustard

½ teaspoon turmeric

1 teaspoon salt

1. Preheat the oven to 400°F.

2. Bring the olive oil to medium heat in the pressure cooker. Add the potatoes, onion, peppers, garlic, and parsley, and sauté for 3 minutes. Lock the lid in place and bring to high pressure; maintain pressure for 6 minutes. Remove from the heat and quick-release the pressure.

3. Combine the tofu, soymilk, cornstarch, nutritional yeast, mustard, turmeric, and salt in a blender or food processor until smooth, then pour the tofu mixture into the cooked potato mixture.

4. Spoon the mixture into an oiled quiche or pie pan. Bake for 45 minutes, or until the frittata is firm, then remove from heat and let stand before serving.

Make It a Scramble

To shorten the preparation time for this meal while keeping all of the flavors, try making this dish into a scramble by preparing the entire recipe in the pressure cooker. Skip the step of blending the tofu and omit the cornstarch.

TOFU RANCHERO

Bring Mexican cuisine to the breakfast table with an easy tofu ranchero.

INGREDIENTS
Serves 4

16 ounces firm tofu, drained and mashed

1 teaspoon fresh lemon juice

1 teaspoon salt

½ teaspoon black pepper

½ teaspoon turmeric

2 tablespoons olive oil

¼ cup onion, diced

1 clove garlic, minced

8 corn tortillas

1 cup vegetarian refried beans, warmed

½ cup cheese or vegan cheese

½ cup chipotle salsa

1. Preheat the oven to 350°F. In a large bowl, mash the tofu with your hands or a fork, then stir in the lemon juice, salt, pepper, and turmeric.

2. Bring 1 tablespoon olive oil to medium heat in the pressure cooker. Add the onion and sauté for 3 minutes. Add the garlic and sauté for an additional 30 seconds.

3. Pour in the tofu mixture and stir, then lock the lid into place. Bring to medium pressure and maintain for 6 minutes. Remove from the heat and allow pressure to release naturally.

4. Heat 1 tablespoon olive oil in a small sauté pan over medium heat. Cook the tortillas one at a time, until they begin to brown on each side.

5. Place all eight of the tortillas on one or two baking sheets. Divide the refried beans evenly among the tortillas, then top with the cooked tofu mixture. Sprinkle cheese over each of the tortillas, then bake until the cheese begins to melt.

6. Remove from the oven and top with salsa before serving.

Choosing Salsa

Salsa comes in many delicious and unique varieties. Most are clearly labeled mild, medium, and hot, but one's interpretation of those words can vary greatly. Chipotle salsa has a deep, earthy spice, but you can also use plain tomato salsa or tomatillo salsa in this recipe.

YEASTY TOFU AND VEGGIES ✧

Nutritional yeast has a cheesy flavor and should not be replaced with other types of yeast.

INGREDIENTS
Serves 4

1 16-ounce package extra-firm tofu

2 tablespoons vegetable oil

2 tablespoons soy sauce

1 cup water

½ onion, diced

1 cup broccoli, blanched and chopped

½ green bell pepper, chopped

½ zucchini, chopped

½ cup yellow squash, chopped

¼ cup nutritional yeast

1. Wrap the block of tofu in paper towels and press for 5 minutes by adding weight on top. Remove the paper towels and cut the tofu into ½"-thick pieces. Add 1 tablespoon of oil to the pressure cooker and sauté the tofu until it is light brown on all sides. Add 1 tablespoon of soy sauce and sauté for 10 seconds more. Remove the tofu.

2. Place the water in the pressure cooker along with the steamer tray. Place the tofu on top of the steamer tray. Lock the lid into place; bring to high pressure and maintain for 5 minutes. Remove from the heat and allow pressure to release naturally.

3. Add 1 tablespoon of oil to a large pan and sauté the onion, broccoli, bell pepper, zucchini, and squash until tender. Add the tofu and 1 tablespoon soy sauce and sauté for 1 minute more. Sprinkle the nutritional yeast on top and serve.

PART III
LUNCH

CHAPTER 3

APPETIZERS AND SNACKS

ASPARAGUS WITH YOGURT CRÈME

The steaming liquid will contain delicious asparagus juice. Reserve the liquid to use in another recipe!

INGREDIENTS
Serves 4

2 cups plain whole yogurt

1 cup water

1 pound asparagus, trimmed

1¼ teaspoons salt

1. Make the yogurt crème by putting the yogurt in a fine mesh strainer over a bowl and putting it in the refrigerator for about 4 hours or until it has reached the consistency of sour cream.

2. Place water in the pressure cooker and add the steamer basket.

3. Lay asparagus flat in steamer basket. If it does not fit in one layer, make a second layer perpendicular to the first. Sprinkle with salt. Close and lock the lid.

4. Turn the heat up to high and when the cooker reaches pressure, lower to the minimum needed to maintain pressure. Cook for 2–3 minutes at high pressure.

5. When time is up, open the pressure cooker by releasing pressure.

6. Serve with yogurt crème.

Yogurt Crème Versus Sour Cream
A crème made of whole, plain yogurt contains about 75 percent less fat than sour cream but is equally tangy and refreshing.

BABA GANNOUJ

Serve with toasted pita chips or as a vegetable dip.

INGREDIENTS
Yields 1½ cups

1 tablespoon olive or sesame oil

1 large eggplant

4 cloves garlic, peeled and minced

½ cup water

3 tablespoons fresh parsley

½ teaspoon salt

2 tablespoons fresh lemon juice

2 tablespoons tahini

1 tablespoon extra-virgin olive oil

1. Add the olive or sesame oil to the pressure cooker and bring to temperature over medium heat. Peel and dice the eggplant and add it to the pressure cooker. Sauté the eggplant in the oil until it begins to get soft. Add the garlic and sauté for 30 seconds. Add the water.

2. Lock on the lid. Bring to high pressure; maintain pressure for 4 minutes. Remove the pan from the heat, quick-release the pressure, and remove the lid.

3. Strain the cooked eggplant and garlic and add to a food processor or blender along with the parsley, salt, lemon juice, and tahini. Pulse to process. Scrape down the side of the food processor or blender container if necessary. Add the extra-virgin olive oil and process until smooth.

BAKED POTATO SKINS

Steaming and then baking the potato skins, instead of frying, gives you a healthier version of this popular appetizer. Use the excess potato for a side of mashed potatoes.

INGREDIENTS
Serves 6

6 Idaho potatoes

2 cups water

1 tablespoon vegetable oil

8 ounces shredded Cheddar cheese, or vegan Cheddar, such as Daiya Cheddar Style Shreds

⅛ cup soy bacon bits, such as Bac-Os

4 tablespoons thinly sliced scallions

¼ cup sour cream, or soy sour cream

1. Preheat the oven to 400°F.

2. Wash the potatoes, then slice each in half lengthwise. Pour water into the pressure cooker. Add the steamer basket and arrange the potatoes in one or two layers.

3. Lock the lid into place. Bring to high pressure; maintain pressure for 10 minutes. Quick-release the pressure, then remove the lid.

4. Remove the potatoes from the pressure cooker and scoop out the inside, leaving a ¼"-thick shell.

5. Brush the scooped-out shell of each potato with oil and arrange on an ungreased baking sheet.

6. Cook the potato skins for 15 minutes, or until the edges begin to brown, then remove from the oven.

7. Fill the potato skins with the cheese and bake for an additional 5 to 10 minutes, or until the cheese has melted.

8. Top each skin with soy bacon bits, sliced scallions, and a dollop of sour cream.

BLACK BEAN DIP

To give this dip a little kick, you can substitute canned jalapeño peppers for the mild green chilies or add 2 teaspoons of chipotle powder.

INGREDIENTS
Serves 12

1 cup dried black beans

2 cups water

1 tablespoon olive oil

1 small onion, peeled and diced

3 cloves garlic, peeled and minced

1 14½-ounce can diced tomatoes

2 4-ounce cans mild green chilies, finely chopped

1 teaspoon chili powder

½ teaspoon dried oregano

¼ cup fresh cilantro, finely chopped

Salt, to taste

1 cup Monterey jack cheese, grated, or vegan Monterey jack cheese, such as Follow Your Heart Monterey Jack Cheese Alternative

1. Add the beans and water to a container; cover and let the beans soak 8 hours at room temperature.

2. Add the oil and the onions to the pressure cooker; sauté for 3 minutes or until the onion is soft. Add the garlic and sauté for 30 seconds.

3. Drain the beans and add them to the pressure cooker along with the tomatoes, chilies, chili powder, and oregano. Stir well. Lock the lid into place. Bring to high pressure; maintain pressure for 12 minutes. Remove from heat and allow pressure to release naturally for 10 minutes.

4. Quick-release any remaining pressure. Remove the lid. Transfer the cooked beans mixture to a food processor or blender. Add the cilantro and process until smooth. Taste for seasoning; add salt if desired.

5. Transfer the dip to a bowl. Stir in the cheese. Serve warm.

Other Bean Options

Bean dips are delicious when made with a variety of dried beans. To complement the flavors in this recipe, use black beans, pinto beans, or white beans. If you're pressed for time, use canned beans instead of dried beans, but be sure to drain the liquid first.

TEXAS CAVIAR

Prepare this dip up to two days in advance and store in a covered container in the refrigerator.

INGREDIENTS
Yields 5 cups

1 cup dried black-eyed peas

8 cups water

1 pound cooked corn kernels

½ onion, diced

½ bell pepper, diced

1 pickled jalapeño, finely chopped

1 medium tomato, diced

2 tablespoons fresh cilantro

¼ cup red wine vinegar

2 tablespoons olive oil

1 teaspoon salt

½ teaspoon ground black pepper

½ teaspoon ground cumin

1. Rinse and soak the black-eyed peas in 4 cups of water for 1 hour. Drain and rinse.

2. Add the black-eyed peas and remaining 4 cups of water to the pressure cooker. Lock the lid into place; bring to high pressure and maintain for 11 minutes. Remove from the heat and allow pressure to release naturally.

3. Pour the drained black-eyed peas into a large mixing bowl; add all remaining ingredients and stir until combined.

4. Refrigerate 1–2 hours before serving.

CIPOLLINE AGRODOLCE
(SWEET AND SOUR PEARL ONIONS) 🌱

You can also make this recipe with regular onions that have been quartered, but they will not keep their shape as well as pearl or pearl baby.

INGREDIENTS
Serves 6

1 pound Cipolline (pearl onions), outer layer removed

½ cup water

⅛ teaspoon salt

1 bay leaf

4 tablespoons balsamic vinegar

1 tablespoon honey

1 tablespoon flour

1. Put the onions in the pressure cooker with water, salt, and the bay leaf. Close and lock the lid.

2. Turn the heat up to high and when the cooker reaches pressure, lower to the minimum needed to maintain pressure. Cook for 5–6 minutes at low pressure (3 minutes at high pressure).

3. While the onions are cooking, combine the vinegar, honey, and flour in a small saucepan. Stir over low heat until well combined (about 30 seconds).

4. When time is up, open the pressure cooker by releasing pressure.

5. Pour the balsamic vinegar mixture over the onions and mix well. Remove bay leaf.

6. Transfer to serving dish and serve, or let sit overnight in refrigerator prior to serving.

Impostors!
Pearl onions are actually closer relatives to leeks than to onions.

CHICKPEA-PARSLEY-DILL DIP 🌿

Try any combination of fresh herbs, such as basil, thyme, or mint, in this versatile dip.

INGREDIENTS
Yields 2 cups

1 cup dried chickpeas

8 cups water

3 tablespoons olive oil

2 cloves garlic, minced

⅛ cup fresh parsley

⅛ cup fresh dill

1 tablespoon fresh lemon juice

2 tablespoons water

¾ teaspoon salt

1. Add the chickpeas and 4 cups water to the pressure cooker. Lock the lid into place; bring to high pressure for 1 minute. Remove from the heat and quick-release the pressure.

2. Drain the water, rinse the chickpeas, and add to the pressure cooker again with the remaining 4 cups of water. Let soak for 1 hour.

3. Add 1 tablespoon olive oil. Lock the lid into place; bring to high pressure and maintain for 20 minutes. Remove from the heat and allow pressure to release naturally. Drain chickpeas and water.

4. Add the drained, cooked chickpeas, garlic, parsley, dill, lemon juice, and water to a food processor or blender. Blend for about 30 seconds.

5. With the lid still in place, slowly add the remaining oil while still blending, then add the salt.

JALAPEÑO CHEESE DIP

To eliminate the spice, just leave the pickled jalapeños out of this recipe.

INGREDIENTS
Serves 12

2 tablespoons butter, or vegan margarine

2 tablespoons flour

1 cup milk, or unsweetened vegan soymilk

8 ounces shredded Cheddar cheese, or vegan Cheddar such as Daiya Chedder Style Shreds

8 ounces shredded Colby cheese, or more vegan Cheddar

½ cup canned tomatoes

½ cup pickled jalapeños

2 tablespoons lemon juice

Salt and pepper, to taste

1. In the pressure cooker, soften butter over medium-high heat and gradually add flour until you have a paste. Add milk and stir until it has thickened and there are no lumps. Bring the mixture to a boil.

2. Add the cheeses and stir until smooth. Add the tomatoes and jalapeños and secure the lid on the pressure cooker. Cook on medium until the pressure-indicator rises. Lower heat and cook for 3 minutes.

3. Allow the pressure to release and remove the lid. Add the lemon juice, salt, and pepper.

Vegan Cheese
Vegan cheese is made from a variety of plant-based ingredients. Some of the most popular ingredients are soy, nuts, oils, and tapioca flour.

SOUTH OF THE BORDER CHICKEN DIP

You can adjust the heat of this dip depending on what type of salsa or chili powder you use. Alternatively, to add more heat you can add some crushed red pepper flakes and use jalapeño-jack cheese.

INGREDIENTS
Serves 24

3 slices bacon, diced

2 tablespoons olive oil

1 medium white onion, peeled and diced

3 cloves garlic, peeled and minced

½ cup fresh cilantro, minced

⅓ cup salsa

¼ cup ketchup

½ cup chicken broth

1 teaspoon chili powder

1 pound chicken breast tenders, finely diced

Optional: 1 tablespoon all-purpose flour

1 cup 4 ounces Monterey jack cheese, grated

½ cup sour cream

Salt and freshly ground black pepper, to taste

1. Add the bacon and oil to the pressure cooker; bring to temperature and add the onion, garlic, and cilantro. Sauté for 3 minutes or until the onion is soft. Stir in the salsa, ketchup, broth, chili powder, and diced chicken. Lock the lid into place and bring to low pressure; maintain pressure for 6 minutes.

2. Remove the lid and simmer over medium heat to thicken the sauce. If needed, whisk the flour into the dip, bring to a boil, and then simmer for 2 minutes or until the flour taste is cooked out. Lower the heat and add the cheese, stirring constantly until it is melted into the dip. Fold in the sour cream. Taste for seasoning and add salt and pepper if desired. Serve warm with baked corn or flour tortilla chips.

TACO CHIPS DIP

Spoon Taco Chips Dip over shredded iceberg lettuce. Top with grated Monterey jack cheese, guacamole, and sour cream. Serve with baked tortilla chips.

INGREDIENTS
Serves 16

1 cup dried kidney beans

2 cups water

¼ cup olive oil

1 large onion, peeled and diced

1 pound ground beef or turkey

2 cloves garlic, peeled and minced

1 8-ounce can tomato sauce

1 cup beef broth

1 tablespoon light brown sugar

2 teaspoons chili powder

1 teaspoon ground cumin

Optional: Dried red pepper flakes, to taste

Salt, to taste

1. Put the beans and water in a covered container and let soak at room temperature overnight. When ready to prepare the dip, drain the beans.

2. Bring the olive oil to temperature in the pressure cooker. Add the onion and sauté for 3 minutes or until softened. Add the ground beef or turkey; stir and break apart until the meat is no longer pink. Drain off any fat rendered from the meat. Add the garlic and stir into the meat.

3. Add the beans, tomato sauce, broth, brown sugar, chili powder, cumin, and red pepper flakes if using. Stir well.

4. Lock the lid into place and bring to high pressure; maintain pressure for 10 minutes. Remove from the heat and allow pressure to release naturally for 10 minutes. Quick-release any remaining pressure and remove the lid. Stir the dip, crushing the beans into the mixture. For a smooth dip, use an immersion blender or transfer the dip to a food processor or blender and process. Taste for seasoning and add salt if needed. Serve warm.

Sodium-Free Version
You can eliminate the salt entirely from this dish if you substitute Mrs. Dash Southwest Chipotle or Tomato Basil Garlic seasoning blend for some of the chili powder and the dried red pepper flakes. Use Mrs. Dash Extra Spicy seasoning blend if you prefer a hot, spicy dip.

WARM SPINACH-ARTICHOKE DIP

Serve with toasted pita points or slices of warm baguette.

INGREDIENTS
Yields 4 cups

1 medium-sized artichoke

2 cups water

1 teaspoon lemon juice

1 tablespoon butter, or vegan margarine, such as Earth Balance

1 cup frozen spinach, thawed, chopped

8 ounces cream cheese, softened, or soy cream cheese

16 ounces sour cream, or soy sour cream

⅓ cup grated Parmesan, or vegan Parmesan

¼ teaspoon garlic powder

¼ teaspoon salt

1. Trim the sharp points off the artichoke and cut off the end of the stem.

2. Put the metal rack in the bottom of the pressure cooker. Add water and lemon juice.

3. Lock the lid into place; bring to high pressure and maintain for 6 to 8 minutes. Remove from the heat and allow pressure to release naturally.

4. Remove the artichoke and coarsely chop.

5. In a large saucepan over medium heat, melt the butter, then add the spinach and chopped artichoke hearts.

6. Add all remaining ingredients, stir, and let cook for 5 minutes. Serve warm.

Serving Options

This recipe calls for serving the dip warm, but chilling the dip and serving cool is also delicious. After cooking, let the dip cool to room temperature, then store in the refrigerator in an airtight container. Let cool for at least 3 hours before serving.

HUMMUS

Hummus can come in a wide variety of flavors. Add roasted red peppers, roasted garlic, or sun-dried tomatoes to spice up this basic recipe.

INGREDIENTS
Yields 2 cups

1 cup dried chickpeas

8 cups water

¼ cup plus 1 tablespoon olive oil

2 teaspoons cumin

¾ teaspoon pepper

¾ teaspoon salt

⅓ cup lemon juice

1 teaspoon garlic

⅓ cup tahini

1. Add the chickpeas and 4 cups water to the pressure cooker. Lock the lid into place; bring to high pressure for 1 minute. Remove from the heat and quick-release the pressure.

2. Drain the water, rinse the beans, and add to the pressure cooker again with the remaining 4 cups water. Let soak for 1 hour.

3. Add 1 tablespoon olive oil. Lock the lid into place; bring to high pressure and maintain for 20 minutes. Remove from heat and allow pressure to release naturally. Drain beans and water.

4. Place all the ingredients, including the drained and cooked chickpeas, in a food processor and blend until mixture has achieved a creamy texture. Serve chilled or at room temperature.

LEMON AND ROSEMARY CANNELLINI CREAM

You can use either Italian cannellini or navy beans for this recipe.

INGREDIENTS
Serves 6

2 tablespoons vegetable oil

1 scallion, chopped

1½ cups dried cannellini beans, rinsed

3 cups water

Juice and zest of 1 lemon

½ teaspoon white pepper

1 sprig rosemary, finely chopped, and 1 whole rosemary sprig

1 tablespoon extra-virgin olive oil

1. In the preheated pressure cooker add the oil and scallion and sauté until softened.

2. Add the beans and water. Close and lock the lid.

3. Turn the heat up to high and when the cooker reaches pressure, lower to the minimum needed to maintain pressure. Cook 25–30 minutes at high pressure.

4. Open with the natural-release method—move the pressure cooker to a cool burner and wait for the pressure to come down on its own (about 15 minutes). For electric pressure cookers, disengage the "keep warm" mode or unplug and open when the pressure indicator has gone down (20–30 minutes).

5. Drain the beans, let them cool, and pour them into a food processor. Add lemon juice, zest, pepper, rosemary, and olive oil. Purée until smooth.

6. Pour into serving dish and garnish with fresh rosemary sprig.

MINI CABBAGE ROLLS

You can improve the flavor of these cabbage rolls by adding diced roasted red pepper instead of raw red bell pepper.

INGREDIENTS
Yields 30 rolls

1 medium head Savoy cabbage

3 cups water, divided

1 pound lean ground beef

1 cup long-grain rice

1 red bell pepper, seeded and minced

1 medium onion, peeled and diced

1 cup vegetable stock

1 tablespoon extra-virgin olive oil

2 tablespoons minced fresh mint

1 teaspoon dried tarragon

1 teaspoon salt

½ teaspoon freshly ground black pepper

2 tablespoons lemon juice

1. Wash the cabbage. Remove the large, outer leaves and set aside. Remove the remaining cabbage leaves and place them in the pressure cooker. Pour in 1 cup water and lock on the lid. Bring to low pressure; maintain the pressure for 1 minute. Quick-release the pressure. Drain the cabbage leaves in a colander and then move them to a cotton towel.

2. In a mixing bowl add the ground beef, rice, bell pepper, onion, stock, oil, mint, tarragon, salt, and pepper to a bowl. Stir to combine.

3. Place the reserved (uncooked) cabbage leaves on the bottom of the pressure cooker to keep the rolls from getting scorched.

4. Remove the stem running down the center of each steamed cabbage leaf and tear each leaf in half lengthwise. Place 1 tablespoon of the ground beef mixture in the center of each cabbage piece. Loosely fold the sides of the leaf over the filling and then fold the top and bottom of the leaf over the folded sides. As you complete them, place each stuffed cabbage leaf in the pressure cooker.

5. Pour 2 cups water and the lemon juice over the stuffed cabbage rolls. Close and lock the lid.

6. Turn the heat up to high and when the cooker reaches pressure, lower to the minimum needed to maintain pressure. Cook 15–20 minutes at high pressure.

7. Open with the natural-release method—move the pressure cooker to a cool burner and wait for the pressure to come down on its own (about 15 minutes). For electric pressure cookers, disengage the "keep warm" mode or unplug and open when the pressure indicator has gone down (20–30 minutes).

8. Carefully move the stuffed cabbage rolls to a serving platter, piercing each one with a toothpick.

ROASTED GARLIC SPREAD

Garlic is known for being pungent, but a lesser-known quality is that it may be able to help prevent heart disease and cancer.

INGREDIENTS

Yields ½ cup

2 whole heads garlic

1 cup water

½ cup butter, softened, or vegan margarine such as Earth Balance

2 tablespoons fresh basil

2 tablespoons fresh oregano

½ teaspoon salt

1. Cut the tops off of each head of garlic.

2. Pour water into the pressure cooker, then add the steamer basket. Add the garlic.

3. Lock the lid into place; bring to high pressure and maintain for 2 minutes. Remove from the heat and allow pressure to quick-release.

4. Once the garlic has cooled, peel away the paper until you are left with only the cloves.

5. In a small bowl, mash the cloves then add the butter, basil, oregano, and salt. Refrigerate for 1 hour before serving.

SAVORY CHEESECAKE

For this dish, you'll need a pressure cooker that's large enough to accommodate a 7-inch springform pan placed on a trivet or rack. (For 8 main dish servings, serve this savory cheesecake with a green salad, crusty bread, and fresh fruit.)

INGREDIENTS
Serves 16

2 teaspoons unsalted butter, melted

¼ cup toasted walnuts, finely chopped

3 8-ounce packages cream cheese

3 large eggs

2 teaspoons fresh lemon juice

1 teaspoon sage

⅛ teaspoon freshly ground white pepper

1 cup Gorgonzola cheese, crumbled

2 cups hot water

1. Coat the bottom and sides of a 7-inch springform pan with melted butter. Place a 16" × 16" piece of plastic wrap on top of an equal-sized piece of aluminum foil. Put the springform pan in the center of the plastic wrap–topped foil; form and crimp the foil around the springform pan to seal the bottom of the pan.

2. Pour the walnuts into the pan; turn the pan so that the walnuts cling to the butter and coat the bottom and sides of the pan.

3. Cut the cream cheese into 1-inch squares and add to a food processor; process until smooth. Add the eggs, lemon juice, sage, and pepper. Process for 1 minute, scrape down the bowl, and then process until smooth. Add the Gorgonzola cheese and pulse to mix the cheese into the cream-cheese mixture. Pour the mixture into the springform pan.

4. Place a trivet or rack on the bottom of the pressure cooker. Pour in the hot water. Crisscross two 24" × 2" strips of foil on the counter and place the springform pan in the center. Cover the cheesecake mixture with a piece of foil treated with nonstick spray; lightly crimp this foil topper to keep in place over the pan. Bring the ends of the foil strips up over the springform pan; hold onto the strips and use them to lower the pan into the pressure cooker until it rests on the rack or trivet.

5. Lock on the lid and bring to high pressure; maintain the pressure for 16 minutes. Remove from the heat and allow pressure to release naturally. Remove the lid and lift the cheesecake from the pan. Remove the foil cover from the springform pan. Carefully use a piece of paper towel to sop up any moisture that may have accumulated on top of the cheesecake. Let the cheesecake cool to room temperature, then refrigerate overnight. To serve, remove the cheesecake from the springform pan, cut into pieces, and allow to come to room temperature.

STEAMED ARTICHOKES

Although primarily cultivated in Europe in the countries around the Mediterranean, artichokes are widely available in the United States.

INGREDIENTS

Serves 6

6 artichokes

1 cup water

Juice of 1 lemon

1. Clean the artichokes by cutting off the top one-third and removing the tough exterior leaves.

2. Place artichokes upright in the steamer basket.

3. Fill the pressure cooker base with water and lemon juice, and then lower the steamer basket into the cooker. Close and lock the lid.

4. The cooking time will depend on the size of the artichokes. A large globe artichoke that almost fills the pressure cooker could take 10 minutes, while medium artichokes only need about 5.

5. Turn the heat up to high and when the cooker reaches pressure, lower to the minimum needed to maintain pressure. Cook for 5–10 minutes at high pressure.

6. When time is up, open the pressure cooker by releasing pressure.

7. Lift very carefully out of the pressure cooker (artichokes will be so tender they may fall apart) and serve.

Artichoke Stems Are Edible!

If you are lucky enough to buy fresh artichokes with the stems attached, be sure to use them in this recipe. You can cut them off so the artichokes will stand straight. Peel off the exterior with a potato peeler. Slice the stems into 2-inch pieces and boil them in the water below, while the artichokes steam above. They are as delicious as the artichoke heart!

STEAMED SPRING ROLLS

Serve with Spicy Peanut Sauce (Chapter 15) or a sweet and sour dipping sauce.

INGREDIENTS
Serves 12

1 cup cabbage, shredded

1 cup bamboo shoots, sliced

¼ cup cilantro, chopped

2 cloves garlic, minced

5 shiitake mushrooms, sliced

2 carrots, grated

1 teaspoon soy sauce

1 teaspoon rice wine vinegar

12 spring roll wrappers

2 cups water

1. Combine the cabbage, bamboo shoots, cilantro, garlic, mushrooms, carrots, soy sauce, and rice wine vinegar in a medium bowl. Stir until just combined.

2. Place the spring roll wrappers on a flat surface.

3. Top each wrapper with an equal amount of the cabbage mixture, making a row down the center. Roll up the wrappers, tuck in the ends, and place side by side in the pressure cooker steamer basket.

4. Add water to the pressure cooker and lower in the steamer basket.

5. Lock the lid into place. Bring to high pressure; maintain pressure for 3 minutes. Quick-release the pressure, then remove the lid.

STEAMY CARROT COINS

Carrots can really showcase the vitamin and flavor-saving capabilities of pressure cookers. Taste them un-dressed, or try them with any of the sauces or dips in this chapter!

INGREDIENTS
Serves 6

1 pound thick carrots, peeled and sliced into ¼-inch thick coins

1 cup water

1. Fill the pressure cooker base with water. Fill the steamer basket with carrot coins and lower the basket into the cooker. Close and lock the lid.

2. Turn the heat up to high and when the cooker reaches pressure, lower to the minimum needed to maintain pressure. Cook 3–4 minutes at low pressure (1–2 minutes at high pressure).

3. When time is up, open the pressure cooker by releasing pressure.

4. Pour into serving dish immediately to stop the cooking.

STUFFED GRAPE LEAVES

A medium (about 5-ounce) lemon will yield about 2 teaspoons of lemon zest and 2–3 tablespoons of juice.

INGREDIENTS
Serves 16

⅓ cup olive oil

4 scallions, minced

⅓ cup fresh mint, minced

⅓ cup fresh parsley, minced

3 cloves garlic, peeled and minced

1 cup long-grain white rice

2 cups vegetable broth

1 teaspoon salt

¼ teaspoon freshly ground black pepper

½ teaspoon lemon zest, grated

1 16-ounce jar grape leaves

2 cups water

½ cup fresh lemon juice

1. Bring the oil to temperature in the pressure cooker over medium-high heat. Add the scallions, mint, and parsley; sauté for 2 minutes or until the scallions are soft. Add the garlic and sauté for an additional 30 seconds. Add the rice and stir-fry in the sautéed vegetables and herbs for 1 minute. Add the broth, salt, pepper, and lemon zest; stir to mix. Lock the lid into place. Bring to high pressure; maintain pressure for 8 minutes.

2. Quick-release the pressure. Remove lid and transfer the rice mixture to a bowl.

3. Drain the grape leaves. Rinse them thoroughly in warm water and then arrange them rib-side up on a work surface. Trim away any thick ribs. Spoon about 2 teaspoons of the rice mixture on each grape leaf; fold the sides of each leaf over the filling and then roll it from the bottom to the top. Repeat with each leaf. Pour the water into the pressure cooker. Place a steamer basket in the pressure cooker and arrange the stuffed grape leaves seam-side down in the basket. Pour the lemon juice over the stuffed grape leaves and then press heavy plastic wrap down around them.

4. Lock the lid into place. Bring to high pressure; maintain pressure for 10 minutes.

5. Quick-release the pressure. Remove the lid. Lift the steamer basket out of the pressure cooker and, leaving the plastic in place, let the stuffed grape leaves rest for 5 minutes. Serve hot or cold.

SWEET AND SOUR "MEATBALLS"

Worcestershire sauce typically contains anchovies, but some grocery store brands omit this ingredient, making it vegetarian.

INGREDIENTS
Yields 12 "meatballs"

½ cup white sugar

2 tablespoons pineapple juice

⅓ cup white vinegar

⅔ cup water

2 tablespoons soy sauce

2 tablespoons vegetarian Worcestershire sauce

1 tablespoon ketchup

2 tablespoons cornstarch

1 pound vegetarian ground beef, such as Gimme Lean Beef

½ onion, diced

1 clove garlic, minced

½ cup panko bread crumbs

1. In the pressure cooker, bring the sugar, pineapple juice, vinegar, water, soy sauce, Worcestershire sauce, ketchup, and cornstarch to a boil over high heat. Stir continuously until the mixture has thickened, then remove from heat.

2. In a large mixing bowl, combine the vegetarian ground beef, onion, garlic, and bread crumbs, and mix until well combined. (Using your hands is the easiest method.)

3. Roll the "beef" mixture into 12 meatballs; add them to the sauce in the pressure cooker.

4. Lock the lid into place. Bring to high pressure; maintain pressure for 5 minutes. Quick-release the pressure, then remove the lid. Serve warm.

Panko Bread Crumbs

Panko is a type of bread crumb made from white bread without crusts. It typically creates a crispier texture when used as the coating on food than regular bread crumbs. To make your own, bake crustless white bread crumbs until they are dry, but not browned.

BOILED PEANUTS

Use "green" raw peanuts, not cooked or dried nuts.

INGREDIENTS
Serves 16

2 pounds raw peanuts

12 cups water

⅓ cup salt

1. Rinse the peanuts under cold water then place in the pressure cooker. Add the water and salt.

2. Lock the lid in place; bring to 10 pounds of pressure, or a medium setting, and cook for 45 minutes. Remove from the heat and allow pressure to release naturally.

3. Let the peanuts cool in the water, then drain.

Cajun Peanuts

Add a little flavor to plain boiled peanuts by adding Cajun seasoning to the water when boiling. Try a preblended seasoning or make your own by combining red pepper, black pepper, cayenne pepper, garlic powder, and salt.

TOMATILLO SALSA

Serve with corn tortilla chips or as an accompaniment to Black Bean Dip (see recipe in this chapter).

INGREDIENTS
Serves 8

1 pound tomatillos, paper removed

Water, as needed

2 jalapeños, stemmed, seeded, and chopped

½ onion, chopped

½ cup cold water

½ cup chopped cilantro

2 teaspoons salt

1. Cut the tomatillos in half and then place in the pressure cooker. Add enough water to cover the tomatillos.

2. Lock the lid into place; bring to high pressure and maintain for 2 minutes. Remove from the heat and allow pressure to release naturally.

3. Add the drained, cooked tomatillos, jalapeños, onion, and cold water to a food processor or blender. Blend until well combined.

4. Add the cilantro and salt and pulse until combined.

5. Chill the salsa before serving.

CHAPTER 4

SOUPS

BEEF STOCK

The resulting concentrated broth can be kept for 1 or 2 days in the refrigerator or frozen for up to 3 months. This stock is rather concentrated, so combine one part stock with one part water or to taste.

INGREDIENTS
Serves 12

1 tablespoon vegetable oil

1½ pounds bone-in chuck roast

1 pound cracked or sliced beef bones

1 large onion, quartered

2 large carrots, peeled and cut in two

2 stalks celery, cut in two

4 cups water, or to cover

1. In an uncovered pressure cooker heat the oil over high heat. Brown the meat and bones on all sides. Reduce heat to medium and add the onion, carrots, celery, and enough water to cover all ingredients. Close and lock the lid.

2. Turn the heat up to high and when the cooker reaches pressure, lower the heat to the minimum needed to maintain pressure. Cook for 60–90 minutes at high pressure.

3. Open with the natural-release method—move the pressure cooker to a cool burner and wait for the pressure to come down on its own (about 15 minutes). For electric pressure cookers, disengage the "keep warm" mode or unplug the cooker and open when the pressure indicator has gone down (20–30 minutes).

4. Strain or use a slotted spoon to remove the roast and beef bones. Reserve the roast and the meat removed from the bones for another use; discard the bones.

5. Cool and refrigerate the broth overnight. Remove and discard the hardened fat.

BEEF-VEGETABLE SOUP

Make Beef-Vegetable Soup a tomato-based dish by substituting 2 (15-ounce) cans of diced tomatoes for the beef broth.

INGREDIENTS
Serves 8

7 large carrots

2 stalks celery, finely diced

1 large sweet onion, peeled and diced

8 ounces fresh mushrooms, cleaned and sliced

1 tablespoon extra-virgin olive oil

1 teaspoon butter, melted

1 clove garlic, peeled and minced

4 cups beef broth

6 medium potatoes, peeled and diced

1 tablespoon dried parsley

¼ teaspoon dried oregano

¼ teaspoon dried rosemary

1 bay leaf

Salt and freshly ground black pepper, to taste

1 3-pound chuck roast

1 10-ounce package frozen green beans, thawed

1 10-ounce package frozen whole kernel corn, thawed

1 10-ounce package frozen baby peas, thawed

1. Peel the carrots. Dice 6 of the carrots and grate 1. Add the grated carrot, celery, onion, mushrooms, oil, and butter to the pressure cooker. Stir to coat the vegetables in the oil and butter. Lock the lid into place. Bring to low pressure; maintain pressure for 1 minute. Quick-release the pressure and remove the lid.

2. Stir in the garlic. Add the broth, diced carrots, potatoes, dried parsley, oregano, rosemary, bay leaf, salt, and pepper. Trim the roast of any fat and cut the meat into bite-sized pieces; add to the pressure cooker and stir in the vegetables. Lock the lid into place and bring to high pressure; maintain pressure for 15 minutes. Quick-release the pressure and remove the lid.

3. Remove and discard the bay leaf. Stir in the green beans, corn, and peas; cook for 5 minutes or until the vegetables are heated through. Taste for seasoning and add additional salt, pepper, and herbs if needed.

Tasty Substitutions

Add a bit more flavor to this soup by substituting several strips of bacon cut into bite-sized pieces for the oil. The bacon bits themselves will be absorbed into the dish and provide extra crunch and zing. Another alternative is using canned French onion soup in place of some of the beef broth.

BORSCHT

If fresh tomatoes are available, you can substitute about a pound of diced vine-ripened tomatoes for the canned tomatoes.

INGREDIENTS
Serves 6–8

1½ tablespoons olive oil or ghee

1 clove garlic, peeled and minced

½ pound lamb, cut into ½-inch pieces

1 small yellow onion, peeled and diced

1 pound red beets

1 small head cabbage, cored and chopped

1 15-ounce can diced tomatoes

7 cups beef broth

¼ cup red wine vinegar

2 bay leaves

1 tablespoon lemon juice

Beet greens

Salt and freshly ground black pepper, to taste

Sour cream

Optional: Fresh dill

1. Add the oil or ghee, garlic, and lamb to pressure cooker. Brown the lamb over medium heat, stirring frequently to keep the garlic from burning. Add the onion and sauté until transparent.

2. Peel and dice the beets. Save the beet greens; rinse well and cover them with cold water until needed.

3. Add the beets, cabbage, tomatoes, beef broth, vinegar, bay leaves, and lemon juice to the pressure cooker.

4. Lock the lid into place and bring to low pressure; maintain pressure for 10 minutes. Remove from the heat and quick-release the pressure.

5. Chop the reserved beet greens and stir into the other ingredients in the pressure cooker.

6. Lock the lid into place, return the pan to the heat, and bring to low pressure; maintain pressure for 5 minutes.

7. Remove from heat and allow pressure to release naturally. Taste for seasoning and add salt and pepper to taste.

8. Ladle soup into bowls and garnish each bowl with a heaping tablespoon of sour cream and some fresh dill if using.

Vegetarian Borscht
Omit the lamb and substitute water or vegetable broth for the beef broth. Decrease the first pressure-cooking time to 5 minutes. If desired, add freshly grated orange or lemon zest to taste when you stir in the beet greens.

CHICKEN NOODLE SOUP

One taste of this dish and you'll never want to eat chicken noodle soup out of a can again!

INGREDIENTS
Serves 8–10

1 tablespoon butter

1 tablespoon olive or vegetable oil

6 medium carrots, peeled and sliced

3 stalks celery, diced

1 large sweet onion, peeled and diced

4 pounds bone-in chicken thighs and breasts

½ teaspoon sea or kosher salt

1 teaspoon dried parsley

¼ teaspoon dried thyme

2 cups chicken broth

4 cups water

2 cups medium egg noodles

1 cup frozen baby peas, thawed

Freshly ground black pepper, to taste

1. Melt the butter and bring to temperature with the oil in the pressure cooker over medium heat. Add the carrots and celery; sauté for 2 minutes. Add the onion; sauté for 3 minutes or until the onion is soft. Add the chicken, salt, parsley, thyme, and chicken broth. Lock the lid into place and bring to low temperature; maintain pressure for 20 minutes. Remove from the heat and quick-release the pressure. Remove the lid.

2. Use tongs or a slotted spoon to transfer the chicken pieces to a cutting board. Remove and discard the skin. Once the chicken is cool enough to handle, remove the meat from the bones; shred the meat or cut it into bite-sized pieces. Return the chicken to the pressure cooker.

3. Return the pressure cooker to medium heat. Stir in the water; bring to a boil. Add the egg noodles and cook according to package directions. Stir in the thawed peas. Taste for seasoning and add additional salt if needed, and pepper, to taste.

Homemade Egg Noodle Taste

For richer chicken noodle soup with that homemade egg noodle taste, beat 1 or 2 large eggs in a small bowl. Whisk in some of the chicken broth from the soup (to temper the eggs), and then stir the egg mixture into the soup about 2 minutes before the noodles are cooked through.

CHICKEN STOCK

You can use the carcass of a previously roasted chicken for this recipe, too! Now, you have concentrated chicken stock that you can use as-is, or add water for a milder flavor. Keep in the fridge for up to three days or freeze portioned in plastic containers for up to three months.

INGREDIENTS
Yields 8 cups

1 tablespoon olive oil

2 pounds bone-in chicken pieces

1 bunch fresh parsley

2 carrots, peeled and cut in half

1 yellow onion, quartered

3 celery stalks, cut in half

1 bunch fresh thyme

1 tablespoon sea salt

6 cups water

1. Preheat the pressure cooker on low heat for 2–3 minutes, then add olive oil. When that begins to shimmer, add the chicken pieces. Turn the heat to medium and brown all of the pieces well, turning frequently (about 7–10 minutes). Then add the parsley, carrots, onion, celery, thyme, and salt.

2. Pour in just enough water to cover the vegetables. Close and lock the pressure cooker lid.

3. Turn the heat up to high and when the cooker reaches pressure, lower the heat to the minimum needed to maintain pressure. Cook for 20–25 minutes at high pressure.

4. Open with the natural-release method—move the pressure cooker to a cool burner and wait for the pressure to come down on its own (about 15 minutes). For electric pressure cookers, disengage the "keep warm" mode or unplug the cooker and open when the pressure indicator has gone down (20–30 minutes).

5. Pour stock through strainer into a large mixing bowl. Let the ingredients cool enough for you to pick through them and pull out any remaining chicken and vegetables. Set this aside to use with the broth as a chicken soup or as a filling for other recipes.

6. Let the liquid cool for about an hour before covering with plastic wrap. Refrigerate overnight.

7. The next day, take the stock out of the refrigerator and spoon off the fat that has gathered at the top. If it has not solidified (it can depend on how much fat was on the pieces of chicken you used for the stock), you can remove the top layer by dropping a paper towel over the top and removing it as soon as it has begun to absorb. You may need to do this several times to fully remove the top layer and clarify the stock.

CHICKEN-VEGETABLE SOUP

Transform Chicken-Vegetable Soup into a tomato-based meal by substituting 2 15-ounce cans of diced tomatoes for the chicken broth.

INGREDIENTS
Serves 8

7 large carrots

2 stalks celery, finely diced

1 large sweet onion, peeled and diced

8 ounces fresh mushrooms, cleaned and sliced

1 tablespoon extra-virgin olive oil

1 teaspoon butter, melted

1 clove garlic, peeled and minced

4 cups chicken broth

6 medium potatoes, peeled and diced

1 tablespoon dried parsley

¼ teaspoon dried oregano

¼ teaspoon dried rosemary

1 bay leaf

2 strips orange zest

Salt and freshly ground black pepper, to taste

8 chicken thighs, skin removed

1 10-ounce package frozen green beans, thawed

1 10-ounce package frozen whole kernel corn, thawed

1 10-ounce package frozen baby peas, thawed

1. Peel the carrots. Dice 6 of the carrots and grate 1. Add the grated carrot, celery, onion, mushrooms, oil, and butter to the pressure cooker. Stir to coat the vegetables in the oil and butter. Lock the lid into place. Bring to low pressure; maintain pressure for 1 minute. Quick-release the pressure and remove the lid.

2. Stir in the garlic. Add the broth, diced carrots, potatoes, dried parsley, oregano, rosemary, bay leaf, orange zest, salt, pepper, and chicken thighs. Lock the lid into place and bring to high pressure. Remove from the heat and allow pressure to release naturally for 5 minutes. Quick-release any remaining pressure and remove the lid.

3. Use a slotted spoon to remove the thighs, cut the meat from the bone and into bite-sized pieces, and return it to the pot. Remove and discard the orange zest and bay leaf. Return the uncovered pressure cooker to medium heat. Stir in the green beans, corn, and peas; cook for 5 minutes or until the vegetables are heated through. Taste for seasoning and add additional salt, pepper, and herbs if needed.

Pot Pie–Style Servings

This soup is also delicious if you use a roux to thicken the broth and serve it pot pie–style: ladled over split buttermilk biscuits. You can buy biscuits in the freezer aisle, but they only take about half an hour to make if you want to fix them from scratch.

CORN CHOWDER

For an extra kick, drain and dice 2 4-ounce cans of green chilies and add them to the chowder.

INGREDIENTS

Serves 6

2 tablespoons butter, or vegan margarine, such as Earth Balance

4 large leeks

4 cups vegetable stock

2 cups water

6 medium russet or Idaho baking potatoes, peeled and diced

1 bay leaf

Salt and freshly ground black pepper, to taste

1½ cups fresh or frozen corn

½ teaspoon dried thyme

Pinch sugar

½ cup heavy cream, or unsweetened soymilk

1. Melt the butter in the pressure cooker over medium heat. Cut off the root end of the leeks and discard any bruised outer leaves. Slice the leeks. Add to the pressure cooker and sauté for 2 minutes. Stir in the stock, water, and potatoes. Add the bay leaf, salt, and pepper.

2. Lock the lid into place and bring to high pressure; maintain pressure for 4 minutes. Quick-release the pressure and remove the lid. Remove and discard the bay leaf.

3. Stir in the corn, thyme, sugar, and cream. Bring to temperature, stirring occasionally.

MANHATTAN CLAM CHOWDER

The clams and their liquid will be salty, so wait until the chowder is cooked to add any salt. Serve with oyster crackers, dinner rolls, or toasted garlic bread.

INGREDIENTS
Serves 6

4 6½-ounce cans minced clams

4 slices bacon

2 stalks celery, finely diced

4 large carrots, peeled and finely diced

1 large sweet onion, peeled and diced

1 pound red potatoes, peeled and diced

1 28-ounce can diced tomatoes

2 cups tomato or V-8 juice

1 teaspoon dried parsley

¼ teaspoon dried thyme

⅛ teaspoon dried oregano

½ teaspoon freshly ground black pepper

Sea salt, to taste

1. Drain the clams. Reserve the liquid to add along with the other liquid. Set the clams aside.

2. Dice the bacon and add to the pressure cooker. Fry over medium-high heat until the bacon is crisp enough to crumble.

3. Add the celery and carrots; sauté for 3 minutes. Add the onion; sauté for 3 minutes or until the onion is soft.

4. Stir in the potatoes; stir-fry briefly in the bacon fat and vegetable mixture to coat the potatoes in the fat.

5. Stir in the clam liquid, undrained tomatoes, tomato or V-8 juice, parsley, thyme, oregano, and pepper.

6. Lock the lid into place and bring to high pressure; maintain pressure for 5 minutes. Lower the heat to warm and allow pressure to drop naturally for 10 minutes. Quick-release any remaining pressure and remove the lid.

7. Stir in the reserved clams. Bring to a simmer (but do not boil); simmer for 5 minutes or until the clams are heated through. Taste for seasoning and add salt if needed.

NEW ENGLAND CLAM CHOWDER

The clams and their liquid will be salty, so wait until the chowder is cooked to add any salt. Serve with oyster crackers or toasted, buttered sourdough bread.

INGREDIENTS
Serves 4

4 6½-ounce cans chopped clams

4 slices bacon

1 stalk celery, finely diced

2 large shallots, peeled and minced

1 pound red potatoes, peeled and diced

2½ cups unsalted chicken or vegetable broth

Optional: 1 tablespoon fresh thyme, chopped

1 cup frozen corn, thawed

2 cups milk

1 cup heavy cream

Sea salt and freshly ground black pepper, to taste

1. Drain the clams. Reserve the liquid to add along with the broth. Set the clams aside.

2. Dice the bacon and add to the pressure cooker. Fry over medium-high heat until the bacon is crisp enough to crumble. Add the celery; sauté for 3 minutes.

3. Add the shallots; sauté for 3 minutes. Stir in the potatoes; stir-fry briefly in the bacon fat and vegetable mixture to coat the potatoes in the fat. Stir in the clam liquid, broth, and thyme if using.

4. Lock the lid into place and bring to high pressure; maintain pressure for 5 minutes. Lower the heat to warm and allow pressure to drop naturally for 10 minutes. Quick-release any remaining pressure and remove the lid.

5. Stir in the corn, milk, cream, and reserved clams. Bring to a simmer (but do not boil); simmer for 5 minutes or until everything is heated through. Taste for seasoning and add salt and pepper if needed.

SALMON CHOWDER

For a serving variation, place the salmon fillets on top of tossed salad greens and drizzle Green Peppercorn Sauce over the salmon and salad. Garnish with some of the fennel leaves. Have oyster crackers or saltines available for those who wish to add it to their chowder.

INGREDIENTS
Serves 4

4 teaspoons freshly squeezed lemon juice

4 6-ounce salmon fillets, skin removed

1 tablespoon olive or vegetable oil

1 large leek

1 large fennel bulb

4 medium Yukon Gold potatoes, peeled and diced

1 teaspoon sea salt

4 cups water

1 bay leaf

Optional: Green Peppercorn Sauce (see sidebar)

1. Sprinkle ½ teaspoon of lemon juice over each side of the salmon fillets. Bring the oil to temperature in the pressure cooker over medium heat.

2. Trim, thinly slice, wash, and drain the leek, patting it dry with a paper towel if necessary.

3. Add the leek to the pressure cooker; sauté for 2 minutes or until it begins to wilt.

4. Quarter the fennel bulb, then thinly slice the quarters. Add the fennel and diced potatoes to the pressure cooker along with the salt, water, and bay leaf.

5. Lock the lid into place and bring to high pressure; maintain pressure for 7 minutes. Quick-release the pressure and remove the lid.

6. Place the salmon fillets in the pressure cooker. Lock the lid back into place and bring to high pressure; maintain pressure for 1 minute. Remove from heat and allow pressure to release naturally.

7. Remove and discard the bay leaf. Use a slotted spoon to lift each salmon fillet into a bowl or, if you wish to serve the salmon separate from the chowder, to a serving plate.

8. Taste the chowder for seasoning and add more salt if needed. Ladle the chowder into bowls. Top the salmon with Green Peppercorn Sauce if desired.

Green Peppercorn Sauce

In a small bowl, whisk together ¾ cup mayonnaise, 1 teaspoon Dijon mustard, 1 teaspoon freshly squeezed lemon juice, 2 tablespoons extra-virgin olive oil, and 3 tablespoons of crushed green peppercorns.

SEAFOOD CHOWDER

Clam juice is salty, so if you're using it in this chowder, wait until after you taste for seasoning to add any salt. Serve with a tossed salad and dinner rolls.

INGREDIENTS
Serves 6

2 tablespoons butter

2 large leeks

4 cups fish broth or clam juice

2 cups water

6 medium russet or Idaho baking potatoes, peeled and diced

1 bay leaf

Salt and freshly ground black pepper, to taste

1 pound scrod or other firm whitefish

½ teaspoon dried thyme

½ cup heavy cream

1. Melt the butter in the pressure cooker over medium heat. Cut off the root end of the leeks and discard any bruised outer leaves. Slice the leeks. Rinse in running water to remove any dirt; drain and dry. Add to the pressure cooker and sauté in the butter for 2 minutes. Stir in the broth, water, and potatoes. Add the bay leaf, salt, and pepper.

2. Lock the lid into place and bring to high pressure; maintain pressure for 4 minutes. Quick-release the pressure and remove the lid. Remove and discard the bay leaf.

3. Cut the fish into bite-sized pieces and add to the pressure cooker. Simmer for 3 minutes or until the fish is opaque and flakes easily. Stir in the thyme and cream.

4. Leave the pan on the heat, stirring occasionally, until the cream comes to temperature. Taste for seasoning; add additional salt and pepper if needed.

CREAM OF CHESTNUT SOUP

This soup is very rich, so make very small servings if being used as an opener to a meal. Serve it with a swirl of cream and freshly ground nutmeg.

INGREDIENTS
Serves 8

½ pound dried chestnuts or 1 16-ounce can or vacuum-packed jar chestnuts

3 tablespoons butter

1 stalk celery, roughly chopped

1 onion, roughly sliced

1 sprig sage

¼ teaspoon white pepper

1 bay leaf

1 medium potato, peeled and roughly chopped

4 cups chicken broth

2 tablespoons dark rum

¼ teaspoon ground nutmeg

1. Place dry chestnuts in a large bowl and cover with water. Let them soak in the refrigerator overnight. Drain and rinse. If using canned or jarred chestnuts, drain and rinse.

2. Melt butter in an uncovered pressure cooker over medium heat. Add celery, onion, sage, and pepper and sauté until the onions are soft (about 5 minutes). Add the bay leaf, potato, chestnuts, and broth. Close and lock the lid.

3. Turn the heat up to high and when the cooker reaches pressure, lower the heat to the minimum needed to maintain pressure. Cook for 15–20 minutes at high pressure.

4. Open with the natural-release method—move the pressure cooker to a cool burner and wait for the pressure to come down on its own (about 15 minutes). For electric pressure cookers, disengage the "keep warm" mode or unplug the cooker. After 10 minutes, release the rest of the pressure using the valve.

5. Remove the bay leaf and add the rum and nutmeg. Purée the contents of the pressure cooker with an immersion blender.

Go Fresh Instead

Fresh chestnuts are only available during several weeks in a year. You can use 1½ pounds of fresh chestnuts instead of the dried or jarred chestnuts. To remove shells from fresh chestnuts boil them whole in your pressure cooker for 10 minutes and open with the natural method. Drain the water, then strain the chestnuts and peel immediately.

CREAM OF MUSHROOM SOUP

Puréed potatoes help to thicken creamy soups.

INGREDIENTS

Serves 4

¼ cup butter, or vegan margarine, such as Earth Balance

1 yellow onion, diced

2 cups white mushrooms, sliced

2 potatoes, peeled and diced

2 cloves garlic, minced

¼ cup white wine

3 cups milk, or unsweetened soymilk

1 teaspoon dried thyme

1 cup béchamel sauce

Salt and pepper, to taste

1. Add the butter to the pressure cooker and sauté the onions until golden brown. Add the mushrooms, potatoes, and garlic and continue sautéing for about 5 minutes more.

2. Add the white wine, soymilk, thyme, and béchamel sauce.

3. Lock the lid into place and bring to high pressure. Once the pressure is achieved, turn the heat to low and cook for about 8 minutes. Remove from the heat and allow pressure to release naturally.

4. Purée the soup in a food processor or blender. Taste for seasoning and add salt and pepper if needed.

Variations

This soup has mild flavors that are perfect as a base for additional flavors. Try adding vegetables, such as steamed green bean pieces or spinach, or chunks of vegetarian chicken, for a cream of chicken soup.

CREAMY ASPARAGUS SOUP

To sneak protein into this soup, try adding 1 cup cooked navy beans to the soup before blending.

INGREDIENTS

Serves 4–6

2 pounds asparagus

2 tablespoons butter, or vegan margarine, such as Earth Balance

1 large onion, diced

1½ teaspoons salt

⅛ teaspoon cayenne pepper

5 cups vegetable stock

¼ cup milk, or unsweetened soymilk

1 teaspoon lemon juice

1. Trim the hard ends off the asparagus and cut it into 1" pieces. Add the butter to the pressure cooker and sauté the onion until golden brown. Add the asparagus, salt, and cayenne pepper and sauté for about 5 minutes.

2. Add the vegetable stock. Lock the lid into place and bring to high pressure. Once the pressure is achieved, turn the heat to low and cook for about 5 minutes. Remove from the heat and allow pressure to release naturally.

3. Add the milk and lemon juice to the soup and purée in a food processor or blender.

CREAMY LIMA BEAN SOUP

Be very careful when blending hot soups. Do not overfill the blender, and be sure to use a kitchen towel to hold the lid in place during blending.

INGREDIENTS
Serves 4–6

2 cups dried lima beans

Water, as needed, plus ½ cup

1 tablespoon olive oil

1 small onion, diced

1 clove garlic, minced

2 cups vegetable stock

Salt and pepper, to taste

2 tablespoons chives, sliced

1. Rinse the lima beans; soak for 8 hours in enough water to cover them by more than 1". Drain.

2. Heat the oil in the pressure cooker and sauté the onion until golden brown. Add the garlic and cook for 1 minute more.

3. Add the stock, ½ cup water, and lima beans. Lock the lid into place and bring to high pressure. Cook for 6 minutes. Remove from the heat and allow pressure to release naturally.

4. Purée the soup in a food processor or blender.

5. Season with salt and pepper, then garnish with chives before serving.

CREAMY WHITE BEAN AND GARLIC SOUP

White bean purée is a great alternative for achieving a creamy texture in soups.

INGREDIENTS
Serves 8

2 cups dried great northern beans

Water, as needed

3 tablespoons olive oil

1 onion, sliced

6 cloves garlic, minced

6 cups vegetable stock

1 bay leaf

1 tablespoon rosemary, chopped

1 teaspoon lemon juice

Salt and pepper, to taste

1. Rinse the beans; soak for 8 hours in enough water to cover them by more than 1". Drain.

2. Bring the oil to temperature in the pressure cooker over medium heat. Add the onion and sauté until golden brown. Add the garlic and sauté for about 1 minute.

3. Add the vegetable stock, bay leaf, and the rosemary.

4. Lock the lid into place and bring to high pressure. Cook for 10 minutes. Remove from the heat and allow pressure to release naturally.

5. Remove the bay leaf. Purée the soup in a food processor or blender. Add the lemon juice. Taste for seasoning and add salt and pepper if needed.

CUBAN BLACK BEAN SOUP

As with almost any bean dish, you can add diced celery and carrot slices to this soup when you add the onion. In fact, adding some along with another cup of chicken broth will let you increase the servings.

INGREDIENTS
Serves 8

½ pound bacon, chopped

1 green bell pepper, seeded and diced

1 large yellow onion, peeled and diced

8 ounces smoked sausage

3 cloves garlic, peeled and minced

2 teaspoons paprika

½ teaspoon ground cumin

½ teaspoon chili powder

¼ teaspoon coriander

1 bay leaf

6 cups chicken broth or water

1 smoked ham hock or smoked turkey wing

1 pound dried black beans, soaked overnight, rinsed and drained

⅛ teaspoon cayenne pepper or dried red pepper flakes

½ cup dry sherry

1 tablespoon red wine vinegar

Salt and freshly ground black pepper, to taste

1. Add bacon to the pressure cooker and fry over medium-high heat until the bacon begins to render its fat. Reduce the heat to medium and add the green pepper; sauté for 3 minutes. Stir in the onion. Slice or dice the smoked sausage and stir into the onion; sauté for 3 minutes or until the onion is tender. Stir in the garlic along with the paprika, cumin, chili powder, coriander, bay leaf, broth or water, ham hock or turkey wing, and beans. Lock the lid into place and bring to high pressure; maintain pressure for 30 minutes. Remove from the heat and allow pressure to release naturally, leaving the lid in place for at least 20 minutes. Remove the lid.

2. Remove the ham hock or turkey wing and take the meat off of the bones; return meat to the pot. Remove and discard the bay leaf. Use a potato masher or immersion blender to partially pureé the soup. Return the uncovered pan to medium heat and bring to a simmer. Stir in the cayenne pepper or dried red pepper flakes, sherry, and vinegar. Simmer for 20 minutes. Taste for seasoning; add salt and pepper as needed and adjust the herbs, chili powder, and cayenne pepper or red pepper flakes if desired.

CURRY CHICKPEA BISQUE

Make this Middle Eastern soup as spicy or mild as you'd like.

INGREDIENTS

Serves 8

2 cups dried chickpeas

Water, as needed

3 tablespoons extra-virgin olive oil

½ onion, diced

2 cloves garlic, minced

1 teaspoon fresh ginger

1 teaspoon garam masala

2–3 teaspoons curry powder

2 cups vegetable stock

1 14-ounce can coconut milk

Salt and pepper, to taste

1. Rinse the chickpeas; soak for 8 hours in enough water to cover them by more than 1". Drain.

2. Add the oil to the pressure cooker and sauté the onion until golden brown. Add the garlic, ginger, garam masala, and curry powder, and sauté for an additional minute.

3. Add the stock and coconut milk. Lock the lid into place and bring to high pressure. Maintain for 20 minutes and then remove from the heat. Allow pressure to release naturally.

4. Purée the soup in a food processor or blender. Taste for seasoning and add salt and pepper, if needed.

DHAL

Serve spread on toasted flatbread or as a vegetable dip.

INGREDIENTS

Yields 2 cups

1 tablespoon olive oil

1 teaspoon unsalted butter, or vegan margarine

1 small onion, peeled and diced

2 teaspoons fresh ginger, grated

1 serrano chili pepper, seeded and finely diced

1 clove garlic, peeled and minced

½ teaspoon garam masala

¼ teaspoon ground turmeric

½ teaspoon dry mustard

1 cup dried yellow split peas

2 cups water

¼ cup plain yogurt or sour cream, or soy sour cream, such as Tofutti Sour Supreme

2 tablespoons fresh cilantro, minced

1. Add the oil and butter to the pressure cooker and bring to temperature over medium heat. Add the onion, ginger, and chili pepper; sauté for 3 minutes or until soft. Add the garlic, garam masala, turmeric, and dry mustard; sauté for an additional minute. Stir in the split peas. Pour in the water.

2. Lock on the lid. Bring the pressure cooker to high pressure; maintain for 8 minutes. Remove from the heat and allow pressure to release naturally. Transfer the cooked split pea mixture to a bowl; stir until cooled.

3. Add the yogurt or sour cream; whisk until smooth. Stir in the cilantro.

EGG DROP SOUP

The eggs for this soup are not cooked under pressure but added at the end, taking advantage of the very hot broth.

INGREDIENTS
Serves 6

½ teaspoon ginger

1 star anise

2 cloves

3 fennel seeds

⅛ teaspoon cinnamon

2 teaspoons white pepper

8 ounces cherry tomatoes, halved

4 cups water

2 cups chicken broth

4 eggs, whisked

2 green scallions, chopped

1. Put spices (ginger, star anise, cloves, fennel seeds, cinnamon, and white pepper) in a tea ball or bouquet garni bag. Add the spices, tomatoes, water, and broth to the pressure cooker. Close and lock the lid.

2. Turn the heat up to high. When the cooker reaches pressure, lower the heat to the minimum needed to maintain pressure. Cook for 5–7 minutes at high pressure.

3. Open the pressure cooker by releasing pressure.

4. While stirring clockwise with one hand, slowly pour in the whisked eggs with the other, creating thin strands.

5. Sprinkle with green scallions and serve.

FISH STOCK

If you know how you'll be using the fish stock, you can season it with herbs accordingly. A common seasoning combination is bay leaf, thyme, parsley, and fennel seed.

INGREDIENTS
Yields about 8 cups

1 pound fish heads, bones, and trimmings

6 black peppercorns

2 stalks celery, cut to fit in pan

1 carrot, scrubbed and cut in quarters

1 small onion, peeled and quartered

8 cups cold water

Optional: ½ cup dry white wine

1. Add all ingredients to the pressure cooker, only pouring in enough water to take the liquid to the fill line. Bring to a boil over medium-high heat; skim and discard any foam from the surface.

2. Lock the lid into place and bring to low pressure; maintain pressure for 15 minutes. Remove from heat and allow pressure to release naturally.

3. Remove the lid and pour through a fine-mesh strainer, using a spatula to push on the solids in the strainer to release the liquid. Discard the solids. Cool; refrigerate for a day or freeze for up to 3 months.

FRENCH ONION SOUP

Red wine can be used as a substitute for beef broth, an ingredient typically found in French onion soup.

INGREDIENTS
Serves 4

¼ cup extra-virgin olive oil

4 Vidalia onions, sliced

4 cloves garlic, minced

1 tablespoon dried thyme

1 cup red wine

4 cups vegetable stock

Salt and pepper, to taste

4 slices French bread

4 ounces Swiss cheese, or vegan cheese such as Daiya Mozzarella Style Shreds

1. Pour the extra-virgin olive oil into the pressure cooker and sauté the onions over medium-high heat until golden brown. Add the garlic and sauté for 1 minute. Add the thyme, red wine, and vegetable stock.

2. Lock the lid into place and bring to high pressure. Once the pressure is achieved, turn the heat to low and cook for 8–10 minutes. Remove from the heat and allow pressure to release naturally for 20 minutes. Quick-release any remaining pressure and remove the lid.

3. Taste for seasoning, and add salt and pepper if needed.

4. Preheat the oven to the broiler setting. Lightly toast the slices of French bread. To serve, ladle the soup into a broiler-safe bowl, place a slice of the toasted French bread on top of the soup, put a slice of the cheese on top of the bread, and place the soup under the broiler until the cheese has melted.

FRESH TOMATO SOUP

This soup celebrates the simple, yet wondrous, summery taste of fresh vine-ripened tomatoes. You can add sautéed onion or shallots and herbs if you wish.

INGREDIENTS
Serves 4

8 medium fresh tomatoes

¼ teaspoon sea salt

1 cup water

½ teaspoon baking soda

2 cups milk, half-and-half, or heavy cream, or unsweetened soymilk

Freshly ground black pepper, to taste

1. Wash, peel, seed, and dice the tomatoes. Add them and any tomato juice you can retain to the pressure cooker. Stir in the salt and water. Lock the lid into place. Place the pressure cooker over medium heat and bring to low pressure; maintain pressure for 2 minutes. Quick-release the pressure and remove the lid.

2. Stir the baking soda into the tomato mixture. Once it's stopped bubbling and foaming, stir in your choice of milk, half-and-half, or cream. Cook and stir for several minutes or until the soup is brought to temperature. Add pepper, to taste.

GREEK MEATBALL SOUP

This recipe is adapted from a Greek soup (youvarlakia avgolemono). The traditional version doesn't have the vegetables added to the broth, but those vegetables make this soup a one-pot meal. Serve the soup topped with some feta cheese and with crusty bread.

INGREDIENTS
Serves 6

1 pound lean ground beef

¼ pound ground pork

1 small onion, peeled and minced

1 clove garlic, peeled and minced

6 tablespoons uncooked converted long-grain white rice

1 tablespoon dried parsley

2 teaspoons dried dill or mint

1 teaspoon dried oregano

Salt and freshly ground black pepper, to taste

3 large eggs

6 cups chicken or vegetable broth, or water

1 medium onion, peeled and chopped

1 cup baby carrots, each sliced into thirds

2 large potatoes, peeled and cut into cubes

1 stalk celery, finely chopped

2 tablespoons masa harina (corn flour)

⅓ cup fresh lemon juice

1. In a large bowl, mix the meat, onion, garlic, rice, parsley, dill or mint, oregano, salt, pepper, and 1 of the eggs. Shape into small meatballs and set aside.

2. Add 2 cups of broth or water to the pressure cooker. Add the meatballs, onion, carrots, potatoes, and celery, and then pour in the remaining broth or water to cover the meatballs and vegetables. Lock the lid into place and bring to low pressure; maintain pressure for 10 minutes. Remove from the heat and allow pressure to release naturally. Remove the lid. Use a slotted spoon to move the meatballs to a soup tureen; cover and keep warm.

3. Return the pan to medium heat and bring to a simmer. In a small bowl or measuring cup, beat the two remaining eggs and then whisk in the corn flour. Gradually whisk in the lemon juice. Ladle in about a cup of the hot broth from the pressure cooker, doing so in a slow, steady stream, beating continuously until all of the hot liquid has been incorporated into the egg–corn flour mixture. Stir this mixture into the pressure cooker. Stir and simmer for 5 minutes or until mixture is thickened. Taste for seasoning and adjust if necessary. Pour over the meatballs and serve.

HAM BROTH

Using this broth for ham and bean soup improves the soup's flavor in the same way that adding a ham bone to the cooking liquid does. Adding ¼ cup of ham broth for every ¾ cup of chicken broth can give a boost to potato soup, too.

INGREDIENTS
Yields about 3½ cups

1 3-pound bone-in ham or 3 pounds ham bones

1 large onion, peeled and quartered

12 baby carrots

2 stalks celery, halved

4 cups water

1. Add all ingredients to the pressure cooker. Lock the lid into place and bring to low pressure; maintain for 45 minutes. Remove from the heat and allow pressure to release naturally. The ham is done if the meat pulls away from the bone.

2. Strain; discard the celery and onion. Reserve any ham removed from the bones and the carrots for another use. Once cooled, cover and refrigerate the broth overnight. Remove and discard any hardened fat. The broth can be kept for 1 or 2 days in the refrigerator or frozen up to 3 months.

ITALIAN PASTA AND BEAN SOUP

Experiment with the types of grains and beans in this soup. Smaller pastas and couscous work well in this soup.

INGREDIENTS
Serves 10

1 pound dried cannellini beans

Water, as needed, plus 6 cups

1 tablespoon extra-virgin olive oil

4 medium carrots, peeled and diced

2 stalks celery, diced

2 medium onions, peeled and diced

3 cloves garlic, peeled and minced

1 teaspoon dried basil

1 teaspoon dried oregano

1 bay leaf

1 teaspoon dried parsley

4 cups vegetable stock or mushroom broth

1½ cups small macaroni or small shell pasta

Salt and freshly ground black pepper, to taste

1. Rinse the cannellini; soak for 8 hours in enough water to cover them by more than 1". Drain.

2. Bring the oil to temperature in the pressure cooker over medium heat. Add the carrots and celery; sauté for 3 minutes. Add the onion; sauté for 3 minutes or until the vegetables are soft. Add the garlic, basil, and oregano; sauté for 30 seconds.

3. Add 6 cups water, beans, and bay leaf. Lock the lid into place and bring to high pressure; maintain pressure for 10 minutes. Remove from the heat and allow pressure to release naturally.

4. Remove and discard the bay leaf. Add the parsley, and vegetable stock or mushroom broth. Return to the heat and bring to a boil; stir in the macaroni or shells. Cook pasta to al dente according to package directions. Taste for seasoning and add salt and pepper if needed.

LENTIL SOUP

Any color lentils—red, yellow, brown, or green—will work in lentil soup.

INGREDIENTS

Serves 4–6

1 tablespoon olive oil

1 yellow onion, sliced

4 cloves garlic, minced

1 carrot, sliced

5 plum tomatoes, chopped

2 teaspoons dried tarragon

1 teaspoon dried thyme

1 teaspoon paprika

6 cups vegetable stock

2 cups lentils

2 bay leaves

Salt and pepper, to taste

1. Heat the olive oil in the pressure cooker; add the onion and sauté until they begin to turn golden. Add the garlic and carrot and continue sautéing for 2–3 minutes.

2. Add the remaining ingredients except salt and pepper. Lock the lid into place and bring to high pressure. Once the pressure is achieved, turn the heat to low and cook for 8 minutes. Remove from the heat and allow pressure to release naturally.

3. Remove the bay leaves and season to taste with salt and pepper.

MINESTRONE

Minestrone is filled with nutrients and is substantial enough to stand on its own as a light meal.

INGREDIENTS
Serves 6

2 tablespoons olive oil

1 large onion, peeled and diced

2 cloves garlic, peeled and minced

2 large carrots, peeled and diced

2 leeks, white part only, cleaned and diced

½ head cabbage, cored and roughly chopped

2 stalks celery, diced

2 14½-ounce cans diced tomatoes

¼ teaspoon dried rosemary

1 teaspoon dried parsley

¼ teaspoon dried oregano

4½ cups vegetable stock

½ cup dried elbow macaroni

½ cup Arborio rice

Salt and freshly ground black pepper, to taste

1. Add the olive oil to the pressure cooker over medium heat. Add the onion and sauté for 3 minutes or until the onion is soft. Stir in the garlic, carrots, leeks, cabbage, celery, undrained tomatoes, rosemary, parsley, oregano, and vegetable stock.

2. Lock the lid into place and bring to low pressure; maintain pressure for 5 minutes. Remove from the heat and quick-release the pressure.

3. Stir in the macaroni and rice.

4. Lock the lid into place and bring to high pressure; maintain pressure for 7 minutes. Remove from the heat and naturally release the pressure. Remove the lid.

5. Taste for seasoning and add salt, pepper, and additional herbs if needed.

MUSHROOM-BARLEY SOUP

The portobello cap will bring umami, the fifth flavor, to this soup.

INGREDIENTS
Serves 6

2 tablespoons butter, or vegan margarine such as Earth Balance

1 tablespoon olive or vegetable oil

2 stalks celery, diced

1 large carrot, peeled and diced

1 large sweet onion, peeled, halved, and sliced

2 cloves garlic, peeled and minced

1 portobello mushroom cap, diced

8 ounces button mushrooms, cleaned and sliced

1 bay leaf

½ cup pearl barley

6 cups water

Optional: 2 tablespoons vermouth or brandy

Salt and freshly ground black pepper, to taste

1. Melt the butter and bring the oil to temperature in the pressure cooker over medium heat. Add the celery and carrot; sauté for 2 minutes. Add the onion and sauté for 3 minutes or until the onion is soft and transparent. Stir in the garlic and mushrooms; sauté for 5 minutes or until the mushrooms release their moisture and the onion begins to turn golden.

2. Stir in the bay leaf, barley, water, and vermouth or brandy (if using). Lock the lid into place and bring to high pressure; maintain pressure for 20 minutes. Remove from the heat and allow pressure to release naturally.

3. Remove the lid. Remove and discard the bay leaf. Taste for seasoning and add salt and pepper if needed. Serve.

MUSHROOM BROTH

Fresh broth can be refrigerated for 2 or 3 days or frozen for 3 months.

INGREDIENTS
Yields 8 cups

4 carrots, washed and cut into large pieces

2 large leeks, well cleaned and cut into large pieces

2 large onions, peeled and quartered

1 celery stalk, chopped

5 whole cloves

Pinch dried red pepper flakes

2 cups fresh mushrooms, sliced

8½ cups water

1. Put all ingredients in the pressure cooker. Lock the lid into place and bring to low pressure; maintain pressure for 15 minutes.

2. Remove from the heat and allow pressure to release naturally. Strain for a clear stock.

Mushroom Varieties

You can use button mushrooms for a mellow flavor, or for a more intense flavor, try portobello mushroom caps cleaned of the black gills. You could also try wild mushrooms like chanterelles or shiitake.

OLD FASHIONED POTATO SOUP

Top with soy bacon bits and shredded cheese to turn this into a baked potato soup.

INGREDIENTS
Serves 4

¼ cup extra-virgin olive oil

½ cup onion, diced

½ cup celery, sliced

4 cups potatoes, peeled and diced

3 cups vegetable stock

2 cups béchamel sauce

Salt and pepper, to taste

Optional: Chopped chives or parsley

1. Add the oil to the pressure cooker and sauté the onion and celery over medium-high heat for about 5 minutes. Add the potatoes and vegetable stock. Lock the lid into place and bring to high pressure. Once the pressure is achieved, turn the heat to low and cook for 8–10 minutes. Remove from the heat and allow pressure to release naturally for 20 minutes. Quick-release any remaining pressure and remove the lid.

2. Bring the soup to a simmer in the pressure cooker and slowly stir in the béchamel sauce to thicken.

3. Taste for seasoning and add salt and pepper if needed. Garnish with chives or parsley.

PASTA AND CHICKPEA MINESTRONE

Once the garbanzo beans are soaked and ready to go they only need about 15 minutes under pressure and 10 more minutes of rest to be fully cooked. This minestrone is delicious topped with a dusting of Pecorino Romano cheese.

INGREDIENTS
Serves 6

1 cup dried chickpeas

7 cups water, divided

1 tablespoon olive oil

1 onion, chopped

1 carrot, chopped

1 celery stalk, chopped

1 sprig rosemary

1 sprig sage

1 bay leaf

1 clove garlic, pressed

2 tablespoons tomato purée or one spoon of tomato concentrate

3 cups water

1 cup dilatini (or other small pasta shape)

2 teaspoons salt

1 teaspoon pepper

1. Soak chickpeas in 4 cups water for at least 24 hours; drain and set aside.

2. Heat olive oil in an uncovered pressure cooker over medium heat. Sauté the onion, carrot, and celery until softened. Add rosemary, sage, bay leaf, and garlic and stir for about a minute. Then add the garbanzo beans, 3 cups water, and tomato purée. Close and lock the lid.

3. Turn the heat up to high and when the cooker reaches pressure, lower the heat to the minimum needed to maintain pressure. Cook for 13–18 minutes at high pressure.

4. Open with the natural-release method—move the pressure cooker to a cool burner and wait for the pressure to come down on its own (about 15 minutes). For electric pressure cookers, disengage the "keep warm" mode or unplug the cooker and open when the pressure indicator has gone down (20–30 minutes).

5. Bring the contents of the pressure cooker to a boil, uncovered, and add pasta. Cook until pasta is tender, about 8–10 minutes.

6. Season with salt and pepper before serving.

Less Gassy Chicks!

Changing the chickpeas' soaking water often can remove some of the indigestible sugars which could translate into gas after being consumed. Strain and rinse the beans and soaking container every 6 hours or so (2 or three times during the soak).

PORK BROTH

Pork broth is seldom called for in recipes, but it can add layers of flavor when mixed with chicken and ham broth in potato, bean, or vegetable soups. You can also use it as the liquid in your favorite meatball recipe.

INGREDIENTS
Yields about 3½ cups

1 3-pound bone-in pork butt roast

1 large onion, peeled and quartered

12 baby carrots

2 stalks celery, cut in half

4 cups water

1. Add all ingredients to the pressure cooker. Lock the lid into place and bring to low pressure; maintain pressure for 45 minutes.

2. Remove from heat and allow pressure to release naturally. Remove the lid and check that the roast has reached an internal temperature of 160°F. The pork should be tender and pull away from the bone. If not, lock the lid back into place and cook on low pressure for another 10–15 minutes.

3. Strain; discard the celery and onion. Reserve the pork roast and carrots for another use. Once cooled, cover and refrigerate the broth overnight. Remove and discard the hardened fat. The broth can be kept for 1 or 2 days in the refrigerator, or frozen up to 3 months.

PORTUGUESE KALE SOUP

Collard greens can be substituted for the kale, but doing so will change the flavor somewhat.

INGREDIENTS
Serves 6

1 pound kale

1 tablespoon extra-virgin olive oil

1 large yellow onion, peeled and thinly sliced

½ pound linguica or kielbasa, sliced

4 large potatoes, peeled and diced

4 cups chicken broth

2 15-ounce cans cannellini beans, rinsed and drained

Salt and freshly ground black pepper, to taste

1. Trim the large ribs from the kale. Slice it into thin strips. Put the kale strips into a bowl of cold water and soak for an hour; drain well.

2. Add the oil, onions, and linguica or kielbasa to the pressure cooker; stir to combine. Place over medium heat; sauté for 5 minutes or until the onions are soft. Add the potatoes, chicken broth, drained kale, and beans. Lock the lid into place and bring to low pressure; maintain pressure for 8 minutes. Remove from the heat and allow pressure to release naturally for 5 minutes. Quick-release any remaining pressure and remove the lid. Taste for seasoning and add salt and pepper to taste.

POSOLE

Posole is a traditional Mexican soup that has corn as the main ingredient.

INGREDIENTS
Serves 8

2 cups hominy

8 cups water

2 tablespoons olive oil

½ onion, diced

2 yellow squash, diced

2 zucchini, diced

2 cloves garlic, minced

1 cup tomato, diced

2 dried Ancho chilies

2 bay leaves

8 cups vegetable stock

2 teaspoons dried oregano

1 teaspoon dried thyme

1 teaspoon saffron

1 teaspoon salt

1 tablespoon lime juice

1 avocado, pitted and sliced

1. Add the hominy and 4 cups water to the pressure cooker. Lock the lid into place; bring to high pressure for 1 minute. Remove from the heat and quick-release the pressure.

2. Drain the water, rinse the hominy, and add to the pressure cooker again with the remaining 4 cups water. Let soak for 1 hour. Drain and set aside.

3. Add the olive oil to the empty pressure cooker and bring to medium heat. Add the onion, squash, and zucchini; sauté for 5 minutes. Add the garlic and sauté for an additional 30 seconds.

4. Add all remaining ingredients except for the avocado; stir. Lock the lid into place; bring to high pressure and maintain for 20 minutes. Remove from the heat and allow pressure to release naturally.

5. Spoon into serving bowls and top each with ⅛ of the sliced avocado.

SCOTCH BROTH

Scotch Broth is not a broth in the traditional sense. Instead, it's the name for a barley soup.

INGREDIENTS
Serves 4

2 leeks, white part only

4 lamb shoulder chops

⅓ cup pearl barley

1 large carrot, peeled and diced

1 stalk celery, thinly sliced

2 medium potatoes, peeled and diced

6 cups water

Salt and freshly ground black pepper, to taste

Optional: Fresh parsley, minced

Dice the white part of the leeks; rinse well and drain. Add the leeks to the pressure cooker along with the lamb chops, barley, carrot, celery, potatoes, water, salt, and pepper. Lock the lid into place and bring to high pressure; maintain pressure for 9 minutes. Remove from the heat and quick-release the pressure. Remove the lid. Taste for seasoning and add additional salt and pepper if needed. Transfer a lamb chop to each of four bowls and ladle the soup over the meat. Garnish with parsley if desired.

SPLIT PEA SOUP

This soup tastes even better if you refrigerate it overnight and heat it up to serve the next day. It's hearty enough to stand alone as the main dish. Serve with crusty bread.

INGREDIENTS

Serves 6

4 strips bacon, diced

1 large sweet onion, peeled and diced

2 large potatoes, peeled and diced

2 large carrots, peeled and sliced

1 cup dried green split peas, rinsed

4 cups chicken broth

2 smoked ham hocks

Optional: 1 10-ounce package frozen peas, thawed

Salt and freshly ground black pepper, to taste

1. Add the bacon to the pressure cooker. Fry it over medium heat until the bacon begins to render its fat. Add the onion; sauté for 3 minutes or until soft. Stir in the diced potatoes; sauté for 3 minutes. Add the carrots, split peas, broth, and ham hocks. Lock the lid into place and bring to low pressure; maintain pressure for 15 minutes. Remove from the heat and allow pressure to release naturally.

2. Remove the lid. Use a slotted spoon to remove the ham hocks; allow to cool until the meat can be removed from the bones. Taste the split peas. If they're not cooked through, lock the lid back into place and cook at low pressure for another 5 minutes; remove from the heat and quick-release the pressure. If the split peas are cooked through and tender, stir the ham removed from the hocks into the soup. If desired, use an immersion blender to pureé the soup.

3. Return the soup to medium heat and bring to a simmer. If desired, stir in the peas and cook until they're heated. Taste for seasoning and add salt and pepper if needed.

THAI CARROT SOUP

Carrots are loaded with vitamin A and help maintain good vision. Coconut milk is very rich, so eat this soup in small portions or make it a meal.

INGREDIENTS
Serves 8

1 tablespoon olive oil

1 onion, diced

2 cloves garlic, minced

3 teaspoons curry powder

1 bay leaf

1 pound carrots, peeled and roughly chopped

4 cups vegetable stock

1 cup unsweetened coconut milk

1 teaspoon salt

½ teaspoon pepper

¼ cup thinly sliced basil

1. Heat olive oil in an uncovered pressure cooker over medium heat. Sauté the onion until soft. Add the garlic and curry powder and sauté for an additional 30 seconds. Then, add the rest of the ingredients except for the basil. Close and lock the lid.

2. Turn the heat up to high and when the cooker reaches pressure, lower the heat to the minimum needed to maintain pressure. Cook for 5–7 minutes at high pressure.

3. Open with the natural-release method—move the pressure cooker to a cool burner and wait for the pressure to come down on its own (about 15 minutes). For electric pressure cookers, disengage the "keep warm" mode or unplug the cooker. After 10 minutes, release the rest of the pressure using the valve.

4. Remove the bay leaf. Pureé using an immersion blender. Add salt and pepper. Garnish individual bowls with basil.

Chiffonade
Chiffonade is a technique for cutting herbs and greens. To chiffonade basil, stack the cleaned and dried leaves, roll the leaves loosely, and slice from end to end. You'll be left with thin ribbons of basil.

TORTILLA SOUP

Turn this soup into a complete meal by adding pieces of cooked vegetarian chicken, such as Morningstar Farms Meal Starters Chik'n Strips or Gardein Seasoned Bites.

INGREDIENTS
Serves 6–8

2 tablespoons olive oil

1 large onion, chopped

2 cloves garlic, minced

2 tablespoons soy sauce

7 cups vegetable stock

2 cups tomato, diced

1 cup corn kernels

1 teaspoon chipotle powder

1 teaspoon cayenne pepper

2 teaspoons ground cumin

2 teaspoons salt

1 teaspoon dried oregano

10 small corn tortillas, sliced

8 ounces shredded Monterey jack cheese, or vegan cheese, such as Daiya Mozzarella Style Shreds

1. Add the olive oil to the pressure cooker and bring to medium heat. Sauté the onions until just soft, about 3 minutes. Add the garlic and sauté for an additional 30 seconds.

2. Add the soy sauce, stock, tomato, corn, chipotle powder, cayenne, cumin, salt, and oregano; stir.

3. Lock the lid into place; bring to medium pressure and maintain for 15 minutes. Remove from the heat and quick-release the pressure.

4. While the soup is cooking, slice the corn tortillas into thin strips and place on an ungreased baking sheet. Bake in a 450°F oven for about 10 minutes, or until they turn golden brown. Remove from heat and set aside.

5. Use an immersion blender or a regular blender to purée the soup.

6. Serve with cooked tortilla strips and 1 ounce of shredded cheese on each bowl of soup.

Chipotle Powder

Chipotle powder is made from ground chipotle peppers, a type of dried jalapeño. They bring a smoky spiciness to dishes but can be replaced with cayenne pepper or chili powder.

TURKEY BROTH

This method will result in a highly concentrated turkey broth. In most cases, for a cup of regular turkey broth you can mix ½ cup of this broth with ½ cup water.

INGREDIENTS
Yields about 3 cups

3 pounds bone-in turkey pieces

1 large onion, peeled and quartered

2 large carrots, scrubbed

1 stalk celery

Salt and freshly ground black pepper, to taste

4 cups water

1. Add the turkey and onion to the pressure cooker. Cut the carrot and celery each into several pieces; add them. Add the salt, pepper, and water.

2. Lock the lid into place and bring to low pressure; maintain pressure for 20 minutes. Remove from the heat and allow pressure to release naturally.

3. Strain, discarding the cooked vegetables. Remove any meat from the bones and save for another use; discard the skin. Cool the broth and refrigerate overnight. Remove and discard the hardened fat.

Using the Turkey Carcass
You can really get your money's worth out of your Thanksgiving Butterball by substituting the carcass for the 3 pounds of turkey pieces called for in this recipe. This broth can be kept in the refrigerator for 1 or 2 days or frozen for up to 3 months.

TURKEY DRUMSTICKS AND VEGETABLE SOUP

Measure the turkey drumsticks to make sure they'll fit in your pressure cooker. It's okay if the end of the bone touches the lid of the cooker, as long as it doesn't block the vent.

INGREDIENTS
Serves 6

1 tablespoon extra-virgin olive oil

1 clove garlic, peeled and minced

2 15-ounce cans diced tomatoes

6 medium potatoes, peeled and cut into quarters

6 large carrots, peeled and sliced

12 small onions, peeled

2 stalks celery, finely diced

½ ounce dried mushrooms

¼ teaspoon dried oregano

¼ teaspoon dried rosemary

1 bay leaf

2 strips orange zest

Salt and freshly ground black pepper, to taste

2 1¼-pound turkey drumsticks, skin removed

1 10-ounce package frozen green beans, thawed

1 10-ounce package frozen whole kernel corn, thawed

1 10-ounce package frozen baby peas, thawed

Fresh parsley or cilantro

1. Add the oil to the pressure cooker and bring to temperature over medium heat. Add the garlic and sauté for 10 seconds.

2. Stir in the tomatoes, potatoes, carrots, onions, celery, mushrooms, oregano, rosemary, bay leaf, orange zest, salt, and pepper. Stand the two drumsticks meaty-side down in the pan.

3. Lock the lid and bring to high pressure; maintain high pressure for 12 minutes.

4. Remove from heat and allow the pressure to drop naturally, and then use the quick-release method for your cooker to release the remaining pressure if needed.

5. Remove the drumsticks, cut the meat from the bone and into bite-sized pieces, and return the meat to the pot.

6. Stir in the green beans, corn, and peas; cook over medium heat for 5 minutes. Remove and discard the orange zest and bay leaf. Taste for seasoning and add salt and pepper if needed.

UKRAINIAN SAUSAGE SOUP

Ukrainian smoked ham sausage is heavily seasoned with garlic. If you use kielbasa or another type of smoked sausage, add the optional garlic to the recipe.

INGREDIENTS
Serves 8

1½ cups dried red kidney beans

5 cups water

1 tablespoon vegetable oil

2 jalapeño peppers, seeded and diced

1 large onion, peeled and diced

8 ounces kielbasa or Ukrainian smoked
   ham sausage

1 bay leaf

1 tablespoon chili powder

1 teaspoon dried oregano

½ teaspoon freshly ground black pepper

¼ teaspoon cayenne pepper

Optional: 4 cloves garlic, peeled and
   minced

3 cups beef broth

1 15-ounce can diced tomatoes

½ cup tomato sauce

2 tablespoons light brown sugar, packed

Salt, to taste

1. Rinse the kidney beans. Put in a container and add enough water to cover them by at least an inch. Cover and let beans soak overnight.

2. Drain the beans and put in the pressure cooker. Add the water and the oil. Lock the lid into place and bring to high pressure; maintain pressure for 12 minutes.

3. Remove from heat and allow pressure to release naturally. Drain the beans and set aside.

4. Add the jalapeño and onion to the pressure cooker. Dice the sausage and add to the pressure cooker along with the bay leaf, chili powder, oregano, black pepper, cayenne pepper, and garlic, if using.

5. Lock the lid into place and bring to low pressure; maintain the pressure for 2 minutes. Quick-release the pressure.

6. Remove the lid and pour in the broth, tomatoes, tomato sauce, brown sugar, and drained beans.

7. Lock the lid into place and bring to high pressure; maintain pressure for 20 minutes. Remove from the heat and allow pressure to release naturally.

8. Remove and discard the bay leaf. Taste for seasoning and add salt if desired. Serve.

VEGETABLE STOCK

Save scraps of vegetables to use to make a homemade stock.

INGREDIENTS
Yields 4 cups

2 large onions, peeled and halved

2 medium carrots, cleaned and cut into large pieces

3 stalks celery, cut in half

1 whole bulb garlic

10 peppercorns

1 bay leaf

4½ cups water

1. Add the onions, carrots, and celery to the pressure cooker. Break the bulb of garlic into individual cloves; peel and add to the pressure cooker. Add the peppercorns, bay leaf, and water to completely cover the vegetables. Lock the lid into place and bring to low pressure; maintain pressure for 10 minutes. Remove from the heat and allow pressure to release naturally.

2. Strain the stock through a fine-mesh strainer or through cheesecloth placed in a colander. Store in a covered container in the refrigerator for 2–3 days, or freeze for up to 3 months.

VIETNAMESE BEEF NOODLE SOUP

This is a simplified, Americanized version of pho, substituting brown sugar for the yellow rock sugar found in Asian markets.

INGREDIENTS
Serves 10

1 3-pound English-cut chuck roast

3 medium yellow onions

1 4-inch piece ginger

5 star anise

6 whole cloves

1 3-inch cinnamon stick

¼ teaspoon salt

2 cups beef broth

Water, as needed

1½–2 pounds small dried or fresh banh pho noodles

4 tablespoons fish sauce

1 tablespoon brown sugar

3 or 4 scallions, green part only, cut into thin rings

⅓ cup fresh cilantro, chopped

Freshly ground black pepper

1. Trim the roast of any fat; cut the meat into bite-sized pieces and add to the pressure cooker. Peel and quarter 2 onions. Cut the ginger into 1-inch pieces. Add the onion and ginger to the pressure cooker along with the star anise, cloves, cinnamon stick, salt, broth, and enough water to cover the meat by about 1 inch. Lock the lid into place and bring to low pressure; maintain pressure for an hour. Remove from the heat and allow pressure to release naturally.

2. About ½ hour before serving, peel the remaining onion; cut it into paper-thin slices and soak them in cold water. For dried rice noodles: Cover them with hot water and allow to soak for 15–20 minutes or until softened and opaque white; drain in colander. For fresh rice noodles: Untangle and place in a colander, then rinse briefly with cold water.

3. Remove the meat from the broth with a slotted spoon; shred the meat. Strain the broth through a fine strainer, discarding the spices and onion; return strained broth to the pressure cooker along with the shredded meat. Bring the meat and broth to a boil over medium-high heat. Stir the fish sauce and brown sugar into the broth. (The broth should taste slightly too strong because the noodles and other ingredients are not salted. Therefore, to test for seasoning, you may want to taste the broth and meat with some noodles. If you desire a stronger, saltier flavor, add more fish sauce. Add more brown sugar to make the broth sweeter if desired. If the broth is already too salty, add some additional water to dilute it.)

4. Blanch the noodles in stages by adding as many noodles to a strainer as you can submerge in the boiling broth without causing the pressure cooker to boil over. The noodles will collapse and lose their stiffness in about 15–20 seconds. Pull strainer from the broth, letting the excess broth clinging to them drain back into cooker. Empty noodles into bowls, allowing each serving to fill about ⅓ of the bowl, and then ladle hot broth and beef over the noodles. Garnish with onion slices, scallions, and chopped cilantro, and finish with freshly ground black pepper.

WHITE BEAN WITH GARLIC AND KALE SOUP

This soup is best enjoyed during the winter, when kale is in peak season.

INGREDIENTS
Serves 8

2 cups dried cannellini beans

Water, as needed

2 tablespoons olive oil

½ cup onion, thinly sliced

6 cloves garlic, thinly sliced

2 teaspoons dried oregano

1 6-ounce can tomato paste

2 tablespoons red wine vinegar

8 cups vegetable stock

3 cups kale, chopped

Salt and pepper, to taste

White Beans

1. Rinse the cannellini; soak for 8 hours in enough water to cover them by more than 1". Drain.

2. Bring the oil to temperature in the pressure cooker over medium heat. Add the onion and sauté until golden brown. Add the garlic and sauté for about 1 minute. Add the rest of the ingredients.

3. Lock the lid into place and bring to high pressure. Cook for about 10 minutes. Remove from the heat and allow pressure to release naturally. Taste for seasoning and add more salt and pepper if needed.

PART IV

VEGETABLES AND GRAINS

CHAPTER 5

VEGETABLES

VEGETABLES

ALOO GOBI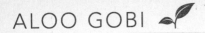

Aloo gobi is a vegetarian Indian dish made from potatoes and cauliflower.

INGREDIENTS
Serves 4–6

2 cups potatoes, peeled and cubed

Water, as needed, plus 2 tablespoons

2 cups cauliflower, chopped

2 tablespoons vegetable oil

1 teaspoon cumin seeds

1 clove garlic, minced

1 teaspoon ginger, minced

1 teaspoon turmeric

1 teaspoon garam masala

1 teaspoon salt

1. Add the potatoes to the pressure cooker and enough water to cover. Lock on the lid. Bring to high pressure; maintain pressure for 4 minutes. Remove the pan from the heat, quick-release the pressure, and remove the lid.

2. Add the cauliflower and reattach the lid. Bring to high pressure; maintain pressure for 2 minutes. Remove the pan from the heat, quick-release the pressure, and remove the lid. Drain all ingredients.

3. Place the vegetable oil in the cleaned pressure cooker over low heat. Add the cumin seeds, garlic, and ginger; cook for 1 minute. Add the turmeric, garam masala, and salt; cook for an additional minute.

4. Stir in 2 tablespoons water, then add the cooked potatoes and cauliflower. Simmer over low heat, stirring occasionally, for 10 minutes.

ASPARAGUS WITH OLIVE OIL DRESSING

Replace the salt with your favorite seasoned salt or herb blend. Asparagus is especially good in spring, and the simpler the recipe, the better the dish.

INGREDIENTS
Serves 4

1½ pounds fresh asparagus

½ cup water

2 tablespoons shallot or red onion, minced

1 tablespoon fresh lemon juice

3 tablespoons extra-virgin olive oil

Salt and freshly ground white or black pepper, to taste

1. Clean the asparagus and snap off the ends. If necessary, peel the stems. Lay flat in the pressure cooker and add the water.

2. Lock the lid into place and bring to high pressure; maintain pressure for 3 minutes. Remove from the heat and allow pressure to release naturally for 2 minutes.

3. In a small bowl or measuring cup, whisk together the shallot or onion, lemon juice, oil, salt, and pepper.

4. Quick-release any remaining pressure and remove the lid. Drain the asparagus and transfer to a serving platter. Pour the dressing over the asparagus. Serve.

ASPARAGUS WITH VEGAN HOLLANDAISE SAUCE

By making this recipe with tofu instead of eggs, you'll eliminate the cholesterol typically found in hollandaise sauce.

INGREDIENTS
Serves 4

1½ pounds fresh asparagus

½ cup water

½ cup silken tofu

1 tablespoon lemon juice

1 teaspoon Dijon mustard

⅛ teaspoon cayenne pepper

⅛ teaspoon turmeric

1 tablespoon vegetable oil

Salt, to taste

1. Trim the end off of each asparagus spear. Lay flat in the pressure cooker and add water. Lock lid into place and bring to high pressure; maintain for 3 minutes. Remove from heat and allow pressure to release naturally for 2 minutes.

2. Add the silken tofu to a food processor and purée until smooth. Add the lemon juice, mustard, cayenne, and turmeric. Blend until well combined. With the food processor still running, slowly add the oil and blend until combined. Season with salt, to taste, to complete the vegan hollandaise.

3. Pour the hollandaise into a small saucepan over low heat and cook until the sauce is warm.

4. Spoon the sauce over the cooked asparagus spears to serve.

LEMON ZEST ASPARAGUS

Lemon zest in the steaming liquid gives this asparagus extra zing.

INGREDIENTS
Serves 4

1 cup water

Zest of 1 lemon

1 pound asparagus

⅛ teaspoon salt

1 tablespoon olive oil

1. Place water and zest in the pressure cooker and add the steamer basket.

2. Lay asparagus flat in steamer basket. If it does not fit in one layer, make a second layer perpendicular to the first and sprinkle with salt. Close and lock the lid.

3. Turn the heat up to high and when the cooker reaches pressure, lower the heat to the minimum needed to maintain pressure. Cook for 2–3 minutes at high pressure.

4. When time is up, open the pressure cooker by releasing pressure.

5. Transfer immediately to serving dish and dress with olive oil before serving.

BRAISED BEET GREENS

Young, fresh greens will cook quicker than older, tougher ones. Adjust the cooking time accordingly.

INGREDIENTS
Serves 4

1 tablespoon olive oil

1 large shallot or small red onion, minced

1 pound beet greens

Salt and pepper, to taste

¼ cup vegetable stock

1 tablespoon white wine

1. Bring the oil to temperature in the pressure cooker over medium heat. Add the shallot or onion; sauté for 3 minutes. Add the beet greens. Sprinkle with salt and pepper. Stir the greens to coat them in the oil. Once they're slightly wilted, add the stock, making sure not to exceed the fill line in your pressure cooker.

2. Lock the lid into place and bring to low pressure; maintain pressure for 1–3 minutes. Quick-release the pressure and remove the lid. Simmer and stir for 1 minute or until the remaining moisture in the pan evaporates.

3. Taste for seasoning, and add more salt and pepper if needed. Add white wine, stir, and serve warm.

GOLDEN BEETS

You can prepare the unpeeled beets ahead of time. Cool them, put them in a zip-closure bag, and refrigerate.

INGREDIENTS
Serves 8

4 large golden or red beets

1 cup water

1 tablespoon olive oil

1 teaspoon salt

½ teaspoon freshly ground black pepper

1. Scrub the beets and trim both ends. Place the beets on the rack in the pressure cooker. Pour in the water. Close and lock the lid.

2. Turn the heat up to high. When the cooker reaches pressure, lower the heat to the minimum needed to maintain pressure. Cook for 15–20 minutes at high pressure.

3. When time is up, open the pressure cooker by releasing pressure.

4. Test the beets to see if they are fully cooked. If beets aren't tender, pressure cook for another minute.

5. Remove beets from pressure and let cool. When they are cool enough to handle, use a paring knife to remove the peel. Slice the beets and season with oil, salt, and pepper.

WHOLE WHITE BEETS

Spring beets are two vegetables in one, the root and the greens!

INGREDIENTS
Serves 4

3 whole white beets

Water, as needed

1 teaspoon salt

1 tablespoon olive oil

2 cloves garlic, minced

1 lemon wedge, squeezed (about 1 teaspoon lemon juice)

1. Cut the greens from the beets and wash well: Immerse them in a large bowl of water and swish them around. Let sit for 30 minutes, then lift them out of the water, leaving all of the dirt and sand at the bottom of the bowl. Place greens in a strainer and drain.

2. Put the beet roots in the pressure cooker, fill with just enough water to cover and add salt. Close and lock the lid.

3. Turn the heat up to high and when the cooker reaches pressure, lower the heat to the minimum needed to maintain pressure. Cook for 5–7 minutes at high pressure.

4. When time is up, open the pressure cooker by releasing pressure.

5. Strain out the beets and greens. Peel the beets (tugging on the thin skin with a paper towel) and cut into pieces. Heat the oil in a sauté pan over medium-high heat. When oil is hot, add the beets and sear for about 3 minutes. Add garlic and beet greens to the pan. Stir frequently and cook until the stems are tender.

6. Transfer to serving dish and squirt with lemon.

Red Beet Variation

This recipe also works with red beets. Cook them a little longer (20–25 minutes instead of the time listed in the recipe) and be extra careful when peeling. You may want to sauté the greens separately just to keep them green.

BROCCOLI AND CITRUS SALAD

Spicy, tangy and sweet, this salad is the perfect accompaniment to fish and meats. Reserve the steaming liquid in the refrigerator and use it to add flavor to another recipe.

INGREDIENTS
Serves 6

VINAIGRETTE

Zest and juice of 1 orange

1 teaspoon hot pepper flakes

1 tablespoon capers

2 tablespoons extra-virgin olive oil

1 teaspoon salt

¼ teaspoon ground black pepper

SALAD

2 pounds broccoli florets, trimmed

2 seedless oranges, peeled and sliced thinly

1. Make the vinaigrette by combining all ingredients in a small container. Seal, shake well, and set aside.

2. Place 1 cup of water in the pressure cooker and add the steamer basket. Fill the basket with broccoli florets and close and lock the lid.

3. Turn the heat up to high and when the cooker reaches pressure, lower to the minimum needed to maintain pressure. Cook 4–6 minutes at low pressure (2–3 minutes at high).

4. When time is up, open the pressure cooker by releasing pressure.

5. Place broccoli and sliced oranges on a serving platter. Drizzle salad with the vinaigrette.

BROCCOLI IN LEMON-BUTTER SAUCE

Serve as a side dish or toss with pasta for a complete meal.

INGREDIENTS
Serves 6

4 cups broccoli florets

¼ teaspoon salt

1 cup water

4 tablespoons butter, melted, or vegan margarine, such as Earth Balance

1 tablespoon fresh lemon juice

¼ teaspoon Dijon mustard

1. Put the broccoli, salt, and water in the pressure cooker. Lock the lid into place and bring to low pressure; maintain pressure for 2 minutes.

2. Remove the pressure cooker from the heat, quick-release the pressure, and remove the lid. Drain and transfer the broccoli to a serving bowl.

3. While the broccoli cooks, whisk together the butter, lemon juice, and mustard. Pour over the cooked broccoli and toss to coat.

SAUTÉED BROCCOLI RABE

Broccoli rabe, also known as rapini, can be prepared in the same way as broccoli.

INGREDIENTS
Serves 6

1 pound broccoli rabe, trimmed

1 teaspoon salt

1 cup water

2 tablespoons olive oil

2 cloves garlic, sliced

2 shallots, sliced

Pepper, to taste

1. Put the broccoli rabe, salt, and water in the pressure cooker. Lock the lid into place and bring to low pressure; maintain pressure for 2 minutes.

2. Remove the pressure cooker from the heat, quick-release the pressure, and remove the lid. Drain and transfer the broccoli to a bowl.

3. In the cleaned pressure cooker or in a sauté pan, bring the olive oil to medium heat. Add the garlic and shallots; sauté for 1 minute, stirring often. Add the broccoli rabe and sauté for an additional minute, until heated through and coated with the olive oil mixture.

4. Season with pepper, to taste.

SPICY BRAISED BROCCOLI

A quick and delicious veggie dish that can also be served on top of rice, pasta, or your favorite grain!

INGREDIENTS
Serves 4

1 tablespoon olive oil

3 cloves garlic, crushed

⅛ teaspoon hot pepper flakes

1 pound broccoli florets, trimmed

¼ teaspoon salt

⅛ teaspoon pepper

¾ cups water

1. Heat olive oil in an uncovered pressure cooker over medium heat. Add garlic and hot pepper flakes and cook for 30 seconds, stirring constantly. Add broccoli and cook about 5 minutes, stirring infrequently so that the edges can become golden.

2. Sprinkle with salt and pepper and add water. Close and lock the lid.

3. Turn the heat up to high and when the cooker reaches pressure, lower the heat to the minimum needed to maintain pressure. Cook for 2–3 minutes at high pressure.

4. When time is up, open the pressure cooker by releasing pressure.

5. Remove to serving dish immediately to avoid overcooking.

WARM BROCCOLI CAESAR SALAD

This salad is the perfect accompaniment for grilled chicken breasts. Serve over torn romaine leaves if desired.

INGREDIENTS

Serves 6

4 cups broccoli florets

¼ teaspoon salt

1 cup water

2 large hard-boiled eggs

2 cloves garlic, peeled and sliced

2 canned anchovies, rinsed and drained

1 tablespoon fresh lemon juice

¼ teaspoon Dijon mustard

2 tablespoons mayonnaise

2 tablespoons Parmigiano-Reggiano
   cheese, freshly grated

¼ cup extra-virgin olive oil

Additional salt, to taste

Freshly ground black pepper, to taste

1. Put the broccoli in the pressure cooker along with the salt and water. Lock the lid into place and bring to low pressure; maintain pressure for 2 minutes.

2. Remove the pressure cooker from heat, quick-release the pressure, and remove the lid. Drain and transfer the broccoli to a serving bowl.

3. Chop the egg whites and add to the serving bowl with the broccoli. Add the egg yolks to a blender or food processor along with the garlic, anchovies, lemon juice, mustard, mayonnaise, and cheese; process until smooth.

4. Gradually drizzle in the olive oil and process until oil is completely incorporated into the dressing.

5. Pour the dressing over the broccoli and chopped egg whites. Stir to mix. Season with salt and pepper to taste. Serve.

PAN-SEARED BRUSSELS SPROUTS

Pan-searing Brussels sprouts brings out a buttery sweetness that is otherwise missing from the vegetable.

INGREDIENTS

Serves 4

1 pound Brussels sprouts

2 tablespoons olive oil

¼ cup water

Salt and pepper, to taste

1. Trim the stems of the Brussels sprouts and remove the discolored outer leaves. Cut in half, from the stem to the top, and place into a medium bowl. Add 1 tablespoon of the oil and gently toss until coated.

2. Add the remaining tablespoon of oil to the pressure cooker and bring to medium-high heat. Place the Brussels sprouts in the pressure cooker and cook for about 5 minutes, stirring often, or until the sides begin to brown. Add the water.

3. Lock on the lid. Bring to high pressure; maintain pressure for 1 minute. Remove the pan from the heat, quick-release the pressure, and remove the lid. Season with salt and pepper, to taste.

RED, WHITE, AND GREEN BRUSSELS SPROUT SALAD

If fresh pomegranate is not available, rehydrate dried cranberries by putting them in the steaming liquid, below the Brussels sprouts.

INGREDIENTS
Serves 6

1 pound Brussels sprouts

1 cup water

1 tablespoon olive oil

1 teaspoon salt

¼ teaspoon pepper

½ cup pine nuts, toasted

Seeds of 1 medium pomegranate

1. Remove the outer leaves and trim the stems of the Brussels sprouts. Cut larger sprouts in half to get them to a uniform size for even cooking.

2. Prepare the pressure cooker by pouring in water and adding the steamer basket. Put the sprouts in the basket. Close and lock the lid.

3. Turn the heat up to high and when the cooker reaches pressure, lower to the minimum needed to maintain pressure. Cook 3–4 minutes at high pressure.

4. When time is up, open the pressure cooker by releasing pressure.

5. Quickly move the sprouts to a serving dish to stop the cooking.

6. Toss Brussels sprouts in olive oil, salt, and pepper. Sprinkle with pine nuts and pomegranate seeds.

BEER-BRAISED SAVOY CABBAGE

You could also braise cabbage in wine, stock, or the reserved steaming liquid from another recipe.

INGREDIENTS
Serves 6

1 medium Savoy cabbage

1 tablespoon butter

1 medium onion, sliced

¾ cup beer

Buying Savoy Cabbage

Buy a whole head of cabbage. Presliced or shredded cabbage begins to lose its vitamins almost immediately.

1. Slice the cabbage in half, and then into strips. Wash and dry the cabbage strips. Heat butter in an uncovered pressure cooker over medium heat. Add the onion and cook, stirring occasionally, until softened.

2. Add the cabbage and beer. Close and lock the lid.

3. Turn the heat up to high and when the cooker reaches pressure, lower to the minimum needed to maintain pressure. Cook 3–5 minutes at high pressure.

4. When time is up, open the pressure cooker by releasing pressure.

5. Transfer to serving platter immediately to stop the cooking, and serve warm or at room temperature.

GERMAN RED CABBAGE

Red wine will help preserve the color of the cabbage. Serve with smoked pork chops or other pork entrées.

INGREDIENTS
Serves 8

4 slices bacon, diced

2 Granny Smith apples

1 medium onion, peeled and diced

½ cup Merlot, sweet red wine, or apple juice

⅓ cup light brown sugar, packed

3 tablespoons red wine vinegar

1 2½-pound red cabbage

Salt and freshly ground black pepper, to taste

1. Add the bacon to the pressure cooker; fry over medium-high heat until crisp. Use a slotted spoon to remove the bacon to paper towels; set aside.

2. Peel the apples, remove the cores, and slice them. Reduce the heat to medium and add the apples and onion. Sauté for 3 minutes or until the onion is soft. Stir in the wine, brown sugar, and vinegar.

3. Wash the cabbage and remove and discard the outer leaves. Quarter the cabbage. Remove and discard the core. Slice the quarters into thin strips.

4. Gradually add to the pressure cooker, at first filling the pressure cooker to the top and loosely covering until the cabbage wilts, freeing up more space in the pan.

5. Stir in enough of the remaining cabbage to bring the pressure cooker to the fill line.

6. Lock the lid into place and bring to high pressure; maintain pressure for 8 minutes.

7. Remove the pressure cooker from the heat, quick-release the pressure, and remove the lid. Stir and then use a slotted spoon to transfer the cabbage to a serving bowl. Stir in the reserved crisp bacon. Season with salt and pepper to taste.

KIMCHI-STYLE CABBAGE

If you can't find Korean chili powder, substitute plain chili powder, which is also made from crushed red peppers.

INGREDIENTS
Yields 1 quart

1 clove garlic, minced

1 teaspoon ginger, minced

1 bunch scallions, sliced

½ cup water

¼ cup soy sauce

1 tablespoon Korean chili powder

4 cups Napa cabbage, cut into 2" pieces

1 cup carrots, julienned

1. Add the garlic, ginger, scallions, water, soy sauce, and chili powder to the pressure cooker and stir well. Add the cabbage and carrots.

2. Lock on the lid. Bring to high pressure; maintain pressure for 2 minutes. Remove the pan from the heat, quick-release the pressure, and remove the lid.

Kimchi

Kimchi is a popular Korean condiment that is often used as the base for other recipes. Traditional recipes call for fermenting the mixture until pickled, but you can make "kimchi-style" cabbage by pressure cooking the ingredients instead of fermenting.

RED CABBAGE AND APPLES

Red wine will help preserve the color of the cabbage. Serve with any pork entrées.

INGREDIENTS
Serves 8

1 tablespoon olive oil

1 medium onion, diced

2 Granny Smith apples, peeled, cored, and sliced

½ cup Merlot

3 tablespoons red wine vinegar

1 2½-pound red cabbage

1 teaspoon salt

¼ teaspoon freshly ground black pepper

1. Heat olive oil in an uncovered pressure cooker over medium heat. Sauté the onion until soft.

2. Add the apples and stir in the wine and vinegar.

3. Quarter the cabbage and remove and discard the core. Slice the quarters into thin strips.

4. Gradually add cabbage to the pressure cooker, at first filling the pressure cooker to the top and loosely covering until the cabbage wilts, freeing up more space in the pan.

5. Stir in enough of the remaining cabbage to bring the pressure cooker to the fill line. Close and lock the lid.

6. Turn the heat up to high and when the cooker reaches pressure, lower the heat to the minimum needed to maintain pressure. Cook for 2–4 minutes at high pressure.

7. When time is up, open the pressure cooker by releasing pressure.

8. Transfer the cabbage to a serving bowl using a slotted spoon. Season with salt and pepper.

SOY-GLAZED BOK CHOY

Any type of bok choy—such as Chinese cabbage or baby bok choy—works well in this recipe.

INGREDIENTS
Serves 4

1 pound bok choy

½ cup water, plus 2 teaspoons warm water

¼ cup soy sauce

1 teaspoon rice wine vinegar

1 teaspoon peanut oil

1 teaspoon ginger, minced

1 teaspoon cornstarch

1. Trim the ends off the bok choy and slice in half lengthwise. Add to the steamer basket, then pour in ½ cup water.

2. Lock on the lid. Bring to high pressure; maintain pressure for 1 minute. Remove the pan from the heat, quick-release the pressure, and remove the lid. Remove the steamer basket and drain water.

3. Add the soy sauce, rice wine vinegar, peanut oil, and ginger to the pressure cooker and bring to medium heat. Combine the cornstarch with remaining 2 teaspoons of water then slowly add to the pressure cooker, stirring constantly. Add the bok choy and stir until it's completely coated.

4. Lock on the lid. Bring to high pressure; maintain pressure for 1 minute. Remove the pan from the heat, quick-release the pressure, and remove the lid.

CARROTS IN MILK

A side dish that is sure to be appreciated by children of all ages!

INGREDIENTS
Serves 4

1 pound thick carrots, peeled and cut into 1-inch chunks

¾ cup fat-free milk

¼ cup water

½ teaspoon salt

¼ teaspoon nutmeg

1 tablespoon olive oil

1 tablespoon flour

1. Fill the pressure cooker with carrots, milk, water, salt, nutmeg, and oil. Close and lock the lid.

2. Turn the heat up to high and when the cooker reaches pressure, lower the heat to the minimum needed to maintain pressure. Cook 3–4 minutes at high pressure.

3. When time is up, open the pressure cooker by releasing pressure.

4. With a slotted spoon, carefully remove carrots to serving dish and place uncovered pressure cooker over medium heat.

5. Add flour and heat until thickened, stirring constantly.

6. Pour sauce over carrots and serve.

GINGERED CARROTS

Boost the flavor in this dish by adding a dash of cinnamon or allspice after cooking.

INGREDIENTS

Serves 4

1 pound carrots, peeled and sliced diagonally

2 tablespoons vegetable oil

1 teaspoon fresh ginger, minced

1 cup water

½ teaspoon salt

¼ teaspoon black pepper

1. Add the carrots, oil, ginger, and water to the pressure cooker. Stir to mix. Close and lock the lid.

2. Turn the heat up to high and when the cooker reaches pressure, lower the heat to the minimum needed to maintain pressure. Cook for 1 minute at high pressure. When time is up, open the pressure cooker by releasing pressure.

3. Strain carrots, season with salt and pepper, and serve.

Fresh versus Ground Ginger

Ground ginger is more pungent than fresh and has a slightly different taste, so it is recommended that you don't substitute one for the other in all recipes. In this recipe, however, either will work well. If using ground ginger, use ⅛ teaspoon or less.

TIE-DYED BABY CARROTS

The name of this recipe comes from the beautiful mottled color the beets give to the carrots.

INGREDIENTS

Serves 8

8 small red beets

1 1-pound bag peeled baby carrots

¼ cup water

Butter, to taste

Salt and freshly ground black pepper, to taste

1. Scrub and peel the beets and trim the ends; quarter the beets. Add the baby carrots to the pressure cooker and put the beets on top. Pour in the water.

2. Lock the lid into place and bring to high pressure; maintain pressure for 8 minutes.

3. Remove the pressure cooker from heat, quick-release the pressure, and remove the lid.

4. Test the beets and carrots to determine whether or not they're cooked through.

5. If they're not yet tender, return the pan to medium heat. Add more water if necessary, and bring to a simmer. Simmer loosely covered until the vegetables are tender.

6. Once they're cooked through, drain off any excess moisture and transfer to a serving bowl. Top with butter, salt, and pepper to taste.

SOUTHERN-STYLE COLLARDS

Collard greens are a Southern staple typically flavored with animal fat, but a flavorful vegetarian version can be made by adding liquid smoke and soy sauce to the broth.

INGREDIENTS
Serves 4–6

1 pound collard greens

1 tablespoon olive oil

½ onion, diced

1 clove garlic, minced

1 chipotle chili pepper

4 cups vegetable stock

1 teaspoon liquid smoke

1 tablespoon soy sauce

1 teaspoon white vinegar

Salt and pepper, to taste

1. To prepare the greens, cut away the tough stalks and stems and discard any leaves that are bruised or yellow. Wash the collards two or three times thoroughly to remove the grit, chop into large pieces, and set aside.

2. Bring the pressure cooker to medium heat. Add the olive oil, onion, garlic, and chipotle pepper. Cook until the onions begin to soften, about 5 minutes. Add all remaining ingredients, except salt and pepper, and the chopped collards; stir well.

3. Lock the lid into place and bring to high pressure; maintain pressure for 10 minutes. Remove from the heat and allow pressure to release naturally.

4. Remove the chipotle before serving. Season with salt and pepper, to taste.

CORN ON THE COB

"Shuck" means to peel off the husk and silk from the corn prior to cooking.

INGREDIENTS
Serves 4

4 ears fresh sweet corn, shucked

½ cup water

1 tablespoon butter, or vegan margarine, such as Earth Balance

Salt and black pepper, to taste

1. Place the rack in the pressure cooker and place the corn on the rack. Pour in the water.

2. Lock the lid into place and bring to low pressure; maintain pressure for 3 minutes. Remove the pressure cooker from heat, quick-release the pressure, and remove the lid.

3. Spread ¼ of the butter over each ear of corn and season with salt and pepper, to taste.

Corn's Peak Season

Corn is at its best during the peak season summer month of July. Whenever possible, use fresh fruits and vegetables for the biggest nutritional punch, but if fresh is not an option, frozen fruits and vegetables are a good alternative.

CILANTRO-LIME CORN ON THE COB

Dress up plain corn on the cob with seasoned butter. To add a little more kick, increase the amount of cayenne pepper.

INGREDIENTS

Serves 4

4 ears fresh sweet corn, shucked

½ cup water

2 tablespoons butter, or vegan margarine, such as Earth Balance

2 tablespoons cilantro, chopped

2 teaspoons fresh lime juice

½ teaspoon salt

½ teaspoon cayenne pepper

1. Place the rack in the pressure cooker and place the corn on the rack. Pour in the water.

2. Lock the lid into place and bring to low pressure; maintain pressure for 3 minutes. Remove the pressure cooker from heat, quick-release the pressure, and remove the lid.

3. In a small bowl, combine the butter, cilantro, lime juice, salt, and cayenne pepper until well blended.

4. When the corn is cool enough to handle, spread ¼ of the mixture on each ear of corn.

CREAMED CORN 🌿

Creamed corn is an almost soupy vegetable side dish that is popular in the Midwest and South.

INGREDIENTS
Serves 8

8 ears sweet corn, shucked

½ cup water

2 teaspoons butter, or vegan margarine, such as Earth Balance

2 teaspoons flour

1 cup milk, or unsweetened soymilk

2 teaspoons salt

1 teaspoon sugar

1. Place the rack in the pressure cooker and place the corn on the rack. Pour in the water.

2. Lock the lid into place and bring to low pressure; maintain pressure for 3 minutes. Remove the pressure cooker from heat, quick-release the pressure, and remove the lid.

3. When the corn is cool enough to handle, place each ear of corn over a large mixing bowl and remove the kernels from the corn with a knife, using long downward strokes and rotating the cob as you go.

4. Take half of the kernels and pulse in a food processor until just smooth.

5. In a small pan, melt the butter, then stir in the flour, being careful not to brown. Slowly stir the milk into the roux, and stir until smooth.

6. Add all of the corn to the saucepan, bring to a boil, reduce heat, and simmer for 10 minutes. Add salt and sugar before removing from heat.

CRANBERRY SAUCE

You can make this cranberry sauce several days in advance, store it in the refrigerator, and then bring it back to temperature on the stove. For additional flavor, stir in some orange liqueur, bourbon, or brandy.

INGREDIENTS
Serves 6

1 12-ounce bag fresh cranberries

1 cup sugar

½ cup water, apple juice, or pineapple juice

Pinch salt

1 tablespoon frozen orange juice concentrate

Optional: Cinnamon and ground cloves, to taste

1. Rinse and drain the cranberries. Remove and discard any stems or blemished cranberries.

2. Add the cranberries to the pressure cooker along with the sugar, water or juice, and salt. Lock the lid into place and bring to high pressure; maintain pressure for 6 minutes.

3. Remove from heat and allow pressure to release naturally for 10 minutes. Remove the lid.

4. Stir in the orange juice concentrate. Stir well, breaking the cranberries apart with a spoon or mashing them slightly with a potato masher.

5. Taste for seasoning and adjust if necessary, stirring in additional sugar if needed and the cinnamon and cloves if desired. Serve warm or chilled.

EGGPLANT CAPONATA

This versatile dish can be served hot, at room temperature, or cold.

INGREDIENTS
Serves 8

¼ cup extra-virgin olive oil

¼ cup white wine

2 tablespoons red wine vinegar

1 teaspoon ground cinnamon

1 large eggplant, peeled and diced

1 medium onion, diced

1 medium green bell pepper, diced

1 medium red bell pepper, diced

2 cloves garlic, minced

1 14½-ounce can diced tomatoes

3 stalks celery, diced

½ cup oil-cured olives, pitted and chopped

½ cup golden raisins

2 tablespoons capers, rinsed and drained

Salt and freshly ground black pepper, to taste

1. Add all ingredients except salt and pepper to the pressure cooker. Stir well to mix. Lock the lid into place and bring to low pressure; maintain pressure for 8 minutes.

2. Remove from heat and quick-release the pressure. Remove the lid and stir the contents of the pressure cooker. Taste for seasoning and add salt and pepper, to taste.

Serving Suggestions

Caponata is often served as a salad but it has other uses as well. Try it as a sandwich spread on Italian bread, a dipping sauce for toasted baguette rounds, or relish.

MASHED EGGPLANT AND TOMATO SALAD

Serve this dish as a salad or as a dip with pita bread. It can be enjoyed hot or cold.

INGREDIENTS
Serves 4–6

1 large eggplant, peeled and diced

½ cup water

3 tablespoons olive oil

3 cloves garlic, minced

2 cups tomatoes, chopped

2 teaspoons lemon juice

1 teaspoon paprika

1 teaspoon salt

2 tablespoons parsley

1. Add the eggplant and water to the pressure cooker. Lock on the lid. Bring to high pressure; maintain pressure for 4 minutes. Remove the pan from the heat, quick-release the pressure, and remove the lid. Drain and set aside.

2. Add the olive oil to the pressure cooker over medium heat. Add the garlic and sauté for 30 seconds. Add the cooked eggplant, tomatoes, lemon juice, paprika, and salt.

3. Lock on the lid. Bring to high pressure; maintain pressure for 2 minutes. Remove the pan from the heat, quick-release the pressure, and remove the lid.

4. Stir in the parsley, then serve.

FENNEL COOKED IN WHITE WINE

To make a fennel purée, use a slotted spoon to transfer it to a food processor after completing step 2. Pulse until smooth, adding some of the cooking liquid if necessary.

INGREDIENTS
Serves 4

4 fennel bulbs

1 tablespoon butter, or vegan margarine, such as Earth Balance

1 tablespoon olive oil

1 small onion, diced

1 cup white wine

Salt and pepper, to taste

1. Cut off the tops and bottoms of the fennel bulbs and remove the two outer leaves. Thoroughly rinse the bulbs under cold running water. Dice the bulbs. Set aside.

2. Bring the butter and oil to temperature in the pressure cooker over medium heat. Add the onion; sauté for 3 minutes. Stir in the diced fennel; sauté for 3 minutes. Stir in the wine. Lock the lid into place and bring to low pressure; maintain for 8 minutes.

3. Quick-release the pressure and remove the lid. Simmer until the fennel is cooked through and soft. Add salt and pepper, to taste.

MILK-BRAISED FENNEL

An unusual accompaniment to meat.

INGREDIENTS
Serves 4

2 large fennel bulbs

¾ cup fat-free milk

¼ cup water

½ teaspoon salt

¼ teaspoon nutmeg

1 tablespoon olive oil

1 tablespoon flour

1 teaspoon freshly ground pepper

1. Remove the green tips of the fennel and reserve them for garnish. Slice the bulbs into ¼" thick slices.

2. Fill the pressure cooker with fennel, milk, water, salt, nutmeg, and oil. Close and lock the lid.

3. Turn the heat up to high and when the cooker reaches pressure, lower the heat to the minimum needed to maintain pressure. Cook 3–4 minutes at high pressure.

4. When time is up, open the pressure cooker by releasing pressure.

5. With a slotted spoon, carefully remove fennel slices to serving dish and place uncovered pressure cooker over medium heat.

6. Add flour and heat until thickened, stirring constantly.

7. Pour sauce over fennel garnish with green fronds and season with pepper before serving.

FRESH GREEN BEANS WITH TOASTED SESAME

If fresh green beans are unavailable, you can use frozen beans instead.

INGREDIENTS

Serves 4

2 cups water

1 pound fresh green beans

1 tablespoon olive oil

2 tablespoons toasted sesame seeds

Salt and pepper, to taste

1. Fill the bottom of the pressure cooker with water. Place the steamer basket in the pressure cooker.

2. Trim the ends off the green beans and place in the steamer basket.

3. Secure the lid; cook on high until the pressure indicator rises. Lower heat and cook for 5 minutes.

4. Remove the green beans from the pressure cooker and toss in the olive oil.

5. Sprinkle sesame seeds over green beans and season with salt and pepper.

GREEN BEAN AND PINE NUT SALAD

The pressure cooker can bring the bright color back to frozen green beans. The bright flavor shines in this simple salad.

INGREDIENTS

Serves 4

1 pound fresh or frozen green beans

1 cup water

¼ cup toasted pine nuts

2 teaspoons white balsamic vinegar

1 tablespoon olive oil

1. Lay green beans in steamer basket.

2. Place water in the pressure cooker and add the steamer basket. Close and lock the lid.

3. Turn the heat up to high and when the cooker reaches pressure, lower the heat to the minimum needed to maintain pressure. Cook for 5–7 minutes at high pressure.

4. When time is up, open the pressure cooker by releasing pressure.

5. Transfer to serving dish and dress with pine nuts, vinegar, and olive oil

SOUTHERN ITALIAN GREEN BEANS AND TOMATOES

To keep the green beans from overcooking, they are steamed over the tomatoes. You can use fresh or frozen green beans for this recipe.

INGREDIENTS
Serves 6

1 tablespoon olive oil

1 clove garlic, crushed

2 cups tomatoes, chopped (or 14.5-ounce can chopped tomatoes)

1 pound green beans, trimmed

¼ teaspoon salt

1 sprig basil, chopped

1 tablespoon extra-virgin olive oil

1. Heat olive oil in an uncovered pressure cooker over medium heat. Add garlic and cook until golden. Add the tomatoes and stir well.

2. Add the steamer basket filled with the green beans. Sprinkle with salt.

3. Turn the heat up to high and when the cooker reaches pressure, lower the heat to the minimum needed to maintain pressure. Cook for 5–7 minutes at low pressure (3 minutes at high pressure).

4. When time is up, open the pressure cooker by releasing pressure.

5. Pull out the steamer basket and mix the green beans with the tomato sauce. Check for doneness. If the green beans need to cook a little more, simmer them together with the sauce on low heat, without the lid.

6. When fork tender, move the mixed contents to a serving bowl, and sprinkle with basil and olive oil. Serve warm or at room temperature.

Tomato Magic

In Italy, meats and vegetables are cooked in tomato sauce. So you can do this recipe with just about any vegetable!

KALE WITH RED PEPPER FLAKES AND CUMIN

Kale can be enjoyed while still tough and chewy, or completely softened. Adjust cooking times to reach the consistency you enjoy.

INGREDIENTS
Serves 4

2 cups water

½ teaspoon salt, plus more to taste

8 cups kale, washed, drained, and chopped

1 tablespoon olive oil

1 clove garlic, minced

1 teaspoon dried red pepper flakes

½ cup vegetable stock

½ teaspoon cumin

1. Bring water to a boil in the pressure cooker. Stir in ½ teaspoon salt. Blanch kale for 1 minute, drain, and set aside.

2. Add the olive oil to the pressure cooker over medium heat. Add the garlic and red pepper flakes; cook for 30 seconds. Add the vegetable stock, cumin, and kale, then stir.

3. Lock the lid into place and bring to high pressure; maintain pressure for 6 minutes. Remove from the heat and allow pressure to release naturally. Remove the lid, and serve.

OKRA WITH CORN AND TOMATO

The "goo" that comes out of okra while cooking helps to thicken liquids.

INGREDIENTS
Serves 8

4 ears fresh sweet corn, shucked

½ cup water

1 teaspoon olive oil

¼ cup red onion, diced

1 pound okra, tops removed and cut into ½" rounds

2 cups tomatoes, chopped

1 cup vegetable stock

2 teaspoons salt

1 teaspoon cayenne pepper

1. Place the rack in the pressure cooker and place the corn on the rack. Pour in the water.

2. Lock the lid into place and bring to low pressure; maintain pressure for 3 minutes. Remove the pressure cooker from heat, quick-release the pressure, and remove the lid.

3. When the corn is cool enough to handle, place each ear of corn over a large mixing bowl and remove the kernels from the corn with a knife, using long downward strokes and rotating the cob as you go.

4. After cleaning the pressure cooker, add the olive oil over medium heat, then sauté the onion until just soft.

5. Add the okra, tomatoes, vegetable stock, salt, and cayenne, then stir.

6. Lock the lid into place and bring to high pressure; maintain pressure for 3 minutes. Remove the pressure cooker from heat, quick-release the pressure, and remove the lid. Stir in the corn before serving.

PARSNIP PURÉE

The techniques in this recipe are inspired by Julia Child's famous preparation of the dish.

INGREDIENTS
Serves 4

1 pound parsnips, peeled and diced

Water, as needed

3 tablespoons butter, or vegan margarine, such as Earth Balance

½ teaspoon salt

½ teaspoon pepper

1. Place the parsnips in the pressure cooker and add enough water to just cover.

2. Lock on the lid. Bring to high pressure; maintain pressure for 3 minutes. Remove the pan from the heat, quick-release the pressure, and remove the lid. Remove the parsnips but reserve the cooking water.

3. Add the drained parsnips and ¼ cup cooking water to a food processor. Blend until smooth, adding more water if necessary.

4. Return the purée to the cleaned pressure cooker or a saucepan. Add the butter, salt, and pepper, and cook over low heat for 10 minutes, stirring often, before serving.

MUSHY PEAS

This is a great use for frozen peas—or pressure steam fresh peas instead.

INGREDIENTS
Serves 6

1 tablespoon olive oil

1 scallion, finely chopped

1 pound frozen peas

1 sprig mint

1 cup water

Salt and pepper to taste (about 1 and ¼ teaspoon)

1. Heat olive oil in an uncovered pressure cooker over medium heat. Add the scallion and sauté until softened.

2. Add the peas, mint, and water. Close and lock the lid.

3. Turn the heat up to high and when the cooker reaches pressure, lower to the minimum needed to maintain pressure. Then, begin counting 2–3 minutes cooking time at high pressure.

4. When time is up, open the pressure cooker by releasing pressure.

5. Remove mint sprig. Drain about ½ of cooking liquid and mash or pureé to desired thickness. Add salt and pepper to taste.

PEPERONATA (FAUX ROASTED PEPPERS)

This Italian pepper recipe is extremely flexible. You can also serve this as an appetizer, piled onto crispy crostini, or as a sauce, mixed in with freshly cooked pasta.

INGREDIENTS
Serves 6

1 tablespoon vegetable oil

1 red onion, thinly sliced into strips

2 red bell peppers, seeded and thinly sliced

2 yellow bell peppers, seeded and thinly sliced

1 green bell pepper, seeded and thinly sliced

2 cloves garlic, chopped, divided

3 ripe tomatoes, chopped (or 14.5-ounce can of chopped tomatoes)

1 bunch basil, chopped

2 tablespoons olive oil

½ teaspoon salt

¼ teaspoon pepper

1. Heat vegetable oil in an uncovered pressure cooker over medium heat. Add onion and sauté until soft.

2. Add the peppers and let one side of the peppers brown without stirring—about 5 minutes. Then add the tomatoes and half of the garlic and mix well. Close and lock the pressure cooker.

3. Turn the heat up to high and when the cooker reaches pressure, lower the heat to the minimum needed to maintain pressure. Cook for 5 minutes at high pressure.

4. When time is up, open the pressure cooker by releasing pressure.

5. Remove the peppers with tongs and put them immediately in a serving bowl. Add the rest of the garlic, basil, olive oil, salt, and pepper.

6. Mix well and serve.

BOOZY TATERS

Here's something a little different to do with your potatoes. They don't have a strong wine flavor, but just a little something "extra."

INGREDIENTS
Serves 6

1 tablespoon olive oil

5 medium potatoes, peeled and diced

2 teaspoons salt

1 teaspoon black pepper

1 sprig rosemary, chopped

1 cup of Marsala, Vin Santo, or any other sweet dry wine

1. Heat olive oil in an uncovered pressure cooker over medium heat. When the oil is hot add the potatoes, salt, pepper, and rosemary.

2. Add the wine, and stir, scraping the bottom of the pan. Close and lock the lid.

3. Turn the heat up to high and when the cooker reaches pressure, lower the heat to the minimum needed to maintain pressure. Cook for 6 minutes at high pressure.

4. When time is up, open the pressure cooker by releasing pressure.

5. Serve warm.

BRAISED FINGERLING POTATOES

Braising is a technique that involves browning food first and then slowly cooking in liquid until softened.

INGREDIENTS
Serves 3–4

2 tablespoons extra-virgin olive oil

1 pound fingerling potatoes, halved (root to stem)

1 cup vegetable stock

4 whole garlic cloves

1 tablespoon rosemary, chopped

1 tablespoon thyme, chopped

Salt and pepper, to taste

1. Add 2 tablespoons olive oil to the pressure cooker and cook the potatoes over medium-high heat 3 minutes on each side. Add the vegetable stock and whole garlic cloves to the pressure cooker.

2. Lock the lid into place and bring to high pressure. Once the pressure is achieved, turn the heat to low and cook for 5 minutes. Remove from the heat and allow pressure to release naturally.

3. Drain the potatoes and garlic in a colander. Put the potatoes in a mixing bowl and mince the cooked garlic.

4. Add the garlic, rosemary, and thyme to the potatoes, then season with salt and pepper to taste.

DILL POTATO SALAD

Instead of—or in addition to—fresh dill, you can use minced dill pickles in this potato salad recipe.

INGREDIENTS
Serves 6–8

1 cup water

2 pounds red potatoes, quartered

½ cup mayonnaise, or vegan mayonnaise, such as Vegenaise

1 teaspoon yellow mustard

1 teaspoon cider vinegar

1 tablespoon fresh dill, chopped

Salt and pepper, to taste

½ cup red onion, chopped

½ cup celery, chopped

1. Add the water and the potatoes to the pressure cooker. Lock the lid into place and bring to high pressure. Once the pressure is achieved, turn the heat to low and cook for 3–4 minutes. Remove from the heat and allow pressure to release naturally. Drain the potatoes and rinse with cold water.

2. Whisk together the mayonnaise, yellow mustard, cider vinegar, dill, salt, and pepper.

3. Combine the potatoes with the chopped onion and celery and then add the mayonnaise mixture.

4. Season with more salt and pepper, if necessary.

GARLIC PARSLEY MASHED POTATOES

Russet potatoes are also commonly called Idaho potatoes.

INGREDIENTS
Serves 6–8

1 cup water

8 cups russet potatoes, quartered

8 tablespoons butter, or vegan margarine, such as Earth Balance

½ onion, diced

4 cloves garlic, minced

½ cup milk, or unsweetened soymilk

½ cup parsley

2 teaspoons salt

½ teaspoon black pepper

1. Pour the water into the pressure cooker and add the potatoes. Lock the lid into place and bring to high pressure. Once the pressure is achieved, turn the heat to low and cook for 5 minutes. Remove from the heat and allow pressure to release naturally.

2. Drain the potatoes into a colander. Add the butter to the pressure cooker and sauté the onion and garlic for about 3 minutes. Add the milk and potatoes, and remove the pressure cooker from the heat. Mash the potatoes using a potato masher or electric mixer.

3. Mix in the parsley, salt, and pepper, and serve.

HERB ROASTED FINGERLING POTATOES

These potatoes will brown nicely during the sauté and look like they're from the oven! Very small new or baby potatoes can also be used.

INGREDIENTS

Serves 6

4 tablespoons vegetable oil

2 pounds fingerling potatoes

3 cloves garlic, skin on

1 sprig rosemary, chopped

½ cup chicken stock

1 teaspoon salt

¼ teaspoon pepper

1. Heat vegetable oil in an uncovered pressure cooker over medium heat. Add as many potatoes as will cover the base of your pressure cooker.

2. Roll the potatoes around and brown the outside on all sides (8–10 minutes). Remove from pressure cooker and repeat with rest of potatoes, garlic, and rosemary. With a sharp knife, pierce each potato in the center. Return potatoes to the pressure cooker and pour in the stock. Close and lock the lid.

3. Turn the heat up to high and when the cooker reaches pressure, lower the heat to the minimum needed to maintain pressure. Cook for 5 minutes at high pressure.

4. Open with the natural-release method—move the pressure cooker to a cool burner and wait for the pressure to come down on its own (about 15 minutes). For electric pressure cookers, disengage the "keep warm" mode or unplug the cooker and open when the pressure indicator has gone down (20–30 minutes).

5. Remove the outer skin of the garlic cloves (and serve whole or smash, to taste). Then, sprinkle everything with salt and pepper and serve.

Pressure Pans

Some stove-top pressure cooker manufacturers make a low, wide pressure cooker that is called a "pressure pan" or "pressure braiser." If you have one, it's perfect for this recipe because of the wide area in which to sauté the potatoes—no need to do it in batches!

LIGHT SCALLOPED POTATOES

Using plain yogurt to replace heavy cream and most of the butter makes this a creamy and light dish.

INGREDIENTS
Serves 6

2 cups plain whole yogurt

5 potatoes, peeled and thinly sliced

1 teaspoon salt

1 teaspoon white pepper

1 teaspoon nutmeg

½ cup grated parmesan cheese

1 tablespoon butter, cut in small cubes

½ cup bread crumbs

1. Place the yogurt in a fine mesh strainer over a bowl and let drain in the refrigerator for about 4 hours. Discard liquid and set thickened yogurt aside.

2. In a heat-proof baking dish that will fit inside your pressure cooker without touching the sides, layer the potatoes and yogurt, sprinkling each layer of potato with salt, pepper, and nutmeg. Continue working in layers until the container is full. Top with parmesan cheese and butter.

3. Place water in the pressure cooker and add the steamer basket (or trivet) and lower the uncovered baking dish into the pressure cooker. Close and lock the lid.

4. Turn the heat up to high and when the cooker reaches pressure, lower the heat to the minimum needed to maintain pressure. Cook for 15 minutes at high pressure.

5. Open with the natural-release method—move the pressure cooker to a cool burner and wait for the pressure to come down on its own (about 15 minutes). For electric pressure cookers, disengage the "keep warm" mode or unplug the cooker and open when the pressure indicator has gone down (20–30 minutes).

6. Carefully remove the container from the pressure cooker.

7. Sprinkle with bread crumbs and slide under the broiler until the top is crisp before serving.

Make and Use a Foil Sling

Getting a heat-proof container in the pressure cooker is easy. The hard part is pulling it out when it's hot and slippery! Use a foil sling to lower and lift containers from the pressure cooker: Fold an extra-long piece of aluminum foil in half. Place a heat-proof dish in the middle of the strip, lift up the sides and use as handles to lower into the pressure cooker. Fold the "handles" down during pressure cooking, and when pressure cooking is finished, unfold the handles and pull your containers out of the pressure cooker.

POTATO AND PARSLEY SALAD

Steaming the potatoes already cut helps them to keep their shape. This way, there's no risk of cutting a hot potato and finding out that it's too soft, turning your salad into an unintended purée.

INGREDIENTS
Serves 6

⅓ cup finely chopped white onion

3 tablespoons white wine vinegar

½ teaspoon black pepper

3 pounds red or new potatoes, cut in 1-inch cubes

1 cup water

½ teaspoon salt

4 tablespoons extra-virgin olive oil

1 bunch parsley, finely chopped

1. Place onion in a small bowl with the vinegar and pepper and set aside to macerate.

2. Place potatoes in the steamer basket. Place water in the pressure cooker and add the steamer basket. Sprinkle with salt. Close and lock the lid.

3. Turn the heat up to high and when the cooker reaches pressure, lower the heat to the minimum needed to maintain pressure. Cook for 10 minutes at high pressure.

4. Open with the natural-release method—move the pressure cooker to a cool burner and wait for the pressure to come down on its own (about 15 minutes). For electric pressure cookers, disengage the "keep warm" mode or unplug the cooker and open when the pressure indicator has gone down (20–30 minutes).

5. When cooking is finished, transfer potatoes to a mixing bowl and dress them with the vinegar and onion mixture. When they have cooled to room temperature (about 10 minutes) add the salt, olive oil, and parsley.

6. Serve immediately or chill overnight in the refrigerator.

POTATO PICCATA

Piccata typically means a dish that contains butter, lemon, and herbs.

INGREDIENTS
Serves 4

2 cups water

4 russet potatoes, sliced

2 tablespoons butter, or vegan margarine, such as Earth Balance

1 onion, julienned

1 red pepper, sliced

¼ cup vegetable stock

2 tablespoons fresh lemon juice

¼ cup parsley

Salt and pepper, to taste

1. Pour the water into the pressure cooker and add the potatoes. Lock the lid into place and bring to high pressure. Once the pressure is achieved, turn the heat to low and cook for 5 minutes. Remove from the heat and allow pressure to release naturally.

2. Drain the potatoes in a colander. Add the butter to the pressure cooker and sauté the onion and red pepper until the onion begins to turn golden brown. Add the potatoes, stock, and lemon juice. Cook for an additional 3–5 minutes.

3. Remove from the heat and add the parsley. Add salt and pepper to taste.

Julienne

Julienne is a type of cut that turns food into long, thin, matchstick-like pieces. Each julienned piece is typically ⅛" to ¼" thick.

POTATO RISOTTO ✍

Risotto is typically made with Arborio rice, but the same technique can be applied to a finely diced potato for a unique twist.

INGREDIENTS

Serves 6

2 leeks (white part only)

¼ cup plus 1 tablespoon olive oil

3 sprigs fresh thyme

3 pounds russet potatoes

2 cups dry white wine

2 quarts mushroom broth

4 cups fresh spinach leaves

Salt and pepper, to taste

1. Thinly slice leeks crosswise into semicircles and rinse. Add ¼ cup olive oil to the pressure cooker and sauté the leeks until translucent. Add the thyme and cook for 10 minutes.

2. Peel the potatoes. Cut into ⅛" slices and then into ⅛" dice. In a small bowl, toss the potatoes with 1 tablespoon olive oil to thinly coat.

3. Add the potatoes to the pressure cooker and cook for 3 minutes. Deglaze with the wine and reduce until the potatoes are dry. Add the leek mixture and the broth to the potatoes. Lock the lid into place and bring to high pressure. Once the pressure is achieved, turn the heat to low and cook for 5 minutes. Allow pressure to release naturally and remove the lid.

4. Continue to cook and stir the potato risotto without the lid on until all the liquid has been absorbed. Julienne the spinach leaves and add to the risotto once the potatoes are cooked.

5. Season with salt and pepper, to taste.

POTATOES AU GRATIN

Panko bread crumbs are made from bread without crust and are almost always vegan.

INGREDIENTS
Serves 4

1 cup water

8 cups potatoes, peeled and diced

2 cups Béchamel sauce (Chapter 5)

1 cup Cheddar cheese, shredded, or vegan Cheddar, such as Daiya Cheddar Style Shreds

Salt and pepper, to taste

1 cup bread crumbs

1. Pour the water into the pressure cooker and add the potatoes. Lock the lid into place and bring to high pressure. Once the pressure is achieved, turn the heat to low and cook for 5 minutes. Remove from the heat and allow pressure to release naturally. Drain the potatoes in a colander.

2. In a saucepan, heat the béchamel sauce, then mix in the cheese, and cook until the cheese is melted. Add salt and pepper to taste.

3. Put the potatoes into a casserole dish and pour the béchamel mixture over the potatoes, mixing gently. Sprinkle the bread crumbs over the top of the potatoes and bake at 400°F for 15 minutes, or until the bread crumbs are golden brown.

Au Gratin
Similar to scalloped, au gratin means a dish topped with a sauce or bread crumbs and baked until a crust forms on top.

ROSEMARY MASHED POTATOES

These basic flavors can be used in other potato dishes if you're not in the mood for mashed potatoes. Instead, try roasting quartered red potatoes or whole fingerlings with rosemary.

INGREDIENTS
Serves 6–8

1 cup water

8 cups russet potatoes, quartered

¼ cup extra-virgin olive oil

4 cloves garlic, minced

1 tablespoon rosemary

½ cup milk, or unsweetened soymilk

2 teaspoons salt

½ teaspoon black pepper

1. Pour the water into the pressure cooker and add the potatoes. Lock the lid into place and bring to high pressure. Once the pressure is achieved, turn the heat to low and cook for 5 minutes. Remove from the heat and allow pressure to release naturally.

2. Drain the potatoes into a colander. Add the olive oil to the pressure cooker and sauté the garlic and rosemary until the garlic begins to turn golden brown. Add the milk and potatoes and remove the pressure cooker from the heat. Mash the potatoes using a potato masher or electric mixer.

3. Season with salt and pepper, adding more if necessary.

SCALLOPED POTATOES

Many recipes that are traditionally baked in an oven can be steamed in a pressure cooker instead.

INGREDIENTS
Serves 4

2 tablespoons butter, or vegan margarine, such as Earth Balance

½ cup onion, julienned

2 cloves garlic, minced

3 cups béchamel sauce

1 teaspoon salt

¼ teaspoon black pepper

4 potatoes, thinly sliced

2 cups water

1. Add the butter to the pressure cooker and sauté the onion until it begins to turn golden brown. Add the garlic and sauté for 1 minute more. Add the béchamel sauce, salt, and pepper, and cook until the sauce has thickened. Pour the sauce into a bowl and set aside.

2. Thinly slice the potatoes. Grease a small pressure cooker–safe casserole dish with nonstick spray or butter. Place half of the potatoes on the bottom of the casserole dish. Cover the potatoes with half of the béchamel sauce. Make another layer of potatoes and sauce, and then cover the casserole dish in aluminum foil.

3. Place the steamer rack into the pressure cooker. Add the water and place the casserole dish in the pressure cooker.

4. Lock the lid into place and bring to high pressure. Once the pressure is achieved, turn the heat to low and cook for about 15 minutes. Remove from the heat and allow pressure to release naturally.

5. Remove the casserole dish from the pressure cooker and serve.

Scalloped

Scalloped traditionally means a dish that is covered in sauce and bread crumbs. You can skip the bread crumbs to make a crust out of a well-cooked sauce instead.

TWICE-COOKED POTATOES

Cooking the potatoes for the first time in a pressure cooker will shorten the cooking time and help lock in nutrients.

INGREDIENTS
Serves 4

2 cups water

4 russet potatoes, not peeled

1 cup sour cream, or vegan sour cream, such as Tofutti Sour Supreme

½ cup milk, or unsweetened soymilk

¼ cup butter, or vegan margarine

1 teaspoon salt

½ teaspoon black pepper

1 cup shredded Cheddar cheese, or vegan Cheddar, such as Daiya Cheddar Style Shreds

4 green onions, sliced

1. Pour the water into the pressure cooker and add the potatoes. Lock the lid into place and bring to high pressure. Maintain for 20 minutes, then remove from the heat and allow pressure to release naturally.

2. Drain the potatoes in a colander. Cut the potatoes in half lengthwise and scoop the flesh of the potatoes into a bowl. Set potato skins aside.

3. Add the sour cream, milk, butter, salt, and pepper to the potato filling in the bowl. Mash the filling with a potato masher or electric mixer.

4. Spoon the blended mixture back into the potato skins and top with Cheddar cheese.

5. Preheat the oven to 350°F. Place the potatoes on a baking sheet, and cook for 15 minutes. Garnish with green onions before serving.

CHIPOTLE AND THYME MASHED SWEET POTATOES

To substitute fresh thyme for dried thyme, use ½ tablespoon of the fresh herb.

INGREDIENTS
Serves 4–6

2 cups water

6 cups sweet potatoes, cubed

4 tablespoons butter, or vegan margarine, such as Earth Balance

3 cloves garlic, minced

½ teaspoon dried chipotle pepper

½ teaspoon dried thyme

Salt and pepper, to taste

1. Pour the water into the pressure cooker and add the sweet potatoes. Lock the lid into place and bring to high pressure. Once the pressure is achieved, turn the heat to low and cook for 5 minutes. Remove from the heat and allow pressure to release naturally.

2. Drain the potatoes into a colander. Add the butter to the pressure cooker and sauté the garlic for about 2 minutes. Remove the pressure cooker from the heat. Add the sweet potatoes, chipotle pepper, and thyme. Mash the potatoes using a potato masher or electric mixer.

3. Season with salt and pepper, to taste.

CURRIED YAMS AND POTATOES

Growing your own potatoes is easy, especially if you live in a cooler climate. Purchase seed potatoes from your local gardening store, and use organic fertilizers to keep them healthy.

INGREDIENTS
Serves 8

1 tablespoon ghee or butter

1 small onion, peeled and finely diced

2 tablespoons curry paste

3 cloves garlic, peeled and minced

4 large yams, peeled and diced

1 large potato, peeled and diced

¼ cup applesauce

¼ cup water

1 cup frozen baby peas, thawed

Optional: Plain yogurt

Optional: Mango Chutney (Chapter 16)

Optional: 1 cucumber, peeled and sliced

1. Melt the ghee or butter in the pressure cooker and bring to temperature over medium-high heat. Add the onion; sauté for 3 minutes.

2. Stir in the curry paste and garlic; sauté for 2 minutes. Stir in the diced yams and potato; sauté for several minutes or until the pan is sticky and the mixture is about to burn. Stir in the applesauce and water.

3. Lock the lid into place and bring to low pressure; maintain pressure for 5 minutes. Remove from the heat and allow pressure to release naturally.

4. Remove the lid. Stir and slightly mash the potato mixture. Add the peas. Stir into the potatoes. Cover and let rest for a few minutes to bring the peas to temperature.

5. If desired, serve with a dollop of plain yogurt and Mango Chutney over each serving and garnish with cucumber slices.

MAPLE-GLAZED SWEET POTATOES

You can remove the sugar from this recipe by replacing it with a sweetener, such as Splenda.

INGREDIENTS
Serves 2–4

1 cup water

4 cups sweet potatoes, diced

1 tablespoon butter, or vegan margarine, such as Earth Balance

¼ cup maple syrup

1 tablespoon brown sugar

⅓ cup chopped pecans

1. Add the water and the sweet potatoes to the pressure cooker. Lock the lid into place and bring to high pressure. Once the pressure is achieved, turn the heat to low and cook for 5 minutes. Remove from the heat and allow pressure to release naturally.

2. Drain the sweet potatoes in a colander. Preheat the oven to 375°F. Place the butter, syrup, and sugar in a small bowl and microwave for about 30 seconds, or until the butter is melted. In a medium mixing bowl, toss the sweet potatoes, butter mixture, and pecans, then pour into the casserole dish. Bake for 10 minutes.

MEDITERRANEAN SWEET POTATO SALAD

Serve this salad at room temperature or chilled after refrigerating for a few hours.

INGREDIENTS
Serves 4

¼ cup olive oil

1 onion, diced

2 cloves garlic, minced

1 teaspoon cumin

1 teaspoon paprika

¼ cup fresh lemon juice

1 cup water

3 cups sweet potatoes, peeled and cubed

¼ cup green olives

3 tablespoons parsley, chopped

Salt and pepper, to taste

1. Add the olive oil to the pressure cooker and sauté the onion until it begins to turn golden brown. Add the garlic, cumin, paprika, and lemon juice; cook for about 2 minutes. Pour into a bowl and set aside.

2. Add the water and the sweet potatoes to the pressure cooker. Lock the lid into place and bring to high pressure. Once the pressure is achieved, turn the heat to low and cook for about 5 minutes. Remove from the heat and allow pressure to release naturally.

3. Drain the sweet potatoes in a colander. In a large bowl, toss the onion mixture with the potatoes.

4. Add the olives and parsley and season with salt and pepper, to taste.

THAI SWEET POTATOES

This dish is a soup that can be served over rice noodles and topped with a cooked egg to make it a complete meal. For more spice, use Thai red curry paste instead of green curry paste.

INGREDIENTS
Serves 6

2 tablespoons peanut or vegetable oil

1 red bell pepper, seeded and sliced

1 yellow bell pepper, seeded and sliced

1 orange bell pepper, seeded and sliced

1 large onion, peeled and sliced

2 cloves garlic, peeled and minced

1 tablespoon Thai green curry paste

3 large sweet potatoes, peeled and diced

1 14-ounce can unsweetened coconut milk

¼ cup water

1 teaspoon fresh lemon or lime juice

1½ cups snow peas or green beans

1½ tablespoons fresh cilantro, minced

1. Bring the oil to temperature over medium heat. Add the bell pepper slices; sauté for 2 minutes.

2. Add the onion slices; sauté for 3 minutes or until the vegetables are soft. Add the garlic and curry paste; sauté for 1 minute.

3. Stir in the sweet potatoes, coconut milk, water, and lemon or lime juice. Lock the lid into place and bring to high pressure; maintain pressure for 3 minutes.

4. Remove the pressure cooker from heat, quick-release the pressure, and remove the lid. Taste for seasoning, adding more curry paste if desired.

5. Cut the snow peas or green beans into 1-inch segments. Stir into the sweet potato mixture in the pressure cooker.

6. Return the pressure cooker to medium heat and bring to a simmer. Maintain the simmer for 3 minutes or until the vegetables are cooked to tender-crisp. Stir in the cilantro. Serve.

STEAMED PUMPKIN

Make your own pumpkin purée to use in pies or pasta sauce!

INGREDIENTS
Serves 6

1 medium (4-pound) pumpkin, cut into large pieces and seeded

1 cup water

1. Place pumpkin pieces in the pressure cooker skin-side down. Pour in the water. Close and lock the lid.

2. Turn the heat up to high and when the cooker reaches pressure, lower the heat to the minimum needed to maintain pressure. Cook for 8–10 minutes at high pressure.

3. Open with the natural-release method—move the pressure cooker to a cool burner and wait for the pressure to come down on its own (about 15 minutes). For electric pressure cookers, disengage the "keep warm" mode or unplug the cooker and open when the pressure indicator has gone down (20–30 minutes).

4. When cool enough to handle, peel off and discard the skin. Mash pumpkin with a fork or purée with an immersion blender.

Save the Seeds!

Rinse the seeds well and spread in an even layer on a cookie sheet to dry. Then toss them with vegetable oil and salt, return them to the cookie sheet, and roast at 300°F for 30 minutes, shaking the pan every 10 minutes.

CREAMED RADISHES

Braised radishes are another easy side dish. Just cover your radishes in enough water to cover them; add some butter, sugar, salt, and pepper; and bring to a boil. Simmer for 10–12 minutes or until radishes are tender.

INGREDIENTS
Serves 4

24 large red radishes

2 tablespoons butter

2 tablespoons all-purpose flour

1 cup chicken broth or water

⅓ cup heavy cream

Salt and freshly ground white or black pepper, to taste

1. Rinse and drain the radishes. Cut off the tops, leaving about 1 inch of the stem. Reserve some of the small leaves for garnish. Cut the radishes in half lengthwise.

2. Melt the butter in the pressure cooker over medium heat. When the butter begins to foam, whisk in the flour and then gradually whisk in the broth or water. Stir in the radishes.

3. Lock the lid into place and bring to low pressure; maintain pressure for 5 minutes. Remove from the heat and allow pressure to release naturally for 5 minutes. Quick-release any remaining pressure and remove the lid.

4. Use a slotted spoon to transfer the radishes to a serving bowl. Return the pressure cooker to medium heat and bring to a boil. Whisk in the cream; boil and stir for 2 minutes or until thickened.

5. Pour over the radishes. Add salt to taste and sprinkle liberally with pepper. Garnish with the reserved radish leaves.

RATATOUILLE

Ratatouille is sometimes served over potatoes. This version adds the potatoes to the dish. You can serve this Ratatouille over whole-grain pasta or topped with toasted garlic croutons.

INGREDIENTS
Serves 4

2 tablespoons extra-virgin olive oil

2 zucchini, sliced

1 Japanese eggplant, peeled and sliced

1 small onion, thinly sliced

1 green bell pepper, diced

2 medium potatoes, peeled and diced

8 ounces fresh mushrooms, sliced

1 28-ounce can diced tomatoes

3 tablespoons tomato paste

3 tablespoons water

2 cloves garlic, minced

1 teaspoon oregano

1 teaspoon basil

⅛ teaspoon dried red pepper flakes

Salt and fresh black pepper, to taste

Parmigiano-Reggiano cheese, grated, or vegan mozzarella, such as Daiya Mozzarella Style Shreds

1. Coat the bottom and sides of the pressure cooker with oil. Add the remaining ingredients except cheese in layers in the order given. Lock the lid into place and bring to low pressure; maintain pressure for 6 minutes.

2. Remove from heat and quick-release the pressure. Remove the lid, stir, and taste for seasoning, adjusting if necessary. Serve topped with the grated cheese.

LIGHTER RATATOUILLE

The original version of this dish lightly fries each vegetable before combining. Here, we skip the frying step and steam everything in its own juices.

INGREDIENTS
Serves 4

2 tablespoons extra-virgin olive oil

½ cup water (if using an electric pressure cooker)

2 7-inch zucchini, washed and sliced

1 small or Japanese eggplant, peeled and sliced

1 small onion, peeled and thinly sliced

1 green bell pepper, seeded and diced

8 ounces fresh mushrooms, cleaned and sliced

1 28-ounce can diced tomatoes

3 tablespoons tomato paste

3 tablespoons water

2 cloves garlic, peeled and minced

1 teaspoon basil

1 teaspoon oregano

⅛ teaspoon dried red pepper flakes

1 teaspoon salt

½ teaspoon freshly ground black pepper

½ cup grated Parmigiano-Reggiano cheese

1. Coat the bottom and sides of the pressure cooker with oil. If using an electric pressure cooker, add water. Layer the remaining ingredients, except cheese, in the order given. Close and lock the lid.

2. Turn the heat up to high and when the cooker reaches pressure, lower the heat to the minimum needed to maintain pressure. Cook for 6 minutes at high pressure.

3. When time is up, open the pressure cooker by releasing pressure.

4. Remove the lid, stir, and taste for seasoning, adjusting if necessary. Serve topped with the grated cheese.

MASHED RUTABAGAS AND PARSNIPS

Unlike many mashed root vegetable dishes where you can substitute milk for the cream or sour cream, this dish needs the added fat to offset the strong flavors of the vegetables.

INGREDIENTS
Serves 4

1 ¾-pound rutabaga, peeled, quartered, and sliced

2 parsnips, peeled and sliced

2 tablespoons butter

¼ teaspoon salt

¼ water

¼ cup heavy cream

¼ cup sour cream

Nutmeg, freshly grated

1. Add the rutabaga, parsnips, butter, salt, and water to the pressure cooker. Lock the lid into place and bring to low pressure; maintain pressure for 8 minutes.

2. Remove from heat and allow pressure to release naturally for 10 minutes. Quick-release any remaining pressure and remove the lid.

3. Drain any excess moisture from the vegetables or put the pressure cooker over low heat for few minutes. Transfer to a food processor; pulse to pureé the vegetables. Gradually add the cream as you pulse the vegetables until they reach their desired consistency. Once the vegetables are pureéd, transfer them to a serving bowl and stir in the sour cream. Taste for seasoning and add additional salt and sour cream if desired. Garnish with the nutmeg. Serve.

STEWED GREEN TOMATOES

This dish is great for green tomatoes that have not had time to ripen on the vine.

INGREDIENTS
Serves 4

1 olive oil

2 tablespoons onion, minced

4 large green tomatoes, sliced

¾ cup water

½ teaspoon sugar

½ teaspoon salt

¼ teaspoon paprika

½ teaspoon curry powder

½ cup plain bread crumbs

1 tablespoon fresh parsley, chopped

1. In a preheated pressure cooker over medium heat, add the oil and onion and sauté for 2 minutes. Add the tomatoes, water, sugar, salt, paprika, and curry powder. Stir to mix. Close and lock the lid.

2. Turn the heat up to high and when the cooker reaches pressure, lower the heat to the minimum needed to maintain pressure. Cook for 8 minutes at high pressure.

3. Open with the natural-release method—move the pressure cooker to a cool burner and wait for the pressure to come down on its own (about 15 minutes). For electric pressure cookers, disengage the "keep warm" mode or unplug the cooker and open when the pressure indicator has gone down (20–30 minutes).

4. Remove lid from pressure cooker. Return to medium heat and bring to a simmer. Stir in bread crumbs. Simmer and stir until thickened. Top with parsley.

BUTTERNUT SQUASH

Winter is the peak season for this squash, which is loaded with vitamin A.

INGREDIENTS
Serves 4–6

2 pounds butternut squash, peeled and cubed into 1" pieces

Water, as needed

2 tablespoons butter or vegan margarine such as Earth Balance

1 tablespoon brown sugar

1 teaspoon salt

1. Add the butternut squash, and enough water to cover the squash, to the pressure cooker. Lock the lid into place and bring to high pressure; maintain pressure for 4 minutes. Remove from the heat and quick-release pressure.

2. Drain the liquid, then place the squash in a medium-sized mixing bowl. Stir in the butter, brown sugar, and salt.

SPAGHETTI SQUASH

Spaghetti squash looks like (and can be used like) strands of pasta. Top with marinara sauce or olive oil for a low-carb dish.

INGREDIENTS
Serves 4

2 pounds spaghetti squash, halved lengthwise

½ cup water

1 tablespoon olive oil

1 teaspoon salt

1. Scoop out the center of the squash, including the seeds, and discard.

2. Place the squash face down in the steamer basket, then add water.

3. Lock the lid into place and bring to high pressure; maintain pressure for 10 minutes. Remove from the heat and quick-release pressure.

4. When squash is cool enough to handle, use a fork to scoop the strands of "spaghetti" from the squash and place in a medium bowl.

5. Drizzle the olive oil and sprinkle salt on top before serving.

SUCCOTASH

Succotash can be made with a variety of beans, but the staple ingredients are lima beans and corn.

INGREDIENTS
Serves 4

2 tablespoons butter, or vegan margarine, such as Earth Balance

½ cup bell pepper, chopped

1 cup fresh lima beans

1 cup whole kernel corn

1 cup tomatoes, chopped

1 cup water

1 teaspoon salt

1. Bring the pressure cooker to medium heat; add the butter and bell pepper. Sauté for 3 minutes, or until the bell pepper begins to soften.

2. Add the lima beans, corn, tomatoes, water, and salt. Stir well.

3. Lock the lid into place and bring to high pressure; maintain pressure for 10 minutes. Remove from heat and quick-release the pressure.

SWISS CHARD AND VEGETABLES IN PARMESAN SAUCE

This rich side dish also goes well with something as simple as leftover roast turkey or chicken.

INGREDIENTS

Serves 8

½ cup water

1 pound Swiss chard

1 onion, peeled and sliced

3 stalks celery, diced

2 carrots, sliced on the diagonal

1 pound Brussels sprouts

1 zucchini

1 cauliflower

4 tablespoons butter

4 cloves garlic, peeled and minced

½ cup Parmigiano-Reggiano cheese, grated

⅛ teaspoon dried red pepper flakes, crushed

½ cup whole milk

1. Add the water to the pressure cooker.

2. Wash and drain the chard. Remove and discard the tough stems. Tear the chard into bite-sized pieces. Set aside.

3. Layer the onion, celery, carrots, and chard into the pressure cooker. Wash and drain Brussels sprouts. Remove and discard the outer leaves. Cut in half and add on top of the chard. Slice the zucchini and put on top of the Brussels sprouts. Divide the cauliflower into large florets and add on top of the zucchini.

4. Close and lock the lid.

5. Turn the heat up to high and when the cooker reaches pressure, lower the heat to the minimum needed to maintain pressure. Cook for 3 minutes at high pressure.

6. When time is up, open the pressure cooker by releasing pressure.

7. Drain the vegetables and transfer them to a serving bowl.

8. Melt the butter in the uncovered pressure cooker over medium heat. Stir in the garlic and sauté for 30 seconds to 1 minute, being careful not to let the garlic burn. Stir in the cheese and pepper flakes. Slowly whisk in the milk.

9. Continue to cook and stir until the sauce is smooth and bubbling. Pour over the vegetables. Toss to coat the vegetables. Serve.

MASHED TURNIPS

Serve this low-carb dish in place of mashed potatoes.

INGREDIENTS
Serves 4

4 medium turnips, peeled and diced

1 small onion, diced

½ cup vegetable stock

¼ cup sour cream, or vegan sour cream, such as Tofutti Sour Supreme

Salt and pepper, to taste

1. Add the turnips, onion, and stock to the pressure cooker. Lock the lid into place and bring to high pressure; maintain pressure for 5 minutes. Remove from the heat and allow pressure to release naturally for 10 minutes.

2. Use a slotted spoon to transfer turnips to a serving bowl, reserving the broth in the pressure cooker. Use a hand-held mixer or immersion blender to purée the turnips, adding some of the broth from the pressure cooker if necessary.

3. Stir in the sour cream. Taste for seasoning, and add salt and pepper if necessary.

Flavor Variations
Some of the ingredients one would typically use in mashed potatoes also work well in mashed turnips. A couple of unique ingredients to try are nutmeg or horseradish, but not both in the same dish.

SAVORY TURNIP GREENS

Use fresh or frozen turnip greens for best flavor and optimal nutrition.

INGREDIENTS
Serves 4

1 pound turnip greens

1 tablespoon olive oil

½ onion, diced

1 clove garlic, minced

1 teaspoon dried red pepper flakes

2 cups vegetable stock

1 teaspoon Dijon mustard

Salt and pepper, to taste

1. To prepare the greens, cut away the tough stalks and stems. Wash the turnip greens, chop into large pieces, and set aside.

2. Bring the pressure cooker to medium heat. Add the olive oil, onion, garlic, and red pepper flakes. Cook until the onion begins to soften, about 5 minutes. Add the vegetable stock, mustard, and chopped turnip greens; stir well.

3. Lock the lid into place and bring to high pressure; maintain pressure for 5 minutes. Remove from the heat and allow pressure to release naturally. Add salt and pepper, to taste.

SEASONED BABY TURNIPS

The allspice in this dish makes it go well with Chinese barbecued ribs, but it will work well with just about any meat entrée.

INGREDIENTS
Serves 4

4 baby turnips

½ cup water

½ teaspoon salt

3 tablespoons butter

1 small onion, peeled and sliced

½ teaspoon sugar

¼ teaspoon freshly ground black pepper

¼ teaspoon ground allspice

2 tablespoons fresh lemon juice

Optional: 1 tablespoon fresh parsley, minced

1. Clean, peel, and quarter the turnips. Place the rack in the pressure cooker. Pour in the water. Place the turnips on the rack and sprinkle them with the salt.

2. Lock the lid into place and bring to low pressure; maintain pressure for 8 minutes. Remove the pressure cooker from the heat, quick-release the pressure, and remove the lid.

3. Transfer the turnips to a serving bowl; set aside. Remove the rack and discard any water remaining. Wipe out the pressure cooker; add the butter and melt over medium heat. Add the onion; sauté for 3 minutes. Stir in the sugar, pepper, allspice, and lemon juice. Whisk and cook until the sugar is dissolved into the sauce. Add the turnips and toss to coat them in the sauce. Transfer back to the serving bowl. Sprinkle the parsley over the top if using.

TURNIP AND CARROT PURÉE

The nutmeg in this recipe makes it a great side dish on a crisp fall evening or for Thanksgiving dinner.

INGREDIENTS
Serves 6

2 cups turnips, peeled and quartered

2 cups carrots, peeled and cut into 2" pieces

2 cups water

1 teaspoon salt

2 tablespoons extra-virgin olive oil

½ teaspoon nutmeg, freshly grated

2 tablespoons sour cream, or vegan sour cream, such as Tofutti Sour Supreme

1. Put the turnips, carrots, water, and salt in the pressure cooker. Lock the lid into place and bring to high pressure; maintain pressure for 8 minutes. Remove the pressure cooker from the heat, quick-release the pressure, and remove the lid.

2. Drain the vegetables. Return them to the pressure cooker and set it at low heat for 1–2 minutes to evaporate any residual moisture. Mash the vegetables together with the oil, nutmeg, and sour cream. Taste for seasoning, and add additional salt if needed. Serve.

TURNIP GREENS IN OLIVE OIL

Try using 1 shallot in place of the garlic to give the turnips a different flavor. Serve in place of a salad or as a vegetable side dish.

INGREDIENTS
Serves 4

10 cups turnip greens, shredded

½ cup chicken broth or water

1 clove garlic, peeled and crushed

½ teaspoon salt

4 teaspoons extra-virgin olive oil

Freshly ground black pepper, to taste

½ cup pecans, pine nuts, or pistachios, toasted

1. Rinse and drain the turnip greens. Add to the pressure cooker along with the broth or water, garlic, and salt.

2. Lock the lid into place and bring to low pressure; maintain pressure for 3 minutes. Remove from heat and allow pressure to release naturally for 5 minutes. Quick-release any remaining pressure and remove the lid.

3. Drain the turnip greens and transfer to a serving bowl. Toss with the oil. Add the pepper.

4. Taste for seasoning and add additional salt if needed. Stir in the toasted nuts. Serve.

SPICY AND MINTY ZUCCHINI

This easy and quick recipe packs lots of flavor!

INGREDIENTS
Serves 4

1 tablespoon olive oil

⅛ teaspoon hot pepper flakes

2 cloves garlic, smashed

1 pound zucchini, sliced into rounds

½ teaspoon salt

½ cup water (if using an electric pressure cooker)

1 bunch fresh mint, chopped

1. Heat olive oil in an uncovered pressure cooker over medium heat. Add pepper flakes, garlic, and half of the zucchini. Brown one side of the zucchini until golden. Then add the rest of the zucchini, stir well, and add salt. For electric pressure cookers, add ½ cup of water. Close and lock the lid.

2. Turn the heat up to high and when the cooker reaches pressure, lower the heat to the minimum needed to maintain pressure. Cook for 4–5 minutes at low pressure (1–2 minutes at high pressure).

3. When time is up, open the pressure cooker by releasing pressure.

4. Quickly remove the zucchini from the cooker to a serving dish to stop cooking. Sprinkle with fresh mint leaves, and serve hot or at room temperature.

WINTER VEGETABLE MEDLEY

Any earthy herbs, such as rosemary, thyme, or sage, will work well in this delicious recipe.

INGREDIENTS
Serves 4–6

2 tablespoons olive oil

1 sprig rosemary

3 carrots, peeled and sliced

1 large sweet potato, diced and peeled

6 red potatoes, quartered

2½ cups butternut squash, peeled and cubed

1 cup water

Salt and pepper, to taste

1. Bring the olive oil and rosemary to medium heat in the pressure cooker. Add all of the vegetables, stirring until well coated, and cook for 5 minutes.

2. Add the water, then lock on the lid. Bring to high pressure; maintain pressure for 6 minutes. Remove the pan from the heat, slowly release the pressure, and remove the lid. Drain the water.

3. Season with salt and pepper, to taste, and remove the rosemary sprig before serving.

ZESTY MASHED ROOT VEGETABLES

Serve as a substitute for mashed potatoes. The carrots add a touch of sweetness. The horseradish in this dish makes it especially good with roast beef.

INGREDIENTS
Serves 8

1 cup water

2 pounds potatoes, peeled and diced

½ pound carrots, peeled and diced

1½ pounds white turnips, peeled and diced

1 teaspoon salt

4 tablespoons butter

1 cup heavy cream

2 teaspoons prepared horseradish

Freshly ground black pepper, to taste

1. Add the water, potatoes, carrots, turnips, and salt to the pressure cooker in that order.

2. Lock the lid into place and bring to high pressure; maintain pressure for 7 minutes. Remove from the heat and allow pressure to release naturally for 10 minutes.

3. Quick-release any remaining pressure and remove the lid. Drain the vegetables and put them in a large serving bowl. Set aside and keep warm.

4. Wipe out the pressure cooker. Melt the butter and add ⅔ cup of the cream. Heat to low simmer over medium heat.

5. Mash the vegetables, stirring in the heated butter-cream mixture. Gradually add the remaining ⅓ cup of the cream if needed.

6. Stir in 1 teaspoon horseradish; taste for seasoning and add additional salt and the remaining horseradish if needed. Season to taste with pepper. Serve.

CHAPTER 6

GRAINS

BULGUR STUFFING

Bulgur is a healthier alternative to white bread in stuffing.

INGREDIENTS
Serves 4–5

1 cup bulgur

3 cups vegetable stock

2 tablespoons butter, or vegan margarine, such as Earth Balance

½ onion, diced

½ cup celery rib, diced

½ cup chopped mushrooms

½ teaspoon dried thyme

½ teaspoon dried sage

½ teaspoon salt

¾ teaspoon black pepper

1. Add the bulgur and vegetable stock to the pressure cooker.

2. Lock the lid into place; bring to high pressure and maintain for 9 minutes. Remove from the heat and allow pressure to release naturally.

3. In a large sauté pan over medium heat, melt the butter and sauté the onion and celery until soft, about 7 minutes. Add the mushrooms, thyme, sage, salt, and pepper, and sauté for an additional 2 minutes.

4. Pour the vegetable mixture into the cooked bulgur and stir until well combined.

Tasty Substitutions
Turn this dish into a cranberry stuffing by adding dried cranberries and chopped pecan pieces instead of the mushrooms and celery.

COUSCOUS

Couscous is really a type of pasta cut into tiny balls, but it is often served as a grain, with vegetables as a topping or on the side.

INGREDIENTS
Serves 4

1 cup couscous

2 cups water

1. Add the couscous and water to the pressure cooker.

2. Lock the lid into place; bring to high pressure and maintain for 2 minutes. Remove from the heat and allow pressure to release naturally.

3. Fluff with a fork before serving or using in a recipe.

COUSCOUS-STUFFED RED PEPPERS

Pine nuts are also known as pinoli or pignol, and are most commonly known for being a key ingredient in pesto.

INGREDIENTS
Serves 4

1 cup couscous

2 cups water

2 tablespoons pine nuts

4 ounces crumbled feta cheese, or vegan feta, such as Sunergia Soy Feta Cheese

1 teaspoon dried oregano

1 teaspoon salt

4 large red bell peppers, stemmed and seeded

1. Preheat the oven to 350°F. Add the couscous and water to the pressure cooker.

2. Lock the lid into place; bring to high pressure and maintain for 2 minutes. Remove from the heat and allow pressure to release naturally.

3. While the couscous is cooking, toast the pine nuts in a small sauté pan over low heat, stirring often to avoid burning. Once they begin to turn golden brown, remove from heat.

4. When the couscous is done, remove the lid of the pressure cooker. Fluff the couscous, and add the cooked pine nuts, feta, oregano, and salt. Stir well to combine.

5. Stuff one-fourth of the couscous mixture into each of the red bell peppers and place in an ungreased baking dish. Bake for 15 minutes, or until the pepper begins to soften.

OLIVE AND PEPPER COUSCOUS SALAD

Kalamata olives are a type of black olive that will add a "meaty" flavor to this dish and are a recommened variety for your mixed olives.

INGREDIENTS
Serves 4

1 cup couscous

2 cups water

½ cup mixed olives, pitted and chopped

1 red bell pepper, diced

1 clove garlic, minced

1 teaspoon olive oil

1 teaspoon red wine vinegar

1 teaspoon salt

1. Add the couscous and water to the pressure cooker.

2. Lock the lid into place; bring to high pressure and maintain for 2 minutes. Remove from the heat and allow pressure to release naturally.

3. Fluff the couscous with a fork. Add all remaining ingredients and stir until combined. Add additional salt, to taste.

4. Refrigerate for 2 hours before serving.

POLENTA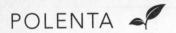

Polenta works as a hot cereal or a side dish. Substitute broth for some or all of the water if you'll be serving it as a side dish.

INGREDIENTS

Serves 6

1 cup yellow cornmeal

4 cups cold water

½ teaspoon salt

1 tablespoon butter

1. In a bowl or measuring cup, mix together the cornmeal, 1 cup cold water, and salt. Set aside.

2. Bring the remaining 3 cups water to a boil in the pressure cooker over medium heat. Stir in the moistened cornmeal mixture and the butter.

3. Continue to cook and stir until the mixture comes to a low boil or begins to bubble.

4. Lock the lid into place and bring to low pressure; maintain pressure for 10 minutes.

5. Remove the pressure cooker from heat, quick-release the pressure, and remove the lid. Stir and taste for seasoning; add additional salt if needed. Serve warm.

CREAMY THYME POLENTA

To substitute fresh herbs in this recipe, increase the amount of thyme to 1 tablespoon.

INGREDIENTS

Serves 4–5

3½ cups water

½ cup coarse polenta

½ cup fine cornmeal

1 cup corn kernels

1 teaspoon dried thyme

1 teaspoon salt

1. Add all of the ingredients to the pressure cooker and stir.

2. Lock the lid into place and bring to high pressure; maintain pressure for 10 minutes. Remove from the heat and quick-release the pressure. Season with additional salt, if necessary.

PAN-FRIED POLENTA WITH MARINARA

Similar to grits, polenta is made from boiled cornmeal, and can be enjoyed firm or creamy in dishes such as Creamy Thyme Polenta (previous).

INGREDIENTS
Serves 4–5

2 tablespoons butter, or vegan margarine, such as Earth Balance

½ onion, diced

2 cloves garlic, minced

4 cups vegetable stock, or water

1 teaspoon salt

½ teaspoon thyme

½ cup cornmeal

½ cup coarse polenta

1 cup corn kernels, canned or fresh

¼ cup olive oil

2 cups marinara sauce

1. Add the butter to the pressure cooker and sauté the onion until it begins to turn golden brown. Add the garlic and sauté for 1 minute more. Add the stock or water, salt, and thyme, and bring to a boil. Slowly add the cornmeal, coarse polenta, and corn, stirring so they will not clump.

2. Lock the lid into place and bring to high pressure; maintain pressure for 10 minutes. Remove from the heat and quick-release the pressure. Allow the polenta to cool and firm for at least 30 minutes.

3. When the polenta is firm, cut into 2½" squares, and remove from the pressure cooker. Add the olive oil to a sauté pan and fry the polenta squares until brown on both sides. Serve with marinara sauce.

Flavor Variations
Jazz up this dish by adding cooked vegetables to the polenta before you allow it to cool. Chopped and sautéed leeks are a nice addition, as well as fresh sautéed bell pepper.

QUINOA

Quinoa is an excellent source of protein for vegans and vegetarians.

INGREDIENTS
Serves 4

1 cup quinoa

2 cups water

1. Add the quinoa and water to the pressure cooker.

2. Lock the lid into place; bring to high pressure and maintain for 6 minutes. Remove from the heat and allow pressure to release naturally.

3. Fluff with a fork before serving or using in a recipe.

QUINOA ARTICHOKE HEARTS SALAD

The amount of dressing called for in this recipe is a suggestion. You may wish to use more or less dressing, depending on how strongly the dressing you're using is seasoned.

INGREDIENTS
Serves 4

1 cup pecans

1 cup quinoa

2½ cups water

2 cups frozen artichoke hearts

2 cups cherry or grape tomatoes, halved

½ small red onion, thinly sliced

¼ cup Italian salad dressing

2 heads Belgian endive

1. Rough chop the pecans and add them to the pressure cooker over medium heat. Dry roast for several minutes, stirring continuously to prevent the nuts from burning. The pecans are sufficiently toasted when they're fragrant and slightly brown. Transfer to a bowl and set aside to cool.

2. Add the quinoa and water to the pressure cooker. Lock the lid into place and bring to high pressure; maintain pressure for 2 minutes. Remove from the heat and allow pressure to release naturally for 10 minutes. Quick-release any remaining pressure. Transfer to a colander; drain and rinse under cold water. Drain well and transfer to a large bowl.

3. While the quinoa is cooking, prepare the artichoke hearts according to package directions and then plunge into cold water to cool and stop the cooking process. When cooled, cut into quarters.

4. Stir the artichoke hearts into the quinoa along with the tomatoes and red onion. Toss with the salad dressing. At this point, the quinoa mixture can be covered and refrigerated until ready to serve. This allows the flavors to blend. However, if you'll be refrigerating the quinoa mixture for more than 1 hour, leave the cherry or grape tomatoes whole rather than halving them.

5. To prepare the salad, separate the endive leaves. Rinse, drain, and divide them between 4 plates. Top each with one-fourth of the quinoa mixture. Sprinkle ¼ cup of the toasted pecans over the top of each salad.

Tasty Substitutions
Customize this dish to your liking by choosing your favorite dressing in place of Italian. A creamy dressing, such as a vegetarian Caesar or creamy dill, is a delicious option.

HERB AND QUINOA STUFFED TOMATOES

This healthy treat is a great way to "disguise" quinoa for those who think they don't like it!

INGREDIENTS
Serves 4

1 cup water

4 large tomatoes

1 cup cooked quinoa

1 stalk celery, chopped

1 tablespoon garlic, minced

2 tablespoons chopped fresh oregano

2 tablespoons chopped fresh parsley

½ teaspoon salt

¼ teaspoon pepper

1. Place water in the pressure cooker and add the steamer basket.

2. Remove the core from each tomato and discard. Scoop out the seeds, leaving the walls of the tomato intact.

3. In a small bowl, stir together the quinoa, celery, garlic, oregano, parsley, salt, and pepper. Divide evenly among the four tomatoes. Place the filled tomatoes in a single layer on the steamer basket.

4. Turn the heat up to high and when the cooker reaches pressure, lower the heat to the minimum needed to maintain pressure. Cook for 5–7 minutes at high pressure.

5. When time is up, open the pressure cooker by releasing pressure.

TOMATO, GARLIC, AND PARSLEY QUINOA SALAD

The combination of tomato, garlic, and parsley goes well with just about any grain, so if you don't like quinoa, substitute couscous or rice instead.

INGREDIENTS

Serves 4

1 cup quinoa

2 cups water

2 tablespoons olive oil

2 cloves garlic, minced

1 cup diced tomatoes

¼ cup chopped parsley

1 tablespoon lemon juice

1 teaspoon salt

1. Add the quinoa and water to the pressure cooker.

2. Lock the lid into place; bring to high pressure and maintain for 6 minutes. Remove from the heat and allow pressure to release naturally. Fluff with a fork.

3. In a small sauté pan, add the olive oil over medium heat. Sauté the garlic for 30 seconds, then add the tomatoes, parsley, and lemon juice. Sauté for an additional minute.

4. Stir the tomato mixture and salt into the cooked quinoa in the pressure cooker. Season with additional salt, to taste.

BARLEY RISOTTO 🌱

If you're not a fan of Parmigiano-Reggiano cheese, you can substitute crumbled blue cheese or grated Cheddar cheese to taste.

INGREDIENTS
Serves 4

1 tablespoon butter, or vegan margarine, such as Earth Balance

1 tablespoon olive oil

1 large onion, diced

1 clove garlic, minced

1 stalk celery, finely minced

1½ cups pearl barley, well rinsed

⅓ cup dried mushrooms

4 cups vegetable stock

2¼ cups water

1 cup Parmigiano-Reggiano cheese, grated, or vegan cheese, such as Daiya Mozzarella Style Shreds

2 tablespoons fresh parsley, minced

Salt, to taste

1. Bring the butter and oil to temperature in the pressure cooker over medium heat. Add the onion; sauté for 3 minutes or until the onion is soft. Add the garlic; sauté for 30 seconds. Stir in the celery and barley until the barley is coated with the fat. Add the mushrooms, stock, and water. Lock the lid into place and bring to high pressure; maintain pressure for 18 minutes. Quick-release the pressure and remove the lid.

2. Drain off any excess liquid not absorbed by the barley, leaving just enough to leave the risotto slightly soupy. Reduce heat to low and stir in the cheese and parsley. Taste for seasoning, and add salt if needed.

Flavor Variations

To further enhance the earthy flavor of the mushrooms and barley, add ½ teaspoon of dried thyme and ½ teaspoon of dried sage instead of fresh parsley.

PEPPERY BROWN RICE RISOTTO

If you avoid alcohol, replace the wine in this recipe with ¼ cup vegetable stock.

INGREDIENTS

Serves 8

2 medium leeks

1 small fennel bulb

3 tablespoons butter, or vegan margarine, such as Earth Balance

2 cups short-grain brown rice, rinsed and drained

½ teaspoon salt

2½ cups water

¼ cup white wine

¾ cup fontina cheese, grated, or vegan cheese, such as Daiya Mozzarella Style Shreds

1½ teaspoons freshly ground or cracked black pepper

1. Cut the leeks into quarters lengthwise, and then slice into ½" slices; wash thoroughly, drain, and dry.

2. Clean the fennel. Trim the fronds from the fennel, chop, and set aside. Dice the bulb.

3. Melt the butter in the pressure cooker over medium heat. Add the leeks and fennel bulb; sauté for 1 minute or until the leeks begin to wilt.

4. Add the rice and stir-fry into the leeks until the rice begins to turn golden brown. Stir in the salt, water, and white wine.

5. Lock the lid into place and bring to high pressure; maintain pressure for 20 minutes. Remove from the heat and allow pressure to release naturally for 10 minutes. Quick-release any remaining pressure. Remove the lid.

6. Fluff the rice with a fork. Stir in the cheese, fennel fronds, and pepper. Taste for seasoning and add additional salt if needed.

Italian Cheese

Fontina is an Italian cheese with a mild flavor that is creamy and melts easily. Mozzarella is a more common alternative to fontina in this recipe.

PUMPKIN RISOTTO

This seasonal risotto will make for a unique entrée on any Thanksgiving table.

INGREDIENTS
Serves 6–8

1 tablespoon olive oil

1 cup diced sweet yellow onion

2 cups Arborio rice

1 cup white wine

2 cups vegetable stock

2 cups water

1 cup canned pumpkin purée

1 teaspoon grated ginger

1 teaspoon grated nutmeg

Salt and pepper, to taste

1. Bring the olive oil to medium heat in the pressure cooker. Sauté the onion until translucent. Add the rice and sauté until opaque, about 4 minutes.

2. Add the white wine and stir until the liquid is absorbed. Add the vegetable stock and 1 cup water.

3. Lock the lid into place; bring to high pressure and maintain for 6 minutes. Quick-release the pressure and remove the lid.

4. Add the remaining cup of water, pumpkin purée, ginger, and nutmeg. Simmer over medium heat until the liquid is absorbed.

5. Season with salt and pepper, to taste, before serving.

SHRIMP RISOTTO

Add a vegetable to the Shrimp Risotto by stirring in 1 cup of thawed frozen baby peas when you add the shrimp. A fresh tomato salad goes well with this rich, creamy dish.

INGREDIENTS
Serves 4

2 tablespoons extra-virgin olive oil

1 small onion, peeled and diced

1 teaspoon fennel seeds

3 cloves garlic, peeled and minced

1½ cups Arborio rice

2 tablespoons tomato paste

Pinch saffron threads

¼ cup dry white vermouth

3 cups chicken broth

1 pound medium shrimp, peeled and deveined

Salt and freshly ground black pepper, to taste

1. Bring the oil to temperature in the pressure cooker over medium-high heat. Add the onion and fennel seeds; sauté for 3 minutes or until the onions are softened.

2. Add the garlic, rice, tomato paste, and saffron; stir until the rice is evenly colored. Stir in vermouth and broth.

3. Lock the lid into place and bring to high pressure; maintain pressure for 6 minutes. Quick-release the pressure and remove the lid.

4. Stir in the shrimp; simmer for 2 minutes or until the shrimp are pale pink and cooked through.

5. Taste for seasoning and add salt and pepper if needed. Serve immediately.

VEGETABLE RISOTTO WITH BEET GREENS

You can substitute water or vegetable broth for the chicken broth and make this a vegetarian meal.

INGREDIENTS
Serves 4

¼ cup extra-virgin olive oil

1 clove garlic, peeled and minced

1 portobello mushroom

1 small Asian eggplant, sliced

1 small zucchini, sliced

1 large red bell pepper, seeded and cut in quarters

1 medium onion, peeled and thickly sliced

Salt and freshly ground black pepper, to taste

¼ cup butter

1 cup Arborio rice

½ cup dry white wine

2 cups chicken broth

2 cups young beet greens, sliced

¼ cup fresh basil, sliced

½ cup Parmigiano-Reggiano cheese, grated

1. Ten minutes before you'll be grilling the vegetables, add the oil and garlic to a small bowl; stir to mix and set aside to infuse the flavor of the garlic into the oil.

2. Preheat the grill or a grill pan over medium-high heat. Remove the stem and black gills from the mushroom cap; slice the cap.

3. Brush all sides of the eggplant slices, zucchini slices, bell pepper quarters, mushroom slices, and onion with the oil.

4. Place vegetables on the grill rack or in the grill pan. Sprinkle with salt and pepper.

5. Turning once, grill the vegetables for several minutes on each side or until softened and slightly charred. Set aside to cool, and then coarsely chop.

6. Bring the remaining garlic-infused oil and 3 tablespoons of the butter to temperature in the pressure cooker over medium heat.

7. Add the rice and stir it to coat it in the oil-butter mixture. Stir in the wine and broth.

8. Lock the lid into place and bring to high pressure; maintain pressure for 7 minutes. Remove from the heat, quick-release the pressure, and remove the lid.

9. Add the chopped grilled vegetables, beet greens, and basil. Cover the pressure cooker (but do not lock the lid into place).

10. Let rest, covered, for 5 minutes or until greens are wilted. Stir in cheese and remaining butter. Taste for seasoning and add additional salt and pepper to taste.

WILD MUSHROOM RISOTTO

Exotic mushrooms such as shiitakes, hen of the woods, and oysters add earthy flavor and diverse textures. For a budget-friendly mushroom, choose portobello.

INGREDIENTS
Serves 6

1 tablespoon olive oil

½ onion, diced

1 clove garlic, minced

2 cups arborio rice

6 cups vegetable stock

2 cups assorted exotic mushrooms, chopped

1 tablespoon butter, or vegan margarine, such as Earth Balance

Salt and pepper, to taste

1. Heat the olive oil in the pressure cooker over medium heat. Add the onion and sauté until just soft, about 3 minutes. Add the garlic and sauté for an additional 30 seconds. Add the rice and sauté for 4 minutes or until the rice becomes opaque.

2. Add 5 cups of the vegetable stock. Lock the lid into place; bring to high pressure and maintain for 6 minutes. Quick-release the pressure and remove the lid.

3. Stir in the remaining stock and mushrooms and let simmer over medium heat until the liquid is absorbed.

4. Add the butter to the risotto and season with salt and pepper just before serving.

Risotto Technique
The technique used to make risotto results in a creamy consistency without the use of milk or soymilk. Instead, the creaminess is achieved by gradually adding stock to rice, while stirring.

BROWN RICE AND VEGETABLES

Add seasoning blend herbs and spices to the rice and water or broth in Step 1. This versatile side dish will go with just about any entrée.

INGREDIENTS
Serves 8

1 cup brown rice

1½ cups water or chicken broth

1 small turnip, peeled and diced

1 pound banana squash, peeled and diced

½ cup baby carrots, quartered

1 small zucchini, peeled, quartered lengthwise, and sliced

3 stalks Swiss chard, leafy greens chopped and stems diced

1 cup broccoli florets, coarsely chopped

⅓ cup water chestnuts, diced

Salt and freshly ground black pepper, to taste

1. Rinse and drain the rice. Bring the rice and water or broth to a boil in the pressure cooker over high heat.

2. Lock the lid into place and adjust heat to bring to low pressure; maintain pressure for 10 minutes.

3. Remove from the heat and allow pressure to release naturally. Remove the lid.

4. Add the turnip, squash, carrots, zucchini, chard, broccoli, and water chestnuts. Stir to mix with the rice.

5. Lock the lid into place, return the pan to the heat, and bring to low pressure; maintain pressure for 1 minute.

6. Remove from the heat and allow pressure to release naturally. Remove the lid.

7. Fluff the rice and vegetables with a fork. Taste for seasoning and add salt and pepper to taste. Serve.

Recipe Versatility

You can use whatever vegetables you have on hand; just dice or slice the vegetable pieces according to the length of time it takes that vegetable to cook. The longer the cooking time, the smaller the dice. For example, butternut squash and carrots are slow cookers, so you should dice those into smaller pieces than onions and celery.

BROWN RICE SALAD

This is the type of salad that will benefit if you experiment with different flavors. Serve this main-dish salad with honey-mustard dressing over salad greens.

INGREDIENTS

Serves 6

2 cups long-grain brown rice, rinsed and drained

4½ cups chicken broth

1 whole chicken breast, skin removed

1½ teaspoons salt

3 green onions, finely diced

2 large carrots, peeled and diced

2 stalks celery, sliced

1 small red bell pepper, seeded and diced

3 tablespoons mayonnaise

1 teaspoon Dijon mustard

1 teaspoon honey

2 tablespoons butter, melted

2 tablespoons apple cider vinegar

½ cup extra-virgin olive oil

2 hard-boiled eggs, peeled and chopped

Salt and freshly ground white pepper, to taste

2 tablespoons fresh parsley, finely chopped

1. Add the rice, broth, chicken, and salt to the pressure cooker. Lock the lid into place and bring to high pressure; maintain pressure for 12 minutes.

2. Remove from heat, quick-release the pressure, and remove the lid. Transfer the chicken to a cutting board. Fluff the rice with a fork and transfer it to a bowl. Once rice has cooled, toss it with the onions, carrots, celery, and bell pepper.

3. To make the dressing, whisk together the mayonnaise, mustard, honey, melted butter, and vinegar, and then slowly whisk in the olive oil.

4. Fold in the chopped boiled eggs. Taste for seasoning and add salt and pepper to taste and more honey if desired.

5. Pour half of the dressing over the rice salad mixture in the bowl. Stir to mix, adding more dressing if desired. Sprinkle the fresh parsley over the salad. Serve.

CHICKEN CAESAR RICE

You're used to Caesar salads and Caesar wraps, but have you tried Caesar dressing with rice and vegetables? Serve with garlic bread.

INGREDIENTS

Serves 6

2 tablespoons olive oil

2 pounds boneless, skinless chicken breasts

1 cup long-grain white rice, rinsed and drained

1 14-ounce can chicken broth

½ cup bottled Caesar salad dressing

4 cloves garlic, peeled and minced

1 tablespoon dried Italian herbs blend

1 cup frozen broccoli florets, thawed

1 cup frozen cauliflower pieces, thawed

1 cup frozen sliced carrots, thawed

½ cup pimento-stuffed olives, sliced

½ cup Parmigiano-Reggiano cheese, grated

1. Bring the oil to temperature in the pressure cooker over medium heat. Cut the chicken into bite-sized pieces and add to the pressure cooker.

2. Stir fry for 5 minutes or until lightly browned. Stir in the rice, broth, dressing, garlic, and Italian herb blend.

3. Lock the lid into place and bring to high pressure; maintain pressure for 8 minutes. Quick-release the pressure and remove the lid.

4. Stir the mixture in the pressure cooker. Add the thawed frozen vegetables and green olives to the top of the chicken and rice mixture.

5. Lock the lid back into place and bring to high pressure; maintain pressure for 2 minutes.

6. Remove from the heat and allow pressure to release naturally. Remove the lid. Stir in the cheese, fluffing the rice with a fork. Transfer to a serving bowl. Serve hot.

CHINESE BLACK RICE

Chinese black rice can be used in savory or sweet dishes. For a sweet approach, try adding coconut milk and sugar.

INGREDIENTS
Serves 4

1 cup Chinese black rice

2 cups vegetable stock

1 teaspoon rice wine vinegar

1 teaspoon Chinese five-spice powder

½ teaspoon salt

1. Add the rice and stock to the pressure cooker.

2. Lock the lid into place; bring to high pressure and maintain for 15 minutes. Remove from the heat and allow pressure to release naturally.

3. Once the pressure has released, open the lid and stir in the rice wine vinegar, Chinese five-spice powder, and salt.

COCONUT RICE

The combination of coconut, currants, and spices transforms this rice into a succulent dish. It is especially good served with a curry entrée.

INGREDIENTS
Serves 4

2 tablespoons butter or vegetable oil

1 cup extra long-grain white rice, rinsed and drained

½ cup unsweetened coconut, flaked or grated

2¼ cups water

¼ cup currants

½ teaspoon ground cinnamon

1 teaspoon anise seed

⅛ teaspoon ground cloves

½ teaspoon salt

1. Bring the butter or oil to temperature in the pressure cooker over medium heat. Add the rice, stirring well to coat it in the fat.

2. Add the coconut, water, currants, cinnamon, anise seed, cloves, and salt. Lock the lid into place and bring to high pressure; maintain the pressure for 3 minutes. Turn off the heat and let the pressure drop naturally for 7 minutes.

3. Quick-release any remaining pressure and remove the lid. Fluff the rice with a fork. Drain off any excess moisture. Taste for seasoning and adjust if necessary. Serve.

CONFETTI RICE

For a healthy, fiber-rich alternative, use brown rice instead of white rice. It's the same thing, except the bran layer and all of its nutrients have not been removed from the brown rice.

INGREDIENTS
Serves 6

3 tablespoons butter

1 small red onion, peeled and diced

2 cloves garlic, peeled and diced

1 cup long-grain white rice, rinsed and drained

3 cups frozen mixed vegetables, thawed

1 14-ounce can chicken broth

¼ cup fresh lemon juice

1 tablespoon ground cumin or herb blend

½ teaspoon salt

½ teaspoon freshly ground black pepper

1. Melt the butter in the pressure cooker over medium heat. Add the onion; sauté for 3 minutes or until soft. Add the garlic; sauté for 30 seconds.

2. Add the rice and stir it to coat it in the butter; sauté until the rice becomes translucent. Add the remaining ingredients. Stir to mix.

3. Lock the lid into place and bring to high pressure; maintain pressure for 7 minutes. Remove from the heat and allow pressure to release naturally. Remove the lid. Fluff the rice with a fork. Taste for seasoning and adjust if necessary.

CRANBERRY-PECAN PILAF

To make this a complete meal, add vegan beef, such as Gardein Beefless Tips.

INGREDIENTS
Serves 4

1 cup long-grain white rice

2 cups vegetable stock

⅔ cup dried cranberries

1 teaspoon dried thyme

1 bay leaf

1 cup pecan pieces

2 tablespoons butter, or vegan margarine, such as Earth Balance

Salt and pepper, to taste

1. Add the rice, vegetable stock, cranberries, thyme, and bay leaf to the pressure cooker.

2. Lock the lid into place and bring to high pressure; maintain pressure for 5 minutes. Remove from the heat and allow pressure to release naturally.

3. Stir in the pecans and butter, then season with salt and pepper. Remove bay leaf before serving.

Serving Suggestions
Turn this pilaf into a holiday dinner centerpiece by serving it in a cooked acorn squash or small pumpkin.

CREOLE CHICKEN AND RICE

Serve this with cornbread or baked corn tortillas. Have hot sauce at the table for those who wish to add it.

INGREDIENTS
Serves 6

2 tablespoons vegetable oil

2 pounds boneless, skinless chicken breasts

1 medium white onion, peeled and diced

1 large green bell pepper, seeded and diced

4 cloves garlic, peeled and minced

1 teaspoon dried rosemary, crushed

1 teaspoon dried thyme

1 teaspoon paprika

¼ teaspoon dried red pepper flakes

½ cup white wine

1 28-ounce can diced tomatoes

1 14-ounce can chicken broth

2 cups frozen okra, thawed and sliced

1 cup frozen whole kernel corn, thawed

2 large carrots, peeled and sliced

1 cup long-grain white rice, rinsed and drained

½ cup fresh cilantro, chopped, packed

1 bay leaf

Salt and freshly ground black pepper, to taste

1. Bring the oil to temperature in the pressure cooker. Cut the chicken into bite-sized strips.

2. Add to the oil along with the onion and green pepper; sauté for several minutes or until the chicken is slightly browned and the onion is soft.

3. Add the garlic, rosemary, thyme, paprika, and red pepper flakes; sauté for 2 minutes or until the herbs begin to release their aroma.

4. Pour in the wine; deglaze the pan, scraping up any bits stuck to the bottom of the pan.

5. Add the remaining ingredients. Stir to mix. Lock the lid into place and bring to high pressure; maintain pressure for 7 minutes.

6. Remove from the heat and allow pressure to release naturally. Remove the lid. Remove and discard the bay leaf. Fluff the rice with a fork. Taste for seasoning and adjust if necessary. Serve.

HOPPIN' JOHN

Hoppin' John is a Southern dish traditionally eaten on New Year's Day. This version is hopped up by adding carrots to make it a one-dish meal.

INGREDIENTS
Serves 6–8

½ pound thick-cut bacon, diced

1 stalk celery, finely diced

1 1-pound bag baby carrots

1 large onion, peeled and diced

2 15-ounce cans black-eyed peas, rinsed and drained

1 cup long-grain white rice, rinsed and drained

4 cups chicken broth

Salt and freshly ground black pepper, to taste

1. Fry the bacon in the pressure cooker over medium heat until the fat begins to render out of the bacon. Add the celery; sauté for 2 minutes.

2. Shred 4 baby carrots and add them to the pan with the celery; sauté for another minute. Add the onion and sauté for 3 minutes or until the onions are soft.

3. Dice the remaining baby carrots and add them to the pressure cooker. Stir in the black-eyed peas, rice, and chicken broth.

4. Lock the lid into place and bring to high pressure; maintain pressure for 7 minutes. Remove from the heat and allow pressure to release naturally. Remove lid and stir. Taste for seasoning; add salt and pepper if needed.

PAELLA

Turmeric is a budget-friendly alternative to saffron in any recipe.

INGREDIENTS
Serves 4–6

3 tablespoons olive oil

1 medium onion, chopped

1 cup grated carrot

1 red bell pepper, seeded and chopped

1 cup green peas, fresh or frozen

1 clove garlic, minced

1 cup basmati rice

1½ teaspoons turmeric

2 cups vegetable stock

¼ cup chopped parsley

Salt and pepper, to taste

1. Add the olive oil to the pressure cooker over medium heat and sauté the onion, carrot, bell pepper, and peas until they begin to soften, about 5 minutes. Add the garlic, rice, and turmeric, and stir until well coated.

2. Add the vegetable stock and parsley. Lock the lid into place; bring to high pressure and maintain for 7 minutes. Remove from the heat and allow pressure to release naturally.

3. Season with salt and pepper, to taste, before serving.

VEGAN CHORIZO PAELLA

Trader Joe's grocery store chain carries a delicious kind of vegan chorizo sausage.

INGREDIENTS
Serves 4

¼ cup olive oil

14 ounces sliced vegetarian chorizo sausage, 1" slices

1 cup onion, diced

4 cloves garlic, minced

½ cup fresh parsley, chopped

1 14-ounce can diced tomatoes, drained

1 cup grated carrot

1 red bell pepper, seeded and chopped

1 cup green peas, fresh or frozen

1½ teaspoons turmeric

1 cup basmati rice

2 cups vegetable stock

Salt and pepper, to taste

1. Add the oil to the pressure cooker and sauté the sausage until it is browned. Remove the sausage and add the onion, garlic, half the parsley, tomatoes, carrot, red bell pepper, peas, and turmeric. Sauté for 3–5 minutes. Add the rice and stock and return the sausage to the pressure cooker. Bring to a boil.

2. Lock the lid into place; bring to high pressure and maintain for 7 minutes. Remove from the heat and allow pressure to release naturally.

3. Garnish with the rest of the parsley. Season with salt and pepper, to taste, before serving.

STUFFED HEAD OF CABBAGE

If you prefer, you can substitute lean ground pork, lamb, chicken, or turkey for the ground beef. Serve with pumpernickel or whole-grain country bread.

INGREDIENTS
Serves 6

1 pound lean ground beef

¼ cup butter

2 large sweet onions, peeled and diced

4 cloves garlic, peeled and minced

1 tablespoon dried parsley

2 tablespoons dried dill

1 teaspoon dried thyme

1 large carrot, peeled and diced

2 stalks celery, diced

1 cup long-grain white rice

2 cups beef or chicken broth, divided

2 14-ounce cans diced tomatoes, divided

1 teaspoon sugar

2 teaspoons salt, divided

1 teaspoon freshly ground black pepper, divided

1 large head green cabbage

¼ cup olive oil

1 small sweet onion, peeled and sliced

1 small green pepper, seeded and diced

1 tablespoon light brown sugar

2 teaspoons dried oregano

1. Add the ground beef to the pressure cooker. Fry it until cooked through over medium-high heat, breaking it apart as you do so. Drain and discard rendered fat. Transfer the cooked ground beef to a bowl and keep warm.

2. Reduce heat to medium. Melt the butter in the pressure cooker and bring it to temperature.

3. Add the 2 large diced onions; sauté for 3 minutes or until it begins to soften. Add the garlic; sauté for 30 seconds.

4. Mix in the parsley, dill, thyme, carrot, celery, rice, cooked ground beef, 1 cup of the broth, 1 can of the undrained tomatoes, sugar, 1 teaspoon of the salt, and ½ teaspoon of the pepper.

5. Lock the lid into place and bring to high pressure; maintain pressure for 6 minutes.

6. Remove the pressure cooker from heat, quick-release the pressure, and remove the lid. Stir and mix the ground beef–rice mixture.

7. Wash and dry the cabbage. Remove the outer leaves and the core. Use a paring knife to hollow out the cabbage, leaving at least a 2-inch-thick shell.

8. Center the cabbage shell on a 24-inch length of cheesecloth. Spoon the ground beef–rice mixture into the cabbage shell, mounding it over the top of the opening. Pull the cheesecloth up and over the top of the cabbage.

9. Add the olive oil to the pressure cooker and bring it to temperature over medium heat.

10. Add the sliced sweet onion and diced green pepper; sauté for 3 minutes or until the onion is soft.

11. Stir in brown sugar, oregano, remaining tomatoes, remaining broth, salt, and pepper. Stir well. Place the steamer basket in the sauce in the pressure cooker.

Continued on the next page

STUFFED HEAD OF CABBAGE
continued

12. Lift the cabbage by the ends of the cheesecloth and place it in the steamer basket.

13. Lock the lid into place and bring to high pressure; maintain pressure for 10 minutes. Remove the pressure cooker from the heat, quick-release the pressure, and remove the lid.

14. Transfer the cabbage to a serving platter by using tongs to hold the ends of the cheesecloth and a spatula to steady the bottom of the cabbage.

15. Carefully pull the cheesecloth out from the under the cabbage. Cut the cabbage into serving wedges.

16. Remove the steamer basket from the pressure cooker and pour the sauce over the cabbage wedges. Serve.

THREE GRAIN PILAF

Millet is a good source of protein and B vitamins.

INGREDIENTS
Serves 4

2 tablespoons extra-virgin olive oil

½ cup scallions, sliced

1 cup jasmine rice

½ cup millet

½ cup quinoa

2½ cups vegetable stock or water

Salt and pepper, to taste

1. Add the olive oil to the pressure cooker and sauté the scallions for 2–3 minutes. Add the grains and sauté for 2–3 minutes more. Add the stock or water and bring to a boil.

2. Lock the lid into place and bring to high pressure; maintain pressure for 4 minutes. Remove from the heat and allow pressure to release naturally for 5 minutes.

3. Quick-release any remaining pressure and remove the lid. Fluff the pilaf with a fork. Taste for seasoning and add salt and pepper if necessary.

VEGETABLE RICE PILAF

Instant pilaf that comes in cardboard boxes at the supermarket is no match for this dish.

INGREDIENTS

Serves 4

1 tablespoon butter, or vegan margarine, such as Earth Balance

1 tablespoon vegetable oil

½ small yellow onion, thinly sliced

2 cloves garlic, minced

1½" pieces fresh ginger, peeled and grated

1 serrano pepper, seeded and minced

1½ cups cauliflower florets, quartered

1 cup green beans, cleaned and cut into 1" pieces

½ cup carrot, peeled and sliced diagonally

1 teaspoon ground cumin

½ teaspoon ground turmeric

¼ teaspoon cardamom seeds

1 teaspoon chili powder

⅛ teaspoon ground cloves

⅛ teaspoon hot paprika

½ teaspoon salt

1 cup long-grain white rice

1½ cups water

¼ cup slivered almonds, toasted

1. Melt the butter in the pressure cooker over medium heat. Add the oil and bring to temperature.

2. Add the onion, garlic, ginger, and serrano pepper; sauté for 2 minutes. Stir in the cauliflower, green beans, carrot, cumin, turmeric, cardamom seeds, chili powder, ground cloves, paprika, salt, rice, and water.

3. Lock the lid into place and bring to high pressure; maintain pressure for 6 minutes. Remove from the heat and allow pressure to release naturally for 15 minutes. Quick-release any remaining pressure and remove the lid.

4. Fluff rice with a fork. Transfer to a serving bowl. Top with toasted almonds.

VEGGIE BIRYANI

This Indian rice dish will serve 2 as a vegetarian main course or 4 as a side dish.

INGREDIENTS

Serves 4

1 tablespoon vegetable oil

2 teaspoons turmeric

2 teaspoons garam masala

⅛ teaspoon cayenne pepper

1 onion, peeled and sliced

1 teaspoon garlic, minced

1 teaspoon ginger, minced

4 ounces fresh mushrooms, sliced

1 small green bell pepper, seeded and diced

1 cup basmati rice, rinsed and drained

½ cup small cauliflower florets

1 carrot, diced

1½ cups vegetable stock

½ cup frozen peas, thawed

½ teaspoon salt

1. Heat oil in an uncovered pressure cooker over medium heat. Add the turmeric, garam masala, cayenne pepper, and onion. Cook, stirring, until the onion begins to turn golden. Add the remaining ingredients and mix well. Close and lock the lid.

2. Turn the heat up to high and when the cooker reaches pressure, lower the heat to the minimum needed to maintain pressure. Cook for 4–5 minutes at high pressure.

3. Open with the natural-release method—move the pressure cooker to a cool burner and wait for the pressure to come down on its own (about 15 minutes). For electric pressure cookers, disengage the "keep warm" mode or unplug the cooker and open when the pressure indicator has gone down (20–30 minutes).

WHEAT BERRY SALAD ✿

For an elegant presentation, place a teaspoon of Wheat Berry Salad on individual sections of baby romaine hearts.

INGREDIENTS
Serves 12

1½ tablespoons vegetable oil

6¾ cups water

1½ cups wheat berries

1½ teaspoons Dijon mustard

1 teaspoon sugar

1 teaspoon sea salt

½ teaspoon freshly ground black pepper

¼ cup white wine vinegar

½ cup extra-virgin olive oil

½ small red onion, peeled and diced

1⅓ cups frozen corn or peas, thawed

1 medium zucchini, peeled, grated, and drained

2 stalks celery, finely diced

1 red bell pepper, seeded and diced

4 green onions, diced

¼ cup sun-dried tomatoes, diced

¼ cup fresh parsley, chopped

1. Add the oil, water, and wheat berries to the pressure cooker. Lock the lid into place and bring to high pressure; maintain pressure for 50 minutes. Remove from the heat and quick-release the pressure. Fluff with a fork. If the grains aren't yet as tender as you'd like, simmer and stir the mixture for a few minutes, adding more water if necessary. When done to your liking, drain and transfer to a large bowl.

2. Make the dressing by puréeing the mustard, sugar, salt, pepper, vinegar, olive oil, and red onion in a food processor or blender. Start by stirring ½ cup dressing into the cooled wheat berries. Toss the seasoned wheat berries with remaining ingredients. Taste for seasoning; add additional salt, pepper, or dressing if needed. Cover and refrigerate any leftover dressing for up to 3 days.

Tasty Substitutions

You can add a bit more flavor to this salad by substituting tomato juice or vegetable stock for some of the wheat berry cooking liquid.

WILD RICE CASSEROLE

This side dish casserole goes great with roast turkey or chicken. It's especially good if you mix in some shiitake mushrooms with the fresh button mushrooms.

INGREDIENTS

Serves 4

2 tablespoons butter

1 small sweet onion, peeled and diced

4 ounces fresh button mushrooms, cleaned and sliced

1 cup wild rice, rinsed and drained

½ cup pecans, chopped and toasted

2 teaspoons Mrs. Dash Garlic and Herb Seasoning Blend

2 cups chicken broth

Salt and freshly ground black pepper, to taste

1. Melt the butter in the pressure cooker over medium heat. Stir in the onion and mushrooms; sauté for 5 minutes or until the mushrooms have given off their moisture and begin to brown. Stir in the wild rice, pecans, seasoning blend, and broth.

2. Lock the lid into place and bring to high pressure; maintain pressure for 20 minutes. Remove from the heat and allow pressure to release naturally.

3. Fluff rice with a fork and drain off any excess moisture. Taste for seasoning and add salt and pepper if needed.

CHAPTER 7

PASTA

BOW TIE PASTA IN A SAGE BEURRE BLANC SAUCE

Sage is an herb with an earthy and slightly minty flavor.

INGREDIENTS
Serves 6–8

Water, as needed

1 pound bow tie pasta

1 tablespoon extra-virgin olive oil

1 cup white mushrooms, sliced

1 small red onion, julienned

2 cloves garlic, minced

1 cup white wine

2 tablespoons white wine vinegar

¾ cup cold butter, or vegan margarine, such as Earth Balance

1 cup tomatoes, diced

1 teaspoon dried sage

Salt and pepper, to taste

1. Fill the pressure cooker with enough water to cover the pasta. Bring the water to a boil. Add the pasta. Lock the lid into place and bring to high pressure; maintain pressure for 5 minutes. Use the natural-release method to release the pressure and then remove the lid. Set the pasta aside.

2. Add the olive oil to a pan and sauté the mushrooms and onion until golden brown. Add the garlic and sauté for an additional 30 seconds. Add the wine and vinegar, and let reduce for about 3 minutes. Add the cold butter to the pan, 1 tablespoon at a time, stirring it constantly into the wine to create an emulsion.

3. Once the butter has emulsified, add the tomatoes, sage, and salt and pepper, to taste. Toss with the pasta before serving.

BROCCOLI–PINE NUT PASTA SALAD

Broccoli contains over 5 grams of protein per cup, making it a good staple ingredient in anyone's diet.

INGREDIENTS
Serves 6–8

Water, as needed

1 pound rotini

⅓ cup pine nuts, toasted

1 head broccoli, blanched and chopped

1 red bell pepper, chopped

½ onion, diced

2 cloves garlic, minced

2 tablespoons red wine vinegar

⅓ cup extra-virgin olive oil

Salt and pepper, to taste

1. Fill the pressure cooker with enough water to cover the pasta. Bring the water to a boil. Add the pasta. Lock the lid into place and bring to high pressure; maintain pressure for 7 minutes. Use the natural-release method to release the pressure and then remove the lid. Pour the pasta and run cold water over it until cooled. Set the pasta aside.

2. In a sauté pan over low heat, toast the pine nuts until they are golden brown. Be careful not to burn them.

3. In a large bowl, combine the pine nuts, broccoli, red pepper, onion, garlic, vinegar, olive oil, and pasta. Taste for seasoning and add salt pepper if needed.

CHICKEN AND VEGETABLE ALFREDO

You don't often find this many vegetables in comfort food. In this case, they're needed to offset all that rich, tasty, high-fat content from the butter, cream, and cheese.

INGREDIENTS
Serves 4

2 tablespoons olive oil

1½ pounds boneless, skinless chicken breasts

1 small onion, peeled and diced

1 red bell pepper, seeded and diced

8 ounces fresh mushrooms, cleaned and sliced

4 cloves garlic, peeled and minced

1 tablespoon dried basil

1 teaspoon dried thyme

⅛ teaspoon freshly ground nutmeg

¼ teaspoon freshly ground black pepper

1 14-ounce can chicken broth

8 ounces sugar snap peas, sliced diagonally

½ cup sliced carrots

1½ cups broccoli florets

1½ cups cauliflower segments

¼ cup Parmigiano-Reggiano cheese, grated

1 stick butter, softened

1 cup heavy cream

8 ounces uncooked linguini

1. Bring the oil to temperature in the pressure cooker over medium heat. Cut the chicken into bite-sized pieces and add to the pressure cooker; stir-fry for 5 minutes or until they begin to brown. Add the onion and red bell pepper; sauté for 3 minutes. Add the sliced mushrooms; sauté for 3 minutes or until the mushrooms have released their moisture. Add the garlic, basil, thyme, nutmeg, pepper, and broth. Stir to combine. Lock the lid into place and bring to low pressure; maintain pressure for 3 minutes. Remove from the heat and quick-release the pressure. Remove the lid.

2. Add the sugar snap peas, carrots, broccoli, and cauliflower to the pressure cooker. Return the pressure cooker to the heat, lock the lid into place, and bring to low pressure; maintain pressure for 3 minutes. Remove from the heat and quick-release the pressure.

3. Whip the cheese into the butter and then blend with the cream. Return the pressure cooker to medium heat. Stir in the cream mixture; cook and stir for 3 minutes or until the cream mixture is heated through.

4. Cook the linguini according to package directions. Top the noodles with the sauce and additional grated cheese if desired.

If You Prefer
You can substitute 2 1-pound bags of thawed frozen stir-fry mixed vegetables for the sugar snap peas, carrots, broccoli, and cauliflower called for in the recipe. If you do so, reduce the pressure-maintaining time for the vegetables to 1 minute.

CHICKEN TORTELLINI

You can substitute broccoli florets for the asparagus. Serve with a tossed salad and garlic bread.

INGREDIENTS
Serves 6

3 slices bacon, diced

¼ cup plus 3 tablespoons butter

4 shallots, peeled and minced

1 tablespoon dried parsley

1½ pounds boneless, skinless chicken breasts

1 small carrot, peeled and finely sliced

1 8-ounce package dried cheese tortellini

1 teaspoon dried tarragon

2 cups chicken broth

1 pound asparagus

2 teaspoons all-purpose flour

¼ cup whole milk

¼ cup heavy cream

½ cup Parmigiano-Reggiano cheese, grated

Salt and freshly ground black pepper, to taste

1. Fry the bacon in the pressure cooker over medium heat until it is crisp. Stir in ¼ cup of the butter, shallots, and parsley; sauté for 3 minutes. Cut the chicken into bite-sized pieces and add it to the pressure cooker along with the carrot, tortellini, tarragon, and broth. Stir. Lock the lid into place and bring to high pressure; maintain pressure for 6 minutes.

2. Quick-release the pressure and remove the lid. Clean and trim the asparagus, cut it into 2-inch pieces, and add it to the pressure cooker. Lock the lid into place and bring to low pressure; maintain pressure for 2 minutes.

3. Quick-release the pressure and remove the lid. Combine the remaining 3 tablespoons of butter with the flour and then whisk it into the milk and cream; stir in the cheese. Bring the contents of the pressure cooker to a simmer and slowly stir in the flour mixture. Cook and stir for 3 minutes or until the sauce is thickened and the flour taste is cooked out of the sauce. Taste for seasoning and add salt and pepper to taste. Transfer to a serving bowl or platter. Top with additional cheese if desired.

A Heavier Sauce

You can omit the flour if you use ½ cup of the heavy cream for the sauce instead of the combination of milk and cream. This is a good option if you're making the sauce for someone who adheres to a gluten-free diet (make sure you have gluten-free tortellini).

FETTUCCINE WITH SMOKED SALMON SAUCE

You can substitute smoked trout, smoked whitefish, or crisp bacon for the smoked salmon.

INGREDIENTS

Serves 6

¼ cup olive oil

2 cups fettuccine

4 cups chicken broth

½ teaspoon sea salt

¼ teaspoon freshly ground white pepper

1 teaspoon dried thyme

3 tablespoons butter

½ cup sour cream

2 green onions, cleaned and diced

1 pound smoked salmon, in bite-sized pieces

⅓ cup Parmigiano-Reggiano cheese, grated

1. Bring the oil to temperature in the pressure cooker over medium heat. Stir in the fettuccine, broth, salt, pepper, and thyme. Lock the lid in place and bring to high pressure; maintain pressure for 8 minutes. Quick-release the pressure and remove the lid.

2. Drain the pasta if necessary. Transfer to a serving bowl. Cut the butter into small chunks and toss with the pasta. Add the sour cream; stir to combine. Add the green onion and smoked salmon; toss to mix. Top with the grated cheese. Serve.

FRESH SPINACH–WHITE WINE ANGEL HAIR PASTA

This light pasta dish can be made alcohol-free by substituting vegetable stock and 1 teaspoon of vinegar for the white wine.

INGREDIENTS

Serves 6–8

Water, as needed

1 pound angel hair pasta

1 tablespoon olive oil

¼ yellow onion, diced

2 cloves garlic, minced

½ cup white wine

¼ cup water, or as needed

1 tablespoon butter, or vegan margarine

1 tablespoon flour

Salt and pepper, to taste

1 cup steamed spinach

1. Fill the pressure cooker with enough water to cover the pasta. Bring the water to a boil. Add the pasta. Lock the lid into place and bring to high pressure; maintain pressure for 4 minutes. Use the natural-release method to release the pressure and then remove the lid. Set the pasta aside.

2. In a medium saucepan over low heat, add the olive oil, onion, and garlic. Cook until the onions are soft, about 5 minutes. Add the white wine and water, then bring to a low simmer. Continue simmering for about 10 minutes.

3. Add the butter and flour, stirring until completely combined and the sauce begins to thicken. If the sauce becomes too thick, add more water until you reach the desired consistency, then season with salt and pepper.

4. In a large mixing bowl, combine the spinach, pasta, and white-wine sauce, then toss until the pasta is completely coated.

GNOCCHI AND MUSHROOMS IN ROSEMARY ALFREDO SAUCE

Gnocchi can be made from flour or potato but is typically treated like pasta in cooking, regardless of the main ingredient. Some stores carry vegetarian prepackaged gnocchi, such as Delallo brand, or you can try making your own.

INGREDIENTS
Serves 2–3

Water, as needed

16 ounces uncooked gnocchi

1 tablespoon extra-virgin olive oil

½ cup mushrooms, sliced

1 teaspoon fresh lemon juice

2 cups béchamel sauce

½ cup Parmesan cheese, or vegan
  Parmesan or mozzarella

½ cup tomatoes, diced

1 teaspoon rosemary, chopped

Salt and pepper, to taste

1. Fill the pressure cooker with enough water to cover the gnocchi. Bring the water to a boil. Add the gnocchi. Lock the lid into place and bring to high pressure; maintain pressure for 1 minute. Use the natural-release method to release the pressure and then remove the lid. Drain the gnocchi and set aside.

2. Add the olive oil to a pan over medium heat and sauté the mushrooms for about 1 minute. Add the gnocchi and sauté for 1 minute more.

3. Deglaze the pan with the lemon juice, then add the béchamel sauce and Parmesan cheese, and allow it to reduce until desired consistency is reached.

4. Stir in the tomatoes and rosemary. Taste for seasoning, and add salt and pepper, if necessary.

ORZO-STUFFED TOMATOES

Any type of larger tomato will work for this recipe. Use what is in season and available at a store near you.

INGREDIENTS
Serves 4

Water, as needed

½ cup orzo pasta

4 beefsteak or large vine-ripe tomatoes

1 cup fresh mozzarella, chopped, or vegan
  mozzarella, such as Daiya Mozzarella
  Style Shreds

2 cloves garlic, minced

2 tablespoons fresh basil, minced

2 tablespoons fresh parsley, minced

Salt and pepper, to taste

2 tablespoons extra-virgin olive oil

1. Fill the pressure cooker with enough water to cover the pasta. Bring the water to a boil. Add the pasta. Lock the lid into place and bring to high pressure; maintain pressure for 3 minutes. Use the natural-release method to release the pressure and then remove the lid. Set the pasta aside.

2. Preheat the oven to 350°F. Cut the tops off the tomatoes and scoop out the pulp. Roughly chop the pulp with a knife and place it in a medium bowl. Add the orzo, mozzarella, garlic, basil, parsley, and salt and pepper to taste.

3. Combine the tomatoes with orzo mixture and place them on a baking sheet. Drizzle the olive oil over the tomatoes and bake them in the oven for 15–20 minutes.

PASTA FAGIOLE

This Italian dish is often served as a soup, but this less brothy version can be served as a main course pasta dish, too.

INGREDIENTS
Serves 6–8

Water, as needed

1 pound spaghetti pasta

4 cups cooked pinto beans

4 cups marinara sauce

1 cup mozzarella cheese, or vegan mozzarella, such as Daiya Mozzarella Style Shreds

⅛ cup basil, chopped

1. Fill the pressure cooker with enough water to cover the pasta. Bring the water to a boil. Add the pasta. Lock the lid into place and bring to high pressure; maintain pressure for 6 minutes. Use the natural-release method to release the pressure and then remove the lid. Set the pasta aside.

2. Preheat the oven to the broiler setting. Place one serving of pasta in a small bowl. Cover with the pinto beans and then with the marinara sauce. Sprinkle some of the mozzarella cheese on top. Repeat with remaining servings. Place under the oven broiler until the cheese melts. Garnish with basil and serve.

PASTA PRIMAVERA WITH VEGETABLES

This light pasta dish is perfect for a mild spring day.

INGREDIENTS
Serves 6–8

Water, as needed

1 pound dry bow tie pasta

1 tablespoon extra-virgin olive oil

1½ cups squash, chopped

1½ cups zucchini, chopped

1 head broccoli, chopped

½ cup sun-dried tomatoes

2 cloves garlic

1 cup white wine

¾ cup cold butter or vegan margarine, such as Earth Balance

¼ cup basil, chopped

Salt and pepper, to taste

1. Fill the pressure cooker with enough water to cover the pasta. Bring the water to a boil. Add the pasta. Lock the lid into place and bring to high pressure; maintain pressure for 5 minutes. Use the natural-release method to release the pressure and then remove the lid. Drain and set the pasta aside.

2. While the pasta is cooking, add the olive oil to a pan over medium-low heat and sauté the squash, zucchini, broccoli, and sun-dried tomatoes until they begin to turn golden brown. Add the garlic and the white wine. Allow the white wine to reduce for about 2–3 minutes.

3. Add the butter to the pan, stirring constantly into the wine to create an emulsion.

4. Once the butter has melted, pour the sauce and veggies over the pasta and stir to coat. Garnish with the basil. Taste for seasoning, and add salt and pepper if necessary.

PASTA PUTTANESCA

Rumor has it that this popular dish was invented by prostitutes, but depending on who is telling the story, the creator varies.

INGREDIENTS
Serves 6–8

Water, as needed

1 pound linguine

2 teaspoons olive oil

2 cloves garlic, slivered

1 tablespoon fresh basil, chopped

2 tablespoons capers

¼ cup kalamata olives, pitted and halved

1 teaspoon dried red pepper flakes

1 tablespoon brine (juice from the olives)

1 14-ounce can crushed tomatoes, drained

Salt and pepper, to taste

1. Fill the pressure cooker with enough water to cover the pasta. Bring the water to a boil. Add the pasta. Lock the lid into place and bring to high pressure; maintain pressure for 6 minutes. Use the natural-release method to release the pressure and then remove the lid. Drain with a colander and set the pasta aside.

2. In a sauté pan over medium heat, warm the oil. Add the garlic and cook for 2–3 minutes. Stir in the basil, capers, olives, and red pepper flakes and cook for 2 more minutes.

3. Stir in the brine and crushed tomatoes and simmer over low heat for 10–15 minutes. Season with salt and pepper to taste.

4. Combine the sauce with the linguine and serve.

PASTA SALAD WITH TOMATO, ARUGULA, AND FETA

Serve this pasta salad at room temperature or after chilling in the refrigerator for at least 2 hours.

INGREDIENTS
Serves 6–8

Water, as needed

1 pound dry rotini pasta

2 Roma tomatoes, diced

2 cloves garlic, minced

1 red bell pepper, diced

2 tablespoons white wine vinegar

⅓ cup extra-virgin olive oil

2 cups arugula or spinach, chopped

1 cup feta cheese or vegan feta cheese

Salt and pepper, to taste

1. Fill the pressure cooker with enough water to cover the pasta. Bring the water to a boil. Add the pasta. Lock the lid into place and bring to high pressure; maintain pressure for 7 minutes. Use the natural-release method to release the pressure and then remove the lid. Drain the pasta, then run cold water over the pasta until cooled. Set aside.

2. In a large bowl, mix the tomatoes, garlic, red bell pepper, vinegar, olive oil, arugula or spinach, and feta. Mix in the pasta and add salt and pepper to taste.

PORTOBELLO STROGANOFF

Beef is commonly used in stroganoff recipes, but you can make a vegetarian or vegan version by using the "meaty" flavor of portobello mushrooms instead.

INGREDIENTS

Serves 6–8

Water, as needed

1 pound linguine

1 tablespoon extra-virgin olive oil

1 yellow onion, diced

3 cups portobello mushrooms, roughly chopped

1 tablespoon all-purpose flour

4 cups Espagnole (Chapter 15)

½ cup sour cream, or vegan sour cream, such as Tofutti Sour Supreme

1 tablespoon ground mustard

Salt and pepper, to taste

¼ cup chopped parsley

1. Fill the pressure cooker with enough water to cover the pasta. Bring the water to a boil. Add the pasta. Lock the lid into place and bring to high pressure; maintain pressure for 6 minutes. Use the natural-release method to release the pressure and then remove the lid. Set the pasta aside.

2. Heat the oil and sauté the onion and mushrooms. Sprinkle in the flour and cook to a paste. Add the Espagnole sauce and cook at a slow simmer for 20 minutes. Mix the sour cream and mustard together. Pour into the sauce and heat thoroughly. Taste for seasoning, and add salt and pepper if necessary.

3. Serve over the linguine and garnish with the parsley. Serve.

ROTINI WITH RED WINE MARINARA

When cooking pasta in a pressure cooker you only need to add the amount of water the pasta will absorb, which should be enough to just cover the dried pasta.

INGREDIENTS

Serves 6–8

Water, as needed

1 pound dry rotini pasta

1 tablespoon extra-virgin olive oil

½ yellow onion, diced

3 cloves garlic, minced

1 16-ounce can crushed tomatoes

½ cup red wine

1 teaspoon sugar

⅛ cup basil, chopped

Salt and pepper, to taste

1. Fill the pressure cooker with enough water to cover the pasta. Bring the water to a boil. Add the pasta. Lock the lid into place and bring to high pressure; maintain pressure for 7 minutes. Use the natural-release method to release the pressure and then remove the lid. Drain the pasta and set aside.

2. Add the olive oil to a pan over medium heat and sauté the onion until it begins to caramelize. Add the garlic and sauté for an additional 30 seconds. Add the crushed tomatoes, red wine, and sugar and simmer for about 10 minutes.

3. Add the basil. Taste for seasoning, and add salt and pepper if necessary.

SAUSAGE WITH BOW TIE PASTA

Serve with a tossed salad and garlic bread.

INGREDIENTS
Serves 6

1 pound ground sausage

1 tablespoon olive oil

1 large onion, peeled and diced

3 cloves garlic, peeled and minced

3 cups chicken broth

1 cup tomato sauce

2 teaspoons dried parsley

½ teaspoon ground fennel

1 teaspoon dried basil

½ teaspoon sugar

¼ teaspoon freshly ground black pepper

⅛ teaspoon dried red pepper flakes

3 cups bow tie pasta

¼ cup heavy cream

Salt, to taste

½ cup Parmigiano-Reggiano cheese, grated

1. Add the sausage to the pressure cooker over medium-high heat; break the sausage apart as you stir-fry it for 5 minutes or until it is cooked through and has rendered its fat. Drain and discard the fat. Stir in the oil and onion; sauté for 3 minutes or until the onion is soft. Stir in the garlic; sauté for 30 seconds.

2. Stir in the broth, tomato sauce, parsley, fennel, basil, sugar, pepper, red pepper flakes, and pasta. Reduce the heat to medium, lock the lid into place, and bring to low pressure; maintain pressure for 9 minutes. Quick-release the pressure and remove the lid.

3. Stir in the cream. Taste for seasoning and adjust if necessary. Add salt to taste. Transfer to a serving bowl or platter. Top with the cheese. Serve.

SPICY BEEF MACARONI AND CHEESE

Serve this Southwestern-inspired dish with an avocado salad and baked tortilla chips.

INGREDIENTS

Serves 6

1 pound lean ground beef

1 tablespoon olive or vegetable oil

1 small yellow onion, peeled and diced

1 jalapeño pepper, seeded and minced

2 cloves garlic, peeled and minced

2 cups bottled salsa

1 3-ounce can tomato paste

2 tablespoons chili powder

3 cups uncooked penne or ziti pasta

Water, as needed

8 ounces sharp Cheddar cheese, grated

1. Add the ground beef to the pressure cooker. Fry over medium-high heat and break apart until it is cooked through. Drain off and discard fat.

2. Stir in the oil, onion, and jalapeño; sauté for 3 minutes or until onion is tender. Stir in the garlic and sauté for 30 seconds.

3. Stir in the salsa, tomato paste, chili powder, and pasta. Pour in enough water to cover all of the ingredients.

4. Lock the lid into place and bring to low pressure; maintain pressure for 6 minutes. Remove from the heat and allow pressure to release naturally. Remove the lid. Drain off and discard any excess moisture.

5. Stir in the cheese. Cover the pressure cooker for 3 minutes to allow time for the cheese to melt. Stir again. Taste for seasoning and adjust if necessary. Serve.

VEGETABLE LINGUINE IN WHITE BEAN ALFREDO SAUCE 🌱

Vegan white bean alfredo mimics the taste of the dairy-based version but only contains a fraction of the fat!

INGREDIENTS
Serves 6–8

Water, as needed

1 pound dry linguine

1 tablespoon olive oil

1 cup red bell pepper, diced

1 cup tomato, diced

3–4 cups White Bean Alfredo Sauce (Chapter 15) or vegan version of White Bean Alfredo Sauce

¼ cup basil, chopped

Salt and pepper, to taste

1. Fill the pressure cooker with enough water to cover the pasta. Bring the water to a boil. Add the pasta. Lock the lid into place and bring to high pressure; maintain pressure for 6 minutes. Use the natural-release method to release the pressure and then remove the lid. Drain the pasta, then set aside.

2. While the pasta is cooking, heat the olive oil in a pan over medium heat. Sauté the red bell pepper until it just begins to soften, about 3 minutes, then remove from heat.

3. In a large bowl, combine cooked pasta with the sautéed red pepper, fresh tomatoes, sauce, and basil.

4. Stir gently, and add salt and pepper to taste.

WHOLE WHEAT FETTUCCINE WITH MUSHROOM CREAM SAUCE

Whole wheat pasta has a slightly different flavor and texture than regular pasta, and it pairs well with the earthy flavor of mushrooms.

INGREDIENTS
Serves 6–8

Water, as needed

1 pound whole wheat fettuccine

2 tablespoons butter, or vegan margarine, such as Earth Balance

1 cup mushrooms, sliced (try button, shiitake, oyster, or portobello)

2 cloves garlic, minced

1 tablespoon all-purpose flour

1¼ cups milk, or unsweetened soymilk

1 tablespoon fresh parsley, chopped

1 tablespoon fresh lemon juice

Salt and pepper, to taste

1. Fill the pressure cooker with enough water to cover the pasta. Bring the water to a boil. Add the pasta. Lock the lid into place and bring to high pressure; maintain pressure for 7 minutes. Use the natural-release method to release the pressure and then remove the lid. Set the pasta aside.

2. Melt 1 tablespoon of the butter in a sauté pan, then add the mushrooms and garlic. Sauté until the mushrooms are soft, about 4 minutes. Remove from the pan and set aside.

3. Melt the second tablespoon of butter, then stir in the flour and cook for about 1 minute to make a roux. Gradually stir in the milk, stirring continuously until smooth.

4. Add the cooked mushrooms, parsley, lemon juice, salt, and pepper and cook for 1–2 minutes.

5. Pour the sauce over warm pasta and serve immediately.

CHAPTER 8

BEANS, CHICKPEAS, AND LENTILS

ADZUKI BEANS

Adzuki beans are an Asian bean that is typically enjoyed sweetened, but they can be served savory, too.

INGREDIENTS

Serves 4

1 cup dried adzuki beans

4 cups water

1 tablespoon vegetable oil

1 teaspoon salt

1. Add the beans, water, oil, and salt to the pressure cooker.

2. Lock the lid into place; bring to high pressure and maintain for 8 minutes. Remove from the heat and allow pressure to release naturally.

BEER-LIME BLACK BEANS

Try a Mexican beer, such as Negra Modelo, Tecate, or Corona to complement the beans in this recipe.

INGREDIENTS

Serves 8

2 cups dried black beans

14 cups water

1 tablespoon vegetable oil

½ red onion, diced

1 clove garlic, minced

2 teaspoons salt

2 12-ounce bottles light-colored beer, such as an ale

¼ cup cilantro, chopped

1 tablespoon lime juice

1. Add the beans and 8 cups water to the pressure cooker. Lock the lid into place; bring to high pressure for 1 minute. Remove from the heat and quick-release the pressure.

2. Drain the water, rinse the beans, and add to the pressure cooker again with the remaining 6 cups water. Soak for 1 hour.

3. Lock the lid into place; bring to high pressure and maintain for 10 minutes. Remove from the heat and quick-release the pressure.

4. Remove the lid and add the oil, onion, garlic, salt, and beer to the pressure cooker, then stir. Lock the lid into place; bring to high pressure and maintain for 2 minutes. Remove from the heat and allow pressure to release naturally.

5. Stir in the chopped cilantro and lime juice before serving.

BLACK BEAN–CILANTRO FRITTERS

For an extra-crunchy exterior, try rolling the fritters in panko bread crumbs before frying.

INGREDIENTS
Serves 8–10

1 cup black beans

8 cups water

1 tablespoon vegetable oil

1 teaspoon salt

1 red bell pepper, diced

1 jalapeño, minced

½ cup onion, diced

¼ cup cilantro

1 cup flour

1 cup cornmeal

1 tablespoon baking powder

½ cup heavy cream, or unsweetened soymilk

2 eggs, beaten, or 2 teaspoons cornstarch mixed with 2 tablespoons water

2 quarts canola oil, for frying

Salt and pepper, to taste

1. Add the beans and 4 cups water to the pressure cooker. Lock the lid into place; bring to high pressure for 1 minute. Remove from the heat and quick-release the pressure.

2. Drain the water, rinse the beans, and add to the pressure cooker again with the remaining 4 cups water. Soak for 1 hour.

3. Add the vegetable oil and salt. Lock the lid into place; bring to high pressure and maintain for 12 minutes. Remove from the heat and allow pressure to release naturally. Drain and set aside.

4. In a bowl, combine the red bell pepper, jalapeño, onion, cilantro, and black beans.

5. In another bowl combine the flour, cornmeal, baking powder, heavy cream, and 2 eggs. Add the vegetable and bean mixture to the flour mixture and stir until well combined. Form the batter into 1" fritters.

6. In a large pot, heat the oil to 350°F and fry the fritters until golden brown, about 3–4 minutes. Season with salt and pepper.

Egg Replacements
Other options for replacing eggs in fritters are using mixes, such as Ener-G Egg Replacer, or tofu. If using tofu, use half a cup of soft tofu to replace two eggs.

BLACK BEAN SALAD

Can be served as a side dish or on top of your favorite rice or pasta.

INGREDIENTS
Serves 6

2 cups black beans, soaked

4 cups water

1 tablespoon vegetable oil

1 clove garlic, smashed

1 bay leaf

2 medium tomatoes, chopped

1 cup fresh or frozen corn kernels

½ red onion, finely chopped

3 teaspoons olive oil

1 teaspoon lemon juice

1 teaspoon salt

¼ teaspoon white pepper

1 sprig fresh oregano

1. Add beans, water, oil, garlic, and bay leaf to the pressure cooker. Close and lock the lid.

2. Turn the heat up to high and when the cooker reaches pressure, lower the heat to the minimum needed to maintain pressure. Cook for 6–8 minutes at high pressure.

3. Open with the natural-release method—move the pressure cooker to a cool burner and wait for the pressure to come down on its own (about 15 minutes). For electric pressure cookers, disengage the "keep warm" mode or unplug the cooker. After 10 minutes, release the rest of the pressure using the valve.

4. Strain the beans and discard the bay leaf. Let cool. Mix in tomatoes, corn, onion, olive oil, lemon juice, salt, and pepper. Sprinkle with fresh oregano leaves before serving.

BOSTON BAKED BEANS

The pressure cooker helps give these beans the flavor that usually comes from slow baking. If you're short on prep time, substitute ¼ cup dried minced onion or onion flakes for the diced onion.

INGREDIENTS
Serves 8

1 pound dried small white beans

6 cups water

4 slices bacon, diced

2 medium sweet onions, peeled and diced

4 cloves garlic, peeled and minced

3½ cups chicken broth

2 teaspoons dried mustard

¼ teaspoon freshly ground black pepper

¼ cup molasses

½ cup ketchup

¼ brown sugar

1 teaspoon Worcestershire sauce

1 teaspoon cider vinegar

Salt, to taste

Optional: Smoked paprika

1. Wash and drain the dried beans. Soak them overnight in 6 cups water, or enough to cover them by more than 1 inch.

2. Fry the bacon in the pressure cooker over medium-high heat until the bacon begins to render its fat. Lower the heat to medium and add the onion; sauté for 3 minutes or until the onions are soft. Stir in the garlic; sauté for 30 seconds. Add the drained soaked beans, broth, dried mustard, and pepper.

3. Lock the lid into place and bring to low pressure; maintain pressure for 20 minutes. Remove from the heat and allow pressure to release naturally.

4. Remove the lid; the beans should still be somewhat soupy at this point. Stir in the molasses, ketchup, brown sugar, Worcestershire sauce, and vinegar. Stir to mix. Taste and add another ¼ cup of molasses if you prefer a heartier taste. Return the pan to the heat, lock the lid into place, and bring to low pressure; maintain pressure for 5 minutes. Remove from the heat and allow pressure to release naturally.

5. Remove the lid. Stir the beans and taste for seasoning. Add salt to taste and additional Worcestershire sauce if needed. If the beans are still too soupy, return to the heat and simmer them, stirring occasionally, until thickened. Stir in the smoked paprika if using. Serve.

CANNELLINI AND MINT BEAN SALAD

This refreshing salad can be served as a side dish or on top of your favorite rice or pasta.

INGREDIENTS
Serves 6

2 cups cannellini beans, soaked

4 cups water

1 tablespoon vegetable oil

1 clove garlic, smashed

1 bay leaf

3 teaspoons olive oil

1 teaspoon white wine vinegar

1 teaspoon salt

¼ teaspoon white pepper

1 sprig fresh mint, chopped

1. Add beans, water, oil, garlic, and bay leaf to the pressure cooker. Close and lock the lid.

2. Turn the heat up to high and when the cooker reaches pressure, lower the heat to the minimum needed to maintain pressure. Cook for 6–8 minutes at high pressure.

3. Open with the natural-release method—move the pressure cooker to a cool burner and wait for the pressure to come down on its own (about 15 minutes). For electric pressure cookers, disengage the "keep warm" mode or unplug the cooker. After 10 minutes, release the rest of the pressure using the valve.

4. Strain the beans and discard the bay leaf. Dress with olive oil, vinegar, salt, and pepper. Sprinkle with mint before serving.

CHIPOTLE-THYME BLACK BEANS

There are actually 5 different varieties of black beans. But when you purchase black beans, they are often just labeled as "black beans."

INGREDIENTS
Serves 8

2 cups dried black beans

16 cups water

1 tablespoon vegetable oil

1 teaspoon chipotle powder

2 teaspoons fresh thyme, minced

1 teaspoon salt

1. Add the beans and 8 cups water to the pressure cooker. Lock the lid into place; bring to high pressure for 1 minute. Remove from the heat and quick-release the pressure.

2. Drain the water, rinse the beans, and add to the pressure cooker again with the remaining 8 cups water. Let soak for 1 hour.

3. Add the vegetable oil, chipotle, thyme, and salt. Lock the lid into place; bring to high pressure and maintain for 12 minutes. Remove from the heat and allow pressure to release naturally.

CUBAN BLACK BEANS AND RICE

Cuban cuisine is a combination of African, Caribbean, and Spanish cuisines.

INGREDIENTS
Serves 6

3 tablespoons olive or vegetable oil

1 medium green bell pepper, seeded and diced

1 stalk celery, finely diced

1 carrot, peeled and grated

1 onion, diced

2 cloves garlic, minced

1 cup medium- or long-grain white rice

1 cup dried black beans, soaked overnight

2 cups vegetable stock

2 teaspoons paprika

½ teaspoon cumin

¼ teaspoon chili powder

1 bay leaf

1 teaspoon salt

¼ teaspoon black pepper

1. Heat olive oil in an uncovered pressure cooker over medium heat. Sauté green bell pepper, celery, carrot and onion until the onion is soft, about 5 minutes. Add the garlic and rice and stir everything together until the rice begins to toast. Then add the beans, stock, paprika, cumin, chili powder, and bay leaf. Close and lock the lid.

2. Turn the heat up to high and when the cooker reaches pressure, lower the heat to the minimum needed to maintain pressure. Cook for 3–5 minutes at high pressure.

3. Open with the natural-release method—move the pressure cooker to a cool burner and wait for the pressure to come down on its own (about 15 minutes). For electric pressure cookers, disengage the "keep warm" mode or unplug the cooker. After 10 minutes, release the rest of the pressure using the valve.

4. Stir and add salt and pepper to taste. Remove bay leaf before serving.

The Bay Leaf
Bay leaf comes from the bay laurel plant and is most commonly used to season soups and stews. When used whole, they should be removed from a dish before serving.

DINNER LOAF

You won't be missing the meatloaf on your dinner table if you try this dinner loaf instead!

INGREDIENTS
Serves 6–8

1 cup dried pinto beans

8 cups water

1 tablespoon vegetable oil

1 teaspoon salt

1 cup onion, diced

1 cup chopped walnuts

½ cup plain dried oats

1 egg, beaten, or 1 teaspoon cornstarch combined with 1 tablespoon water

¾ cup ketchup

1 teaspoon garlic powder

1 teaspoon dried basil

1 teaspoon dried parsley

Salt and pepper, to taste

1. Add the beans and 4 cups water to the pressure cooker. Lock the lid into place; bring to high pressure for 1 minute. Remove from the heat and quick-release the pressure.

2. Drain the water, rinse the beans, and add to the pressure cooker again with the remaining 4 cups water. Soak for 1 hour.

3. Add the vegetable oil and salt. Lock the lid into place; bring to high pressure and maintain for 11 minutes. Remove from the heat and allow pressure to release naturally. Drain the beans and pour into a large mixing bowl.

4. Combine the rest of the ingredients with the beans. Spread the mixture into a loaf pan and bake at 350°F for 30–35 minutes.

Mock Meatloaf

There are many ingredients you can use to make mock meatloaf. For the easiest option, use vegetarian ground beef, such as Gimme Lean Ground Beef, instead of real meat in your favorite recipe.

EDAMAME-SEAWEED SALAD

There are many types of edible seaweed. The most popular varieties include aramae, hijiki, and wakame.

INGREDIENTS
Serves 4

1 cup edamame, shelled

8 cups water, plus more as needed

1 tablespoon vegetable oil

½ cup dried arame, chopped

1 tablespoon sesame oil

1 clove garlic, minced

½ teaspoon fresh ginger, minced

1 teaspoon rice wine vinegar

1 teaspoon salt

1. Add the edamame and 4 cups water to the pressure cooker. Lock the lid into place; bring to high pressure for 1 minute. Remove from the heat and quick-release the pressure.

2. Drain the water, rinse the edamame, and add to the pressure cooker again with the remaining 4 cups water. Soak for 1 hour.

3. Add the vegetable oil. Lock the lid into place; bring to high pressure and maintain for 11 minutes. Remove from the heat and allow pressure to release naturally. Drain and set aside.

4. While the edamame is cooking, cover the arame with water in a small bowl and let sit for 7 minutes. Drain and set aside.

5. In a small sauté pan, heat the sesame oil over medium heat. Add the garlic and ginger and sauté for 30 seconds. Add the vinegar and salt, then the cooked edamame and arame; Serve warm or chilled.

LIMA BEANS

All beans should be finished using the natural-release method.

INGREDIENTS
Serves 4

1 cup dried lima beans

4 cups water

4 cups vegetable stock

1 tablespoon vegetable oil

1. Add the beans and water to the pressure cooker. Lock the lid into place; bring to high pressure for 1 minute. Remove from the heat and quick-release the pressure.

2. Drain the water, rinse the beans, and add to the pressure cooker again with the vegetable stock. Let soak for 1 hour.

3. Add the vegetable oil. Lock the lid into place; bring to high pressure and maintain for 6 minutes. Remove from the heat and allow pressure to release naturally.

NEW ORLEANS RED BEANS AND RICE

Red beans and rice is a New Orleans staple that is traditionally served on Mondays.

INGREDIENTS
Serves 8

2¼ cups dried red kidney beans

16 cups water

3 tablespoons butter, or vegan margarine, such as Earth Balance

1 cup onion, diced

1 cup bell pepper, diced

1 cup celery, diced

2 cloves garlic, minced

6 cups vegetable stock

1 teaspoon liquid smoke

½ teaspoon vegan Worcestershire sauce

1 teaspoon hot sauce (or more if desired)

½ teaspoon dried thyme

1 teaspoon cayenne pepper

2 bay leaves

2 teaspoons salt

8 cups cooked long-grain white rice

1. Add the beans and 8 cups water to the pressure cooker. Lock the lid into place; bring to high pressure for 1 minute. Remove from the heat and quick-release the pressure.

2. Drain the water, rinse the beans, and add to the pressure cooker again with the remaining 8 cups water. Soak for 1 hour.

3. Drain the beans and clean the pressure cooker. Add the butter to the pressure cooker over medium heat. Add the onion, bell pepper, and celery. Sauté until very soft, about 15 minutes. Add the garlic and sauté an additional 30 seconds.

4. Add the vegetable stock, liquid smoke, vegan Worcestershire, hot sauce, thyme, cayenne, bay leaves, and salt.

5. Lock the lid into place; bring to high pressure and maintain for 11 minutes. Remove from the heat and allow pressure to release naturally.

6. Remove the bay leaves before serving and season with additional salt and hot sauce to taste. Serve over cooked white rice.

Make It "Meaty"

Sausage and ham hocks are the most common meats used in red beans and rice. To make a vegetarian "meaty" version, add cooked, sliced vegetarian sausage and chunks of cooked vegetarian bacon right before serving.

NOT REFRIED BEANS

Traditionally, these beans are cooked first and then transferred to a hot pan—hence the "fry" in the refried beans. Instead, we fry the aromatics and cook them with the beans for a more flavorful and healthy "refried" bean.

INGREDIENTS
Serves 6

1 bunch parsley, washed

1 tablespoon vegetable oil

1 onion, chopped

2 cloves garlic, smashed

¼ teaspoon chipotle powder

½ teaspoon cumin

2 cups pinto or borlotti beans, soaked

2 cups water

1 teaspoon salt

1. Separate the parsley leaves from the stems. Chop the stems and set aside, and chop the leaves and set aside.

2. Heat oil in an uncovered pressure cooker over medium heat. Add onion, garlic, chipotle powder, cumin, and parsley stems. Sauté until the onions are soft. Add the beans and water. Close and lock the lid.

3. Turn the heat up to high and when the cooker reaches pressure, lower the heat to the minimum needed to maintain pressure. Cook for 6–8 minutes at high pressure.

4. Open with the natural-release method—move the pressure cooker to a cool burner and wait for the pressure to come down on its own (about 15 minutes). For electric pressure cookers, disengage the "keep warm" mode or unplug the cooker. After 10 minutes, release the rest of the pressure using the valve.

5. Add salt, and using a potato masher, mash about half of the beans. Sprinkle with parsley leaves before serving.

PINTO BEANS

Most beans must be soaked for 4 hours before cooking. You can also try a "quick soak," which is described in this recipe.

INGREDIENTS
Serves 4

1 cup dried pinto beans

8 cups water

1 tablespoon vegetable oil

1 teaspoon salt

1. Add the beans and 4 cups water to the pressure cooker. Lock the lid into place; bring to high pressure for 1 minute. Remove from the heat and quick-release the pressure.

2. Drain the water, rinse the beans, and add to the pressure cooker again with the remaining 4 cups of water. Soak for 1 hour.

3. Add the vegetable oil and salt. Lock the lid into place; bring to high pressure and maintain for 11 minutes. Remove from the heat and allow pressure to release naturally.

RED BEAN FRITTERS

Serve these fritters with a side of sour cream or vegan sour cream, for dipping.

INGREDIENTS
Serves 6–8

1 cup red beans

8 cups water

1 tablespoon olive oil

1 teaspoon salt

1 jalapeño, minced

½ onion, diced

4 cloves garlic, minced

¼ cup cilantro

1 cup flour

1 cup cornmeal

1 tablespoon baking powder

½ cup heavy cream, or unsweetened soymilk

2 eggs, beaten, or 2 teaspoons cornstarch mixed with 2 tablespoons water

2 quarts canola oil, for frying

Salt and pepper, to taste

1. Add the beans and 4 cups water to the pressure cooker. Lock the lid into place; bring to high pressure for 1 minute. Remove from the heat and quick-release the pressure.

2. Drain the water, rinse the beans, and add to the pressure cooker again with the remaining 4 cups water. Soak for 1 hour.

3. Add the olive oil and salt. Lock the lid into place; bring to high pressure and maintain for 11 minutes. Remove from the heat and allow pressure to release naturally. Drain and set aside.

4. In a bowl, combine the jalapeño, onion, garlic, cilantro, and red beans.

5. In another bowl combine the flour, cornmeal, baking powder, heavy cream, and 2 eggs. Add the bean mixture to the flour mixture and stir until well combined. Form the batter into 1" fritters.

6. In a large pot, heat the canola oil to 350°F and fry the fritters until golden brown, about 3–4 minutes. Season with salt and pepper.

Alternate Methods of Preparation
To reduce the amount of oil used in this recipe, pan-fry the fritters instead of deep frying. After the fritters are formed, heat 1 tablespoon of oil in a sauté pan over medium heat and cook the fritters for 3 minutes on each side.

RED BEANS WITH PLANTAINS

Beans served with plantains is a common dish in the West African country of Ghana.

INGREDIENTS
Serves 8

2 cups red beans

16 cups water

4 tablespoons olive oil

2 teaspoons salt, plus more to taste

1 cup onion, diced

4 cloves garlic, minced

1 teaspoon fresh ginger, peeled and minced

½ teaspoon cayenne pepper

1 cup tomatoes, diced

3 ripened plantains, peeled and sliced diagonally

1 cup canola oil

Pepper, to taste

1. Add the beans and 8 cups water to the pressure cooker. Lock the lid into place; bring to high pressure for 1 minute. Remove from the heat and quick-release the pressure.

2. Drain the water, rinse the beans, and add to the pressure cooker again with the remaining 8 cups water. Soak for 1 hour.

3. Add 2 tablespoons olive oil and 2 teaspoons salt. Lock the lid into place; bring to high pressure and maintain for 11 minutes. Remove from the heat and allow pressure to release naturally.

4. While cooking the beans, add the remaining olive oil to a pan and sauté the onion until caramelized. Add the garlic, ginger, and cayenne and sauté 1 minute more. Add the tomatoes and bring to a simmer for 3–5 minutes. Add the mixture to the beans.

5. For the plantains, simply fry in the canola oil. Season with salt and pepper and serve with the red beans.

REFRIED BEANS

Refried beans can be made with black beans or the more commonly used pinto beans. It's typically served as a side dish with Mexican meals.

INGREDIENTS
Serves 8

2 cups dried pinto beans

8 cups water

8 cups vegetable stock

1 tablespoon olive oil

½ onion, diced

½ small jalapeño pepper, seeded and minced

1 clove garlic, minced

½ teaspoon chipotle powder

½ teaspoon cumin

1 teaspoon salt

8 ounces shredded Monterey jack cheese, or vegan Monterey jack cheese, such as Follow Your Heart

1. Add the beans and water to the pressure cooker. Lock the lid into place; bring to high pressure for 1 minute. Remove from the heat and quick-release the pressure.

2. Drain the water, rinse the beans, and add to the pressure cooker again with the stock. Soak for 1 hour.

3. Lock the lid into place; bring to high pressure and maintain for 11 minutes. Remove from the heat and allow pressure to release naturally.

4. In a small sauté pan, heat the oil and sauté the onion, jalapeño, and garlic until just softened, about 5 minutes. Add the chipotle, cumin, and salt, then add the vegetable mixture to the cooked beans and stir.

5. Use a masher or immersion blender to mash the pinto beans, adding more stock if necessary to achieve a creamy consistency.

Minus the Meat
Traditional refried beans are often made with lard, which is not suitable for vegetarians and vegans. To make a vegetarian version, oil and vegetable stock are used instead.

SOUTHERN BLACK-EYED PEAS

Make a meatless version by substituting smoky paprika for the bacon.

INGREDIENTS
Serves 8

½ pound thick-cut bacon, diced

1 stalk celery, finely diced

1-pound bag baby carrots

1 large onion, peeled and diced

3 cups black-eyed peas, soaked

1 cup long-grain white rice, rinsed

4 cups chicken broth

1 teaspoon salt

¼ teaspoon pepper

1. Heat an uncovered pressure cooker over medium heat and add bacon. Fry the bacon until the fat begins to render. Pour out all of the fat, except for about a tablespoon. Add celery, carrots, and onions and sauté until the onions are soft. Add the black-eyed peas, rice, and chicken broth. Close and lock the lid.

2. Turn the heat up to high and when the cooker reaches pressure, lower the heat to the minimum needed to maintain pressure. Cook for 5–7 minutes at high pressure.

3. Open with the natural-release method—move the pressure cooker to a cool burner and wait for the pressure to come down on its own (about 15 minutes). For electric pressure cookers, disengage the "keep warm" mode or unplug the cooker. After 10 minutes, release the rest of the pressure using the valve.

4. Season with salt and pepper and serve.

SOYBEANS

The same cooking time applies to black, yellow, or beige soybeans. Red soybeans (adzuki beans) need 6–9 minutes at high pressure.

INGREDIENTS
Serves 4

2 cups soybeans, soaked

8 cups water

2 tablespoons vegetable oil

1. Put all of the ingredients in the pressure cooker. Close and lock the lid.

2. Turn the heat up to high and when the cooker reaches pressure, lower the heat to the minimum needed to maintain pressure. Cook for 20–22 minutes at high pressure.

3. Open with the natural-release method—move the pressure cooker to a cool burner and wait for the pressure to come down on its own (about 15 minutes). For electric pressure cookers, disengage the "keep warm" mode or unplug the cooker and open when the pressure indicator has gone down (20–30 minutes).

4. Strain and serve.

SPLIT PEAS

Split peas do not need to be soaked before cooking.

INGREDIENTS
Serves 4

2 cups dried split peas

8 cups water

2 tablespoons vegetable oil

1. Put all of the ingredients in the pressure cooker. Close and lock the lid.

2. Turn the heat up to high and when the cooker reaches pressure, lower the heat to the minimum needed to maintain pressure. Cook for 4–6 minutes at high pressure.

3. Open with the natural-release method—move the pressure cooker to a cool burner and wait for the pressure to come down on its own (about 15 minutes). For electric pressure cookers, disengage the "keep warm" mode or unplug the cooker and open when the pressure indicator has gone down (20–30 minutes).

4. Strain and serve.

THREE BEAN SALAD

Cover and refrigerate this salad for at least 2 hours before serving. It can even be made a day in advance and left in the refrigerator overnight.

INGREDIENTS
Serves 8–10

⅓ cup apple cider vinegar

¼ cup sugar

2½ teaspoons salt, plus more to taste

½ teaspoon pepper, plus more to taste

¼ cup olive oil

½ cup dried chickpeas

½ cup dried kidney beans

8 cups water

1 tablespoon vegetable oil

1 cup fresh or frozen green beans, cut into 1" pieces

1 cup flat-leaf parsley, chopped

½ cup onion, diced

½ cup cucumber, diced

1. In a small bowl, whisk together the vinegar, sugar, 1½ teaspoons salt, and pepper. While whisking continuously, slowly add the olive oil. Once well combined, cover and refrigerate.

2. Add the chickpeas, kidney beans, and 4 cups water to the pressure cooker. Lock the lid into place; bring to high pressure for 1 minute. Remove from the heat and quick-release the pressure.

3. Drain the water, rinse the beans, and add to the pressure cooker again with the remaining 4 cups water. Soak for 1 hour.

4. Add the vegetable oil and 1 teaspoon salt. Lock the lid into place; bring to high pressure and maintain for 20 minutes. Quick-release the pressure and open the lid. Add the green beans, lock the lid, and bring to high pressure for an additional 3 minutes. Remove from heat and allow the pressure to release naturally.

5. Drain the cooked beans and add to a large mixing bowl. Stir in all remaining ingredients and dressing. Cover and refrigerate for 2 hours before serving.

Bean Variations

Almost any combination of beans can be used to make a bean salad. Try black beans, pinto beans, and navy beans mixed with Mexican flavors, or adzuki beans, soybeans, and green beans with Japanese flavors.

WHITE BEAN–LEEK PURÉE

Tarragon is a pungent herb that isn't enjoyed by all. If you don't care for tarragon, replace it with sage in this recipe.

INGREDIENTS

Serves 4

1 cup dried cannellini beans

4 cups water

4 cups vegetable stock

1 tablespoon vegetable oil

½ teaspoon salt

1 cup thinly sliced leeks

1 teaspoon lemon juice

2 cloves garlic, minced

¼ teaspoon dried tarragon

1. Add the beans and water to the pressure cooker. Lock the lid into place; bring to high pressure for 1 minute. Remove from the heat and quick-release the pressure.

2. Drain the water, rinse the beans, and add to the pressure cooker again with the stock. Soak for 1 hour.

3. Add the vegetable oil and salt. Lock the lid into place; bring to high pressure and maintain for 10 minutes. Quick-release the pressure.

4. Add all remaining ingredients to the pressure cooker and lock the lid. Bring to high pressure and maintain for 4 minutes. Remove from heat and allow the pressure to release naturally.

5. Pour the beans and remaining liquid into a large food processor or blender and blend until creamy. Season with additional salt, if desired.

WHITE BEANS AND RICE

It may sound like an odd condiment, but a touch of yellow mustard finishes off this dish surprisingly well.

INGREDIENTS
Serves 8

2 cups dried white beans

16 cups water

3 tablespoons canola oil

1 cup onion, diced

1 green bell pepper, chopped

1 stalk celery, chopped

3 cloves garlic, minced

2 bay leaves

¼ teaspoon cayenne pepper

Salt and pepper, to taste

4 cups cooked white rice

1. Add the beans and 8 cups water to the pressure cooker. Lock the lid into place; bring to high pressure for 1 minute. Remove from the heat and quick-release the pressure. Drain the water, rinse the beans, and add to the pressure cooker again with the remaining 8 cups water. Soak for 1 hour. Lock the lid into place; bring to high pressure and maintain for 12 minutes. Remove from the heat and allow pressure to release naturally.

2. Add the oil to a pan and sauté the onion, green pepper, celery, and garlic until they are fragrant and browned. Add the mixture to the pressure cooker along with the bay leaves and cayenne pepper.

3. Lock the lid into place; bring to high pressure and maintain for 10–15 minutes. Remove from the heat and allow pressure to release naturally. Remove bay leaves.

4. Season with salt and pepper and serve over the white rice.

Flavor Variations
Give this dish Italian flair by adding chopped tomatoes, fresh basil, and chopped and pitted kalamata olives.

WHITE BEANS WITH GARLIC AND FRESH TOMATO

Cherry or Roma tomatoes work best for this recipe, but in a pinch, any variety will do.

INGREDIENTS
Serves 4–6

1 cup dried cannellini beans

4 cups water

4 cups vegetable stock

1 tablespoon vegetable oil

1 teaspoon salt

2 cloves garlic, minced

½ cup tomato, diced

½ teaspoon dried sage

½ teaspoon black pepper

1. Add the beans and water to the pressure cooker. Lock the lid into place; bring to high pressure for 1 minute. Remove from the heat and quick-release the pressure.

2. Drain the water, rinse the beans, and add to the pressure cooker again with the stock. Soak for 1 hour.

3. Add the vegetable oil and salt. Lock the lid into place; bring to high pressure and maintain for 10 minutes. Quick-release the pressure.

4. Add all remaining ingredients to the pressure cooker and lock the lid. Bring to high pressure and maintain for 4 minutes. Remove from heat and allow the pressure to release naturally.

WILD RICE AND BLACK SOYBEANS

This combination is easy to make because both wild rice and soybeans need the same pressure-cooking time.

INGREDIENTS
Serves 4

3 cloves garlic, smashed

4 cups vegetable broth

1 cup black soybeans, soaked

1 cup wild rice

1 teaspoon salt

¼ teaspoon pepper

1. Place all ingredients in the pressure cooker. Close and lock the lid.

2. Turn the heat up to high and when the cooker reaches pressure, lower the heat to the minimum needed to maintain pressure. Cook for 22–25 minutes at high pressure.

3. Open with the natural-release method—move the pressure cooker to a cool burner and wait for the pressure to come down on its own (about 15 minutes). For electric pressure cookers, disengage the "keep warm" mode or unplug the cooker and open when the pressure indicator has gone down (20–30 minutes).

4. Stir well and serve.

CHICKPEAS

Did you know that you can also find black chickpeas? The same cooking time also applies to black chickpeas—which are really just dark brown!

INGREDIENTS
Serves 4

2 cups chickpeas, soaked

8 cups water

2 tablespoons vegetable oil

1. Put all of the ingredients in the pressure cooker. Close and lock the lid.

2. Turn the heat up to high and when the cooker reaches pressure, lower the heat to the minimum needed to maintain pressure. Cook for 13–15 minutes at high pressure.

3. Open with the natural-release method—move the pressure cooker to a cool burner and wait for the pressure to come down on its own (about 15 minutes). For electric pressure cookers, disengage the "keep warm" mode or unplug the cooker and open when the pressure indicator has gone down (20–30 minutes).

4. Strain and serve.

Using Dried Chickpeas (Unsoaked)
You can skip the soaking step and make this recipe using dried chickpeas. Cover the chickpeas with water and pressure cook for 30 to 40 minutes at high pressure. Open with the natural-release method and strain and rinse before serving.

CHANA MASALA

The main ingredient in the popular Indian dish chana masala is chickpeas.

INGREDIENTS
Serves 4–6

1 cup dried chickpeas

8 cups water

1 tablespoon vegetable oil

1 tablespoon butter, or vegan margarine, such as Earth Balance

½ onion, diced

1 clove garlic, minced

1 teaspoon ground cumin

¼ teaspoon ground cayenne pepper

½ teaspoon ground turmeric

¼ cup tomatoes, diced

½ cup water

1 teaspoon paprika

½ teaspoon garam masala

1 teaspoon salt

1 tablespoon lemon juice

1 teaspoon ginger, grated

1. Add the chickpeas and 4 cups water to the pressure cooker. Lock the lid into place; bring to high pressure for 1 minute. Remove from the heat and quick-release the pressure.

2. Drain the water, rinse the beans, and add to the pressure cooker again with the remaining 4 cups water. Soak for 1 hour.

3. Add the vegetable oil. Lock the lid into place; bring to high pressure and maintain for 20 minutes. Remove from the heat and allow pressure to release naturally. Drain and set chickpeas aside.

4. Add the butter to the pressure cooker over medium heat and sauté the onion and garlic. Add all remaining ingredients, including the cooked chickpeas, and let simmer until the sauce has reduced, about 15–20 minutes.

Indian Cuisine

Indian cuisine varies by regions of the country, but they are all similar. Herbs and spices, such as coriander, curry powder, and garam masala are commonly used, as well as rice and a variety of lentils.

CHICKPEA CAPRESE SALAD

The fresh basil plays double duty. The stems flavor the beans during cooking and the leaves give this dish a classic Caprese feel.

INGREDIENTS
Serves 6

1 bunch basil

2 cups chickpeas, soaked

4 cups water

1 tablespoon vegetable oil

1 clove garlic, smashed

3 medium tomatoes, diced

4 ounces fresh mozzarella cheese, diced

3 teaspoons olive oil

1 teaspoon salt

1 teaspoon white pepper

1. Separate the basil leaves from the stems. Chop the leaves and reserve the stems.

2. Add chickpeas, water, oil, garlic, and basil stems to the pressure cooker. Close and lock the lid.

3. Turn the heat up to high and when the cooker reaches pressure, lower the heat to the minimum needed to maintain pressure. Cook for 13–15 minutes at high pressure.

4. Open with the natural-release method—move the pressure cooker to a cool burner and wait for the pressure to come down on its own (about 15 minutes). For electric pressure cookers, disengage the "keep warm" mode or unplug the cooker. After 10 minutes, release the rest of the pressure using the valve.

5. Strain the beans and discard the basil stems. Rinse chickpeas under water and let cool. In a serving bowl, mix chickpeas, tomatoes, mozzarella, basil leaves, olive oil, salt, and pepper.

CHICKPEA "TUNA" SALAD SANDWICH

Chickpeas are also commonly known as garbanzo beans.

INGREDIENTS
Serves 4

1 cup dried chickpeas

8 cups water

6" piece dried kombu

1 tablespoon vegetable oil

2 tablespoons sweet relish

½ celery stalk, minced

¼ red onion, minced

4 tablespoons mayonnaise, or vegan mayonnaise, such as Vegenaise

1 teaspoon lemon juice

½ teaspoon dried dill

1 teaspoon salt

4 sandwich buns

4 lettuce leaves and 4 slices tomato, optional

1. Add the chickpeas and 4 cups water to the pressure cooker. Lock the lid into place; bring to high pressure for 1 minute. Remove from the heat and quick-release the pressure.

2. Drain the water, rinse the chickpeas, and add to the pressure cooker again with the remaining 4 cups water. Soak for 1 hour.

3. Add the kombu and vegetable oil. Lock the lid into place; bring to high pressure and maintain for 20 minutes. Remove from the heat and allow pressure to release naturally.

4. Once the pressure is released, remove the lid, remove the kombu, and drain the chickpeas.

5. Transfer the drained chickpeas to a large bowl and mash.

6. Add the relish, celery, red onion, mayonnaise, lemon juice, dill, and salt, and stir until well combined. Scoop into a small dish, cover, and refrigerate for 1–2 hours.

7. Divide the mixture evenly over the 4 sandwich buns, top with lettuce and tomato, if desired, and serve.

Kombu

Kombu is a type of edible seaweed that is often sold in sheets. It is often used to flavor soups and other savory dishes because it adds the umami flavor.

WARM CHICKPEA SALAD

In the summer, you can put the salad in an aluminum baking pan and cook it over indirect heat on a covered grill. Or skip the baking part entirely, chill the salad, and serve it cold.

INGREDIENTS
Serves 12

1 pound dried chickpeas

10 cups water

1½ tablespoons vegetable oil

2 teaspoons salt

4 green onions, sliced

1 cup red onion, diced

1 small green bell pepper, diced

1 small red bell pepper, diced

½ cup fresh parsley, minced

1 large carrot, peeled and grated

¼ cup extra-virgin olive oil

2 teaspoons fresh lemon juice

2 teaspoons white wine vinegar

1 tablespoon mayonnaise, or vegan mayonnaise, such as Vegenaise

1 clove garlic, minced

⅛ teaspoon freshly ground white pepper

½ teaspoon dried oregano

¼ cup Parmigiano-Reggiano and Romano cheese, grated, or vegan cheese, such as Daiya Mozzarella Style Shreds

1. Soak chickpeas in 6 cups of water for at least 4 hours or overnight. Drain. Add chickpeas to the pressure cooker along with 4 cups of water and the vegetable oil. Lock the lid in place and bring to high pressure; maintain pressure for 20 minutes. Remove from heat and allow pressure to release naturally. Drain the beans and transfer them to an ovenproof 9" × 13" casserole dish.

2. Add the salt, green onions, red onion, green and red bell peppers, parsley, and carrot to the casserole and toss with the beans.

3. Preheat the oven to 375°F.

4. To prepare the dressing, add the oil, lemon juice, vinegar, mayonnaise, garlic, pepper, and oregano to a small bowl or measuring cup. Whisk to mix. Pour the dressing over the bean mixture; stir to combine. Sprinkle the cheese over the dressed beans. Bake for 6 minutes. Stir before serving.

WASABI-BARBECUE CHICKPEAS

Most bottled barbecue sauces in your local grocery store are vegetarian, but to be sure, read the label before purchasing.

INGREDIENTS

Serves 4

1 cup dried chickpeas

8 cups water, plus 1 tablespoon

2 tablespoons vegetable oil

½ cup onion, diced

1 tablespoon wasabi powder

1 cup barbecue sauce

1. Add the chickpeas and 4 cups water to the pressure cooker. Lock the lid into place; bring to high pressure for 1 minute. Remove from the heat and quick-release the pressure.

2. Drain the water, rinse the chickpeas, and add to the pressure cooker again with the remaining 4 cups water. Soak for 1 hour.

3. Add 1 tablespoon vegetable oil. Lock the lid into place; bring to high pressure and maintain for 20 minutes. Remove from the heat and allow pressure to release naturally. Drain chickpeas and water. Set chickpeas aside.

4. Add the remaining tablespoon of oil to the pressure cooker over medium heat. Sauté the onions until just soft, about 5 minutes.

5. Reconstitute the wasabi powder by combining with 1 tablespoon water, then add to the sautéd onions. Stir i n the barbecue sauce and cooked chickpeas.

6. Lock the lid into place; bring to high pressure and maintain for 3 minutes. Remove from the heat and allow pressure to release naturally.

Wasabi

Wasabi is a condiment also known as Japanese horseradish. It has a spicy and pungent flavor that is known to clear nasal passages if enough is consumed.

CURRIED CHICKEN AND LENTILS SALAD

This main dish salad gets its salt from the roasted cashews. If you're using unsalted cashews, you may need to add some salt or have it available at the table.

INGREDIENTS
Serves 6

1 teaspoon vegetable oil

2 pounds boneless, skinless chicken breasts

1 cup dried lentils

2 cups water

2½ teaspoons curry powder

2 small Golden Delicious apples, peeled and diced

1 teaspoon lemon juice

2 cups seedless grapes, cut in half

1 cup roasted cashews

2 stalks celery, diced

½ small red onion, peeled and diced

¾ cup plain yogurt or sour cream

¼ cup mayonnaise

6 cups salad greens

1. Bring the oil to temperature in the pressure cooker over medium-high heat. Cut the chicken into bite-sized pieces; add to the pressure cooker and stir-fry for 5 minutes or until browned. Stir in the lentils, water, and a teaspoon of the curry powder. Halve one of the apples; peel and dice it and add it to the pressure cooker. Coat the cut side of the other half of the apple with the lemon juice to prevent it from turning brown.

2. Lock the lid into place and bring the pressure cooker to low pressure; maintain pressure for 8 minutes. Remove from the heat and allow pressure to release naturally.

3. Transfer the contents of the pressure cooker to a bowl. Once it's cooled, stir in the remaining diced apple, grapes, cashews, celery, and red onion.

4. To make the dressing, mix together the yogurt or sour cream, mayonnaise, and remaining 1½ teaspoons curry powder.

5. For each serving, place 1 cup of the salad greens on a plate. Either mix the dressing into the lentil mixture or add the lentil mixture on top of the lettuce and drizzle with the dressing.

Sweeten the Dressing
Cooking the apples with the lentils cuts some of the heat of the curry powder. The raw apple and grapes in the salad will also sweeten the curry powder taste. But if you still find the taste of the curry powder in the dressing too harsh, you can stir some sugar, honey, or applesauce into the dressing to soften the taste.

ITALIAN LENTILS IN TOMATO SAUCE

This recipe can be served as a side dish, as a sauce for pasta, or over rice.

INGREDIENTS

Serves 6

1 tablespoon olive oil

1 stalk celery, chopped

1 medium green pepper, chopped

1 medium onion, chopped

1 cup dried lentils

1 14.5-ounce can chopped tomatoes

2 cups water

1 tablespoon extra-virgin olive oil

1 teaspoon salt

¼ teaspoon pepper

1. Heat olive oil in an uncovered pressure cooker over medium heat. Add celery, pepper, and onion. Sauté until onion has softened. Then add the lentils, tomatoes, and water and stir well. Close and lock the lid.

2. Turn the heat up to high and when the cooker reaches pressure, lower the heat to the minimum needed to maintain pressure. Cook for 10–12 minutes at high pressure.

3. Open with the natural-release method—move the pressure cooker to a cool burner and wait for the pressure to come down on its own (about 15 minutes). For electric pressure cookers, disengage the "keep warm" mode or unplug the cooker. After 10 minutes, release the rest of the pressure using the valve.

4. Finish with a swirl of extra-virgin olive oil and salt and pepper to taste before serving.

LENTIL PÂTÉ

Pâté is typically made from ground meat, but for a vegetarian version try ground beans or mushrooms.

INGREDIENTS
Serves 8–10

2 cups dried lentils

8 cups water

2 tablespoons olive oil

1 teaspoon salt, plus more to taste

3 tablespoons butter, or vegan margarine, such as Earth Balance

1 cup onion, diced

3 cloves garlic, minced

1 teaspoon red wine vinegar

Pepper, to taste

1. Add the beans, water, 1 tablespoon olive oil, and salt to the pressure cooker.

2. Lock the lid into place; bring to high pressure and maintain for 7 minutes. Remove from the heat and allow pressure to release naturally.

3. Add the butter to a pan and sauté the onion until it begins to turn golden brown. Add the garlic and vinegar, and sauté 1 minute more. Add the mixture to the lentils. Pour the mixture into a food processor and blend until smooth. Taste and season with salt and pepper, if desired.

Serving Suggestions

For an eye-pleasing presentation, pour the pâté into a lightly oiled ramekin and pack tightly. Flip the ramekin over onto a serving dish and gently remove the pâté. Serve with a variety of crackers and baguette slices.

LENTIL-SPINACH CURRY

The once-exotic curry powder can now be found in almost any grocery store. There are several varieties, and any will work in this recipe.

INGREDIENTS
Serves 4

1 cup yellow lentils

4 cups water

1 tablespoon olive oil

½ cup onion, diced

1 clove garlic, minced

½ teaspoon coriander

½ teaspoon turmeric

½ teaspoon curry powder

½ cup tomato, diced

2 cups fresh spinach

1. Add the lentils and water to the pressure cooker. Lock the lid into place; bring to high pressure and maintain for 6 minutes. Quick-release the pressure, then drain the beans. Clean the pressure cooker.

2. Add the oil to the pressure cooker over medium heat. Sauté the onion for 3 minutes; add the garlic, coriander, turmeric, and curry powder and sauté for an additional 30 seconds.

3. Stir in the tomato, fresh spinach, and cooked lentils. Simmer for 10 minutes before serving.

RED LENTIL CURRY

You can simplify the seasoning in this dish by omitting the turmeric and ginger.

INGREDIENTS
Serves 8

2 cups dried lentils

8 cups water

3 tablespoons olive oil

1 teaspoon salt, plus more to taste

1 cup onion, diced

1 teaspoon garlic, minced

1 teaspoon ginger, peeled and minced

3 tablespoons curry powder

1 teaspoon turmeric

1 teaspoon cumin

1 teaspoon chili powder

1 teaspoon sugar

1 6-ounce can tomato paste

Salt and pepper, to taste

1. Add the beans, water, 1 tablespoon oil, and 1 teaspoon salt to the pressure cooker.

2. Lock the lid into place; bring to high pressure and maintain for 7 minutes. Remove from the heat and allow pressure to release naturally.

3. In a pan, add the remaining oil and sauté the onion until it is caramelized. Add the garlic and ginger and sauté for 1 minute more. Add the curry powder, turmeric, cumin, chili powder, sugar, and tomato paste, and bring the mixture to a simmer for 2–3 minutes, stirring constantly.

4. Drain the lentils and add to the curry mixture. Taste for seasoning and add salt and pepper if needed.

YELLOW LENTIL AND SPINACH CURRY

This color combination is particularly attractive, but you can make this curry with any lentils of your choice. Adjust the cooking time accordingly.

INGREDIENTS
Serves 4

1 tablespoon vegetable oil

1 onion, diced

¼ teaspoon red pepper flakes

¼ teaspoon coriander

¼ teaspoon turmeric

⅛ teaspoon cumin

1 cup yellow dried lentils

1 cup chopped tomatoes

½ cup water

2 cups fresh baby spinach, chopped

1. Heat oil in an uncovered pressure cooker over medium heat. Add onion, pepper flakes, coriander, turmeric, and cumin. Sauté until onion has softened, then add lentils, tomatoes, and water. Stir well. Close and lock the lid.

2. Turn the heat up to high and when the cooker reaches pressure, lower the heat to the minimum needed to maintain pressure. Cook for 10–12 minutes at high pressure.

3. Open with the natural-release method—move the pressure cooker to a cool burner and wait for the pressure to come down on its own (about 15 minutes). For electric pressure cookers, disengage the "keep warm" mode or unplug the cooker. After 10 minutes, release the rest of the pressure using the valve.

4. Mix in the baby spinach and serve.

PART V

THE MAIN COURSE

CHAPTER 9

STEWS AND CHILIS

AFRICAN LAMB STEW

You can make this stew in a 2.5-quart pressure fry pan or in a larger pressure cooker. Serve over cooked rice.

INGREDIENTS
Serves 6

1 tablespoon olive or vegetable oil

2 pounds boneless lamb shoulder

1 large onion, peeled and diced

2 cloves garlic, peeled and minced

1 cup dried apricots

⅓ cup raisins

½ cup blanched whole almonds

1 tablespoon fresh ginger, minced

½ teaspoon ground cinnamon

¾ cup red wine

¼ cup freshly squeezed orange juice

½ cup fresh mint leaves, packed

Salt and freshly ground black pepper, to taste

Optional: Additional mint leaves for garnish

1. Bring the oil to temperature in the pressure cooker over medium-high heat. Cut the lamb into bite-sized pieces.

2. Add the lamb to the pressure cooker in batches and brown each batch for 5 minutes or until well browned. Use a slotted spoon to remove lamb; set aside and keep warm.

3. Add the onion to the pressure cooker; sauté for 3 minutes; Stir in the garlic and sauté for 30 seconds.

4. Halve the apricots and add them to the pressure cooker along with the raisins, almonds, ginger, cinnamon, wine, orange juice, and mint leaves.

5. Lock the lid into place and bring to high pressure; maintain pressure for 20 minutes. Remove from the heat and allow pressure to release naturally.

6. Remove the lid, stir, and taste for seasoning. Add salt and pepper to taste. Garnish with fresh mint leaves if desired.

AFRICAN PEANUT STEW

West Africa is the home of the exotic peanut stew.

INGREDIENTS

Serves 4

1 tablespoon peanut oil

1 cup onion, diced

1 red bell pepper, diced

2 cloves garlic, minced

2 tablespoons fresh ginger, minced

1 sweet potato, peeled and cubed

1 14-ounce can diced tomatoes, drained

1 14-ounce can chickpeas, drained

3 cups vegetable stock

½ cup chunky peanut butter

1 tablespoon curry powder

1 teaspoon salt

½ teaspoon black pepper

½ cup coconut milk

1. Bring the peanut oil to medium heat in the pressure cooker. Add the onion and red bell pepper and sauté for 3 minutes. Add the garlic and ginger, and sauté an additional 30 seconds.

2. Add the sweet potato, tomatoes, chickpeas, stock, peanut butter, curry powder, salt, and pepper to the pressure cooker. Lock the lid into place; bring to high pressure and maintain for 10 minutes. Remove from heat and allow pressure to release naturally.

3. Stir in the coconut milk before serving.

BEEF AND GUINNESS STEW

This stew is filled with vegetables and is very flavorful. The small amounts of sugar and cocoa eliminate the bitterness occasionally found in similar stews without being detectable.

INGREDIENTS
Serves 8

2 teaspoons canola oil

1 large onion, diced

2 parsnips, diced

2 carrots, diced

2 stalks celery, diced

3 cloves garlic, minced

2 russet potatoes, peeled and diced

2 tablespoons minced fresh rosemary

2 pounds lean top round roast, cut into 1" cubes

1 tablespoon honey

1 teaspoon salt

½ teaspoon pepper

1 teaspoon unsweetened cocoa powder

1½ cups Guinness extra stout beer

1 cup frozen peas

1. Heat oil in an uncovered pressure cooker over medium heat. Sauté the onion, parsnips, carrots, celery, garlic, potatoes, rosemary, and beef until the ingredients begin to soften and brown. Drain excess fat. Add honey, salt, pepper, and cocoa powder. Pour in the beer. Close and lock the lid.

2. Turn the heat up to high and when the cooker reaches pressure, lower the heat to the minimum needed to maintain pressure. Cook for 13–15 minutes at high pressure.

3. When time is up, open the pressure cooker by releasing pressure.

4. Add the peas and simmer uncovered for 5 minutes before serving.

Lean Cuts of Beef

Leaner cuts like top round are excellent choices for pressure cooking because they are tenderized in no time. Look for cuts that have minimal marbling and trim off any excess fat before cooking. Searing and sautéing are good ways to cook off some external fat before adding the meat to the cooker. Drain any excess fat before pressure cooking.

BRUNSWICK STEW

Original or hickory-smoked barbecue sauce works best in this recipe.

INGREDIENTS
Serves 4

2 tablespoons olive oil

1 onion, chopped

2 stalks celery, sliced

1 bell pepper, diced

1 16-ounce package vegan chicken

1 28-ounce can crushed tomatoes

2 cups uncooked corn kernels

1 cup ketchup

½ cup barbecue sauce

1 tablespoon liquid smoke

1 tablespoon vegan Worcestershire sauce

1 teaspoon salt

½ teaspoon black pepper

1. Heat the olive oil in the pressure cooker over medium heat and sauté the onion, celery, and bell pepper until soft, about 5 minutes. Add the vegan chicken and cook until done according to package directions.

2. Add all remaining ingredients. Lock the lid into place; bring to high pressure and maintain for 30 minutes. Remove from heat and allow pressure to release naturally.

Recipe Origins
Competing cities both claim to be the originator of this popular southern stew. Both Brunswick, Georgia, and Brunswick County, Virginia, take credit for creating this recipe.

CHICKEN IN BEER STEW

Serve this Cajun-inspired stew over brown rice, cornbread, or mashed potatoes. Increase the amount of cayenne pepper if you want a zestier, hotter stew.

INGREDIENTS
Serves 6

1 teaspoon salt

½ tablespoon garlic powder

½ teaspoon cayenne pepper

2 tablespoons unbleached all-purpose flour

2 pounds boneless, skinless chicken thighs

2 tablespoons olive or vegetable oil

1 small green bell pepper, seeded and diced

1 small red bell pepper, seeded and diced

1 stalk celery, diced

1 medium onion, peeled and diced

1 jalapeño pepper, seeded and diced

2 cloves garlic, peeled and minced

1 bay leaf

1 teaspoon marjoram

1 8-ounce can tomato sauce

1 12-ounce bottle dark beer

½ cup chicken broth

2 teaspoons Worcestershire sauce

1 tablespoon bacon fat or lard

Freshly ground black pepper, to taste

1. Add the salt, garlic powder, cayenne pepper, and flour to a large zip-closure plastic bag; shake the bag to mix the spices into the flour.

2. Trim and discard any fat from the chicken thighs and cut them into bite-sized pieces.

3. Add the thigh pieces to the bag and shake to coat them in the seasoned flour.

4. Bring the oil to temperature in the pressure cooker over medium-high heat. Add the chicken in batches; stir-fry for 3–5 minutes or until browned. Reserve leftover seasoned flour.

5. Remove the browned chicken pieces and keep warm.

6. Reduce heat to medium. Add the green bell pepper, red bell pepper, and celery; sauté for 3 minutes.

7. Stir in the onion; sauté for 3 minutes or until the onion is soft. Add the jalapeño pepper and garlic; sauté for 30 seconds.

8. Stir in the bay leaf, marjoram, tomato sauce, beer, chicken broth, and Worcestershire sauce.

9. Lock the lid into place and bring to low pressure; maintain pressure for 20 minutes. Quick-release the pressure and remove the lid. Remove and discard the bay leaf.

10. While the chicken mixture cooks under pressure, bring the bacon fat or lard to temperature in a cast-iron skillet over medium heat.

11. Whisk in the reserved seasoned flour and enough water to make a paste. Cook and stir constantly for about 10 minutes or until the roux turns the color of peanut butter.

12. Whisk some of the juices from the pressure cooker into the roux in the skillet to loosen the mixture, and then stir the roux into the mixture in the pressure cooker.

13. Bring the mixture to a simmer; simmer for 3 minutes or until thickened. Taste for seasoning; add additional salt and Worcestershire sauce, if needed, and black pepper to taste. Serve.

CHICKPEA, CANNELLINI, AND BARLEY STEW

This dish has a very light and delicate flavor. If you find the taste too simple, fry some sage leaves in a little garlic and butter to use for extra flavor and garnish.

INGREDIENTS
Serves 6

1 whole clove

3 coriander seeds

1 heaping cup dried chickpeas, soaked

1 heaping cup dried cannellini (or navy) beans

½ cup perlated barley

1 clove garlic

2 tablespoons vegetable oil

1 teaspoon white pepper

4 cups water

1 teaspoon salt

¼ cup grated pecorino romano cheese

1 tablespoon extra-virgin olive oil

1. Put the clove and coriander seeds in a tea ball, or bouquet garni and place in pressure cooker. Add chickpeas, beans, barley, garlic, oil, white pepper, and water to the pressure cooker. Close and lock the lid.

2. Turn the heat up to high and when the cooker reaches pressure, lower the heat to the minimum needed to maintain pressure. Cook for 15 minutes at high pressure.

3. Open with the natural-release method—move the pressure cooker to a cool burner and wait for the pressure to come down on its own (about 15 minutes). For electric pressure cookers, disengage the "keep warm" mode or unplug the cooker and open when the pressure indicator has gone down (20–30 minutes).

4. Season with salt to taste and top each serving with cheese and a swirl of olive oil.

EGGPLANT STEW

Large, purple eggplants are ideal for this dish, but Japanese eggplants will work, too.

INGREDIENTS
Serves 4

2 medium eggplants, cut into large cubes

1 russet potato, diced

1 14-ounce can chickpeas, drained

6 cups vegetable stock

1 cup tomatoes, diced

1 tablespoon tomato paste

1 tablespoon lemon juice

1 bay leaf

1 teaspoon cumin

½ cup parsley, chopped

2 teaspoons salt

1. Add all of the ingredients to the pressure cooker and lock the lid into place.

2. Bring to low pressure and maintain for 30 minutes. Remove from heat and allow pressure to release naturally.

3. Remove bay leaf and adjust seasoning before serving, if necessary.

FAUX FROGMORE STEW

A 10- or 12-quart pressure cooker is recommended for this recipe. If yours is smaller, just halve all of the ingredients to make sure they will fit.

INGREDIENTS

Serves 6

12 cups water

¼ cup Old Bay seasoning

1 pound red potatoes, whole and unpeeled

6 ears corn on the cob, husked, cleaned, and halved

1 14-ounce package Tofurky sausage cut into 2" pieces

2 whole heads garlic

1. Add the water, Old Bay, and potatoes to the pressure cooker. Lock the lid into place; bring to high pressure and maintain for 5 minutes. Quick-release the pressure.

2. Remove the lid and add all remaining ingredients to the pressure cooker. Lock the lid into place; bring to high pressure and maintain for 5 more minutes. Remove from heat and allow pressure to release naturally.

3. Drain the liquid before serving or remove the vegetables and Tofurky sausage with a slotted spoon.

Old Bay Seasoning

Old Bay is a popular brand of seafood seasoning that comes in bags, liquid, or ground and loose. Any type of Old Bay will work in this recipe, just adjust the amount accordingly. A generic or homemade seafood blend will work just as well.

GUMBO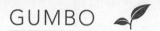

Gumbo is a popular dish across Louisiana that is traditionally made with meat or seafood, but you can use vegetables instead to create "gumbo z'herbes."

INGREDIENTS
Serves 6

½ cup vegetable oil

½ cup flour

1 white onion, diced

1 bell pepper, diced

2 stalks celery, diced

4 cloves garlic, minced

4 cups water

2 cups vegetable stock

1 tablespoon vegan Worcestershire sauce

1 16-ounce package frozen chopped okra

1 tablespoon Cajun seasoning

1 bay leaf

2 teaspoons salt

2 teaspoons black pepper

1 pound vegan chicken, chopped

½ cup flat-leaf parsley, chopped

½ cup scallions, sliced

½ teaspoon filé powder

6 cups cooked white rice

1. Bring the oil and flour to medium heat in the pressure cooker. Stir continuously until the roux achieves a rich brown color, about 25 minutes.

2. Add the onion, bell pepper, celery, and garlic to the roux and sauté for 5 minutes. Add the water and bring to a boil over high heat for 20 minutes.

3. Add the stock, vegan Worcestershire sauce, okra, Cajun seasoning, bay leaf, salt, and pepper. Lock the lid into place; bring to low pressure and maintain for 1 hour. Allow pressure to release naturally.

4. Add all remaining ingredients except the rice and cook over low heat for 10 minutes.

5. Remove the bay leaf and serve over cooked white rice.

Vegan Chicken

Major grocery store chains around the United States carry several varieties of vegan faux meats, making meat-free cooking easier than ever. Morningstar Farms Meal Starter Chik'n Strips are a fast-cooking option commonly sold in the frozen foods section, near breakfast items. Lightlife's Smart Menu Chick'n Strips are another delicious option, usually found near the produce or health foods sections.

TURKEY GUMBO

Filé powder is made from ground dried sassafras leaves; it helps flavor and thicken the gumbo.
For a more robust flavor, add cayenne pepper to taste when you add the black pepper or have hot sauce available at the table.

INGREDIENTS
Serves 4

2 tablespoons olive or vegetable oil

½ pound smoked andouille sausage or kielbasa

1 pound boneless, skinless turkey breast

1 large sweet onion, peeled and diced

4 cloves garlic, peeled and minced

1½ teaspoons dried thyme

1 teaspoon filé powder

¼ teaspoon dried red pepper flakes

½ teaspoon freshly ground black pepper

¼ teaspoon dried sage

½ cup white wine

3 bay leaves

2 stalks celery, sliced

1 large green bell pepper, seeded and diced

1 10-ounce package frozen sliced okra, thawed

½ cup fresh cilantro, minced

1 15-ounce can diced tomatoes

1 14-ounce can chicken broth

1. Bring the oil to temperature in the pressure cooker over medium heat. Add the sausage slices.

2. Cut the turkey into bite-sized pieces and add to the pressure cooker along with the onion.

3. Stir-fry for 5 minutes or until the turkey begins to brown and the onions are transparent.

4. Stir in the garlic, thyme, filé powder, red pepper flakes, black pepper, and sage.

5. Sauté for a minute and then deglaze the pan with the wine, scraping the bottom of the pressure cooker to loosen anything stuck to the bottom of the pan. Stir in the remaining ingredients.

6. Lock the lid into place and bring to low pressure; maintain pressure for 8 minutes. Remove from the heat and allow pressure to release naturally.

7. Remove the lid. Remove and discard bay leaves. Taste for seasoning and adjust if necessary.

HERBED CHICKEN STEW WITH DUMPLINGS

Nothing says comfort food like chicken and dumplings. You can stretch this recipe to 6 or 8 main dish servings if you serve the stew over another favorite comfort food companion: mashed potatoes.

INGREDIENTS
Serves 4

¼ cup unbleached all-purpose flour

½ teaspoon salt

¼ teaspoon freshly ground black pepper

8 bone-in chicken thighs, skin removed

2 tablespoons unsalted butter

2 stalks celery, finely diced

1 large onion, peeled and diced

1 teaspoon dried thyme

12 ounces baby carrots, cut in half

2½ cups chicken broth

½ cup dry white wine or water

2 teaspoons dried parsley

1 bay leaf

1 recipe dumplings

1. Add the flour, salt, and pepper to a large zip-closure plastic bag; shake to mix. Trim the chicken of any fat and add to the bag. Seal the bag and shake to coat the chicken in the seasoned flour.

2. Melt the butter in the pressure cooker over medium-high heat. When the butter begins to bubble, add 4 of the chicken thighs; brown for 3 minutes on each side.

3. Transfer chicken to a platter. Add the remaining thighs and brown them in a similar manner; remove to the platter.

4. Add the celery; sauté for 2 minutes. Add the onion and thyme; sauté for 3 minutes or until the onion is softened.

5. Stir in the carrots, broth, wine or water, parsley, and bay leaf. Return the browned chicken thighs (and their juices) to the pressure cooker.

6. Lock the lid into place and bring to high pressure; maintain pressure for 10 minutes. Quick-release the pressure and remove the lid. Remove and discard the bay leaf.

7. Leave the pressure cooker on the heat, adjusting it to maintain a simmer. Drop heaping teaspoons of the dumpling batter into the simmer stew.

8. Cover loosely to allow a small amount of the steam to escape and cook for 10 to 15 minutes or until the dumplings are puffy and cooked through. Serve.

Dumpling Batter

To make the dumplings, add 2 cups of unbleached all-purpose flour, 1 tablespoon baking powder, and ½ teaspoon salt to a mixing bowl. Stir to combine, then use a pastry blender or two forks to cut in 5 tablespoons of unsalted butter. Stir in 1 large beaten egg and ¾ cup of buttermilk until the mixture comes together.

ITALIAN CHICKPEA AND BARLEY STEW

As a stew, this should have a thick consistency, and not be runny.

INGREDIENTS

Serves 4

1 cup dry chickpeas, soaked

1 cup perlated barley

1 clove garlic, pressed

2 tablespoons olive oil, divided

2 carrots, diced

2 celery stalks, diced

1 large white onion, diced

4 cups water

2 teaspoons salt

1 teaspoon white pepper

1. Add all of the ingredients to the pressure cooker, except for the salt, pepper, and 1 tablespoon olive oil. Close and lock the lid.

2. Turn the heat up to high and when the cooker reaches pressure, lower the heat to the minimum needed to maintain pressure. Cook for 15 minutes at high pressure.

3. Open with the natural-release method—move the pressure cooker to a cool burner and wait for the pressure to come down on its own (about 15 minutes). For electric pressure cookers, disengage the "keep warm" mode or unplug the cooker. After 10 minutes, release the rest of the pressure using the valve.

4. Stir in salt and pepper and serve with a swirl of the remaining olive oil.

KOREAN TOFU STEW

A tablespoon of crushed red pepper may be a little too much for sensitive taste buds. If so, reduce the amount to 1 teaspoon and add more as needed.

INGREDIENTS
Serves 2–4

1 tablespoon sesame oil

½ onion, sliced

1 clove garlic, minced

1 teaspoon fresh ginger, minced

1 cup shredded green cabbage

1 cup shiitake mushrooms, sliced

1 12.3-ounce package soft silken tofu, drained and cubed

1 tablespoon crushed red pepper

1 teaspoon soy sauce

1 teaspoon rice wine vinegar

3" piece kombu

3 cups vegetable stock

2 green onions, sliced

1. Bring the sesame oil to medium heat in the pressure cooker. Add the onion and sauté for 3 minutes. Add the garlic and ginger and sauté an additional 30 seconds.

2. Add the cabbage, mushrooms, tofu, red pepper, soy sauce, vinegar, kombu, and stock to the pressure cooker. Lock the lid into place; bring to low pressure and maintain for 5 minutes. Remove from heat and allow pressure to release naturally.

3. Remove the lid. Discard the kombu and stir in the green onions before serving.

Kombu

Kombu is edible seaweed commonly used in Asian cuisine, and can help give salty flavor and nutrients to food. Be sure to remove large pieces of kombu from your recipes before serving.

MUSHROOM BEEF STEW WITH DUMPLINGS

Wait until the stew is fully cooked before adding any salt and pepper; the amount needed will depend on the type of canned mushrooms and soups you use. Serve this stew with buttered dinner rolls and you have an easy, complete comfort-food meal.

INGREDIENTS
Serves 8

1 3-pound English or chuck roast

2 4-ounce cans sliced mushrooms, drained

1 10¾-ounce can condensed cream of mushroom soup

1 10½-ounce can condensed French onion soup

1 tablespoon Worcestershire sauce

2 cups water

1 24-ounce bag frozen vegetables for stew, thawed

4 cups frozen vegetables, thawed

Salt and freshly ground black pepper, to taste

1. Trim and discard any fat from the roast. Cut into bite-sized pieces and add meat, drained mushrooms, soups, Worcestershire sauce, and water to the pressure cooker.

2. Lock the lid into place and bring to low pressure; maintain pressure for 30 minutes. Quick-release the pressure and remove the lid.

3. Stir in the thawed frozen vegetables. Bring to a simmer and then drop tablespoon-sized dollops of the Quick and Easy Dumplings batter into the bubbling stew.

4. Lock the lid into place and bring to low pressure; maintain pressure for 5 minutes. Quick-release the pressure and remove the lid.

5. Stir the stew, being careful not to break the dumplings apart. (If dumplings aren't yet puffy and cooked through, loosely cover the pan and let the stew simmer for a few more minutes.) Taste for seasoning and add salt and pepper if needed.

Quick and Easy Dumplings

Cut 1 tablespoon shortening or butter into 1½ cups biscuit mix until crumbly. Combine ⅔ cup milk and 1 large beaten egg; add to dry mixture. Stir until just blended. When you cook the dumplings in the stew, small drops of batter will suffice; they expand in the hot liquid.

NEW ENGLAND FISH STEW

Fish is a low-fat meat, which lessens the impact of the cream. To make this a special occasion dish, float a pat of butter on top of each portion. Using heavy cream obviously makes this a richer stew, but you can substitute milk if you prefer.

INGREDIENTS

Serves 4

2 tablespoons butter

1 large onion, peeled and diced

2 stalks celery, diced

4 large carrots, peeled and diced

4 medium potatoes, peeled and cut into ½-inch cubes

1 pound firm-fleshed white fish fillets, cut into ½-inch pieces

2 cups fish stock or clam juice

1 cup cold water

1 bay leaf

½ teaspoon dried thyme

1 cup heavy cream or milk

1 cup fresh or thawed frozen corn kernels

Salt and freshly ground white or black pepper, to taste

Optional: Additional butter

Optional: Fresh parsley

1. Add the butter to the pressure cooker and bring it to temperature over medium heat. Add the onions; sauté for 3 minutes or until soft.

2. Stir in the celery, carrot, and potatoes; sauté for an additional minute. Add the fish, fish stock or clam juice, water, bay leaf, and thyme.

3. Lock the lid in place and bring the pressure cooker to high pressure; maintain pressure for 4 minutes. Quick-release the pressure.

4. Remove the lid, tilting it away from you to allow any excess steam to escape.

5. Remove and discard the bay leaf. Stir in the cream or milk and corn. Taste for seasoning and add salt and pepper, to taste.

6. Simmer until the corn is cooked and the chowder is hot. Transfer to a serving tureen or individual bowls and top with additional butter if desired. Garnish with parsley if desired.

OLD SOUTH CHICKEN STEW

The sugar in this dish offsets the acidity of the tomatoes. The aroma of the bacon fat will transport you back to a time when all Southern cooks kept a container of bacon drippings at the ready.

INGREDIENTS

Serves 8

3 tablespoons bacon fat

8 chicken thighs

2 cups water

1 28-ounce can diced tomatoes

2 large yellow onions, peeled and sliced

¼ teaspoon sugar

½ cup dry white wine or chicken broth

1 10-ounce package frozen lima beans, thawed

1 10-ounce package frozen whole kernel corn, thawed

1 10-ounce package frozen okra, thawed and sliced

1 cup bread crumbs, toasted

3 tablespoons Worcestershire sauce

Salt and freshly ground black pepper, to taste

Optional: Hot sauce, to taste

1. Bring the bacon fat to temperature in the pressure cooker over medium heat. Add 4 chicken thighs skin-side down and fry them until lightly browned.

2. Remove the fried thighs and fry the remaining thighs. Return the first 4 fried thighs to the pressure cooker and add the water, tomatoes, onions, sugar, and wine or chicken broth.

3. Lock the lid into place and bring to high pressure; maintain pressure for 12 minutes. Quick-release the pressure and remove the lid. Remove the chicken.

4. Once chicken is cool enough to handle, remove the meat from the bones and discard the skin and bones. Shred the chicken meat and set aside.

5. Add the lima beans, corn, and okra to the pot. Bring to a simmer and cook uncovered for 30 minutes.

6. Stir in the shredded chicken, bread crumbs, and Worcestershire sauce. Simmer for 10 minutes, stirring occasionally, to bring the chicken to temperature and thicken the stew.

7. Taste for seasoning and add salt and pepper if needed and hot sauce if desired.

OYSTER MUSHROOM STEW

Any type of mushroom will work in this stew, but oyster mushrooms are recommended because of their delicate texture, which mimics fish.

INGREDIENTS
Serves 4

2 tablespoons butter, or vegan margarine, such as Earth Balance

½ cup onions, diced

½ cup celery, diced

1 clove garlic, minced

½ cup béchamel sauce

1 pound oyster mushrooms, chopped

½ cup white wine

2 cups heavy cream, or unsweetened soymilk

½ teaspoon dried thyme

1 teaspoon salt

1 teaspoon lemon juice

Optional: Chopped parsley

1. Heat the butter in the pressure cooker over medium heat. Add the onions and celery and sauté for 5 minutes. Add the garlic and sauté an additional 30 seconds.

2. Add the béchamel sauce, mushrooms, white wine, cream, thyme, and salt. Lock the lid into place; bring to low pressure and maintain for 30 minutes. Remove from heat and allow pressure to release naturally.

3. Once the pressure has released remove the lid and check for consistency. If it is not thick enough return to the burner and simmer over low heat with the lid off. Stir in the lemon juice.

4. Stir in chopped parsley before serving, if desired.

POTATO-KALE STEW

Avoid using russet potatoes in this recipe because they become too mushy when overcooked.

INGREDIENTS
Serves 4

3 cups kale, chopped

1 tablespoon olive oil

2 cloves garlic, minced

4 red potatoes, peeled and quartered

3 cups vegetable stock

1 teaspoon salt

1 teaspoon black pepper

2 15-ounce cans cannellini beans, drained

1 14-ounce can whole tomatoes, drained

1. Trim the kale by removing the tough stalk end of each leaf, then chop the kale leaves into large pieces.

2. Bring the olive oil to medium heat in the pressure cooker. Add the garlic and sauté for 30 seconds.

3. Add all remaining ingredients. Lock the lid into place; bring to high pressure and maintain for 15 minutes. Remove from heat and allow pressure to release naturally.

QUICK AND EASY BEEF STEW

This is a quick and easy way to turn leftover roast beef into a hearty stew. Serve with crackers or dinner rolls and you have an easy, complete comfort-food meal.

INGREDIENTS

Serves 8

2 cups cooked roast beef, cut into bite-sized pieces

1 10¾-ounce can condensed tomato soup

1 10½-ounce can condensed French onion soup

1 tablespoon Worcestershire sauce

2 cups water

1 24-ounce bag frozen vegetables for stew

1 10-ounce box frozen mixed vegetables

1 tablespoon butter

1 tablespoon all-purpose flour

Salt and freshly ground black pepper, to taste

1. Add the roast beef, soups, Worcestershire sauce, water, and frozen vegetables to the pressure cooker.

2. Lock the lid into place and bring to low pressure; maintain pressure for 3 minutes. Remove from heat, quick-release the pressure, and remove the lid.

3. In a small bowl, mix the butter into the flour to make a paste. Ladle about ½ cup of the soup broth into the bowl and whisk into the paste, then pour it into the stew.

4. Place the uncovered pressure cooker over medium-high heat and bring the stew to a boil; boil for 2 minutes, stirring occasionally.

5. Reduce the heat and simmer for an additional 2 minutes or until the stew is thickened. Taste for seasoning, and add salt and pepper if needed.

Starting from Scratch

If you don't have leftover roast beef, you can begin by adding 1 pound of uncooked beef stew meat to the pressure cooker with the condensed French onion soup and water. Lock the lid into place, bring to high pressure, and maintain pressure for 20–30 minutes. Quick-release the pressure and complete the stew by following the other recipe instructions.

TEX-MEX STEW

As its name implies, Tex-Mex is a fusion of the Southwestern flavors of Texas and Mexico. Serve this hearty Tex-Mex Stew over rice along with an avocado salad and cornbread or baked corn chips.

INGREDIENTS
Serves 8

1 3½-pound English or chuck roast

2 tablespoons olive or vegetable oil

1 7-ounce can green chilies

2 15-ounce cans diced tomatoes

1 8-ounce can tomato sauce

1 large sweet onion, peeled and diced

1 green bell pepper, seeded and diced

6 cloves garlic, peeled and minced

1 tablespoon ground cumin

1 teaspoon freshly ground black pepper

Cayenne pepper, to taste

2 tablespoons lime juice

2 jalapeño peppers, seeded and diced

Optional: Beef broth or water

1 bunch fresh cilantro, chopped

1. Trim the fat from the roast and cut the meat into 1-inch cubes. Add the oil to the pressure cooker and bring it to temperature over medium-high heat.

2. Add the beef and stir-fry for 8 minutes or until it's well browned. Stir in the chilies, tomatoes, tomato sauce, onion, bell pepper, garlic, cumin, black pepper, cayenne, lime juice, and jalapeño peppers.

3. If needed, add enough beef broth or water to cover the ingredients in the cooker, but remember not to fill the cooker more than two-thirds full.

4. Lock the lid into place and bring to low pressure; maintain pressure for 1 hour. Remove from heat and allow pressure to release naturally. Remove the lid and stir in the cilantro. Serve immediately.

VEGETABLE ÉTOUFÉE

Onion, celery, and bell pepper, otherwise known as the "holy trinity," are the foundation of many New Orleans dishes.

INGREDIENTS
Serves 6

10 tablespoons butter, or vegan margarine, such as Earth Balance

1 cup white onion, finely diced

1 cup celery, finely diced

1 cup green bell pepper, finely diced

1 clove garlic, minced

2 tablespoons flour

2 ounces tomato paste

2 cups water

2 teaspoons salt

1 teaspoon black pepper

1 tablespoon vegan Worcestershire sauce

½ cup green onion, finely diced

¼ cup parsley, chopped

½ teaspoon cayenne pepper

1 bay leaf

6 cups cooked white rice

1. Melt the butter or margarine in the pressure cooker over medium-low heat. Add the onion, celery, and bell pepper and sauté for 45 minutes, stirring often. Add the garlic and sauté for 1 additional minute.

2. Stir in the flour to make a roux and cook for about 5 minutes. It should still be light in color.

3. Add all remaining ingredients except the rice. Lock the lid into place; bring to medium pressure and maintain for 10 minutes. Remove from heat and allow pressure to release naturally.

4. Remove the bay leaf and serve over cooked white rice.

BLACK BEAN AND LENTIL CHILI

If you prefer hotter chili, substitute a Scotch bonnet or serrano pepper for the jalapeño.

INGREDIENTS
Serves 6

2 tablespoons vegetable oil

1 large Spanish onion, diced

1 jalapeño, seeded and minced

1 clove garlic, minced

1 cup brown or green lentils

1 15½-ounce can black beans, drained and rinsed

1 cup pearl barley

3 tablespoons chili powder

1 tablespoon sweet paprika

1 teaspoon dried oregano

1 teaspoon ground cumin

1 28-ounce can diced tomatoes

6 cups vegetable stock

Optional: 1 12-ounce can chipotle peppers in adobo sauce

Salt and pepper, to taste

1. Bring the oil to temperature in the pressure cooker over medium heat. Add the onion; sauté for 3 minutes. Stir in the jalapeño; sauté for 1 minute.

2. Stir in the garlic; sauté for 30 seconds. Stir in the lentils, black beans, barley, chili powder, paprika, oregano, cumin, undrained tomatoes, and stock. If using, mince 1 or more chipotle peppers and add them along with some sauce to taste.

3. Lock the lid into place and bring to high pressure; maintain for 10 minutes. Remove from the heat and allow pressure to release naturally for 10 minutes. Quick-release any remaining pressure. Remove the lid. Stir and check that the lentils and barley are tender. If not, lock the lid back into place, return to the heat, and bring to pressure for 2–3 more minutes. Remove from heat and allow pressure to release naturally.

4. Remove the lid and return the pan to the heat. Bring to a simmer. Taste for seasoning, and add salt and pepper if needed. Simmer until slightly thickened.

Handling Peppers

Scotch bonnet peppers are some of the hottest peppers in the world and must be handled carefully if you choose to use them in this recipe. Wear gloves while handling and wash your hands thoroughly once gloves are removed.

CHICKEN CHILI

Serve this chili with an avocado or tossed salad. Have sour cream and baked corn tortilla chips at the table.

INGREDIENTS

Serves 4

2 pounds boneless, skinless chicken thighs

2 tablespoons vegetable oil

1 jalapeño pepper, seeded and minced

1 small red bell pepper, seeded and diced

1 small onion, peeled and diced

1 clove garlic, peeled and minced

1 15-ounce can diced tomatoes

1 16-ounce can red kidney beans

1 tablespoon paprika

1 tablespoon tomato paste

1 cup chicken broth

¼ teaspoon dried thyme

¼ teaspoon dried oregano

1 teaspoon chili powder

Salt and freshly ground black pepper, to taste

1. Cut the chicken into bite-sized cubes. Add the oil to the pressure cooker and bring it to temperature over medium heat. Add the chicken and stir-fry for 5 minutes.

2. Add the jalapeño and red pepper; stir-fry with the chicken for 2 minutes. Stir in the onion; sauté for 3 minutes or until tender.

3. Stir in the garlic, tomatoes, rinsed and drained kidney beans, paprika, tomato paste, broth, thyme, oregano, chili powder, salt, and pepper.

4. Lock the lid into place and bring to low pressure; maintain pressure for 10 minutes. Remove the pan from the heat and let pressure release naturally for 10 minutes.

5. Quick-release any remaining pressure and remove the lid. Stir the chili and taste for seasoning; add additional salt, pepper, spices, or herbs if needed.

CINCINNATI CHILI

Cincinnati chili is native to the state of Ohio and is typically eaten over spaghetti or on hot dogs.

INGREDIENTS
Serves 4–6

1 tablespoon olive oil

1 onion, chopped

1 12-ounce package frozen veggie burger crumbles

1 clove garlic, minced

1 cup tomato sauce

1 cup water

2 tablespoons red wine vinegar

2 tablespoons chili powder

½ teaspoon cumin

½ teaspoon ground cinnamon

½ teaspoon paprika

½ teaspoon ground allspice

1 tablespoon light brown sugar

1 tablespoon unsweetened cocoa powder

1 teaspoon hot pepper sauce

16 ounces cooked spaghetti

Optional: Shredded Cheddar, or vegan Cheddar, such as Daiya Cheddar Style Shreds

Optional: Diced white onion or beans

1. Heat the oil in the pressure cooker over medium heat. Add the onion and sauté about 3 minutes. Add the burger crumbles and garlic and cook until the crumbles are heated.

2. Add the tomato sauce, water, vinegar, chili powder, cumin, cinnamon, paprika, allspice, light brown sugar, cocoa powder, and hot sauce. Lock the lid into place; bring to high pressure and maintain for 5 minutes. Quick-release the pressure and remove the lid.

3. Continue to simmer, without the lid, until the sauce has thickened.

4. Serve over cooked pasta and topped with cheese and onions, if desired.

FIVE-PEPPER CHILI 🌿

Sound the alarm! This chili will set mouths aflame.

INGREDIENTS
Serves 6

1 tablespoon vegetable oil

1 onion, diced

1 jalapeño, seeded and minced

1 habanero pepper, seeded and minced

1 bell pepper, diced

1 poblano pepper, seeded and diced

2 cloves garlic, minced

2 14½-ounce cans crushed tomatoes

2 cups fresh tomatoes, diced

2 tablespoons chili powder

1 tablespoon cumin

½ tablespoon cayenne pepper

⅛ cup vegan Worcestershire sauce

4 cups cooked Pinto Beans (Chapter 8)

Salt and pepper, to taste

1. Add the vegetable oil to the pressure cooker and sauté the onion until it has caramelized. Add the jalapeño, habanero, bell, and poblano peppers and sauté for 1 minute more. Add the garlic, crushed tomatoes, fresh tomatoes, chili powder, cumin, cayenne pepper, Worcestershire, beans, salt, and pepper.

2. Lock the lid into place; bring to high pressure and maintain for 12 minutes. Remove from the heat and allow pressure to release naturally. Serve.

GREEN CHICKEN CHILI

Serve with cornbread or tortilla chips. Have sour cream, grated Cheddar or jack cheese, and avocado slices or guacamole available at the table.

INGREDIENTS
Serves 8

1 cup dried pinto beans

8 cups water

2 teaspoons vegetable oil

1 tablespoon olive oil

1 medium onion, peeled and diced

1 large carrot, peeled and diced

2 medium red bell peppers, seeded and diced

2 jalapeño peppers, seeded and diced

4 cloves garlic, peeled and minced

4 4-ounce cans chopped green chili peppers

1 chipotle pepper, seeded and diced

3 pounds mixed meaty chicken pieces, skin removed

4 cups chicken broth

2 tablespoons butter

2 tablespoons unbleached all-purpose flour

Salt and freshly ground black pepper, to taste

1. Rinse the beans; soak them in 3 cups of the water overnight. Drain and add the beans, the remaining 5 cups of water, and vegetable oil to the pressure cooker.

2. Lock the lid into place and bring to high pressure; maintain pressure for 15 minutes. Remove from the heat and allow pressure to release naturally. Strain the beans; set aside. Wash and dry the pressure cooker.

3. Bring the olive oil to temperature in the pressure cooker over medium-high heat. Add the onion; sauté for 3 minutes. Stir in the carrot; sauté for 3 minutes.

4. Stir in the red bell and jalapeño peppers; sauté for 5 minutes or until all vegetables are soft.

5. Add the garlic, canned peppers, chipotle peppers, chicken pieces, and chicken broth.

6. Lock the lid into place and bring to high pressure; maintain pressure for 12 minutes. Quick-release the pressure. Remove the chicken pieces to a bowl.

7. When the chicken is cool enough to handle, remove the meat from the bones, cut or tear it into bite-sized pieces, and return the meat to the pressure cooker. Stir in the beans.

8. Bring the chili to a boil. Blend the butter together with the flour to make a paste, and then whisk it into the chili.

9. Boil for 1 minute and then reduce heat to maintain a simmer for about 5 minutes or until the chili is thickened. Taste for seasoning and add salt and pepper if desired. Serve.

SOUTHWEST CHILI

Southwest cuisine is similar to Mexican and is known for its spiciness.

INGREDIENTS

Serves 4–6

2 cups dried kidney beans

16 cups water

1 tablespoon vegetable oil

1 large onion, diced

1 red bell pepper, diced

1 cup uncooked corn kernels

2 cups fresh tomato, diced

2 tablespoons tomato paste

1 4-ounce can chopped green chilies

8 cups vegetable stock

1 tablespoon chili powder

1 teaspoon ground cumin

1 teaspoon salt

Optional: Chopped cilantro

Optional: Shredded Cheddar, or vegan Cheddar, such as Daiya Cheddar Style Shreds

1. Add the beans and 8 cups water to the pressure cooker. Lock the lid into place; bring to high pressure for 1 minute. Remove from the heat and quick-release the pressure.

2. Drain the water, rinse the beans, and add to the pressure cooker again with the remaining 8 cups of water. Let soak for 1 hour and then drain.

3. Heat the oil in the empty pressure cooker over medium heat. Add the onions and red bell pepper and sauté about 3 minutes. Add the corn, tomato, tomato paste, chilies, stock, chili powder, cumin, and salt. Stir to combine.

4. Lock the lid into place; bring to high pressure and maintain for 15 minutes. Remove from heat and allow pressure to release naturally.

5. If the desired consistency has not been reached, place the chili back on the burner over medium-low heat and simmer with the lid off.

6. Serve topped with cilantro and cheese, if desired.

SPEEDY CHILI CON "CARNE"

Try Boca Ground Crumbles in this fast recipe as a vegan alternative to ground beef.

INGREDIENTS
Serves 4–6

1 tablespoon olive oil

½ cup onion, diced

½ cup bell pepper, diced

1 12-ounce package frozen veggie burger crumbles

2 cloves garlic, minced

1 15-ounce can kidney beans, rinsed and drained

2 cups vegetable stock

1 tablespoon chili powder

½ tablespoon chipotle powder

½ tablespoon cumin

1 teaspoon thyme

1 tablespoon oregano

2 cups fresh tomatoes, diced

1 tablespoon tomato paste

1 tablespoon cider vinegar

2 teaspoons salt

1. Heat the oil in the pressure cooker over medium heat. Add the onion and bell pepper and sauté about 3 minutes. Add the burger crumbles and garlic and cook until the crumbles are heated.

2. Add all remaining ingredients. Lock the lid into place; bring to high pressure and maintain for 10 minutes. Remove from heat and allow pressure to release naturally.

3. If the desired consistency has not been reached, place the chili back on the burner over medium-low heat and simmer with the lid off.

Vegan Beef

In addition to Boca Ground Crumbles there are other types of vegetarian ground beef on the market. Try Gimme Lean Ground Beef Style or Morningstar Farms Crumbles (not suitable for vegans) for a prepackaged option. Or try using rehydrated texturized vegetable protein (TVP).

TEXAS FIREHOUSE CHILI

This no-bean chili is similar to dishes entered into firehouse chili cook-offs all over Texas.

INGREDIENTS

Serves 4

1 pound cubed lean beef

2 tablespoons onion powder

1 tablespoon garlic powder

2 tablespoons Mexican-style chili powder

1 tablespoon paprika

1 teaspoon oregano

½ teaspoon freshly ground black pepper

1 teaspoon white pepper

½ teaspoon cayenne pepper

1 teaspoon chipotle pepper

8 ounces chopped tomatoes

1. Put all ingredients in the pressure cooker. Close and lock the lid.

2. Turn the heat up to high and when the cooker reaches pressure, lower the heat to the minimum needed to maintain pressure. Cook for 15–20 minutes at high pressure.

3. Open with the natural-release method—move the pressure cooker to a cool burner and wait for the pressure to come down on its own (about 15 minutes). For electric pressure cookers, disengage the "keep warm" mode or unplug the cooker and open when the pressure indicator has gone down (20–30 minutes).

4. Simmer, uncovered, over medium heat, for about 5 minutes to reduce the liquids and thicken.

TURKEY CHILI

This dish is perfect for using up your Thanksgiving leftovers. Serve with cornbread or as a topper for baked potatoes and a tossed salad.

INGREDIENTS
Serves 8

2 tablespoons extra-virgin olive oil

3 pounds lean ground turkey

2 large sweet onions, peeled and diced

1 large red bell pepper, seeded and diced

4 cloves garlic, peeled and minced

3 tablespoons chili powder

1½ teaspoons ground cumin

1 teaspoon ground allspice

1 teaspoon ground cinnamon

1 teaspoon ground coriander

1 teaspoon dried oregano

2 15-ounce cans diced tomatoes

¼ cup chicken broth

1 bay leaf

2 tablespoons cornmeal

Salt and freshly ground black pepper, to taste

1. Bring the oil to temperature in the pressure cooker over medium-high heat. Add the turkey and fry it for 5 minutes, occasionally breaking it apart with a spatula.

2. Stir in the onion and bell pepper; stir-fry with the meat for 3 minutes. Stir in the garlic, chili powder, cumin, allspice, cinnamon, coriander, and oregano.

3. Sauté the spices together with the meat for 2 minutes. Stir in the undrained tomatoes, broth, and bay leaf.

4. Lock the lid into place and bring to high pressure; maintain pressure for 10 minutes. Remove from the heat and allow pressure to release naturally. Remove the lid.

5. Return the pressure cooker to the heat. Stir in the cornmeal and simmer for 15 minutes or until the cornmeal thickens the chili. Remove and discard the bay leaf. Stir in salt and pepper to taste.

Cincinnati-Style Turkey Chili

Stir in a teaspoon of cinnamon when you add the other spices. After you simmer the chili and cornmeal together, stir in 2 tablespoons of semisweet chocolate chips and continue to simmer the chili until the chocolate is melted. Serve over cooked spaghetti and topped with grated Cheddar cheese.

WHITE CHICKEN CHILI

Serve like you would any other chili, with cornbread or tortilla chips. Have grated cheese and sour cream available for those who wish to use it to top their chili.

INGREDIENTS
Serves 8

1 tablespoon olive or vegetable oil

1 large white onion, peeled and diced

4 cloves garlic, peeled and minced

2 pounds boneless, skinless chicken breasts

2 teaspoons ground cumin

2 teaspoons dried oregano

¼ teaspoon ground cayenne pepper

1 4-ounce can chopped green chili peppers

2 14-ounce cans chicken broth

2 16-ounce cans white beans

Hot sauce, to taste

Salt and freshly ground white or black pepper, to taste

1. Bring the oil to temperature in the pressure cooker over medium-high heat. Add the onion; sauté for 3 minutes or until the onion is soft.

2. Stir in the garlic; sauté for 30 seconds. Cut the chicken into bite-sized pieces and add to the pressure cooker along with the cumin, oregano, and cayenne pepper; stir-fry for 1 minute.

3. Stir in the undrained can of green chilies and 1 can of the chicken broth. Lock the lid into place and bring to high pressure; maintain pressure for 6 minutes. Quick-release the pressure and remove the lid.

4. Stir in the remaining can of chicken broth and the undrained cans of beans. Bring to a simmer and allow to cook until the beans are brought to temperature. Taste for seasoning and add hot sauce, salt, and pepper to taste. Serve.

Chicken for Later
To make extra chicken to store in the refrigerator for 2 days or to freeze to use later, double the amount of chicken and spices called for and increase the pressure time to 10 minutes. Use a slotted spoon to remove half of the chicken before you add the remaining chili ingredients.

CHAPTER 10

BEEF AND VEAL

BARBECUED BEEF

An English roast tends to pull apart easier, which makes it perfect for beef barbecue sandwiches. You can also serve beef barbecue over your favorite cooked pasta. Top with some grated Cheddar cheese and diced sweet or green onion.

INGREDIENTS

Serves 8

1 3-pound beef English roast

1 cup water

½ cup red wine

½ cup ketchup

1 tablespoon red wine vinegar

2 teaspoons Worcestershire sauce

2 teaspoons mustard powder

2 tablespoons dried minced onion

1 teaspoon dried minced garlic

1 teaspoon cracked black pepper

1 tablespoon brown sugar

1 teaspoon chili powder

½ teaspoon ground cinnamon

¼ teaspoon ground cloves

¼ teaspoon ground ginger

Pinch ground allspice

Pinch dried pepper flakes, crushed

1. Halve the roast and stack the halves in the pressure cooker. Mix together all the remaining ingredients and pour over the beef.

2. Lock the lid into place and bring to low pressure; maintain pressure for 55 minutes. Remove from the heat and allow pressure to release naturally.

3. Use a slotted spoon to remove the beef from the slow cooker; pull it apart, discarding any fat or gristle. Taste the meat and sauce and adjust seasonings if necessary.

4. To thicken the sauce, return the pressure cooker to the heat. Skim any fat off the surface of the sauce and simmer uncovered while you pull apart the beef. Stir occasionally to prevent the sauce from burning.

BARBECUE POT ROAST

Whether you make it with beef or with pork, this barbecue is a delicious part of a casual supper when you serve it on sandwiches along with potato chips and coleslaw.

INGREDIENTS
Serves 8

½ cup ketchup

½ cup apricot preserves

¼ cup dark brown sugar

¼ cup apple cider white vinegar

½ cup teriyaki or soy sauce

Dry red pepper flakes, crushed, to taste

1 teaspoon dry mustard

¼ teaspoon freshly ground black pepper

1 4-pound boneless chuck roast

1½ cups water for beef

1 large sweet onion, peeled and sliced

1. Add the ketchup, preserves, brown sugar, vinegar, teriyaki or soy sauce, red pepper flakes, mustard, and pepper to a gallon-sized plastic freezer bag; close and squeeze to mix. Trim the roast of any fat, cut the meat into 1-inch cubes, and add to the bag. Refrigerate overnight.

2. Add the appropriate amount of water and the cooking rack or steamer basket to a 6-quart or larger pressure cooker. Place half of the sliced onions on the rack or basket. Use a slotted spoon to remove the roast pieces from the sauce and place them on the onions; reserve the sauce. Cover the roast pieces with the remaining onions.

3. Lock the lid in place on the pressure cooker. Place over medium heat and bring to high pressure; maintain for 50 minutes, or 15 minutes per pound (remember: you reduce the weight of the roast when you trim off the fat). Turn off the heat and allow 15 minutes for the pressure to release naturally. Use the quick release to release any remaining pressure, and then carefully remove the lid. Strain the meat, separate it from the onions, and return it to the pan. Pureé the onions in a food processor or blender.

4. Pour the reserved sauce into the cooker and use two forks to pull the meat apart and mix it into the sauce. Bring to a simmer over medium heat. Stir in the onion. Skim the sauce for fat. Add ½ cup of the pan juices to the cooker and stir into the meat and sauce. Reduce the heat to low and simmer for 15 minutes, or until the mixture is thick enough to serve on sandwiches.

BEEF BIRYANI

Biryani is a one-dish meal that is well spiced but not spicy. Traditionally it is made using large amounts of ghee, a type of clarified butter, but pressure cooking it brings out the flavor without adding unnecessary fat.

INGREDIENTS
Serves 6

1 tablespoon ghee

1 onion, sliced

1 pound top round, cut into strips

1 tablespoon minced fresh ginger

2 cloves garlic, minced

½ teaspoon ground cloves

½ teaspoon ground cardamom

½ teaspoon ground coriander

½ teaspoon freshly ground black pepper

½ teaspoon cinnamon

½ teaspoon cumin

1 teaspoon salt

1 cup whole-milk plain yogurt

1 28-once can whole stewed tomatoes

2 cups cooked basmati rice

1. Heat ghee in an uncovered pressure cooker over medium heat. Add onion and sauté until softened. Add the rest of the ingredients except the rice to the pressure cooker.

2. Turn the heat up to high and when the cooker reaches pressure, lower the heat to the minimum needed to maintain pressure. Cook for 13–15 minutes at high pressure.

3. When time is up, open the pressure cooker by releasing pressure.

4. Simmer uncovered until most of the liquid has evaporated (about 10 minutes).

5. Serve over rice.

Make Your Own Ghee

In a heavy-bottomed pan, on low heat, melt an unsalted stick of butter. Simmer until white foam appears, then turn off the heat. Spoon off the foam and discard. Pour though a fine sieve or cheesecloth into jar and refrigerate. The resulting liquid should be clear and golden, like vegetable oil, and solidifies when placed in the refrigerator.

BEEF BOURGUIGNON

This is a classic French recipe that probably originated as a way to tenderize tough cuts of meat. Serve over buttered noodles or mashed potatoes with a salad and a steamed vegetable.

INGREDIENTS
Serves 8

8 slices bacon, diced

1 3-pound boneless English or chuck roast

Salt and freshly ground black pepper, to taste

1 large yellow onion, peeled and diced

2 tablespoons tomato paste

3 cloves garlic, peeled and minced

½ teaspoon thyme

1 bay leaf

4 cups Burgundy

1 large yellow onion, peeled and thinly sliced

½ cup plus 2 tablespoons butter

16 ounces fresh mushrooms, sliced

2 cups beef broth or water

½ cup all-purpose flour

1. Add the bacon to the pressure cooker and fry over medium heat until it renders its fat; remove bacon and reserve for another use. Trim the roast of fat and cut into bite-sized pieces; add the beef pieces to the pressure cooker, sprinkle with salt and pepper to taste, and stir-fry for 5 minutes. Add the diced onion and sauté for 3 minutes or until the onion is tender. Add the tomato paste, garlic, and thyme; stir to coat the meat. Add the bay leaf and stir in enough of the Burgundy to cover the meat in the pan completely, being careful not to exceed the fill line in the pressure cooker. Lock the lid into place and bring to low pressure; maintain pressure for 45 minutes. Remove from heat and allow pressure to release naturally.

2. Add the sliced onion to a microwave-safe bowl along with 2 tablespoons of the butter; cover and microwave on high for 2 minutes. Add the mushrooms; cover and microwave on high for 1 minute. Stir, cover and microwave on high in 30-second increments until the mushrooms are sautéed and the onion is transparent.

3. Quick-release any remaining pressure in the pressure cooker and remove the lid. Stir the mushroom-onion mixture into the pan. Lock the lid into place and bring to low pressure; maintain pressure for 5 minutes.

4. Quick-release the pressure and remove the lid. Stir in any remaining Burgundy and the broth or water. Increase the heat to medium-high and bring the contents of the pan to a boil.

5. In a small bowl or measuring cup, mix the remaining ½ cup of butter together with the flour to form a paste; whisk in some of the pan liquid a little at a time to thin the paste. Strain out any lumps if necessary.

6. Once the contents of the pressure cooker reach a boil, whisk the butter-flour mixture into the meat and juices in the pan; boil for 1 minute. Reduce the heat and simmer uncovered, cooking and stirring for 5 minutes or until the pan juices have been reduced and a gravy results.

BEEF BRAISED IN BEER

You can use a large onion and omit the leek if you wish. Serve with roasted or mashed potatoes and a steamed vegetable.

INGREDIENTS
Serves 4

2 tablespoons Dijon mustard

Salt and freshly ground black pepper, to taste

1 teaspoon paprika

4 beef minute steaks, tenderized

1 tablespoon olive or vegetable oil

1 12-ounce bottle dark beer

2 tablespoons flour

1 tablespoon tomato paste

1 cup beef broth

1 medium yellow onion, peeled and diced

2 large carrots, peeled and diced

1 small stalk celery, finely diced

1 leek, white part only

1. Mix together the mustard, salt, pepper, and paprika. Spread both sides of the meat with the mustard mixture.

2. Bring the oil to temperature in the pressure cooker over medium-high heat. Fry the meat, 2 slices at a time, for 2 minutes on each side. Remove the meat and set aside.

3. Deglaze the pressure cooker with about ¼ cup of the beer, stirring and scraping to loosen any browned bits stuck to the bottom of the pan.

4. Whisk in the flour and the tomato paste. Whisk in the remaining beer. Add the beef back into the pan along with the broth, onion, carrots, and celery. Clean and slice the white part of the leek and add to the pressure cooker.

5. Lock the lid into place and bring to low pressure; maintain the pressure for 15 minutes. Remove from the heat and allow pressure to release naturally.

6. Remove the meat to a serving platter. If desired, use an immersion blender to pureé the pan juices. Taste for seasoning and add additional salt and pepper if needed. Pour over the meat. Serve.

Instead of Minute Steaks

You can substitute 6-ounce slices of beef bottom round or flank steak for the minute steaks. If you do, put each slice between two pieces of plastic wrap and pound them into thin slices before you coat them with the mustard mixture.

BEEF ROAST DINNER

Serve this roast with a tossed salad and warm buttered dinner rolls. Have sour cream at the table for the potatoes.

INGREDIENTS
Serves 6

1 tablespoon vegetable oil

1 stalk celery, finely diced

1 1-pound bag baby carrots

1 large onion, peeled and diced

1 3-pound rump roast

Salt and freshly ground black pepper, to taste

Optional: 1 tablespoon Dijon mustard

6 medium Yukon Gold or red potatoes, scrubbed

3 cups beef broth

Optional: Water

1 tablespoon butter

Optional: Fresh parsley

1. Add the oil to the pressure cooker and bring it to temperature over medium-high heat. Add the celery. Grate 6 of the baby carrots and add to the pan. Sauté for 3 minutes.

2. Add the onion, stir it into the celery and carrots, and push to the edges of the pan. Put the meat in the pan, fat side up. Season with salt and pepper.

3. Brown for 5 minutes and then turn the roast fat-side down. If desired, spread the mustard over the browned top of the roast. Season with salt and pepper.

4. Spoon some of the sautéed celery, carrots, and onion over the top of the roast. Quarter the potatoes; add potatoes and remaining carrots to the top of the meat.

5. Pour in the broth. Add water, if needed, to bring the liquid level with the ingredients in the pressure cooker; remember not to fill the pressure cooker more than two-thirds full.

6. Lock the lid. Bring the cooker to high pressure; lower the heat to maintain pressure for 1 hour.

7. Turn off the heat and let the pan set for 15 minutes to release the pressure; use the quick-release method to release any remaining pressure.

8. Move the roast, potatoes, and carrots to a serving platter; tent with foil and keep warm.

9. Skim the fat from the pan juices. Bring to a boil over medium-high heat; reduce the heat and simmer for 5 minutes, and then whisk in the butter 1 teaspoon at a time. Pour into a gravy boat to serve with the roast. Garnish the roast platter with fresh parsley if desired.

BEEF ROGAN JOSH

Traditionally made with lamb, this lean-beef version is lower in fat but full of flavor. Serve it over rice.

INGREDIENTS

Serves 6

1 tablespoon ghee (or vegetable oil)

1 onion, diced

1 pound cubed bottom round

3 cloves garlic, minced

2 teaspoons minced fresh ginger

2 tablespoons cumin

2 tablespoons coriander

1 tablespoon turmeric

2 teaspoons cardamom

2 teaspoons freshly ground black pepper

1 teaspoon chili powder

1 28-ounce can crushed tomatoes

1 cup whole milk yogurt

1. Heat ghee in an uncovered pressure cooker over medium heat. Sauté onion until softened. Add the rest of the ingredients except for the yogurt to the pressure cooker.

2. Turn the heat up to high and when the cooker reaches pressure, lower the heat to the minimum needed to maintain pressure. Cook for 13–15 minutes at high pressure.

3. When time is up, open the pressure cooker by releasing pressure.

4. Stir in the yogurt and simmer uncovered until thickened, about 10 minutes.

Canned Versus Fresh Tomatoes

While fresh tomatoes are delicious, they cannot always be found at their peak of ripeness and flavor. Canned tomatoes are always "in season" and, as a bonus they already have had their skin removed. Crushed and puréed canned tomatoes have also already been de-seeded.

BRACIOLE

The stuffing in the Braciole already adds substance to this dish, but you can serve it with cooked pasta or garlic bread, too, if you wish. Add a salad and a steamed vegetable for a complete meal.

INGREDIENTS
Serves 4

4 tablespoons extra-virgin olive oil

2 pounds flank steak

Salt and freshly ground black pepper, to taste

3 cloves garlic, peeled and minced

1 cup bread crumbs

1 medium carrot, peeled and grated

½ stalk celery, minced

1 small yellow onion, peeled and minced

1 teaspoon dried oregano

¼ teaspoon dried rosemary

¼ teaspoon dried thyme

2 teaspoons dried parsley

2 ounces freshly grated Parmigiano-Reggiano

2 large eggs

1 teaspoon sugar

1 25-ounce jar pasta sauce

¼ cup tomato juice or beef broth

Optional: Fresh parsley

Optional: Additional freshly grated Parmigiano-Reggiano

1. Rub 2 tablespoons oil over both sides of the steak. Put the steak between 2 pieces of plastic wrap; use a rolling pin, mallet, or the flat surface of a meat tenderizer utensil to pound the meat out until it's ¼-inch thick.

2. Remove the top piece of plastic wrap and season the meat with salt and pepper. Sprinkle the garlic over the meat, and then rub it into the meat.

3. Add the bread crumbs, carrot, celery, onion, oregano, rosemary, thyme, parsley, Parmigiano-Reggiano, and eggs to a bowl; mix well. Use your hands to shape the mixture into a log and place it in the center of the meat.

4. Roll up the steak like a jellyroll so that when you later slice the meat, the slices will be against the grain of the meat; tie with butcher's twine. Cut in half so that the meat will fit the bottom of the pressure cooker.

5. Bring the remaining 2 tablespoons oil to temperature over medium heat in the pressure cooker. Add the meat rolls; brown them for 5 minutes on each side.

6. Stir the sugar into the pasta sauce, and then pour it over the meat. Add the tomato juice or broth. Lock the lid into place and bring to low pressure; maintain pressure for 40 minutes. Remove from the heat and allow pressure to release naturally. Remove the lid.

7. Transfer the meat to a serving platter and tent with aluminum foil. If you want a thicker sauce, return the pressure cooker to medium heat and bring the sauce to a simmer. Simmer while the meat rests for 10 minutes and the sauce thickens. Remove the foil, carve the meat, and spoon the sauce over the meat. Garnish with fresh parsley and serve topped with additional freshly grated Parmigiano-Reggiano if desired.

CITRUS CORNED BEEF AND CABBAGE

If you want, you can slice 6 medium peeled potatoes and add them when you add the cabbage wedges in Step 4, or you can serve this dish with baked or fried potatoes.

INGREDIENTS
Serves 6

Nonstick spray

2 medium onions, peeled and sliced

1 3-pound corned beef brisket

1 cup apple juice

¼ cup brown sugar, packed

2 teaspoons orange zest, finely grated

2 teaspoons prepared mustard

6 whole cloves

6 cabbage wedges

1. Treat the inside of the pressure cooker with nonstick spray. Arrange the onion slices across the bottom of the crock.

2. Trim and discard excess fat from the brisket and place it on top of the onions.

3. Add the apple juice, brown sugar, orange zest, mustard, and cloves to a bowl and stir to mix; pour over the brisket. Lock the lid into place and bring to low pressure; maintain for 45 minutes. Quick-release the pressure and remove the lid.

4. Place the cabbage on top of the brisket. Lock the lid into place and bring to low pressure; maintain pressure for 8 minutes. Quick-release the pressure and remove the lid.

5. Move the cabbage and meat to a serving platter, spooning some of the pan juices over the meat. Tent with aluminum foil and let rest for 15 minutes. Carve the brisket by slicing it against the grain. Remove and discard any fat from the additional pan juices and the cloves. Pour the pan juices into a gravy boat to pass at the table.

If You're Pressed for Space

If there isn't room for the cabbage and the meat, increase the time you maintain the pressure in Step 3 to 55 minutes. Let the pressure release naturally. Wrap the brisket in aluminum foil; keep warm. Add the cabbage to the pressure cooker, lock the lid into place, bring to low pressure, maintain for 8 minutes, quick-release, and proceed with Step 5.

GRANDMA'S POT ROAST

Turn this into two meals for four people by making roast beef sandwiches the next day. The meat will be tender and moist if you refrigerate the leftovers in the pan juices.

INGREDIENTS
Serves 8

1 3-pound boneless chuck roast

1 1-pound bag of baby carrots

2 stalks celery, diced

1 green bell pepper, seeded and diced

1 large yellow onion, peeled and sliced

1 envelope onion soup mix

½ teaspoon black pepper

1 cup water

1 cup tomato juice

2 cloves garlic, peeled and minced

1 tablespoon Worcestershire sauce

1 tablespoon steak sauce

1. Cut the roast into serving-sized portions. Add the carrots, celery, green bell pepper, and onion to the pressure cooker. Place the roast pieces on top of the vegetables and sprinkle with soup mix and black pepper.

2. Add the water, tomato juice, garlic, Worcestershire sauce, and steak sauce to a bowl or measuring cup; mix well and then pour into the pressure cooker.

3. Lock the lid into place and bring to low pressure; maintain pressure for 45 minutes. Remove from the heat and allow pressure to release naturally.

French Dip Sandwiches

Reheat leftover pan juices from the pot roast and serve it as a sauce in which to dip roast beef sandwiches. Be sure to have horseradish and mayonnaise available for those who want to add it to their sandwiches.

HAMBURGER AND CABBAGE

Rather than taking the time to make stuffed cabbage rolls, serve this casserole-style dish instead. You can serve it over cooked rice or with toasted cheese sandwiches.

INGREDIENTS

Serves 6

1½ pounds lean ground beef

1 large sweet onion, peeled and diced

1 15-ounce can diced tomatoes

1 cup tomato juice

1 tablespoon Mrs. Dash Garlic and Herb Seasoning Blend

3 cups coleslaw mix or shredded cabbage

Salt and freshly ground black pepper, to taste

1. Add the ground beef and diced onion to the pressure cooker. Fry over medium-high heat, breaking apart the hamburger. Drain off any rendered fat and discard.

2. Stir in the undrained tomatoes, tomato juice, seasoning blend, and enough coleslaw mix to bring mixture to the fill line.

3. Lock the lid into place and bring to low pressure; maintain pressure for 8 minutes. Remove from heat and allow pressure to release naturally. Remove the lid. Stir. Check seasoning and add salt and pepper to taste.

HUNGARIAN GOULASH

Hungarian goulash is often served with prepared spaetzle or hot buttered egg noodles and cucumber salad (see sidebar). Make the cucumber salad in advance of preparing the goulash so that the cucumbers marinate in the dressing while you make the stew.

INGREDIENTS
Serves 6

1 tablespoon olive or vegetable oil

1 green bell pepper, seeded and diced

4 large potatoes, peeled and diced

3 strips bacon, cut into 1-inch pieces

1 large yellow onion, peeled and diced

2 tablespoons sweet paprika

2½ pounds stewing beef or round steak

1 clove garlic, peeled and minced

Pinch caraway seeds, chopped

2 cups beef broth

1 15-ounce can diced tomatoes

2 tablespoons sour cream, plus more for serving

Salt and freshly ground black pepper, to taste

1. Add the oil, bell pepper, potatoes, bacon, and onion to the pressure cooker over medium heat; sauté for 10 minutes or until the onion is transparent and the fat is rendering from the bacon.

2. Stir in paprika. Trim the beef of any fat and cut it into ½-inch cubes. Stir the beef into the vegetable mixture along with the garlic and caraway seeds.

3. Stir in the beef broth and tomatoes. Lock the lid into place and bring to low pressure; maintain pressure for 30 minutes.

4. Remove from heat and allow pressure to release naturally. Remove lid and stir 2 tablespoons sour cream into the goulash.

5. Taste for seasoning and add salt, pepper, and additional paprika if needed. Serve with additional sour cream on the side, and over prepared spaetzle or egg noodles if desired.

Cucumber Salad

Thinly slice 2 cucumbers; put slices in a bowl and sprinkle with salt. Let rest for 30 minutes. Drain off excess moisture and add 1 thinly sliced onion; 2 tablespoons vinegar; ¼ cup heavy or sour cream; 2 teaspoons sugar; ⅛ teaspoon sweet paprika; a pinch of dill; and freshly ground black pepper. Mix well, cover, and refrigerate until ready to serve.

ITALIAN BOILED BEEF ROAST

The toughest cut of beef can be softened into submission by simply being boiled—tough ligaments and nerves are reduced to gelatin. Serve with a fresh and tangy Italian Salsa Verde (see sidebar).

INGREDIENTS
Serves 6

1 medium onion, halved (ends removed, skin still on)

8 whole cloves

6 cups water

1 large carrot, peeled and halved

1 celery stalk, halved

1 small tomato, chopped

1 bay leaf

1 sprig sage

1 sprig rosemary

2 sprigs thyme

3 tablespoon salt

1 tablespoon black peppercorns

3-pound beef round roast

1. Cut onion in half and remove ends, but leave skin on. Pierce each half with 4 cloves. Place onion halves in pressure cooker.

2. Add water, carrot, celery, tomato, bay leaf, sage, rosemary, thyme, salt, and peppercorns. In the uncovered pressure cooker, bring the contents to a boil over high heat, and then carefully add the meat. If the water does not cover beef, add more until it does. Bring the contents to a boil. Close and lock the lid.

3. Turn the heat up to high and when the cooker reaches pressure, lower the heat to the minimum needed to maintain pressure. Cook for 50–60 minutes at high pressure.

4. Open with the natural-release method—move the pressure cooker to a cool burner and wait for the pressure to come down on its own (about 15 minutes). For electric pressure cookers, disengage the "keep warm" mode or unplug the cooker and open when the pressure indicator has gone down (20–30 minutes).

5. Remove beef to a serving platter and tent loosely with foil. Reduce the broth in the uncovered pressure cooker over high heat for about 5 minutes. Strain the broth and remove visible fat.

6. Thinly slice the meat and pour broth over the slices before serving.

Italian Salsa Verde

Pour ½ cup white wine vinegar over ½ cup unseasoned bread crumbs and set aside. Purée the following in a food processor until smooth: anchovies (optional), teaspoon capers, 2 peeled garlic cloves, 2 bunches parsley (about 4½ ounces), and ¼ cup olive oil. Add the soaked bread crumbs and purée for about 30 seconds to combine. Continue adding more olive oil and pulsing until a sauce consistency is reached. Season with salt and pepper.

MEATBALL SUBS

You can substitute 2 teaspoons dried oregano and 1 teaspoon dried basil for the Italian seasoning blend. Choose the pasta sauce according to what other flavors you want to introduce to the sandwiches: roasted red peppers sauce, mushroom sauce, or traditional marinara sauce.

INGREDIENTS
Serves 6

1 pound lean ground beef

1 large egg

1 small onion, peeled and diced

½ cup bread crumbs

2 tablespoons Parmigiano-Reggiano or Asiago cheese, freshly grated

1 tablespoon Mrs. Dash Classic Italian Medley Seasoning Blend

1 teaspoon garlic powder

Pinch dried red pepper flakes

Salt and freshly ground black pepper, to taste

1 teaspoon sugar

1 28-ounce jar pasta sauce

6 sub buns

3 tablespoons extra-virgin olive oil

1½ cups mozzarella cheese, grated

1. Add the ground beef, egg, onion, bread crumbs, grated Parmigiano-Reggiano or Asiago cheese, Italian seasoning blend, garlic powder, red pepper flakes, salt, and pepper to a mixing bowl. Combine well. Shape into 12 ping pong ball–sized meatballs. Add to the pressure cooker.

2. Stir the sugar into the pasta sauce and pour over the meatballs. Lock the lid into place and bring to low pressure; maintain pressure for 8 minutes. Remove from heat and allow pressure to release naturally. Remove the lid. Skim and discard any fat.

3. Lay the buns flat on a broiling pan. Brush the insides of the buns with the olive oil. Place under the broiler for a few minutes until lightly toasted.

4. Spread 1 tablespoon sauce over the bottom portion of each bun. Halve the meatballs and add 2 meatballs to each bun, cut-side down on the bottom portion of the bun.

5. Top with the grated mozzarella cheese. Return to broiler; broil until cheese is melted and bubbly. Pour remaining sauce into a serving bowl.

Meatball Sub Toppers

Peel and slice a large sweet onion; add the slices to the pressure cooker after you pour in the pasta sauce. Add slices of green and red bell peppers. At the end of Step 2, move the cooked onions and peppers to a serving bowl. Pass at the table for those who want to add them to their sandwiches.

MEATLOAF

Because it's easier to remove it from the pan, this recipe is adjusted for the meatloaf to be cooked in a 2.5-quart pressure fry pan or braiser. Allow an additional 15 minutes under pressure if you're shaping a shorter, taller loaf to fit into a 5-quart pressure cooker.

INGREDIENTS
Serves 4

½ pound lean ground beef

½ pound lean ground pork

½ teaspoon salt

1½ teaspoons freshly ground black pepper

¾ cup oatmeal

1 tablespoon Worcestershire sauce

2 teaspoons dried parsley

1 medium yellow onion, peeled and finely diced

2 stalks celery, finely diced

2 cloves garlic, peeled and minced

1 small red or green bell pepper, seeded and finely diced

¼ cup ketchup

1 cup water

2 tablespoons tomato paste

1. Add the ground beef, ground pork, salt, pepper, oatmeal, Worcestershire sauce, parsley, onion, celery, garlic, and bell pepper to a large bowl. Mix well.

2. Turn the mixture out onto a large piece of waxed paper or plastic wrap. Shape into a large, somewhat flat oval loaf.

3. Wrap and chill in the freezer for 30 minutes or in the refrigerator for at least 2 hours.

4. Bring a 2.5-quart pressure braiser or fry pan to temperature over medium-high heat. Add the meatloaf and brown for 5 minutes. Turn the loaf.

5. Top the meatloaf with the ketchup. Mix water and tomato paste and pour around the meatloaf.

6. Lock the lid into place and bring to high pressure; maintain pressure for 20 minutes. Remove from the heat and allow pressure to release naturally. Serve sliced, topped with some of the pan sauce if desired.

Substitutions and Additions

You can substitute an 8-ounce can of tomato sauce for the water and tomato paste. If you prefer, you can omit the salt and add 1 tablespoon of Mrs. Dash Classic Italian Medley Seasoning Blend, Mrs. Dash Extra Spicy Seasoning Blend, or another favorite salt-free seasoning blend to the meatloaf mixture.

ONION STEAK

Serve over mashed potatoes.

INGREDIENTS
Serves 6

1 tablespoon olive or vegetable oil

4 large onions, peeled and sliced

1½ pounds round steak, cut into 6 pieces

4 cloves garlic, peeled and minced

1 tablespoon dried parsley

1 cup beef broth

1 teaspoon dried thyme

½ teaspoon dried rosemary

Pinch dried red pepper flakes

Salt and freshly ground black pepper, to taste

¼ cup milk

2 tablespoons all-purpose flour

1. Use the oil to coat the bottom of the pressure cooker. In layers, add half of the onions, the meat, and the other half of the onions. Add the garlic, parsley, beef broth, thyme, rosemary, red pepper flakes, salt, and pepper. Lock the lid into place and bring to high pressure; maintain pressure for 14 minutes.

2. Quick-release the pressure and remove the lid. Move the meat to a serving platter; cover and keep warm. Whisk together the milk and flour, and then whisk the milk-flour paste into the onions and broth in the pan. Simmer and stir for 3 minutes or until the onion gravy is thickened and the flour taste is cooked out of the sauce. Pour over the meat or transfer to a gravy boat to pass at the table. Serve.

PEPPER STEAK

If you want to be traditional, serve Pepper Steak over cooked rice, but it's also good over a baked potato or cooked noodles.

INGREDIENTS
Serves 6

1 tablespoon sesame oil

2 tablespoons peanut or vegetable oil

1 large sweet onion, peeled and sliced

3 cloves garlic, peeled and minced

1 pound beef round steak

½ cup beef broth

1 tablespoon sherry

1 teaspoon light brown sugar

1 teaspoon fresh ginger, grated

Pinch dried red pepper flakes

2 tomatoes

1 large green bell pepper, seeded and sliced

4 green onions, sliced

¼ cup soy sauce

2 tablespoons cold water

2 tablespoons cornstarch

1. Bring the oil to temperature in the pressure cooker over medium-high heat. Add the onion; sauté for 3 minutes. Stir in the garlic; sauté for 30 seconds.

2. Cut the round steak into thin strips. Add to the pressure cooker; stir-fry for 3 minutes. Stir in the broth, sherry, brown sugar, ginger, and pepper flakes.

3. Lock the lid into place and bring to high pressure; maintain pressure for 10 minutes. Quick-release the pressure. Remove the lid.

4. Peel the tomatoes and remove the seeds; cut them into eighths. Add to the pressure cooker along with the bell pepper and green onions.

5. Lock the lid into place and bring to low pressure; maintain pressure for 3 minutes. Quick-release the pressure and remove the lid.

6. In a small bowl or measuring cup, whisk together the soy sauce, water, and cornstarch. Stir the cornstarch mixture into the beef mixture in the pressure cooker.

7. Cook uncovered, stirring gently, for 3 minutes or until the mixture is thickened and bubbly.

ROPA VIEJA

Serve this Cuban shredded beef with yellow rice and spicy black beans.

INGREDIENTS
Serves 8

2 pounds top round roast

1 cubanelle pepper, diced

1 large onion, diced

2 carrots, diced

1 28-ounce can crushed tomatoes

2 cloves garlic

1 tablespoon oregano

2 teaspoons cumin

½ cup green pimento-stuffed olives

1. Place all ingredients, except for olives, in the pressure cooker. Close and lock the lid.

2. Turn the heat up to high and when the cooker reaches pressure, lower the heat to the minimum needed to maintain pressure. Cook for 60 minutes at high pressure.

3. Open with the natural-release method—move the pressure cooker to a cool burner and wait for the pressure to come down on its own (about 15 minutes). For electric pressure cookers, disengage the "keep warm" mode or unplug the cooker. After 10 minutes, release the rest of the pressure using the valve.

4. Shred the meat with two forks. Add the olives and mash with a potato masher until well-mixed.

More Uses for Shredded Beef

Use this delicious shredded beef as filling for tacos, burritos, enchiladas, and quesadillas.

SAUERBRATEN

*Sauerbraten is a German dish. (*Sauer *means "sour" and* braten *means "roast meat.") In addition to the potatoes in this recipe, it's often also served with cooked cabbage and dumplings or noodles.*

INGREDIENTS
Serves 8

2 tablespoons olive or vegetable oil

1 stalk celery, diced

1 carrot, peeled and grated

2 large onions, peeled and diced

2 cloves garlic, peeled and minced

2 cups beef broth

1 cup sweet red wine

1 teaspoon dried parsley

½ teaspoon dried thyme

½ teaspoon dried marjoram

4 whole cloves

2 bay leaves

1 teaspoon salt

½ teaspoon freshly ground black pepper

1 3-pound beef sirloin roast

8 medium potatoes, peeled and quartered

¼ cup butter, softened

¼ cup tomato sauce

¼ cup all-purpose flour

½ cup sour cream

1. Bring the oil to temperature in the pressure cooker over medium heat. Add the celery and carrot; sauté for 2 minutes.

2. Add the onions; sauté for 5 minutes or until the onions are softened. Stir in the garlic; sauté for 30 seconds.

3. Stir in the broth, wine, parsley, thyme, marjoram, cloves, bay leaves, salt, and pepper. Add the roast.

4. Lock the lid into place and bring to high pressure; maintain pressure for 1 hour. Remove from the heat and quick-release the pressure.

5. Remove the lid and transfer the roast to a serving platter; tent it with aluminum foil and keep warm.

6. Skim and discard the fat from the pan juices, and then strain the juices. Pour 2 cups of the strained juices into the pressure cooker.

7. Add the potatoes to the pressure cooker. Lock the lid in place and bring to high pressure; maintain pressure for 6 minutes.

8. Quick-release the pressure and remove the lid. Use a slotted spoon to transfer the potatoes to the serving platter.

9. In a small bowl, stir together the butter, tomato sauce, and flour. Bring the pan juices to a high simmer and whisk in the flour mixture.

10. Cook and stir for 5 minutes or until the mixture is thickened. Stir in the sour cream. Pour the sauce into a gravy boat to serve with the beef and sauce.

SHREDDED BEEF BURRITO FILLING

For more heat, substitute jalapeño, poblano, panilla, or Anaheim peppers for the green pepper and use hot enchilada sauce.

INGREDIENTS

Serves 6

1 large sweet onion, peeled and diced

1 large green bell pepper, seeded and diced

1 10-ounce can enchilada sauce

¼ cup water

1 3-pound English roast or beef brisket

1. Add the onion, green pepper, and enchilada sauce to the pressure cooker. Stir in the water. Trim and discard any fat from the roast. Place the roast in the pressure cooker. Lock the lid into place and bring to low pressure; maintain pressure for 50 minutes. Remove from the heat and allow pressure to release naturally.

2. Remove the meat to a cutting board and shred it. Return the shredded beef back into the sauce in the pressure cooker. Return the pan to medium heat; simmer uncovered for a few minutes to bring the meat back up to pressure and thicken the sauce.

Assembling Burritos

For 6 burritos, you'll need 12 10-inch flour tortillas, 2 cups grated Cheddar cheese, 2 cups shredded lettuce, and 1 cup of diced tomatoes. Add some drained meat, cheese, lettuce, and tomato to the center of each tortilla. Fold up the ends and then roll the sides over each other to close the burrito. Have sour cream, avocado, and salsa at the table.

SOUTH AFRICAN GROUND BEEF CASSEROLE

Serve with Yellow Rice, fluffy white rice spiced with turmeric, sugar, cinnamon, and raisins. Fresh slices of tropical fruits like mango or papaya, a refreshing salad, or a good helping of chutney are other good side choices for this dish.

INGREDIENTS
Serves 8

1 cup 1% milk

2 slices stale white bread, torn in small pieces

2 tablespoons peanut oil

2 onions, chopped

1 tablespoon curry powder

¾ teaspoon turmeric

1 teaspoon salt

¼ teaspoon pepper

2 pounds ground beef

2 tablespoons raw sugar

Zest and juice of 1 lemon

¼ cup sliced almonds, toasted

½ cup raisins, soaked and drained

1 tablespoon butter

5 eggs

4 bay leaves

1. Pour milk over bread and set aside.

2. In a large, wide sauté pan over medium heat, heat the oil. Add onions and sauté until soft. Add the curry powder, turmeric, salt, and pepper. Add ground beef to pan and cook, stirring to crumble, until beef is browned and all of the liquid has evaporated (about 5–7 minutes). Turn off the heat and mix in the sugar.

3. Squeeze the bread and add it to the pan (keep the milk to use later for the topping). Add the lemon juice and zest, almonds, and raisins. Mix well. Butter a 7½"-wide heatproof baking dish. Pour mixture into buttered baking dish and flatten slightly.

4. Prepare the pressure cooker by inserting the trivet, or steamer basket, and filling it with one cup of water. Make a foil sling (by folding a long piece of foil into three) and lower the uncovered dish into the pressure cooker. Close and lock the lid.

5. Turn the heat up to high and when the cooker reaches pressure, lower the heat to the minimum needed to maintain pressure. Cook for 15–20 minutes at high pressure.

6. When time is up, open the pressure cooker by releasing pressure.

7. Mix the eggs into the milk to make a custard mixture. Carefully remove the baking dish and pour the custard mixture over the meat. Add the bay leaves and cover with foil. Lower dish into the pressure cooker again.

8. Turn the heat up to high and when the cooker reaches pressure, lower the heat to the minimum needed to maintain pressure. Cook for 3–5 minutes at high pressure.

9. When time is up, open the pressure cooker by releasing pressure. Discard bay leaves.

10. Serve as is, or brown the custard under the broiler.

SLOPPY JOES

Serve on hamburger buns with potato chips and coleslaw. Depending on the size of the buns (and individual appetites), this recipe can be stretched to 8 servings.

INGREDIENTS

Serves 6

1 tablespoon olive oil

1 large sweet onion, peeled and diced

2 cloves garlic, peeled and minced

1½ pounds lean ground beef or ground turkey

½ cup beef broth

¼ cup tomato paste

2 tablespoons light brown sugar

Salt and freshly ground black pepper, to taste

Pinch dried red pepper flakes

½ teaspoon chili powder

1 teaspoon prepared mustard

1 tablespoon Worcestershire sauce

⅛ teaspoon ground cinnamon

Pinch ground cloves

1. Bring the oil to temperature in the pressure cooker over medium-high heat. Add the onion and sauté for 3 minutes. Add the garlic; sauté for 30 seconds.

2. Stir in the remaining ingredients. Lock the lid into place and bring to low pressure; maintain pressure for 10 minutes.

3. Quick-release the pressure and, leaving the pan over the heat, remove the lid. Remove and discard any fat floating on top of the meat mixture.

4. Stir and simmer, breaking apart the cooked ground meat to thicken the sauce. Serve by spooning onto hamburger buns.

SOUTH OF THE BORDER MEATBALLS

Add extra heat to the sauce by adding more canned chipotles, some Mrs. Dash Extra Spicy Seasoning Blend, or hot sauce. Serve these meatballs with some of the sauce over cooked rice. Top with guacamole and sour cream or serve with an avocado salad.

INGREDIENTS

Serves 8

1 tablespoon vegetable oil

1 large onion, thinly sliced

1½ teaspoons garlic powder

1 tablespoon chili powder

¼ teaspoon dried Mexican oregano

2 canned chipotle chili peppers in adobo sauce

1 15-ounce can diced tomatoes

1 cup chicken broth

Salt and freshly ground black pepper, to taste

1½ pounds lean ground beef

½ pound ground pork

1 large egg

1 small white onion, peeled and diced

1 tablespoon chili powder

1½ teaspoons garlic powder

10 soda crackers, crumbled

1. Add oil to the pressure cooker and bring to temperature over medium heat. Add the sliced onion; sauté for 3 minutes or until the onion is transparent.

2. Stir in the garlic powder, chili powder, oregano, chipotles in adobo sauce, undrained tomatoes, broth, salt, and pepper. Simmer uncovered while you prepare the meatballs.

3. Add the ground beef, ground pork, egg, diced onion, chili powder, garlic powder, and crumbled crackers to a large bowl; use hands to mix. Form into sixteen meatballs.

4. Use an immersion blender to pureé the sauce in the pressure cooker. Add the meatballs to the sauce.

5. Lock the lid into place and bring to low pressure; maintain pressure for 12 minutes. Remove from heat and allow pressure to release naturally.

STEAK FAJITAS

You can serve this meat with the thickened sauce over rice or mashed potatoes. Or, if you prefer, you can serve the drained meat and vegetables wrapped in a flour tortilla.

INGREDIENTS
Serves 4

1 pound round steak

1 small onion, peeled and diced

1 small green bell pepper, seeded and diced

Salt and freshly ground black pepper, to taste

2 cups frozen whole kernel corn, thawed

1¼ cups tomato juice

½ teaspoon chili powder

Optional: 1 tablespoon cornstarch

Optional: ¼ cup cold water

1. Trim and discard any fat from the meat. Cut the meat into ½-inch diced pieces and add to the pressure cooker. Stir in the onion, bell pepper, salt, pepper, corn, tomato juice, and chili powder. Lock the lid into place and bring to low pressure; maintain pressure for 12 minutes. Remove from the heat and allow pressure to release naturally for 5 minutes. Quick-release any remaining pressure.

2. Optional: To thicken the sauce, in a small bowl or measuring cup whisk the cornstarch together with the cold water. Return the pressure cooker to medium heat and bring to a simmer; whisk in the cornstarch slurry and cook uncovered for 5 minutes or until the sauce is thickened and the raw cornstarch taste is cooked out of the sauce. Taste for seasoning and add additional salt and pepper if needed.

STUFFED GREEN PEPPERS

For a slightly different taste, substitute an equal amount of pasta sauce for the tomato sauce or add a little sugar and some Italian seasoning to the tomato sauce.

INGREDIENTS

Serves 4

4 medium green bell peppers

1 pound lean ground beef

1 cup cooked rice

2 large eggs

3 cloves garlic, peeled and minced

1 small yellow onion, peeled and diced

Salt and freshly ground black pepper, to taste

Optional: Pinch allspice or nutmeg

½ cup chicken broth

½ cup tomato sauce

1. Cut the tops off the green peppers. Remove and discard the seeds and use a spoon to scrape out and discard some of the white pith inside the peppers. Set aside.

2. Dice any of the green pepper that you can salvage from around the stem and mix well with ground beef, rice, eggs, garlic, onion, salt, pepper, and allspice or nutmeg if using.

3. Evenly divide the meat mixture between the green peppers. Place the rack in the pressure cooker and pour the broth into the cooker.

4. Place the peppers on the rack and pour the tomato sauce over the peppers. Lock the lid into place and bring to low pressure; maintain pressure for 15 minutes.

5. Quick-release the pressure. Remove the peppers to serving plates. Remove the rack and pour the pan juices into a gravy boat to pass at the table.

STUFFED ROUND STEAK

To serve with potatoes, scrub 4 medium potatoes and prick each potato several times with a fork or knife. Add them to the pressure cooker when you add the pasta sauce.

INGREDIENTS

Serves 4

3 tablespoons extra-virgin olive oil

2 pounds round steak

Salt and freshly ground black pepper, to taste

3 cloves garlic, peeled and minced

4 hard-boiled eggs, peeled and sliced

4 large carrots, peeled and grated

1 small yellow onion, peeled and minced

1 cup zucchini, grated and squeezed dry

2 ounces freshly grated Parmigiano-Reggiano

1 25-ounce jar pasta sauce

1 teaspoon sugar

¼ cup tomato juice or beef broth

1. Rub 2 tablespoons oil over both sides of the round steak. Put the steak between 2 pieces of plastic wrap; use a rolling pin, mallet, or the flat surface of a meat tenderizer utensil to pound the meat out flatter. Remove the top piece of plastic wrap and season the meat with salt and pepper. Sprinkle the garlic over the meat, and then rub it into the meat.

2. Down the center of the meat, evenly arrange the egg slices, carrots, onion, zucchini, and half of the Parmigiano-Reggiano. Roll up the steak like a jellyroll and tie with butcher's twine. Cut in half if necessary to fit the meat roll in the bottom of the pressure cooker. Rub the remaining oil over the meat roll.

3. Bring the pressure cooker to temperature over medium-high heat. Add the meat and sear it on all sides. Lower the temperature to medium and pour the pasta sauce over the meat.

4. Add the sugar and tomato juice or broth. Lock the lid into place and bring to low pressure; maintain pressure for 40 minutes. Remove from heat and allow pressure to release naturally.

5. Remove the cover. Transfer the meat to a serving platter. Slice the meat. Pour the sauce over the meat slices and sprinkle the remaining Parmigiano-Reggiano over the meat and pasta sauce. Serve.

SWEDISH MEATBALLS

You can substitute ½ cup (or more to taste) of sour cream for the heavy cream. Serve over egg noodles.

INGREDIENTS

Serves 4

1 slice whole wheat bread

½ cup milk

1 pound lean ground beef

8 ounces lean ground pork

1 large egg

1 small onion, peeled and minced

1 teaspoon dried dill

Salt and freshly ground black pepper, to taste

4 tablespoons butter

¼ cup all-purpose flour

1½ cups beef broth

1 cup water

½ cup heavy cream or sour cream

1. Add the bread to a large bowl. Pour in the milk and soak the bread until the milk is absorbed.

2. Break up the bread and mix it into the beef, pork, egg, onion, dill, salt, and pepper. Form into 12 meatballs and set aside.

3. Add the butter to the pressure cooker and melt it over medium-high heat; whisk in the flour until it forms a paste. Whisk in the broth and water. Bring to a simmer and then add the meatballs.

4. Lock the lid into place and bring to high pressure; maintain pressure for 10 minutes. Remove from the heat and quick-release the pressure.

5. Carefully stir in the cream. Taste for seasoning and add additional salt and pepper if needed. Serve.

SWISS STEAK MEAL

If you prefer a thick gravy, thicken the pan juices with a roux or cornstarch. Remember that you should never fill a pressure cooker more than two-thirds full. When in doubt about cooking times or other issues, check the instruction manual that came with your cooker.

INGREDIENTS
Serves 6

2½ pounds beef round steak, 1" thick

1 tablespoon vegetable oil

Salt and freshly ground pepper, to taste

1 medium yellow onion, peeled and diced

2 stalks celery, diced

1 large green pepper, seeded and diced

1 cup tomato juice

1 cup beef broth or water

6 large carrots, peeled

6 medium white potatoes, scrubbed

Optional: 4 teaspoons butter

1. Cut the round steak into 6 serving-sized pieces. Add the oil and bring it to temperature over medium heat. Season the meat on both sides with salt and pepper.

2. Add 3 pieces of the meat and fry for 3 minutes on each side to brown them. Move to a platter and repeat with the other 3 pieces of meat.

3. Leave the last 3 pieces of browned meat in the cooker; add the onion, celery, and green pepper on top of them.

4. Lay in the other 3 pieces of meat and pour the tomato juice and broth or water over them. Place the carrots and potatoes on top of the meat.

5. Lock the lid into place; bring to high pressure and maintain the pressure for 17 minutes. Remove from the heat and allow pressure to release naturally.

6. Once pressure has dropped, open the cooker and move the potatoes, carrots, and meat to a serving platter. Cover and keep warm.

7. Skim any fat from the juices remaining in the pan. Set the uncovered cooker over medium heat and simmer the juices for 5 minutes.

8. Whisk in the butter, 1 teaspoon at a time, if desired. Taste for seasoning and add additional salt and pepper if needed.

9. Have the resulting gravy available at the table to pour over the meat. Serve immediately.

TURKISH STUFFED EGGPLANT BOATS

In Turkish this dish is called Karniyarik, and all of the ingredients are fried separately and then baked. Here we only lightly brown some of the ingredients and do the rest of the cooking with steam. If you have a low, wide pressure cooker (also known as a pressure pan), you can easily double this recipe to fit in your extra-wide steamer basket!

INGREDIENTS

Serves 6

3 thin, long eggplants

1 tablespoon vegetable oil

4 ounces ground beef

1 small onion, chopped

2 cloves garlic, minced

2 sprigs parsley (stems and leaves divided), chopped

1 large tomato, chopped and drained

1 teaspoon salt

1 teaspoon pepper

3 banana peppers, sliced into strips

1 cup water

1. Poke each eggplant with a fork all around, then slice in half lengthwise.

2. Heat oil in an uncovered pressure cooker over medium heat. Place each eggplant half cut-side down in the pressure cooker and cook until lightly browned. Set aside.

3. Add the beef, onion, and parsley stems to the cooker and sauté until onions have softened and meat has begun to brown (about 5–7 minutes). Add the garlic, tomato, salt, and pepper. Mix thoroughly and turn off the heat.

4. Slice the eggplant halves in the middle with a shallow cut that does not reach the ends or bottom. Arrange halves in the steamer basket and stuff them with the meat mixture. Lay pepper strips over the stuffed eggplant halves.

5. Add one cup of water to the pressure cooker and lower the steamer basket. Close and lock the lid.

6. Turn the heat up to high and when the cooker reaches pressure, lower the heat to the minimum needed to maintain pressure. Cook for 10 minutes at high pressure.

7. When time is up, open the pressure cooker by releasing pressure.

8. Carefully remove the eggplant boats using a long spatula and tongs. Sprinkle with parsley leaves before serving.

UNSTUFFED CABBAGE

Use Italian-seasoned tomatoes and cooked orzo pasta instead of the rice to give this dish a Tuscan flair. If you prefer German flavors, add 1 teaspoon caraway seeds and 2 teaspoons brown sugar.

INGREDIENTS
Serves 6

2 tablespoons extra-virgin olive oil

2 stalks celery, diced

3 large carrots, peeled and diced

1 pound lean ground beef

1 medium yellow onion, peeled and diced

1 clove garlic, peeled and minced

½ teaspoon salt

¼ teaspoon freshly ground black pepper

1 teaspoon sugar

1 15-ounce can diced tomatoes

1½ cups cooked rice

3 cups coleslaw mix or rough-chopped cabbage

1½ cups chicken broth

Optional: ½ cup white wine

1. Bring the oil to temperature over medium heat in the pressure cooker. Add the celery and carrots; sauté for 5 minutes.

2. Add the ground beef and onion; stir-fry until beef is browned and broken apart and onion is transparent. Drain off and discard any excess fat.

3. Add the garlic, salt, pepper, sugar, undrained tomatoes, rice, coleslaw mix or cabbage, and broth; stir into the beef mixture.

4. Use the back of a spoon to press the mixture down evenly in the pan. Add white wine if using, being careful not to exceed the fill line on your pressure cooker.

5. Lock the lid into place and bring to low pressure; maintain for 8 minutes. Remove from heat and allow pressure to release naturally.

6. Uncover and return the pressure cooker to medium heat. Simmer for 15 minutes or until most of the liquid has evaporated.

UNSTUFFED PEPPERS CASSEROLE

You can use a can of whole tomatoes instead of diced if you prefer. Just crush or cut up the tomatoes when you add them to the casserole.

INGREDIENTS

Serves 4

1 pound ground beef

1 tablespoon olive or vegetable oil

1 medium onion, peeled and chopped

2 large green bell peppers, seeded and diced

2½ cups herb-seasoned bread crumbs

1 8-ounce can whole kernel corn, drained

1 14-ounce can diced tomatoes

½ cup beef broth

1 tablespoon butter, melted

1. Add the ground beef to the pressure cooker. Fry over medium-high heat until cooked through. Drain and discard fat. Stir in the oil, onion, and green bell peppers. Sprinkle 1½ cups of the bread crumbs over the beef-onion-pepper mixture.

2. Add the corn in a layer over the bread crumbs and the can of undrained diced tomatoes in a layer over the corn. Drizzle with the beef broth.

3. Lock the lid into place and bring to high pressure; maintain pressure for 3 minutes. Remove from the heat, quick-release the pressure, and remove the lid. Stir well. Taste for seasoning and adjust if necessary.

4. Preheat the oven to 400°F. In a small bowl, mix the remaining bread crumbs with the melted butter.

5. Transfer the contents of the pressure cooker to an ovenproof casserole treated with nonstick spray and sprinkle the buttered bread crumbs over the top.

6. Bake for 10 minutes or until the bread crumbs are golden brown. Remove from the oven and let rest for 10 minutes. Serve.

ITALIAN SUMMER VEAL ROAST

Vitello Tonnato is a popular veal roast in Italy especially enjoyed during hot summer days. The tuna sauce is surprisingly not fishy-tasting.

INGREDIENTS
Serves 8

3 anchovies

1 6-ounce can Italian tuna in olive oil

1 cup good quality mayonnaise

1 tablespoon olive oil

1 2-pound veal roast (or two small ones)

1 onion, roughly sliced

1 carrot, roughly sliced

1 celery stalk, roughly sliced

2 cloves garlic, peeled

1 cup white wine

1 cup water

4 whole cloves

5 bay leaves

1 sprig rosemary

2 teaspoons salt

½ teaspoon white pepper

2 tablespoons capers, rinsed and drained

1. In a blender, purée anchovies, tuna, and mayonnaise until smooth. Refrigerate sauce.

2. Heat olive oil in an uncovered pressure cooker over medium heat. Brown roast on all sides. Add all of the other ingredients. Close and lock the lid.

3. Turn the heat up to high and when the cooker reaches pressure, lower the heat to the minimum needed to maintain pressure. Cook for 20–30 minutes (depending on the thickness of the meat) at high pressure.

4. When time is up, open the pressure cooker by releasing pressure.

5. Remove the roast and place it on a serving platter. Tent with foil and let cool. Strain and reserve the cooking liquid. When the roast is relatively cool, wrap well and refrigerate a few hours.

6. To serve, slice the roast thinly. Remove tuna sauce from refrigerator and thin with reserved cooking liquid, if necessary. Cover veal slices with tuna sauce and sprinkle with capers.

MUSHROOM STUFFED VEAL ROLL

You can just as easily substitute a butterflied pork roast for the veal. Serve with a salad, baked potatoes, steamed vegetable, and dinner rolls.

INGREDIENTS
Serves 8

½ tablespoon unsalted butter

2 tablespoons olive oil, divided

8 ounces fresh button mushrooms, cleaned and sliced

4 ounces fresh shiitake mushrooms, cleaned and sliced

2 large shallots, peeled and minced

2 cloves garlic, peeled and minced, divided

1½ teaspoons salt, divided

3 tablespoons all-purpose flour

½ teaspoon freshly ground black pepper

1 3½-pound boneless veal shoulder roast, butterflied

4 ounces prosciutto, thinly sliced

1 large carrot, peeled and grated

1 stalk celery, finely diced

1 small onion, peeled and diced

1 cup dry white wine

1 cup veal or chicken broth

1. Heat butter and 1 tablespoon olive oil in an uncovered pressure cooker over medium heat. Sauté mushrooms for 3 minutes or until they begin to soften. Stir in the shallots, 1 clove garlic, and 1 teaspoon salt. Sauté for another 10 minutes or until the mushrooms have given off most of their moisture.

2. Add flour, ½ teaspoon salt, and pepper to a bowl; stir to mix and set aside.

3. Place the veal roast cut-side up on a flat working surface. Arrange the prosciutto over the cut side of the roast, overlapping the edges opposite the center of the roast by several inches. Spread all but ¼ cup of the sautéed mushroom mixture over the prosciutto up to where the prosciutto overlaps the edges of the roast. Fold the overlapped edges over the mushroom mixture and then roll the prosciutto-mushroom layers to the center of the roast. Pull the edges of the roast up and over the prosciutto-mushroom roll and secure at 1-inch intervals with butcher's twine.

4. Add the remaining oil to the pressure cooker and bring it to temperature over medium-high heat. Add the roast and brown it for about 5 minutes on each side. Remove roast from the cooker and add the carrot, celery, onion, and remaining clove of garlic to the pressure cooker and sauté for 5 minutes. Deglaze the cooker with the wine and broth, and add the roast on top of the sautéed vegetables. Close and lock the lid.

5. Turn the heat up to high and when the cooker reaches pressure, lower the heat to the minimum needed to maintain pressure. Cook for 25–30 minutes (depending on the thickness) at high pressure.

Continued on the next page

MUSHROOM STUFFED VEAL ROLL
continued

6. Open with the natural-release method—move the pressure cooker to a cool burner and wait for the pressure to come down on its own (about 15 minutes). For electric pressure cookers, disengage the "keep warm" mode or unplug the cooker and open when the pressure indicator has gone down (20–30 minutes).

7. Transfer the roast to a serving platter and tent loosely with aluminum foil; let rest for at least 10 minutes before slicing. Use an immersion blender to pureé the pan juices and vegetables in the pressure cooker.

8. Slice the roast into ½-inch slices and either pour the thickened pan juices over the slices or serve with the sauce on the side.

OSSO BUCO

This Osso Buco recipe is a hybrid, combining today's tradition of adding tomatoes and the nineteenth-century Milanese practice of using allspice and cinnamon. Americans often prefer eating it with a baked potato, steamed vegetable, and tossed salad.

INGREDIENTS
Serves 8

1 cup all-purpose flour

1 teaspoon salt

½ teaspoon freshly ground black pepper

8 veal shanks, cross-cut ½-inch thick

3 tablespoons extra-virgin olive oil

3 tablespoons unsalted butter

1 celery stalk, diced

2 carrots, diced

1 medium onion, peeled and diced

1 cup beef stock

1 head garlic, cut horizontally through the middle

1 28-ounce can diced tomatoes

¼ teaspoon cinnamon

⅛ teaspoon allspice

2 bay leaves

¼ cup dry white wine

1. Place flour, salt, and pepper in a large plastic bag; add the veal shanks to the bag and shake to coat them.

2. Heat olive oil and butter in an uncovered pressure cooker over medium heat. Remove 4 veal shanks from the plastic bag, shake off any excess flour (too much could prevent the cooker from reaching pressure). Brown them on each side for about 5 minutes or until golden. Remove the browned meat to a platter. Repeat with the remaining 4 veal shanks and remove when done.

3. Add the celery, carrots, and onion and sauté until the vegetables start to get some color and develop an intense aroma (about 8 minutes). Deglaze the cooker with the stock, and scrape the bottom of the pan well to incorporate the delicious browned bits into the sauce. Return the veal shanks to the pan. Add the garlic, tomatoes, cinnamon, allspice, bay leaves, and wine. Close and lock the lid.

4. Turn the heat up to high and when the cooker reaches pressure, lower the heat to the minimum needed to maintain pressure. Cook for 18–20 minutes at high pressure.

5. When time is up, open the pressure cooker by releasing pressure.

6. Simmer uncovered for about 5 minutes or until the liquid is reduced. Discard the bay leaf. Carefully remove the tender meat to each plate and cover with generous spoonful of tomato sauce.

Actually . . .
There are several regional variations of Osso Buco: alla Milanese, which is braised in white wine and topped with freshly chopped parsley, garlic, and lemon zest gremolata; alla Romana, in which the veal is cooked with peas; and alla Fiorentina, which includes tomatoes and is similar to this recipe.

CHAPTER 11

POULTRY

BELGIAN-STYLE CHICKEN

Belgium gave us more than just waffles and chocolate. The Belgians are also known for their fried food, including french fries.

INGREDIENTS

Serves 4

3 stalks celery, cut into thirds

1 medium sweet onion, peeled and quartered

¾ teaspoon dried thyme

1 3-pound chicken

Salt, to taste

8 small carrots, peeled

½ cup chicken broth or water

¼ cup dry white wine

3 tablespoons butter

2 cups coarse dried bread crumbs

Optional: Fresh parsley

1. Place the celery pieces in the bottom of the pressure cooker and top with the onion wedges. Sprinkle with the thyme.

2. Rinse the chicken and pat dry. Season the chicken with salt to taste and place it on top of the onions and celery.

3. Place the carrots around and on top of the chicken. Pour in the broth or water and wine.

4. Lock the lid into place and bring to low pressure; maintain pressure for 25 minutes. Remove from the heat and allow pressure to release naturally for 5 minutes. Quick-release any remaining pressure.

5. Melt the butter in a nonstick skillet over medium heat. Add the bread crumbs and cook uncovered, stirring until toasted to a golden brown. Remove from the heat.

6. Transfer the chicken to a serving platter and cut into sections. Use a slotted spoon to move and arrange the vegetables around the chicken.

7. Skim and discard any fat from the pan juices and then pour the juices over the chicken and vegetables.

8. Sprinkle the toasted bread crumbs over the chicken and vegetables. Garnish with fresh parsley if desired. Serve.

CHICKEN BORDEAUX

Serve Chicken Bordeaux with buttered egg noodles, cooked rice, or potatoes prepared your favorite way.

INGREDIENTS
Serves 4

3 tablespoons vegetable oil

1 clove garlic, peeled and crushed

3 pounds chicken pieces

1 teaspoon cracked black pepper

1 cup dry white wine

1 15-ounce can diced tomatoes

4 ounces mushrooms, sliced

1. Bring the oil to temperature in the pressure cooker over medium-high heat. Add garlic; sauté to infuse the garlic flavor into the oil. Remove garlic and discard.

2. Rub chicken with pepper. Arrange the chicken pieces skin-side down in the pressure cooker. Pour in the wine and tomatoes. Add the mushrooms.

3. Lock the lid into place and bring to low pressure; maintain for 10 minutes. Remove from the heat and quick-release the pressure.

4. Remove chicken to a serving platter and keep warm. Return the pressure cooker to the heat and simmer the sauce until it thickens. Pour over the chicken.

CHICKEN CACCIATORE

Serve Chicken Cacciatore with pasta or rice, garlic bread, and a tossed salad.

INGREDIENTS

Serves 4

1 3-pound chicken, cut up

3 tablespoons all-purpose flour

½ teaspoon salt

⅛ teaspoon freshly ground pepper

2 tablespoons vegetable or olive oil

¼ cup diced salt pork

1 large onion, peeled and sliced

2 cloves garlic, peeled and minced

1 tablespoon dried parsley

2 teaspoons Mrs. Dash Classic Italian Medley Seasoning Blend

2 large carrots, peeled and diced

1 stalk celery, diced

1 15-ounce can diced tomatoes

Salt and freshly ground pepper, to taste

½ cup white wine

1 6-ounce can tomato paste

1. Trim and discard any extra fat from the chicken. Add the flour, salt, and pepper to a large zip-closure bag. Add the chicken, seal the bag, and shake to coat the chicken.

2. Bring the oil to temperature in the pressure cooker over medium-high heat. Add the salt pork and sauté until it begins to render its fat.

3. Add the meatier pieces of chicken, skin-side down, and brown until crisp. Add the remaining ingredients except for the tomato paste.

4. Lock the lid into place. Bring to low pressure; maintain pressure for 20 minutes.

5. Remove the pan from the heat and quick-release the pressure. Place the chicken on a serving platter and keep warm.

6. Return the pan to the heat, stir the tomato paste into the sauce in pressure cooker, and simmer for 5 minutes or until thickened. Pour the sauce over chicken.

Italian Medley Seasoning Blend

Mrs. Dash Classic Italian Medley Seasoning Blend is a mixture of garlic, basil, oregano, rosemary, parsley, marjoram, white pepper, sage, savory, cayenne pepper, thyme, bay leaf, cumin, mustard powder, coriander, onion, and red bell pepper. All of the Mrs. Dash blends are salt-free, which makes them a healthy addition to any dish.

CHICKEN IN RED SAUCE

Serve with a hearty tossed salad that includes chopped hard-boiled egg, dressed with lemon vinaigrette.

INGREDIENTS
Serves 4

1½ tablespoons olive oil

4 chicken leg-thigh pieces

Salt and freshly ground pepper, to taste

2 cups water

1 tablespoon paprika

1 medium carrot, scrubbed and halved

1 stalk celery, halved

1 bay leaf

1 1-inch cinnamon stick

Pinch cayenne pepper

2 whole cloves

2 small yellow onions, peeled and halved

½ cup dry sherry

1 tablespoon fresh lemon juice

½ cup slivered almonds, toasted

1. Bring the oil to temperature in the pressure cooker over medium-high heat. Remove and discard the skin from the chicken pieces.

2. Add the chicken to the pressure cooker. Sprinkle the pieces with salt and pepper, to taste.

3. Add the water, paprika, carrot, celery, bay leaf, cinnamon, and cayenne pepper. Stick a whole clove into each onion half; add them to the pressure cooker.

4. Lock the lid in place and bring to low pressure; maintain for 12 minutes. Remove from the heat and let rest for 10 minutes. Quick-release any remaining pressure.

5. Transfer the chicken to a serving platter and keep warm. Remove and discard the carrot and celery pieces, bay leaf, cinnamon stick, and onion.

6. Return the pressure cooker to the heat. Add the sherry and bring to a boil over medium-high heat. Simmer for 3 minutes. Stir in the lemon juice. Pour the sauce over the chicken and top with the almonds.

Lemon Vinaigrette

Whisk 2 tablespoons fresh lemon juice together with ½ teaspoon Dijon mustard, ⅛ teaspoon dried thyme, a pinch of sugar, ⅛ teaspoon salt, and ⅛ teaspoon freshly ground black pepper. Slowly pour ½ cup extra-virgin olive oil into the lemon juice mixture, whisking as you do so. Taste for seasoning and adjust.

CHICKEN IN SPICED ORANGE SAUCE

Serve Chicken in Spiced Orange Sauce over rice. Have soy sauce available at the table.

INGREDIENTS
Serves 8

2 tablespoons butter

3 pounds boneless, skinless chicken thighs

1 teaspoon paprika

½ teaspoon salt

⅛ teaspoon cinnamon

⅛ teaspoon ginger

Pinch ground cloves

½ cup white raisins

½ cup slivered almonds

1½ cups orange juice

1 1-pound bag baby carrots, quartered

1 tablespoon cornstarch

¼ cup cold water

1. Bring the butter to temperature in the pressure cooker over medium heat. Add the chicken thighs and fry for 2 minutes on each side. Add the paprika, salt, cinnamon, ginger, cloves, raisins, almonds, orange juice, and carrots.

2. Lock the lid into place. Bring to low pressure; maintain pressure for 10 minutes. Quick-release the pressure; remove the lid.

3. Combine cornstarch with the water and whisk into the sauce. Stir and cook for 3 minutes or until the sauce is thickened and the raw cornstarch taste is cooked out of the sauce.

CHICKEN IN SWEET ONION SAUCE

Your family will love this rich, succulent one-pot meal. (You'll love it because it's quick and easy.) Serve with a tossed salad and dinner rolls.

INGREDIENTS
Serves 6

1 tablespoon olive oil

1 tablespoon butter or ghee

2 large sweet onions, peeled and diced

8 ounces fresh mushrooms, sliced

6 boneless, skinless chicken breasts

1 10-ounce can cream of mushroom soup

6 medium potatoes, peeled and sliced

1 1-pound bag of baby carrots

2 tablespoons heavy cream

1. Heat the oil and butter or ghee to temperature in the pressure cooker over medium heat. Add the onions; sauté for 2 minutes. Stir in the mushrooms; sauté for 3 minutes.

2. Add the chicken, mushroom soup, potatoes, and carrots to the pressure cooker. Lock the lid in place and bring to low pressure; maintain pressure for 8 minutes. Remove from the heat and let the pressure release naturally.

3. Remove the lid and transfer the carrots, potatoes, and chicken to a serving platter; keep warm.

4. Return the pan to the heat and stir in the cream. Simmer for several minutes and then pour sauce over the chicken and vegetables on the serving platter. Serve immediately.

CHICKEN MASALA

Make this dish tomato-free by omitting the chicken broth and drained tomatoes and substituting an undiluted can of condensed cream of chicken soup. Serve the finished dish over cooked rice with Indian flatbread and a cucumber salad.

INGREDIENTS
Serves 4

2 tablespoons ghee or vegetable oil

1 stalk celery, finely diced

1 medium sweet onion, peeled and diced

1 large carrot, peeled and grated

1½ tablespoons garam masala

1 clove garlic, peeled and minced

⅓ cup flour

½ cup chicken broth

1 14.5-ounce can diced tomatoes, drained

1 cup coconut milk

1 pound boneless, skinless chicken breasts, diced

1 cup frozen peas, thawed

Salt and freshly ground black pepper, to taste

1. Add the ghee or oil to the pressure cooker and bring to temperature over medium heat.

2. Add the celery; sauté for 1 minute. Add the onion; sauté for 3 minutes or until the onion is transparent. Stir in the carrot, garam masala, and garlic; sauté for 1 minute.

3. Stir in the flour, then whisk in the chicken broth. Stir in the tomatoes, coconut milk, and chicken.

4. Lock the lid into place and bring to low pressure. Maintain pressure for 10 minutes. Remove from the heat and allow pressure to release naturally.

5. Remove the lid and stir. If the sauce is too thick, loosen it by stirring in chicken broth or coconut milk a tablespoon at a time.

6. Return pan to medium heat, stir in the peas, and cook until the peas are heated through. Taste for seasoning and add salt and pepper if needed.

Garam Masala Spice Blend

Make your own garam masala spice blend by mixing together 1 tablespoon ground coriander, 2 teaspoons ground cardamom, 1 teaspoon cracked black pepper, 1 teaspoon ground cinnamon, 1 teaspoon Charnushka, 1 teaspoon caraway, ½ teaspoon ground cloves, ½ teaspoon freshly ground China no. 1 ginger, and ¼ teaspoon ground nutmeg. Store in a covered container in a cool, dry place.

CHICKEN PAPRIKASH

This simple recipe takes hardly any time or effort at all. Serve with buttered egg noodles.

INGREDIENTS

Serves 4

2 tablespoons ghee or vegetable oil

1 medium sweet onion, peeled and diced

1 green bell pepper, peeled and diced

5 cloves garlic, peeled and minced

4 chicken breast halves

¼ cup tomato sauce

2 tablespoons Hungarian paprika

1 cup chicken broth

1 tablespoon flour

¾ cup sour cream

Salt and freshly ground black pepper, to taste

1. Bring the ghee or oil to temperature in the pressure cooker over medium-high heat. Add the onion and green pepper; sauté for 3 minutes. Stir in the garlic. Add the chicken pieces skin-side down. Brown chicken for a few minutes.

2. Mix together the tomato sauce, paprika, and chicken broth. Pour over the chicken.

3. Lock the lid into place. Bring to low pressure; maintain pressure for 10 minutes.

4. Remove the pan from the heat and quick-release the pressure. Transfer the chicken to a serving platter and keep warm. Return the pan to the heat.

5. Stir the flour into the sour cream, then stir into the pan juices. Cook and stir until mixture simmers; simmer for 5 minutes or until the broth is thickened. Stir in salt and pepper to taste. Pour sauce over chicken.

CHICKEN PICCATA

If you prefer a more intense lemon flavor, add a teaspoon or two of grated lemon zest to the sauce just before you return the pan to the heat to bring it to a boil.

INGREDIENTS
Serves 6

2 tablespoons olive or vegetable oil

4 shallots, peeled and minced

3 cloves garlic, peeled and minced

6 chicken breast halves

¾ cup chicken broth

⅓ cup fresh lemon juice

1 tablespoon dry sherry

½ teaspoon salt

¼ teaspoon freshly ground white pepper

1 teaspoon dried basil

1 cup pimento-stuffed green olives, minced

2 tablespoons extra-virgin olive oil

1 tablespoon butter

1 tablespoon all-purpose flour

¼ cup sour cream

¼ cup fontinella cheese, grated

Optional: 1 lemon, thinly sliced

1. Bring the oil to temperature in the pressure cooker over medium-high heat. Add the shallots; sauté for 3 minutes. Stir in the garlic.

2. Arrange the chicken breast halves in the pressure cooker, skin-side down. Add the broth, lemon juice, sherry, salt, pepper, basil, and olives. Lock the lid into place. Bring to high pressure; maintain for 10 minutes.

3. Remove from the heat and quick-release the pressure. Use tongs to transfer the chicken to a broiling rack, arranging pieces skin-side up.

4. Brush the skin with the extra-virgin olive oil. Place under the broiler at least 6 inches from the heat and broil to crisp the skin while you finish the sauce.

5. In a small bowl, mix the butter and flour together to form a paste. Stir in 2 tablespoons of the pan juices.

6. Return the pressure cooker to the heat and bring to a boil over medium-high heat. Once it reaches a boil, stir in the flour mixture.

7. Reduce heat to maintain a simmer for 3 minutes or until the mixture is thickened and the raw flour taste is cooked out of the sauce. Stir in the sour cream.

8. Move the chicken from the broiling rack to a serving platter. Pour the sour cream sauce over the chicken. Sprinkle the cheese over the top. Garnish with lemon slices if desired.

CHICKEN STUFFED WITH APRICOTS AND PRUNES

To offset the sweetness of the fruit in this dish, serve with a tossed salad dressed with a sour cream or other creamy dressing and dinner rolls.

INGREDIENTS
Serves 4

1 3-pound chicken

12 pitted prunes, snipped

8 dried apricots, snipped

½ small lemon, cut into 6 thin slices

1 tablespoon vegetable oil

¼ cup finely minced shallots

2 stalks celery, finely minced

1 tablespoon finely minced fresh ginger

1 cup chicken broth

¼ teaspoon salt or to taste

2 medium sweet potatoes, peeled and halved

1 tablespoon grated orange zest

¼ cup Grand Marnier liqueur or orange juice

1. If available, remove the giblets from the chicken cavity. Chop the gizzard, heart, and liver and mix them together with the prunes, apricots, and lemon slices. Add the mixture to the chicken cavity.

2. Bring the oil to temperature in the pressure cooker. Add the shallots and celery; sauté for 2 minutes. Stir in the ginger.

3. Place the chicken, breast-side down, in the pressure cooker. Pour in the broth and add the salt. Place the sweet potatoes around the chicken.

4. Lock the lid into place and bring to low pressure; maintain pressure for 25 minutes. Remove the pan from the heat and quick-release the pressure. Carefully move the sweet potatoes and chicken to a serving platter; keep warm.

5. Stir the orange zest and liqueur or orange juice into the pan juices. Return the pressure cooker to the heat; bring to a boil over medium-high heat. Cook until the alcohol burns off or the sauce thickens slightly. Either pour the sauce over the chicken and potatoes or transfer to a gravy boat to serve the sauce on the side.

CHICKEN TAGINE

Serve over cooked couscous. To prepare couscous, bring 2¼ cups chicken broth to boil in a saucepan. Stir in 2 cups dried couscous. Cover, remove from the heat, and let stand for 5 minutes. Fluff with a fork. Serve.

INGREDIENTS
Serves 6

2 tablespoons butter or ghee

1 tablespoon extra-virgin olive oil

2 large onions, peeled and diced

2 cloves garlic, peeled and minced

2 teaspoons fresh ginger, grated

1 teaspoon ground cumin

½ teaspoon saffron

2 pounds boneless, skinless chicken breast

2 cups chicken broth

1 lemon

2 tablespoons honey

12 large green olives, pitted

2 tablespoons cornstarch

2 tablespoons cold water

2 tablespoons fresh flat-leaf parsley, minced

Salt and freshly ground black pepper, to taste

1. Bring the butter or ghee and oil to temperature in the pressure cooker over medium heat. Add the onion; sauté for 5 minutes.

2. Stir in the garlic, ginger, cumin, and saffron; sauté for 30 seconds. Cut the chicken into bite-sized pieces; add to the pressure cooker and stir-fry for 3 minutes. Stir in the broth, zest from half of the lemon, fresh lemon juice, and honey.

3. Lock the lid into place and bring to high pressure; maintain pressure for 8 minutes. Remove from the heat and quick-release the pressure.

4. Remove the lid; stir in the olives and the zest from the other half of the lemon.

5. In a small bowl, mix together the cornstarch and water, and then whisk that mixture into the chicken mixture in the pressure cooker.

6. Simmer and stir for 3 minutes or until the mixture is thickened and the raw taste is cooked out of the cornstarch. Stir in the parsley. Taste for seasoning, and add salt and pepper if needed.

CHICKEN WITH MUSHROOMS IN WHITE WINE

For a more intense flavor, substitute the white wine for a very strong and aged red—you only need half a cup so use whatever you're serving with dinner.

INGREDIENTS
Serves 6

1 tablespoon olive oil

1 clove garlic, peeled and crushed

3 pounds chicken bone-in pieces

1 teaspoon cracked black pepper

½ cup dry white wine

1 15-ounce can diced tomatoes

4 ounces mushrooms, sliced

2 teaspoons salt

1. Heat olive oil in an uncovered pressure cooker over medium heat. Sauté the garlic until golden. Rub chicken with pepper. Arrange the chicken pieces skin-side down in the pressure cooker and brown well (you may need to work in batches). Remove chicken from pan and deglaze the bottom with wine until the liquid is almost completely evaporated. Arrange all pieces skin-side up in the pressure cooker, then add tomatoes, mushrooms, and salt. Close and lock the lid.

2. Turn the heat up to high and when the cooker reaches pressure, lower the heat to the minimum needed to maintain pressure. Cook for 8–10 minutes at high pressure.

3. When time is up, open the pressure cooker by releasing pressure.

4. Remove chicken to a serving platter and keep warm. In the uncovered pressure cooker, reduce the sauce until thickened. Pour over chicken and serve.

COQ AU VIN

Traditional Coq Au Vin is made with an old rooster, slowly cooked in wine to tenderize the meat. This updated version is simpler but just as good, especially if you use the cognac to add to the authentic flavors of the dish. Serve it over cooked noodles or boiled potatoes.

INGREDIENTS
Serves 8

6 slices smoked bacon, diced

1 tablespoon olive or vegetable oil

2 pounds boneless, skinless chicken thighs

2 pounds boneless, skinless chicken breasts

1 large carrot, peeled and grated

2 stalks celery, sliced

1 1-pound bag pearl onions, thawed

2 cloves garlic, peeled and minced

8 ounces button mushrooms, cleaned and sliced

½ teaspoon dried thyme

2 teaspoons dried parsley

2 cups dry red wine

¼ cup cognac

2 tablespoons cornstarch

3 tablespoons cold water

Salt and freshly ground black pepper, to taste

1. Add the bacon to the pressure cooker and fry it over medium-high heat until crisp. Use a slotted spoon to transfer the cooked bacon to a bowl. Add the oil to the pressure cooker and bring to temperature.

2. Cut the chicken into bite-sized pieces. Brown in batches in the bacon fat and oil in the pressure cooker, transferring it to the bowl with the bacon once it's lightly browned.

3. Add the carrot and celery to the pressure cooker; sauté for 2 minutes. Add the onions; sauté for 3 minutes or until they begin to brown. Add the garlic, mushrooms, thyme, and parsley; sauté for 5 minutes or until the mushrooms have released their moisture.

4. Stir in the wine and cognac. Lock the lid into place and bring to low pressure; maintain pressure for 10 minutes. Remove from heat, quick-release the pressure, and remove the lid.

5. In a bowl, whisk the cornstarch into the water. Return the pressure cooker to medium heat. Bring to a simmer and whisk in the cornstarch slurry.

6. Simmer for 3 minutes or until the sauce is thick and glossy and the cornstarch flavor has cooked out of the sauce. Taste for seasoning and add salt and pepper if needed. Serve.

CURRIED CHICKEN SALAD

If you prepare the chicken the night before and refrigerate it in its own broth, the chicken will be moist beyond belief.

INGREDIENTS

Serves 6

1 medium sweet onion, peeled and quartered

1 large carrot, peeled and diced

1 stalk celery, diced

8 peppercorns

1 cup water

3 pounds chicken breast halves, bone-in and with skin

¼ cup mayonnaise

½ cup sour cream

2–3 tablespoons curry powder

Salt, to taste

½ teaspoon freshly ground black pepper

1½ cups apples, diced

½ cup seedless green grapes, halved

1 cup celery, sliced

1 cup slivered almonds, toasted

2 tablespoons red onion or shallot, diced

1. Add the onion, carrot, celery, peppercorns, water, and chicken to the pressure cooker.

2. Lock the lid into place and bring to high pressure; maintain pressure for 10 minutes.

3. Remove from heat; allow pressure to release naturally for 10 minutes and then quick-release any remaining pressure.

4. Use a slotted spoon to transfer chicken to a bowl. Strain the broth in the pressure cooker and then pour it over the chicken. Allow chicken to cool in the broth.

5. To make the salad, add the mayonnaise, sour cream, curry powder, salt, and pepper to a bowl. Stir to mix. Stir in the apples, grapes, celery, almonds, and red onion or shallot.

6. Remove the chicken from the bones. Discard the bones and skin. Dice the chicken and fold into the salad mixture. Chill until ready to serve.

EAST INDIAN CHICKEN

Serve with cooked rice or couscous and a cucumber salad. Make a tangy vinaigrette for the salad with equal parts rice vinegar and chili sauce, a little sesame oil, and sugar, garlic powder, salt, and pepper to taste.

INGREDIENTS
Serves 6

1 cup water

½ cup plain yogurt

1 tablespoon lemon juice

2 cloves garlic, peeled and minced

2 teaspoons grated fresh ginger or ½
    teaspoon ground ginger

1 teaspoon turmeric

¼ teaspoon salt

1 teaspoon paprika

1 teaspoon curry powder

¼ teaspoon freshly ground black pepper

6 boneless, skinless chicken breasts

2 teaspoons cornstarch

2 teaspoons cold water

1. Mix water, yogurt, lemon juice, garlic, ginger, turmeric, salt, paprika, curry powder, and pepper in a bowl; add the chicken and marinate at room temperature for 1 hour.

2. Pour the chicken and marinade into the pressure cooker. Lock the lid into place and bring to low pressure; maintain pressure for 10 minutes.

3. Remove the pressure cooker from the heat and quick-release the pressure. Transfer the chicken to a serving platter and keep warm.

4. Mix the cornstarch with the cold water. Stir into the yogurt mixture in the pressure cooker.

5. Return the pressure cooker to heat and bring to a boil of medium-high heat. Boil for 3 minutes or until mixture thickens. Pour sauce over the chicken. Serve immediately.

GINGER-CHILI CHICKEN

Serve these thighs and sauce with rice, topped with coleslaw on a hamburger bun, or rolled into flour tortillas with romaine leaves.

INGREDIENTS
Serves 6

1 cup plain yogurt

1 clove garlic, peeled and minced

2 teaspoons fresh ginger, grated

¼ teaspoon cayenne pepper

3 pounds boneless, skinless chicken thighs

1 15-ounce can diced tomatoes

8 teaspoons ketchup

½ teaspoon chili powder

4 tablespoons butter

1 teaspoon sugar

½ cup cashews, crushed

Salt and freshly ground black pepper, to taste

Optional: Plain yogurt or sour cream

Optional: A few drops of red coloring

1. Mix together the yogurt, garlic, ginger, and cayenne pepper in a bowl or zip-closure bag; add the chicken thighs and marinate for 4 hours.

2. Remove the chicken thighs from the marinade and add them to the pressure cooker along with the undrained diced tomatoes, ketchup, and chili powder.

3. Lock the lid into place and bring to low pressure; maintain pressure for 8 minutes. Quick-release the pressure.

4. Use a slotted spoon to move cooked chicken thighs to a serving platter and keep warm.

5. Use an immersion blender to pureé the tomatoes. Whisk in the butter and sugar. Stir in the cashews. Taste for seasoning and add salt and pepper, to taste.

6. If the sauce is spicier than you'd like, stir in some plain yogurt or sour cream 1 tablespoon at a time until you're pleased with the taste. Add red food coloring if desired. Pour over the chicken thighs and serve.

ITALIAN HERB AND LEMON CHICKEN

Black olives are almost never pressure cooked. They have a very strong and decisive flavor that would overwhelm all other flavors if they were to be added to the pressure cooker.

INGREDIENTS
Serves 6

4 lemons

2 cloves garlic

3 sprigs fresh rosemary

2 sprigs fresh sage

½ bunch parsley

5 tablespoons extra-virgin olive oil, divided

1 teaspoon salt

½ teaspoon pepper

1 chicken, cut into parts or package of bone-in chicken pieces, skin removed

½ cup of dry white wine

4 ounces pitted black salt-cured olives (Taggiesche, French, or Kalamata)

1. Juice three lemons and pour the juice in a small bowl. Chop together the garlic, 2 rosemary sprigs, sage, and parsley and add to the lemon juice, along with 4 tablespoons olive oil, salt, and pepper. Mix well and set aside. Place the chicken in a deep dish and cover well with the marinade. Cover with plastic wrap and marinate in the refrigerator for 2–4 hours.

2. Remove chicken from dish, reserving marinade. Heat 1 tablespoon olive oil in an uncovered pressure cooker over medium heat and brown the chicken pieces on all sides for about 5 minutes. Remove chicken from pan and deglaze pan with the white wine. Cook until liquid is almost completely evaporated (about 3 minutes).

3. Return chicken pieces to pressure. Place dark-meat pieces (wings, legs, and thighs) on the bottom of the pan, topped with the breasts. (Breasts should not touch the bottom of the pressure cooker.) Pour in the reserved marinade. Close and lock the lid.

4. Turn the heat up to high and when the cooker reaches pressure, lower the heat to the minimum needed to maintain pressure. Cook for 8–10 minutes at high pressure.

5. When time is up, open the pressure cooker by releasing pressure.

6. Move the chicken pieces out of the cooker onto a serving platter covered with foil and keep warm. Reduce the liquid in the uncovered cooker, over medium-high heat, to ¼ of its amount, or until it becomes thick and syrupy.

7. Pour reduced pan juices over chicken. Slice the remaining lemon and chop 1 sprig of rosemary. Serve chicken garnished with lemon slices, rosemary, and olives.

MUSHROOM CHICKEN WITH POTATOES

This is a wonderful one-pot meal for the whole family. Serve with fresh grilled vegetables or a simple salad of sliced romaine with your favorite dressing.

INGREDIENTS
Serves 6

1 tablespoon olive oil

4 tablespoons butter, divided

2 large onions, peeled and diced

1 pound mushrooms, sliced thinly

4 boneless, skinless chicken breasts cut into bite-sized pieces

4 medium potatoes, peeled and sliced

1 pound carrots, peeled sliced into thick rounds

½ cup chicken broth

2 teaspoons salt

1 teaspoon white pepper

½ cup water

2½ cups whole milk

4 tablespoons flour

1. Heat olive oil and 1 tablespoon butter in an uncovered pressure cooker over medium heat. Sauté the onions until soft (about 5 minutes). Add the mushrooms and sauté for about 3 more minutes. Add the chicken, potatoes, carrots, broth, salt, pepper, and water. Mix well. Close and lock the lid.

2. Turn the heat up to high and when the cooker reaches pressure, lower the heat to the minimum needed to maintain pressure. Cook for 5–7 minutes at high pressure.

3. When time is up, open the pressure cooker by releasing pressure.

4. Add the milk and flour and mix well. Simmer uncovered, stirring frequently until the contents have reached the desired consistency.

PESTO CHICKEN

There's already salt and pepper in the pesto, so there's none called for in this recipe. Have it on the table for those who want to add more.

INGREDIENTS
Serves 4

3 pounds bone-in chicken thighs

⅓ cup pesto

½ cup chicken broth

1 large sweet onion, peeled and sliced

8 small red potatoes, peeled

1 1-pound bag baby carrots

1. Remove the skin and trim the chicken thighs of any fat; add to a large zip-closure bag along with the pesto. Seal and shake to coat the chicken in the pesto.

2. Add the broth and onion to the pressure cooker. Place the trivet or cooking rack on top of the onion. Arrange the chicken on the rack and then add the potatoes and carrots to the top of the chicken.

3. Lock the lid into place. Bring to high pressure; maintain pressure for 11 minutes.

4. Remove the pressure cooker from the heat. Quick-release the pressure. Transfer the chicken, potatoes, and carrots to a serving platter. Use tongs to remove the trivet or cooking rack.

5. Remove any fat from the juices remaining in the pan, then strain the juices over the chicken and vegetables. Serve hot.

Pesto

To make your own pesto, add 9 peeled cloves garlic and ¼ cup each toasted walnuts and pine nuts to a food processor; process for 15 seconds. Add 5 cups fresh basil, ½ teaspoon salt, and 1 teaspoon freshly ground black pepper. Gradually add 1½ cups extra-virgin olive oil; process until puреéd. Makes about 5 cups.

SATAY-FLAVORED CHICKEN

Serve this chicken dish over cooked jasmine rice. Drizzle with the peanut sauce. Serve with Indian flatbread and a cucumber salad.

INGREDIENTS
Serves 4

½ cup coconut milk

1 tablespoon fish sauce

2 teaspoons red curry paste

1 teaspoon light brown sugar

½ teaspoon ground turmeric

¼ teaspoon freshly ground black pepper

1 pound boneless, skinless chicken breasts, cut into bite-sized pieces

1. Add all ingredients to the pressure cooker. Stir to mix. Lock the lid into place and bring to low pressure; maintain pressure for 10 minutes. Remove from the heat and allow pressure to release naturally.

2. Remove the lid, return pan to medium heat, and simmer until the sauce is thickened. Pour over cooked jasmine rice.

Peanut Sauce

In a saucepan, bring a cup of coconut milk to a simmer. Whisk in 3 tablespoons curry paste, ½ cup chunky peanut butter, ½ cup chicken broth, and ¼ cup light brown sugar; simmer for 5 minutes, continuing to whisk and stir until all ingredients are dissolved into the sauce. Remove from the heat and stir in 2 tablespoons tamarind or fresh lime juice and salt to taste.

SPANISH CHICKEN AND RICE

Adapt the heat level of this Spanish Chicken and Rice recipe by choosing between mild, medium, or hot chili powder, according to your tastes. In addition, you can substitute jalapeño pepper for some or all of the green pepper.

INGREDIENTS
Serves 4

2 tablespoons extra-virgin olive or vegetable oil

1 pound boneless chicken breast, cut into bite-sized pieces

1 large green pepper, seeded and diced

1 teaspoon chili powder

1 teaspoon smoked paprika

¼ teaspoon dried thyme

⅛ teaspoon dried oregano

¼ teaspoon freshly ground black pepper

Pinch cayenne pepper

1 medium white onion, peeled and diced

4 ounces fresh mushrooms, sliced

2 cloves garlic, peeled and minced

2 cups chicken broth

1 cup long-grain rice, uncooked

½ cup black olives, pitted and halved

1. Bring the oil to temperature in the pressure cooker over medium heat. Add the chicken, green pepper, chili powder, paprika, thyme, oregano, black pepper, cayenne, and onion; stir-fry for 5 minutes or until the onion is transparent and the chicken begins to brown.

2. Stir in the mushrooms; sauté for 2 minutes. Add the garlic, broth, rice, and olives.

3. Lock the lid into place and bring to high pressure; maintain pressure for 3 minutes. Remove from the heat and allow the pressure to release naturally for 7 minutes.

4. Quick-release any remaining pressure. Uncover and fluff with a fork. Taste for seasoning and add salt and other seasoning if needed.

WHOLE BEER-CAN CHICKEN

Be sure to measure the height of your pressure cooker before buying a chicken. You don't want it to be too tall to fit! If the can doesn't fit in the chicken, use a trivet (pointing up into the cavity) as a stand.

INGREDIENTS
Serves 6

2 tablespoons chopped rosemary (reserve a teaspoon for garnish)

2 tablespoons chopped sage

2 tablespoons chopped thyme

2 tablespoons olive oil

Juice and zest of 1 lemon

1 teaspoon salt

½ teaspoon black pepper

3- to 4-pound chicken

1 can beer

2 bay leaves

1. Prepare the seasoning by mixing the herbs, olive oil, lemon juice, salt, and pepper.

2. Rinse chicken inside and out and pat dry. Tuck the tips of the wings behind the neck opening of the chicken and brush on the seasoning.

3. In a separate pan (or your pressure cooker if it is large enough) brown the seasoned chicken well on all sides, about 10 minutes.

4. Pour ⅓ of the beer out of the can and place half the lemon zest and one bay leaf into the can. Place the can in the middle of the pressure cooker. Lower the chicken over the can of beer so that the can is inside the cavity. Pour any of the remaining seasoning and liquid from the sauté pan over the chicken. Add the remaining lemon zest and bay leaf. Close and lock the lid.

5. Turn the heat up to high and when the cooker reaches pressure, lower the heat to the minimum needed to maintain pressure. Cook for 20–25 minutes at high pressure.

6. Open with the natural-release method—move the pressure cooker to a cool burner and wait for the pressure to come down on its own (about 15 minutes). For electric pressure cookers, disengage the "keep warm" mode or unplug the cooker. After 10 minutes, release the rest of the pressure using the valve.

7. Carefully remove the chicken and the beer can from the pressure cooker. Place the chicken on the serving platter to rest tented with aluminum foil; pour in the remaining beer from the can and discard. Simmer the contents of the uncovered cooker for about 5 minutes or until reduced by half.

8. Strain the pan sauce and pour over the chicken. Sprinkle with fresh rosemary before serving.

BRAISED TURKEY BREAST WITH CRANBERRY CHUTNEY

The cranberry juice will add some sweetness to the cooked cranberries. The optional brown sugar is a suggested amount; sweeten the chutney according to your taste.

INGREDIENTS
Serves 6

2 cups cranberry juice

1 cup whole cranberries

1 large sweet onion, peeled and diced

1 3-pound whole turkey breast

1 teaspoon dried thyme

Salt and freshly ground black pepper, to taste

2 tablespoons butter, melted

1 teaspoon orange zest, grated

1 tablespoon lemon juice

Optional: ¼ cup light brown sugar

1. Place the rack in the pressure cooker. Add the cranberry juice, cranberries, and onion.

2. Rinse the turkey breast and pat dry with paper towels. Sprinkle the thyme, salt, and pepper over the breast. Place the turkey on the rack.

3. Lock the lid into place and bring to low pressure; maintain pressure for 25 minutes. Remove from the heat and allow pressure to release naturally.

4. Transfer the turkey breast to a broiling rack. Brush the skin with the melted butter. Place under the broiler; broil until the skin is browned and crisp.

5. Transfer the turkey to a serving platter and tent with aluminum foil; let rest for 10 minutes before carving.

6. Drain all but about ¼ cup of the juice from the cranberries and onions. Stir in the orange zest and lemon juice.

7. Return the pressure cooker to the heat and bring contents to a boil. Taste and stir in brown sugar to taste. Maintain a low boil until the mixture is thickened. Transfer to a serving bowl and serve with the turkey.

Intensified Cranberry Chutney

Reserve about ¼ cup of the diced onion and wait until you stir in the orange zest and lemon juice to add them to the chutney. The onion will cook until it's crisp-tender. Intensify the flavors by adding a generous amount of freshly ground black pepper at the end of the cooking time.

CRANBERRY AND WALNUT BRAISED TURKEY WINGS

This dish is a perfect solution for a small Thanksgiving feast or a hearty winter meal.

INGREDIENTS

Serves 6

2 tablespoons butter

1 tablespoon vegetable oil

1 teaspoon salt

½ teaspoon pepper

4 turkey wings (about 3 pounds)

1 onion, roughly sliced

1 cup dry cranberries (soaked in boiling water for 5 minutes)

1 cup shelled walnuts

1 bunch fresh thyme, tied with twine

1 cup freshly squeezed orange juice (or prepared juice without sugar)

1. Heat butter and oil in an uncovered pressure cooker over medium heat. Sprinkle salt and pepper over turkey wings. Brown wings on both sides, making sure that the skin side is nicely colored. Remove the wings from the pressure cooker and add the onion. Return wings to the pan, skin-side up, along with cranberries, walnuts, and thyme. Pour the orange juice over the turkey. Close and lock the lid.

2. Turn the heat up to high and when the cooker reaches pressure, lower the heat to the minimum needed to maintain pressure. Cook for 12–15 minutes at high pressure.

3. Open with the natural-release method—move the pressure cooker to a cool burner and wait for the pressure to come down on its own (about 15 minutes). For electric pressure cookers, disengage the "keep warm" mode or unplug the cooker. After 10 minutes, release the rest of the pressure using the valve.

4. Remove and discard the thyme bundle and carefully remove the wings to a serving dish. Tent with foil while you reduce the contents of the liquid in the pressure cooker to about half. Pour the liquid, walnuts, onions, and cranberries over the wings and serve.

Fresh and Canned Cranberries

Substitute the dried cranberries in this recipe with 1½ cups fresh cranberries or 1 cup canned cranberries, drained and rinsed.

MOCK BRATWURST IN BEER

Bavarian seasoning is a blend of Bavarian-style crushed brown mustard seeds, French rosemary, garlic, Dalmatian sage, French thyme, and bay leaves. The Spice House (www.thespicehouse.com) has a salt-free Bavarian Seasoning Blend.

INGREDIENTS

Serves 6

1 stalk celery, finely chopped

1 1-pound bag baby carrots

1 large onion, peeled and diced

2 cloves garlic, peeled and minced

4 slices bacon, cut into small pieces

1 2½-pound boneless turkey breast

1 2-pound bag sauerkraut, rinsed and drained

1 12-ounce can beer

1 tablespoon Bavarian seasoning

Salt and freshly ground pepper, to taste

6 medium red potatoes, washed and pierced

1. Add the ingredients to the pressure cooker in the order given. Lock the lid in place. Bring to low pressure; maintain pressure for 15 minutes.

2. Remove from the heat and allow pressure to release naturally. Taste for seasoning and adjust if necessary. Serve hot.

Bavarian Seasoning Substitution

You can substitute a tablespoon of stone-ground mustard along with ¼ teaspoon each of rosemary, garlic powder, sage, and thyme. Add a bay leaf (but remember to remove it before you serve the meal). Just before serving, taste for seasoning and adjust if necessary.

PETIT TURKEY MEATLOAF

The flavor of this meatloaf can be changed up, depending on what you have on hand. Try freshly chopped Italian flat-leaf parsley, snipped chives, Worcestershire sauce, and a little lemon zest.

INGREDIENTS

Serves 4

1 pound lean ground turkey

1 onion, peeled and diced

1 stalk celery, minced

1 carrot, peeled and grated

½ cup cracker crumbs

½ cup pecorino romano cheese, grated

1 clove garlic, peeled and minced

1 teaspoon freshly chopped basil

1 teaspoon mustard

1 teaspoon sea salt

¼ teaspoon pepper

1 large egg

3 tablespoons ketchup

1. Add all ingredients to a large bowl and mix well. Divide the mixture between 2 mini loaf pans. Pack the mixture down into the pans.

2. Place water in the pressure cooker and add the steamer basket. Lower the little pans onto the basket. Close and lock the lid.

3. Turn the heat up to high and when the cooker reaches pressure, lower the heat to the minimum needed to maintain pressure. Cook for 15–20 minutes at high pressure.

4. Open with the natural-release method—move the pressure cooker to a cool burner and wait for the pressure to come down on its own (about 15 minutes). For electric pressure cookers, disengage the "keep warm" mode or unplug the cooker and open when the pressure indicator has gone down (20–30 minutes).

5. Use oven mitts or tongs to lift the pans out of the pressure cooker. Serve directly from the pans or transfer to a serving platter.

Individual Loaves

Making individual loaves is a great idea no matter how many people you're cooking for. Serve ½ to 1 loaf per person then freeze the remaining individual loaves for a quick meal anytime.

POT PIE–STYLE TURKEY DINNER

If you prefer, you can thicken this dish with ½ cup cornmeal instead of the butter and flour mixture.

INGREDIENTS
Serves 8

1 tablespoon extra-virgin olive oil

1 clove garlic, peeled and minced

4 cups turkey or chicken broth

6 medium potatoes, peeled and diced

6 large carrots, peeled and sliced

1 large sweet onion, peeled and diced

2 stalks celery, finely diced

½ ounce dried mushrooms

¼ teaspoon dried oregano

¼ teaspoon dried rosemary

1 bay leaf

2 1¼-pound turkey drumsticks, skin removed

2 tablespoons all-purpose flour

2 tablespoons butter

1 10-ounce package frozen green beans, thawed

1 10-ounce package frozen whole kernel corn, thawed

1 10-ounce package frozen baby peas, thawed

Salt and freshly ground black pepper, to taste

8 large buttermilk biscuits

1. Add the oil to the pressure cooker and bring to temperature over medium heat. Add the garlic and sauté for 10 seconds.

2. Stir in the broth, potatoes, carrots, onion, celery, mushrooms, oregano, rosemary, and bay leaf. Stand the two drumsticks meaty-side down in the pan, arranging them so they don't block the pressure cooker vent when the lid is in place.

3. Lock the lid and bring to high pressure; maintain pressure for 12 minutes. Remove from the heat and allow the pressure to drop naturally, and then use the quick-release method for your cooker to release the remaining pressure if needed. Remove the drumsticks; cut the meat from the bone and into bite-sized pieces and return it to the pot.

4. Mix the flour together with the butter, and then stir in some of the broth from the pan to make a paste. Return the pan to the heat; bring it to a boil over medium-high heat.

5. Stir in the flour mixture; reduce the heat to medium. Maintain a simmer and stir for 5 minutes or until the broth is thickened.

6. Stir in the green beans, corn, and peas; cook over medium heat for 5 minutes or until the vegetables are heated through. Remove and discard the bay leaf. Taste for seasoning and add salt and pepper if needed.

7. To serve, split the buttermilk biscuits in half and place them opened in serving bowls. Spoon the turkey and vegetables over the biscuits. Serve immediately.

TURKEY À LA KING

Because it's made up of meat, vegetables, and sauce, Turkey à la King is almost a meal in itself.

INGREDIENTS

Serves 4

3 tablespoons ghee or butter

1 pound skinless, boneless turkey breast

1 small sweet onion, peeled and diced

1 cup frozen peas

1 4-ounce can sliced mushrooms, drained

1 2-ounce jar pimentos, drained and diced

1 14-ounce can chicken broth

¼ cup all-purpose flour

½ cup heavy cream

Optional: ½ cup milk

Salt and freshly ground black pepper, to taste

1. Bring the ghee or butter to temperature in the pressure cooker over medium heat.

2. Cut the turkey into bite-sized pieces and add to the pressure cooker along with the onion.

3. Stir-fry for 5 minutes or until the turkey begins to brown and the onions are transparent. Stir in the peas, mushrooms, pimentos, and broth.

4. Lock the lid into place and bring to low pressure; maintain pressure for 6 minutes. Remove from the heat and allow pressure to release naturally.

5. Remove the lid and return the pressure cooker to medium heat. Whisk the flour into the cream.

6. Once the pan juices in the pressure cooker reach a low boil, whisk in the flour-cream mixture.

7. Stir and cook for 3 minutes or until the mixture thickens and the flour taste is cooked out.

8. If the dish gets too thick, whisk in as much of the optional milk as needed to get it to the desired consistency. Taste for seasoning and add salt and pepper if needed.

Leftover Turkey or Chicken

In this recipe, you can substitute 2 or 3 cups of diced cooked turkey or chicken for the skinless, boneless turkey breast. If you do, sauté the onion and stir in the meat with the other ingredients. Reduce the time the dish is cooked under pressure to 2 minutes, and then quick-release the pressure.

TURKEY AND VEGETABLE CASSEROLE

The meat, potatoes, and vegetables are already in this casserole. It's good served over or alongside buttermilk biscuits. Add a tossed salad if you wish.

INGREDIENTS

Serves 6

1 tablespoon extra-virgin olive oil

1 clove garlic, peeled and minced

4 cups chicken broth

6 medium potatoes, peeled and diced

6 large carrots, peeled and sliced

1 large sweet onion, peeled and diced

2 stalks celery, finely diced

½ ounce dried mushrooms

¼ teaspoon dried oregano

¼ teaspoon dried rosemary

1 bay leaf

2 strips orange zest

Salt and freshly ground black pepper, to taste

2 1¼-pound turkey drumsticks, skin removed

1 10-ounce package frozen green beans, thawed

1 10-ounce package frozen whole kernel corn, thawed

1 10-ounce package frozen baby peas, thawed

1. Add the oil to the pressure cooker and bring to temperature over medium heat. Add the garlic and sauté for 10 seconds.

2. Stir in the broth, potatoes, carrots, onion, celery, mushrooms, oregano, rosemary, bay leaf, orange zest, salt, and pepper. Stand the two drumsticks meaty-side down in the pan.

3. Lock the lid and bring to high pressure; maintain pressure for 12 minutes. Remove from heat and allow pressure to drop naturally.

4. Remove the drumsticks, cut the meat from the bone and into bite-sized pieces, and return it to the pot.

5. Stir in the green beans, corn, and peas; cook over medium heat for 5 minutes. Remove and discard the orange zest and bay leaf. Taste for seasoning and add salt and pepper if needed.

TURKEY BREAST IN YOGURT SAUCE

Serve over cooked rice or couscous with a cucumber-yogurt salad. To make the salad, combine plain yogurt, garlic, mint, salt, and ginger. Spritz with lemon juice and add thinly sliced cucumbers.

INGREDIENTS

Serves 6

1 cup plain yogurt

1 teaspoon ground turmeric

1 teaspoon ground cumin

1 teaspoon yellow mustard seeds

¼ teaspoon salt

½ teaspoon freshly ground black pepper

1 pound boneless turkey breast

1 tablespoon ghee or butter

1 1-pound bag baby peas and pearl onions

1. In a bowl large enough to hold the turkey, mix together the yogurt, turmeric, cumin, mustard seeds, salt, and pepper.

2. Cut the turkey into bite-sized pieces. Stir into the yogurt mixture. Cover and marinate in the refrigerator for 4 hours.

3. Melt the ghee or butter in the pressure cooker. Add the turkey and yogurt mixture.

4. Lock the lid into place and bring to low pressure; maintain pressure for 8 minutes. Remove from the heat and let pressure release naturally for 5 minutes. Quick-release any remaining pressure.

5. Remove the lid and stir in the peas and pearl onions. Return pan to medium heat.

6. Simmer and stir until the vegetables are cooked through and the sauce is thickened. Serve immediately.

Cucumber-Yogurt Salad

In a serving bowl, mix together 2 cups of drained plain yogurt and 2 peeled, seeded, and thinly sliced cucumbers. Add 8 fresh chopped mint leaves, 1 peeled and minced clove of garlic, and some salt to a small bowl; crush them together. Stir the mint mixture into the salad. Add more salt if needed. Chill until ready to serve.

TURKEY BREAST ROMANO

You can substitute chicken breast tenders in this recipe. Serve over pasta along with a salad and garlic bread.

INGREDIENTS

Serves 8

½ cup all-purpose flour

½ teaspoon salt

½ teaspoon freshly ground black pepper

2 pounds boneless, skinless turkey breast

2 tablespoons olive oil

1 large sweet onion, peeled and diced

4 cloves garlic, peeled and minced

1 tablespoon dried oregano

1 teaspoon dried basil

2 tablespoons tomato paste

½ cup turkey or chicken broth

1 10-ounce can tomato sauce

1 teaspoon balsamic vinegar

2 4-ounce cans sliced mushrooms, drained

1 tablespoon sugar

8 ounces Romano cheese, grated

1. Add the flour, salt, and pepper to a large zip-closure bag; seal and shake to mix. Cut the turkey into bite-sized pieces. Add to the bag, seal, and shake to coat the turkey in the flour.

2. Bring the oil to temperature in the pressure cooker over medium-high heat. Add the turkey and onion; fry for 5 minutes or until the turkey begins to brown and the onion is transparent.

3. Stir in the garlic, oregano, basil, and tomato paste; sauté for 2 minutes. Stir in the broth, tomato sauce, vinegar, mushrooms, and sugar.

4. Lock the lid into place and bring to low pressure; maintain low pressure for 12 minutes. Remove from heat and allow pressure to release naturally for 10 minutes.

5. Quick-release any remaining pressure. Stir the cooked turkey and sauce; ladle it over cooked pasta and top with grated Romano cheese.

TURKEY BREAST WITH MUSHROOMS

The cooking liquid is thickened at the end of pressure cooking to form a delicious mushroom gravy topping.

INGREDIENTS
Serves 6

1 tablespoon vegetable oil

3 tablespoons butter, divided

1 large onion, peeled and diced

1 pound button mushrooms, sliced

4 cloves garlic, smashed

2-pound boneless turkey breast, sliced

1¾ cups chicken or turkey broth

½ cup sweet Madeira or Port

1 bay leaf

¼ cup all-purpose flour

1 teaspoon salt

½ teaspoon black pepper

1. Heat oil and 1 tablespoon butter in an uncovered pressure cooker over medium heat. Add the onion; sauté for 3 minutes or until transparent. Add the mushrooms; sauté for 3 minutes (stirring infrequently), then add garlic.

2. Push the sautéed vegetables to the sides of the pan and add the turkey breast. Cook the turkey for 3 minutes or until it browns on one side. Turn turkey and add the broth, wine, and bay leaf. Close and lock the lid.

3. Turn the heat up to high and when the cooker reaches pressure, lower the heat to the minimum needed to maintain pressure. Cook for 5–7 minutes at high pressure.

4. Open with the natural-release method—move the pressure cooker to a cool burner and wait for the pressure to come down on its own (about 15 minutes). For electric pressure cookers, disengage the "keep warm" mode or unplug the cooker. After 10 minutes, release the rest of the pressure using the valve.

5. Transfer the turkey to a serving platter and tent with foil.

6. Discard the bay leaf. Over medium heat, add flour and remaining butter to the liquid in the pressure cooker. Whisk constantly and simmer uncovered until thickened (about 5 minutes).

7. Season with salt and pepper and serve turkey breast covered with mushroom gravy.

TURKEY CACCIATORA

This dish is slightly stewy and would be perfect on a pillow of warm polenta (see Chapter 6).

INGREDIENTS
Serves 8

1 tablespoon butter

1 tablespoon olive oil

1 (12-pound) turkey cut into 8 pieces (wings, legs and thighs, and breast)

1 cup red wine

1 onion, roughly diced

1 carrot, roughly diced

1 celery stalk, roughly diced

1 clove garlic, smashed

1 28-ounce can whole tomatoes

2 teaspoons salt

1 teaspoon black pepper

2 sprigs rosemary, divided

1 sprig sage

1 cup of black salt-cured olives (Taggiesche, French, or Kalamata)

1. Heat butter and olive oil in an uncovered pressure cooker over medium heat. Brown the turkey pieces on all sides for about 5 minutes and set aside. Deglaze pan with wine and reduce until it is almost all evaporated (about 3 minutes). Add the onion, carrot, celery, and garlic. Top with turkey pieces. Pour the tomatoes over the turkey and sprinkle with salt and pepper. Add 1 rosemary sprig and sage. Close and lock the lid.

2. Turn the heat up to high and when the cooker reaches pressure, lower the heat to the minimum needed to maintain pressure. Cook for 25–30 minutes at high pressure.

3. Open with the natural-release method—move the pressure cooker to a cool burner and wait for the pressure to come down on its own (about 15 minutes). For electric pressure cookers, disengage the "keep warm" mode or unplug the cooker. After 10 minutes, release the rest of the pressure using the valve.

4. Pour black olives into cooker and stir to warm through. Transfer turkey and sauce to a serving platter and garnish with a sprig of rosemary.

TURKEY IN TARRAGON SAUCE

Serve this delicious turkey with mashed potatoes and steamed asparagus.

INGREDIENTS
Serves 4

2 slices bacon, cut in half

1 pound skinless, boneless turkey breast

1 onion, peeled and diced

2 cloves garlic, peeled and minced

½ cup dry white wine

2 tablespoons minced fresh tarragon

1 cup heavy cream

1 teaspoon salt

½ teaspoon white pepper

1. Cook the bacon in the uncovered pressure cooker over medium heat until crisp. Drain the cooked bacon on paper towels and set aside.

2. Cut the turkey into bite-sized pieces and add to the pressure cooker along with the onion. Sauté for 5 minutes or until the turkey is lightly browned and the onion is transparent. Add garlic and deglaze the pan with the wine. Close and lock the lid.

3. Turn the heat up to high and when the cooker reaches pressure, lower the heat to the minimum needed to maintain pressure. Cook for 7–9 minutes at high pressure.

4. When time is up, open the pressure cooker by releasing pressure.

5. Using a slotted spoon, transfer the cooked turkey to a serving dish and keep warm. Stir the fresh tarragon into the cooker and bring to a simmer. Stir in the cream until incorporated. Add salt and pepper.

6. Pour the sauce over the cooked turkey. Crumble the bacon over the top of the dish and serve.

Fresh Tarragon

Tarragon is a leafy herb that has a licorice flavor. Because of its strong flavor, it pairs nicely with other strong-flavored ingredients such as heavy cream. Other great herbs to use in this recipe are Italian flat-leaf parsley or dill.

TURKEY RATATOUILLE

Serve over cooked pasta or potatoes, or with thick slices of buttered French bread.

INGREDIENTS
Serves 4

1 pound skinless, boneless turkey breast

2 tablespoons olive or vegetable oil

2 medium zucchini, sliced thick

1 medium eggplant, peeled and diced

1 medium sweet onion, peeled and diced

1 medium green bell pepper, seeded and diced

½ pound mushrooms, sliced

1 28-ounce can diced tomatoes

3 tablespoons tomato paste

2 cloves garlic, peeled and minced

2 teaspoons dried basil

¼ teaspoon dried red pepper flakes

Salt and freshly ground black pepper, to taste

Parmigiano-Reggiano cheese, grated

1. Cut the turkey into bite-sized pieces. Bring the oil to temperature over medium heat. Add the turkey and fry for several minutes until it begins to brown.

2. Stir in the zucchini, eggplant, onion, bell pepper, mushrooms, undrained diced tomatoes, tomato paste, garlic, basil, and red pepper flakes.

3. Lock the lid into place. Bring to low pressure; maintain the pressure for 5 minutes. Remove from the heat and quick-release the pressure.

4. Taste for seasoning and add salt and pepper, to taste. Serve topped with grated Parmigiano-Reggiano cheese.

TURKEY THIGHS IN FIG SAUCE

Balsamic vinegar brings out the flavor of the figs in the sauce for this dish, imparting a tart wine-like flavor. If you have room in the pressure cooker, you can add 4 scrubbed Yukon Gold potatoes and cook them along with the thighs.

INGREDIENTS

Serves 4

4 ¾-pound bone-in turkey thighs, skin removed

1 large onion, peeled and quartered

2 large carrots, peeled and sliced

½ stalk celery, finely diced

½ cup balsamic vinegar

2 tablespoons tomato paste

1 cup chicken, turkey, or veal broth

Salt and freshly ground black pepper, to taste

12 dried figs, cut in half

Optional: 1 sprig fresh rosemary, chopped

1. Add the turkey and onion to the pressure cooker. Cut the carrots and celery each into several pieces; add them. Add the balsamic vinegar, tomato paste, and broth to a bowl or measuring cup; whisk to combine and then pour into the pressure cooker. Season with the salt and pepper. Add the figs. Lock the lid into place and bring to high pressure; maintain pressure for 14 minutes. Remove from the heat and allow pressure to release naturally.

2. Remove the lid. Transfer the thighs, carrots, and figs to a serving platter. Tent loosely with aluminum foil and keep warm while you finish the sauce. Strain the pan juices. Discard the onion and celery. Skim and discard any fat. Pour the resulting strained sauce over the thighs. Serve with rosemary.

Concentrated Fig Sauce

Once the turkey legs and vegetables are transferred to a serving platter, skim and discard the fat from the pan juices. Use an immersion blender to pureé the sauce. Bring to a boil over medium-high heat and cook until the sauce is syrupy.

TURKEY IN CREAMY TARRAGON SAUCE

Save some of the white wine to drink with this refined dish. Serve over cooked rice or egg noodles.

INGREDIENTS

Serves 4

4 slices bacon

1 pound skinless, boneless turkey breast

1 medium sweet onion, peeled and diced

2 cloves garlic, peeled and minced

½ cup dry white wine

2 tablespoons fresh tarragon, minced

1 cup heavy cream

Salt and freshly ground black pepper, to taste

1. Cook the bacon in the pressure cooker over medium heat until crisp. Move the cooked bacon to paper towels and set aside.

2. Cut the turkey into bite-sized pieces and add to the pressure cooker along with the onion.

3. Stir-fry for 5 minutes or until the turkey is lightly browned and the onion is transparent. Stir in the garlic and sauté for 30 seconds. Deglaze the pan with the wine.

4. Lock the lid into place and bring to low pressure; maintain low pressure for 8 minutes. Remove from the heat and allow pressure to release naturally.

5. Remove the lid. Use a slotted spoon to transfer the cooked turkey to a serving bowl; keep warm.

6. Return the pressure cooker to medium heat. Stir the fresh tarragon into the pan juices. Bring the pan juices to a simmer. Whisk in the heavy cream; simmer until the cream is heated through.

7. Taste for seasoning and add salt and pepper if desired. Pour the sauce over the cooked turkey. Crumble the bacon over the top of the dish. Serve.

'Tis the Season(ings)

If fresh tarragon isn't available, you can substitute 2 teaspoons of dried tarragon. Or use 2 teaspoons of your favorite seasoning blend, such as Mrs. Dash Onion and Herb Blend, Mrs. Dash Lemon Pepper Seasoning Blend, or Mrs. Dash Garlic and Herb Seasoning Blend. However, if you're using dried herbs, add them at the end of Step 3 instead of in Step 6.

TURKEY WITH MIXED VEGETABLES AND POTATOES

For a real casserole "feel," pour this recipe in a casserole dish, and slide it under the broiler for a few minutes to give it a brown top.

INGREDIENTS
Serves 6

1 tablespoon vegetable oil

¾ pound skinless, boneless turkey breast, cut into bite-sized pieces

2 zucchini, sliced in thick rounds

1 eggplant, peeled and diced

1 onion, peeled and diced

1 green bell pepper, seeded and diced

1 pound potatoes, roughly diced

5 tomatoes, diced (or 28-ounce can)

3 tablespoons tomato paste

2 cloves garlic, peeled and minced

2 teaspoons fresh chopped basil

1 teaspoon salt

¼ teaspoon white pepper

4 tablespoons Pecorino Romano cheese, grated

1. Heat oil in an uncovered pressure cooker over medium heat. Sauté the turkey until it begins to brown. Stir in the zucchini, eggplant, onion, bell pepper, potatoes, tomatoes, paste, garlic, and basil. Stir well. Close and lock the lid.

2. Turn the heat up to high and when the cooker reaches pressure, lower the heat to the minimum needed to maintain pressure. Cook for 5–7 minutes at high pressure.

3. When time is up, open the pressure cooker by releasing pressure.

4. Taste for seasoning and add salt and pepper. Serve topped with grated cheese.

CHAPTER 12

PORK, LAMB, HAM, AND GAME

APPLE HARVEST PORK WESTERN RIBS

Cooking the pork in beer with applesauce adds a German influence to these sandwiches. The North Carolina influence comes from the ketchup-based coleslaw served as the condiment on the sandwiches. To continue the comfort-food theme, serve with baked beans and warm German potato salad.

INGREDIENTS
Serves 12

3 pounds pork Western ribs

1 12-ounce can beer

1 cup unsweetened applesauce

1 large sweet onion, peeled and diced

2 tablespoons brown sugar

½ teaspoon freshly ground black pepper

Salt, to taste

Optional: Orange marmalade or apple jelly

12 hamburger buns

1. Add the pork to the pressure cooker. Do not trim the fat from the ribs; it's what helps the meat cook up moist enough to shred for sandwiches. A lot of the fat will melt out of the meat as it cooks.

2. Pour the beer over the pork. Add the applesauce, onion, brown sugar, black pepper, and salt. Lock the lid into place and bring to low pressure; maintain pressure for 55 minutes. Remove from heat and allow pressure to release naturally.

3. Remove the lid and use a slotted spoon to move the pork to a cutting board. Remove and discard any fat still on the meat. Use two forks to shred the meat. Skim and discard any fat from the top of the pan juices. Stir the shredded pork back into the sauce. Place the pressure cooker over medium heat and bring to a simmer. Taste for seasoning; stir in orange marmalade or apple jelly a tablespoon at a time if you prefer a sweeter barbecue.

4. Spoon the meat onto hamburger buns. Top the meat with a heaping tablespoon of North Carolina–Style Coleslaw.

North Carolina–Style Coleslaw
Add ¾ cup cider vinegar, 1 tablespoon ketchup, 1 tablespoon brown sugar, 1 teaspoon salt, ⅛ teaspoon dried red pepper flakes, and ¾ teaspoon freshly ground black pepper to a large bowl. Whisk to mix, and then stir in a 2-pound bag of coleslaw mix. Add hot sauce, to taste.

BALSAMIC PORK CHOPS WITH FIGS

Serve with baked potatoes, a steamed vegetable, and a tossed salad topped with diced apples and toasted walnuts.

INGREDIENTS
Serves 4

4 1-inch-thick bone-in pork loin chops

Salt and freshly ground black pepper, to taste

2 teaspoons butter or ghee

2 teaspoons extra-virgin olive oil

2 medium sweet onions, peeled and sliced

4 cloves garlic, peeled and minced

½ teaspoon dried thyme

3 tablespoons balsamic vinegar

2 tablespoons dry white wine

½ cup chicken broth

10 ounces dried figs

1. Lightly season the pork chops on both sides by sprinkling them with salt and pepper. Add the butter or ghee and oil to the pressure cooker and bring to temperature over medium-high heat. Add 2 pork chops; brown for 3 minutes on each side. Move chops to a plate and repeat with the other 2 chops. Remove those chops to the plate.

2. Add the onions; sauté for 4 minutes or until the onions are transparent. Stir in the garlic; sauté for 30 seconds. Stir in the thyme and balsamic vinegar. Cook uncovered until the vinegar is reduced by half. Stir in the wine and broth. Add the pork chops, spooning some of the onions over the chops. Place the figs on top.

3. Lock the lid into place and bring to high pressure; maintain pressure for 9 minutes. Remove from the heat and quick-release the pressure. Serve immediately.

Make a Syrupy Sauce
Use a slotted spoon to transfer the pork chops, onions, and figs to a serving platter; cover and keep warm. Return the pressure cooker to medium-high heat. Simmer, uncovered, for 5 minutes or until the pan juices are reduced and coat the back of a spoon. Pour over the pork chops, onions, and figs on the serving platter.

BARBECUE PORK RIBS

By the time this pressure finishes, the meat on these ribs will be falling off the bone. Use this as a standalone dish or for pork sandwiches.

INGREDIENTS

Serves 4

1 cup barbecue sauce

½ cup apple jelly

1 (3") cinnamon stick

6 whole cloves

1 large onion, peeled and diced

1 cup water

3 pounds pork western ribs

1. Add the barbecue sauce, jelly, cinnamon stick, cloves, onion, and water to the pressure cooker. Stir to mix. Add the ribs, ladling some of the sauce over them. Close and lock the lid.

2. Turn the heat up to high and when the cooker reaches pressure, lower the heat to the minimum needed to maintain pressure. Cook for 10–15 minutes at high pressure.

3. Open with the natural-release method—move the pressure cooker to a cool burner and wait for the pressure to come down on its own (about 15 minutes). For electric pressure cookers, disengage the "keep warm" mode or unplug the cooker and open when the pressure indicator has gone down (20–30 minutes).

4. Remove the meat and bones to a serving platter; cover with foil and keep warm. Skim any fat from the sauce in the cooker. Remove and discard the cinnamon stick and cloves.

5. Return the pressure cooker to medium-high heat and simmer uncovered for 15 minutes or until the sauce is reduced to desired thickness. Either remove the meat from the bones and stir back into the sauce or pour the sauce into a gravy boat and pass at the table.

BEER BBQ PORK SLIDERS WITH APPLE

Beer and apples provide a tangy sweetness to these already delicious sandwiches. Serve with a salad or North Carolina–style coleslaw.

INGREDIENTS
Serves 6

1½ pounds pork western ribs

½ cup beer

1 apple, peeled, cored, and roughly sliced

1 onion, peeled and diced

1 teaspoon raw sugar

1 teaspoon salt

½ teaspoon black pepper

12 whole-wheat slider buns or 6 whole-wheat hamburger buns

1. Place ribs in the pressure cooker. Pour in beer and add the apple, onion, sugar, salt, and pepper. Close and lock the lid.

2. Turn the heat up to high and when the cooker reaches pressure, lower the heat to the minimum needed to maintain pressure. Cook for 15–20 minutes at high pressure.

3. Open with the natural-release method—move the pressure cooker to a cool burner and wait for the pressure to come down on its own (about 15 minutes). For electric pressure cookers, disengage the "keep warm" mode or unplug the cooker and open when the pressure indicator has gone down (20–30 minutes).

4. Remove the meat and bones using a slotted spoon to move the pork to a cutting board. Remove and discard any fat still on the meat. Use two forks to shred the meat.

5. Skim and discard any fat from the top of the pan juices. Blend the contents of the pressure cooker, using an immersion blender. Stir the shredded pork back into the cooker and simmer, uncovered on medium heat for 5 minutes. Spoon onto buns and serve.

BUBBLE AND SQUEAK

Adding some ham and bacon to this traditional British dish makes it a complete meal, even if you choose to serve it without a salad. For variety, you can add some chopped celery and grated carrots, too.

INGREDIENTS
Serves 6

6 slices bacon, cut into pieces

1 medium yellow onion, peeled and diced

1 zucchini, grated

3 large potatoes, scrubbed and diced

8 ounces cooked ham, diced

1 small head cabbage, cored and chopped

Salt and freshly ground black pepper, to taste

1. Add the bacon pieces to the pressure cooker; fry until just beginning to crisp over medium-high heat.

2. Reduce heat to medium and add the onion; sauté for 3 minutes or until the onion is softened. Add the zucchini and potatoes and stir into the onion and bacon.

3. Lock the lid into place and bring to low pressure; maintain pressure for 3 minutes. Remove from heat, quick-release the pressure, and remove the lid.

4. Mash the potatoes into the bacon and onions. Spread the ham over the potato mixture, then spread the cabbage over the ham.

5. Lock the lid into place and bring to high pressure; maintain pressure for 3 minutes. Remove from the heat and allow pressure to release naturally. Remove the lid.

6. If necessary, place the pan over low heat until any excess moisture from the cabbage and zucchini evaporates. Add salt and pepper, to taste. To serve, invert onto a serving plate.

CASSOULET

Cassoulet is a simple dish that perfectly melds the flavors of succulent meats and beans. Serve over or with thick slices of toasted French bread.

INGREDIENTS
Serves 8

1 pound dried white beans, rinsed and drained

6 cups cold water

5 cups chicken broth

2 tablespoons olive or vegetable oil

4 whole cloves

1 small white or yellow onion, peeled

2 bay leaves

2 teaspoons dried parsley

½ teaspoon dried thyme

2 large whole bone-in chicken breasts

4 slices bacon, diced

1 large sweet onion, peeled and diced

1 clove garlic, peeled and minced

1 8-ounce package brown-and-serve sausage links

1 14-ounce can diced tomatoes

Optional: Dry white wine, or additional broth or water

1. Soak the beans overnight in the water; drain. Add the beans, chicken broth, and 1 tablespoon oil to the pressure cooker. Place over medium-high heat and bring to a boil.

2. Push the cloves into the onion and add it to the pressure cooker along with the bay leaves, parsley, and thyme. Lock the lid into place and bring to high pressure; maintain pressure for 10 minutes. Remove from the heat and allow pressure to release naturally while you prepare the other ingredients.

3. Quarter each chicken breast. Rub each chicken breast piece with the remaining oil.

4. Remove the lid from the pressure cooker and transfer the beans and broth to a bowl. Cover and keep warm.

5. Wipe out the pressure cooker. Return it to medium-high heat and add the bacon. Fry the bacon until it begins to brown. Add 4 chicken breast quarters. Brown for 5 minutes. Transfer the chicken and cooked bacon to the bowl with the beans. Repeat with the remaining 4 chicken breast pieces.

6. Add the onion; sauté for 3 minutes. Add the garlic; sauté for 30 seconds. Carefully transfer the beans, broth, and browned chicken pieces to the pressure cooker. Add the sausage links and tomatoes. If necessary, add enough white wine, broth, or water to cover the ingredients in the pressure cooker completely.

7. Lock the lid into place and bring to high pressure; maintain pressure for 10 minutes. Remove from heat and allow pressure to release naturally. Remove the lid. Remove and discard the onion studded with cloves and the bay leaves. Transfer the sausage links to a soup tureen. Remove the chicken meat from the bones and add that to the tureen; discard the skin and bones. Mash some of the beans into the pan juices to thicken the sauce and then pour into the tureen. Carefully stir to mix. Taste for seasoning and add salt and pepper if needed.

GERMAN PORK CHOPS AND SAUERKRAUT

Bavarian seasoning is a mix of a blend of Bavarian-style crushed brown mustard seeds, French rosemary, garlic, Dalmatian sage, French thyme, and bay leaves.

INGREDIENTS

Serves 4

1 stalk celery, finely chopped

1 1-pound bag baby carrots

1 large onion, peeled and sliced

1 clove garlic, peeled and minced

4 slices bacon, cut into small pieces

4 1-inch-thick bone-in pork loin chops

1 1-pound bag sauerkraut, rinsed and drained

4 medium red potatoes, peeled and quartered

1 12-ounce can beer

2 teaspoons Bavarian seasoning

Salt and freshly ground pepper, to taste

1. Add the ingredients to the pressure cooker in the order given. Lock the lid in place. Bring to high pressure; maintain pressure for 9 minutes.

2. Remove from the heat and allow pressure to release naturally. Taste for seasoning and adjust if necessary. Serve hot.

GINGER SOY PORK CHOPS WITH BROCCOLI AND RICE

An easy, and unexpected, one-pot meal.

INGREDIENTS
Serves 4

4 boneless pork chops

2 tablespoons soy sauce

½ cup unsweetened pineapple juice

1 tablespoon apple cider vinegar

1 teaspoon raw sugar

1 tablespoon fresh gingerroot, minced

2 cups frozen broccoli florets

1 cup long-grain white rice, rinsed and strained

1½ cups chicken broth

1. Place pork chops in a zip-closure bag and add soy sauce, pineapple juice, cider vinegar, sugar, and ginger. Seal bag and refrigerate for up to 2 hours. Empty the entire contents of the bag into the pressure cooker and discard bag. Close and lock the lid.

2. Turn the heat up to high and when the cooker reaches pressure, lower the heat to the minimum needed to maintain pressure. Cook for 6–8 minutes at high pressure.

3. When time is up, open the pressure cooker by releasing pressure.

4. Add broccoli, rice, and broth. Close and lock the lid.

5. Turn the heat up to high and when the cooker reaches pressure, lower the heat to the minimum needed to maintain pressure. Cook for 3 minutes at low pressure.

6. Open with the natural-release method—move the pressure cooker to a cool burner and wait for the pressure to come down on its own (about 15 minutes). For electric pressure cookers, disengage the "keep warm" mode or unplug the cooker. After 10 minutes, release the rest of the pressure using the valve.

7. Serve immediately.

GROUND PORK AND EGGPLANT CASSEROLE

Ground black pepper contains anticaking agents that can cause stomach upset for some people and can also change the flavor of your dish. That's why dishes always taste better when you grind the pepper yourself. Serve with a tossed salad and toasted garlic bread.

INGREDIENTS
Serves 8

2 pounds lean ground pork

1 large yellow onion, peeled and diced

1 stalk celery, diced

1 green pepper, seeded and diced

4 cloves garlic, peeled and minced

2 medium eggplants, cut into ½-inch dice

⅛ teaspoon dried thyme, crushed

1 tablespoon freeze-dried parsley

3 tablespoons tomato paste

Optional: 1 teaspoon hot sauce

2 teaspoons Worcestershire sauce

Salt and freshly ground pepper, to taste

1 large egg, beaten

½ cup chicken broth

1. Bring the pressure cooker to temperature over medium-high heat. Add the ground pork, onion, celery, and green pepper to the pressure cooker and stir-fry until the pork is no longer pink, breaking it apart as it cooks.

2. Drain and discard any fat rendered from the meat. Add the garlic, eggplants, thyme, parsley, tomato paste, hot sauce (if using), Worcestershire sauce, salt, pepper, and egg; stir to combine.

3. Pour in the chicken broth. Lock the lid into place and bring to low pressure; maintain pressure for 10 minutes. Remove from heat and allow pressure to release naturally.

JAMBALAYA

There are as many versions of Jambalaya as there are Southern cooks. Originally created as a dish to use up leftovers, it's a versatile recipe that you can adjust according to your tastes.

INGREDIENTS
Serves 6

2 tablespoons bacon fat or peanut oil

1 large carrot, peeled and grated

1 stalk celery, finely diced

1 large green bell pepper, seeded and chopped

1 medium yellow onion, peeled and diced

2 green onions, chopped

2 cloves garlic, minced

½ pound pork steak

½ pound boneless, skinless chicken thighs

½ pound smoked sausage, thinly sliced

½ pound cooked ham, diced

1 15-ounce can diced tomatoes, drained

2 cups chicken broth

½ tablespoon dried parsley

½ teaspoon dried thyme

¼ teaspoon hot sauce, or to taste

2 tablespoons Worcestershire sauce

½ pound shrimp, peeled and deveined

Salt and freshly ground pepper to taste

6 servings cooked long-grain brown rice

1. Add the bacon fat or oil to the pressure cooker and bring it to temperature over medium heat.

2. Add the grated carrot, celery, and green bell pepper to the pan; sauté for 3 to 5 minutes or until soft. Add the yellow and green onions and sauté until transparent.

3. Add the garlic and sauté for an additional 30 seconds. Cut the pork and chicken into bite-sized pieces. Add to the pressure cooker and stir-fry for 3 minutes.

4. Stir in the smoked sausage and stir-fry for 3 minutes; add the ham and stir-fry for 1 minute.

5. Stir in the tomatoes, broth, parsley, thyme, hot sauce, and Worcestershire sauce. Lock the lid into place and bring to low pressure; maintain pressure for 8 minutes.

6. Quick-release the pressure. If the shrimp are large, halve them; otherwise, add the shrimp to the pot, cover, and cook over medium heat for 3 to 5 minutes or until shrimp are cooked.

7. Taste for seasoning and add salt and pepper if needed. Serve over the rice or stir the rice into the Jambalaya.

Pressure-Cooked Long-Grain Brown Rice

For 6 servings, add 1 cup long-grain brown rice, 2 cups water or broth, 1 tablespoon oil or butter, and 1 teaspoon salt to a pressure cooker over high heat. Lock the lid and bring to low pressure; maintain pressure for 20 minutes. Remove pan from heat and let sit for 10 minutes. Quick-release any remaining pressure, remove lid, and fluff rice.

MILK-BRAISED PORK LOIN

This recipe is adapted from Marcella Hazan's "Pork Lois Braised in Milk" roast (from The Classic Italian Cookbook*). Hazan's pork loin simmers for an hour and a half! Yours will be ready in just 30 minutes.*

INGREDIENTS
Serves 6

1 tablespoon butter

2 tablespoons olive oil

2-pound pork loin in one piece, with some fat on it, securely tied

2 teaspoons salt

1 teaspoon white pepper

1 bay leaf

2½ cups whole milk

1. Heat butter and olive oil in an uncovered pressure cooker over medium heat. When the butter is melted, add the pork loin, fat-side facing down. Brown thoroughly on all sides, and finish on the side where you began. Add the salt, pepper, and bay leaf. Pour in the milk. If the roast is not covered to the halfway mark, add more milk. Close and lock the lid.

2. Turn the heat up to high and when the cooker reaches pressure, lower the heat to the minimum needed to maintain pressure. Cook for 25–30 minutes at high pressure.

3. Open with the natural-release method—move the pressure cooker to a cool burner and wait for the pressure to come down on its own (about 15 minutes). For electric pressure cookers, disengage the "keep warm" mode or unplug the cooker and open when the pressure indicator has gone down (20–30 minutes).

4. Move the roast to a serving dish tented with tin foil to rest.

5. Discard the bay leaf and reduce the cooking liquid in the uncovered pressure cooker over medium heat for about 5 minutes.

6. Slice the roast and arrange on platter. Pour the warm sauce over the slices and serve.

Curdled Milk?

When the roast is finished cooking, there will be what look like chunks of curdled milk. It's not. It's coagulated milk and they are little bundles of concentrated flavor. If they are not aesthetically pleasing, simply disintegrate them into the rest of the cooking liquid by using an immersion blender.

PORK AND BEANS

If the meat or beans are not tender enough, cover and simmer for 15 more minutes, or lock the lid, bring back to high pressure, and cook at high pressure for another 3 minutes.

INGREDIENTS
Serves 6

2 teaspoons paprika

1 teaspoon garlic powder

¼ teaspoon ground black pepper

½ teaspoon onion powder

⅛ teaspoon cayenne

¼ teaspoon dried oregano

¼ teaspoon dried thyme

2½ pounds pork shoulder, cut into 1½-inch pieces

1½ tablespoons vegetable oil

1 large yellow onion, peeled and diced

6 cups chicken broth or water

2 cups dried white beans, such as great northern or navy

½ pound salt pork or bacon, cut into pieces

1 15-ounce can diced tomatoes

4 cloves garlic, peeled and minced

½ cup packed light brown sugar

2 tablespoons whole grain or Creole mustard

2 teaspoons chili powder

¼ teaspoon salt

1 bay leaf

¼ teaspoon dried thyme

1. Add the paprika, garlic powder, pepper, onion powder, cayenne, oregano, and thyme to a gallon-sized plastic bag; shake to mix. Add the pork pieces and shake the bag to season the meat on all sides. Add the oil to the pressure cooker and bring it to temperature over medium-high heat. Add the pork and stir-fry for about 2 minutes per side or until it just begins to brown. Move the meat to a plate and set aside.

2. Add the onion to the cooker; reduce heat to medium and sauté for 2 minutes or until tender. Add the broth or water.

3. Remove any stones or impurities from the beans, and then stir them into the liquid in the cooker, scraping up any browned bits off the bottom of the pot. (This is important because browned bits that remain on the pan bottom could burn during the pressure process, imparting an unpleasant burnt flavor to the final dish.)

4. Lock the lid into place on the pressure cooker. Bring to high pressure; maintain pressure for 15 minutes.

5. Turn off the burner; leave the pressure cooker in place until it returns to normal pressure. Once the pressure is released, carefully remove the lid to allow excess steam to escape.

6. Add the salt pork, tomatoes, garlic, light brown sugar, mustard, chili powder, salt, bay leaf, thyme, and reserved pork to the cooker; stir to combine. Lock the lid into place; bring the pressure cooker to high pressure and maintain pressure for 15 minutes.

7. Remove from heat and let sit for 10 minutes. Quick-release any remaining pressure and remove the lid.

8. Check for seasoning, and add salt and pepper if needed. Remove and discard the bay leaf. Serve.

PORK LOIN WITH CORNBREAD AND CRANBERRY-PECAN STUFFING

To make apple-walnut stuffing, omit the dried cranberries, apple juice, and pecans. Peel, core, and grate an apple. Substitute chopped walnuts for the pecans. For added moisture, add apple juice or water as needed.

INGREDIENTS
Serves 4

2 tablespoons dried cranberries

2 tablespoons apple juice

2 strips bacon, diced

1 small stalk celery, finely diced

1 small onion, peeled and diced

1 cup cornbread stuffing mix

2 tablespoons pecans, toasted and chopped

1 large egg, beaten

Pinch nutmeg, freshly grated

Salt and freshly ground black pepper, to taste

4 1-inch-thick pork chops

1 tablespoon olive or vegetable oil

1 tablespoon butter

½ cup chicken broth

1. Put the dried cranberries and apple juice in a microwave-safe bowl. Cover and microwave on high for 1 minute to soften the cranberries. Set aside.

2. Fry the bacon in the pressure cooker over medium-high heat until it begins to render its fat. Add the celery; sauté for 2 minutes. Add the onion; sauté for 3 minutes. Pour the contents of the pressure cooker into a bowl.

3. Use a paper towel to blot up some of the excess bacon fat. Mix in the cranberries and apple juice, cornbread stuffing mix, pecans, egg, nutmeg, salt, and pepper. The cornbread stuffing mixture should be moist, but not wet. If some of the stuffing mix is still dry, add apple juice or water a teaspoon at a time until moistened.

4. Trim and discard any excess fat from the pork chops. Cut a pocket into each one, slicing from the outside edge to the bone. Fill each pork chop with a fourth of the stuffing mixture. Press to close. Season each side of the pork chops with salt and pepper.

5. Bring the oil and butter to temperature over medium heat in the pressure cooker. Add the pork chops and brown well on both sides. Pour the broth into the bottom of the pan.

6. Lock the lid into place and bring to high pressure; maintain pressure for 15 minutes. Remove the pressure cooker from the heat, quick-release the pressure, and remove the lid. Serve.

PORK ROAST WITH ROOT BEER GRAVY

Only use regular (not diet) root beer in this recipe. Soft drinks made with artificial sweeteners cannot withstand the heat of the pressure cooker.

INGREDIENTS
Serves 6

1 10-ounce can golden cream of mushroom soup

1 12-ounce can root beer

1 1-ounce envelope dry onion soup mix

1 3-pound pork roast

1. Add the soup, root beer, and onion soup mix to the pressure cooker. Stir to mix. Add the pork roast.

2. Lock the lid in place. Bring to low pressure; maintain pressure for 45 minutes. Remove from the heat and allow pressure to release naturally.

3. Transfer the roast to a serving platter; let rest for 5 minutes before slicing.

4. Skim any fat from the gravy in the pressure cooker. Stir to mix and then transfer to a gravy boat or pour over the sliced meat.

PORK SAUSAGE WITH BELL PEPPERS AND ONIONS

Use a combination of spicy Italian sausage, bratwurst, or mild sausage links, if desired.

INGREDIENTS
Serves 6

6 pork sausages

½ tablespoon vegetable oil

1 large green bell pepper, seeded and sliced

1 large red bell pepper, seeded and sliced

1 large yellow bell pepper, seeded and sliced

1 large onion, sliced

2 cloves garlic, minced

⅓ cup chicken stock

1. Poke each sausage several times with a fork.

2. Heat oil in an uncovered pressure cooker over medium heat. Add half the sausages to the pressure cooker and brown for about 5 minutes. Remove to a plate and brown the remaining sausages. Discard all but one tablespoon of rendered fat in the pressure cooker. Add the peppers and onion and sauté for about 3 minutes or until they begin to soften. Add garlic and return the sausages to the pressure cooker, pushing them down into the peppers and onions. Pour in the stock. Close and lock the lid.

3. Turn the heat up to high and when the cooker reaches pressure, lower the heat to the minimum needed to maintain pressure. Cook for 5–8 minutes at high pressure.

4. When time is up, open the pressure cooker by releasing pressure.

5. Serve with a slotted spoon.

PORK STEAK IN FRUIT SAUCE

Serve this dish over some mashed potatoes and alongside some steam-in-the-bag green beans.

INGREDIENTS

Serves 6

8 pitted prunes

4 8-ounce pork steaks, trimmed of fat

2 small Granny Smith apples, peeled, cored, and sliced

½ cup dry white wine or apple juice

½ cup heavy cream

Salt and freshly ground pepper, to taste

1 tablespoon red currant jelly

Optional: 1 tablespoon butter

1. Add the prunes, pork steaks, apple slices, wine or apple juice, and cream to the pressure cooker. Salt and pepper to taste.

2. Lock the lid into place and bring to high pressure; maintain pressure for 9 minutes. Quick-release the pressure.

3. Remove the meat and fruit to a serving platter. Either leave the pan juices as they are and keep them warm or skim the fat from the liquid in the pressure cooker and use an immersion blender to blend the fruit into the creamy broth.

4. Leave the pressure cooker on the heat and simmer uncovered for 10 minutes or until the mixture is reduced by half and thickened. Whisk in the red currant jelly. Taste for seasoning and add more salt and pepper if needed. Whisk in the butter a teaspoon at a time if you want a richer, glossier sauce. Ladle the sauce over the meat or pour it into a heated gravy boat.

ROAST PORK WITH CINNAMON CRANBERRIES AND SWEET POTATOES

This dish is worthy of a holiday dinner party. Serve with a tossed salad, steamed vegetables, and dinner rolls.

INGREDIENTS
Serves 6

1 3-pound pork butt roast

Salt and freshly ground pepper, to taste

1 16-ounce can sweetened whole cranberries

1 medium onion, peeled and diced

¼ cup orange marmalade

½ cup orange juice

¼ teaspoon ground cinnamon

⅛ teaspoon ground cloves

3 large sweet potatoes, peeled and quartered

Optional: 1 tablespoon cornstarch

Optional: 2 tablespoons cold water

1. Place the pork, fat-side down, in the pressure cooker. Salt and pepper to taste. Combine the cranberries, onion, marmalade, orange juice, cinnamon, and cloves in a large measuring cup; stir to mix and then pour over the pork roast.

2. Arrange the sweet potatoes around the meat. Lock the lid into place and bring to low pressure; maintain pressure for 45 minutes. Remove from heat and allow pressure to release naturally.

3. To serve with a thickened sauce, transfer the meat and sweet potatoes to a serving platter. Cover and keep warm. Skim any fat off of the pan juices, making sure you have 2 cups of juice remaining in the cooker.

4. Return the pressure cooker to medium heat. Combine the cornstarch with the water. Whisk into the liquid in the pressure cooker; simmer and stir for 2 minutes, or the cornstarch flavor has cooked out of the sauce and it is thickened and bubbly.

ROSEMARY PORK SHOULDER WITH APPLES

Using apple juice gives you a sweeter sauce than white wine. Substitute water for the white wine if you want the apples to remain tart. Serve with fried potatoes, a steamed vegetable, and crusty bread or dinner rolls.

INGREDIENTS

Serves 6

1 3½-pound pork shoulder roast

3 tablespoons Dijon mustard

1 tablespoon olive or vegetable oil

½ cup dry white wine, apple juice, or water

2 tart apples, peeled and quartered

3 cloves garlic, peeled and minced

Salt and freshly ground black pepper, to taste

1 teaspoon dried rosemary

1. Coat all sides of the roast with the mustard. Bring the oil to temperature in the pressure cooker over medium-high heat. Add the pork roast; brown the roast on all sides, reducing the heat if necessary to avoid burning the mustard

2. Pour the wine, apple juice, or water around the roast. Working around the roast, use the liquid to deglaze the pan, scraping up any browned bits sticking to the bottom of the pan. Add the apples, garlic, salt, pepper, and rosemary.

3. Lock the lid into place and bring to low pressure; maintain pressure for 45 minutes. Remove from heat and allow pressure to release naturally.

4. Remove the lid. Use a meat thermometer to measure whether the roast has reached an internal temperature of 160°F.

5. Remove the roast to a serving platter. Tent and keep warm while you use an immersion blender to pureé the pan contents. Slice the roast and pour the pureéd juices over the slices. Serve.

SAUSAGES WITH SAUTÉED ONIONS AND GREEN PEPPERS

For this recipe, you can use your choice of 8 bratwurst, 8 Italian sausages, or 16 breakfast sausage links. Serve in steamed or toasted sandwich rolls.

INGREDIENTS
Serves 8

8 sausages

1 tablespoon olive oil

1 large green bell pepper, seeded and sliced

1 large red bell pepper, seeded and sliced

1 large orange bell pepper, seeded and sliced

1 large yellow bell pepper, seeded and sliced

2 large sweet onions, peeled and sliced

2 cloves garlic, peeled and minced

½ cup chicken broth

1. Add half of the sausages to the pressure cooker and brown them over medium-high heat. Remove them to a plate and brown the remaining sausages.

2. Drain and discard any rendered fat in the pressure cooker. Add the olive oil and bring it to temperature. Add the sliced peppers; sauté for 3 minutes or until they begin to get soft. Add the onion slices; sauté for 3 minutes or until the onions are transparent. Add the garlic; sauté for 30 seconds.

3. Return the sausages to the pressure cooker, pushing them down into the peppers and onions. Pour in the broth. Lock the lid into place and bring to high pressure; maintain pressure for 4 minutes. Quick-release the pressure. Serve.

Sausages in Marinara Sauce
Whether you want to serve them in sandwiches or over cooked pasta, these sausages benefit from the addition of a tablespoon of Italian herb blend during the cooking process. To make it even better, stir them into some marinara sauce.

SESAME PORK WITH PINEAPPLE

This dish is similar to the classic Chinese restaurant favorite, Sweet and Sour Pork. Serve it with Chinese noodles or steamed white rice.

INGREDIENTS
Serves 6

1 14-ounce can pineapple chunks

2 pounds pork shoulder

1 tablespoon all-purpose flour

2 tablespoons sesame oil

1 tablespoon raw sugar

⅛ teaspoon mustard powder

½ teaspoon ground ginger

2 tablespoons apple cider vinegar

1 tablespoon soy sauce

4 medium carrots, peeled and sliced

1 large red bell pepper, seeded and diced into 1" pieces

½ pound fresh sugar snap peas

1½ cups fresh broccoli florets, cut into bite-sized pieces

2 cloves garlic, peeled and thinly sliced

1 large onion, peeled and sliced

2 tablespoons cornstarch

2 tablespoons cold water

¼ cup bean sprouts

1 tablespoon sesame seeds

1. Drain pineapple, reserving juice. Set both aside.

2. Cut the pork into bite-sized pieces. Add to a zip-closure bag along with the flour; seal and shake to coat the pork in the flour. Remove pork from bag with tongs and shake off excess flour (too much flour in the cooker could prevent it from reaching pressure).

3. Heat oil in an uncovered pressure cooker over medium heat. Sauté the pork for 3 minutes or until it begins to brown. Deglaze the pan with the pineapple juice; stir and scrape up any bits stuck to the bottom of the pan. Add the sugar, mustard powder, ginger, vinegar, soy sauce, carrots, red pepper, peas, broccoli, garlic, and onion. Close and lock the lid.

4. Turn the heat up to high and when the cooker reaches pressure, lower the heat to the minimum needed to maintain pressure. Cook for 18–20 minutes at high pressure.

5. When time is up, open the pressure cooker by releasing pressure.

6. Using a slotted spoon, remove pork and vegetables to a serving bowl and keep warm.

7. To make the glaze, mix together the cornstarch and water in a small bowl. Stir in some of the pan juices. Put the pressure cooker over medium heat. Bring pan juices to a boil and whisk in the cornstarch mixture.

8. Reduce the heat to maintain a simmer for 3 minutes or until the mixture is thickened. Stir in the bean sprouts and reserved pineapple chunks. Pour over the cooked pork and vegetables in the serving bowl; stir to combine.

9. Sprinkle with sesame seeds and serve.

STUFFED ACORN SQUASH

The hash browns, peas, and sausage will be easier to mix together if the hash browns and peas are still frozen (but broken apart) and the sausage is at room temperature.

INGREDIENTS
Serves 2

1 acorn squash

½ cup frozen country-style hash browns

¼ cup frozen peas

½ pound pork sausage

2 teaspoons extra-virgin olive oil

Salt and freshly ground black pepper to taste

½ cup water

Optional: 2 poached or fried eggs

1. Cut the squash in half lengthwise and scrape out the seeds. Use a fork to prick the inside of each squash half, being careful not to pierce the skin.

2. In a bowl, mix together the hash browns, peas, and sausage. Divide the mixture between the squash halves. Drizzle 1 teaspoon oil over each stuffed squash half. Season with salt and pepper to taste.

3. Place the rack in the pressure cooker. Pour the water into the pressure cooker and then carefully place the squash halves on the rack.

4. Lock the lid into place and bring to high temperature; maintain pressure for 12 minutes. Remove from the heat and allow pressure to release naturally.

5. Use tongs and a spatula to move each squash half to serving plates. Top each with an egg if desired. Serve.

SWEET AND SOUR PORK

Serve over cooked rice or Chinese noodles. Have soy sauce and toasted sesame oil available at the table.

INGREDIENTS
Serves 8

2 pounds pork shoulder

1 tablespoon all-purpose flour

2 tablespoons sesame or peanut oil

1 14-ounce can pineapple chunks

1 tablespoon light brown sugar

⅛ teaspoon mustard powder

½ teaspoon ground ginger

2 tablespoons apple cider vinegar

1 tablespoon low-sodium soy sauce

4 medium carrots, peeled and sliced

1 large red bell pepper, seeded and sliced

½ pound fresh sugar snap peas

2 cups fresh broccoli florets

2 cloves garlic, peeled and thinly sliced

2 large sweet onions, peeled and diced

2 tablespoons cornstarch

2 tablespoons cold water

1 cup bean sprouts

1. Cut the pork into bite-sized pieces. Add to a zip-closure bag along with the flour; seal and shake to coat the pork in the flour.

2. Bring the oil to temperature in the pressure cooker over medium-high heat. Fry the pork for 3 minutes or until it begins to brown. Add the pineapple juice and reserve the pineapple chunks; stir and scrape up any bits stuck to the bottom of the pan.

3. Add the sugar, mustard powder, ginger, vinegar, soy sauce, carrots, red bell pepper, and sugar snap peas. Cut the broccoli florets into bite-sized pieces and add them to the pressure cooker. Add garlic and ¾ onion. Lock the lid into place and bring to low pressure; maintain pressure for 12 minutes.

4. Quick-release the pressure. Use a slotted spoon to transfer all solids from the pressure cooker to a serving bowl; keep warm.

5. To make the glaze, in a small bowl mix together the cornstarch and water. Stir in some of the pan juices. Put the pressure cooker over medium heat. Bring to a boil and then whisk in the cornstarch mixture.

6. Reduce the heat to maintain a simmer for 3 minutes or until the mixture is thickened and the raw cornstarch taste is cooked out of the glaze. Stir in the bean sprouts, reserved pineapple chunks, and onion. Pour over the cooked pork and vegetables in the serving bowl; stir to combine. Serve.

VIETNAMESE PORK CURRY

Pork is one of the most popular meats in Vietnamese dishes. It perfectly picks up the spicy sweetness of this sauce. Serve Vietnamese Pork Curry over cooked rice.

INGREDIENTS
Serves 6

2 pounds boneless pork steaks

1 tablespoon peanut or vegetable oil

1 medium onion, peeled and diced

3 cloves garlic, peeled and minced

1 large eggplant, peeled and diced

1 jalapeño pepper, seeded and diced

3 carrots, peeled and sliced

2 medium waxy potatoes, peeled and diced

1 tablespoon sugar

1 tablespoon fresh ginger, grated

1 teaspoon curry powder

1 star anise

1 cup chicken broth or water

½ diced tomatoes

¼ cup fish sauce

1 tablespoon cold water

1 tablespoon cornstarch

6 green onions

¼ cup fresh cilantro

1. Trim and discard the fat from the pork steaks; cut steaks into bite-sized pieces. Set aside.

2. Bring the oil to temperature in the pressure cooker over medium-high heat. Add the onion; sauté for 3 minutes. Add the garlic; sauté for 30 seconds.

3. Stir in the pork steak, eggplant, jalapeño pepper, carrots, potatoes, sugar, ginger, curry powder, star anise, broth or water, tomatoes, and fish sauce.

4. Lock the lid into place and bring to high pressure; maintain pressure for 20 minutes. Quick-release the pressure. Remove the lid. Remove and discard the star anise.

5. Stir together the water and cornstarch in a small bowl. Whisk into the pork mixture in the pressure cooker.

6. Cook, uncovered, for 5 minutes, stirring until mixture is thickened and bubbly. Stir in the green onions and cilantro. Serve immediately.

GREEK MEATBALLS IN TOMATO SAUCE

You can serve the meatballs and sauce over pasta, beans, or a combination of both. Serve with pita and a salad tossed with a lemon and extra-virgin olive oil vinaigrette and topped with some feta cheese.

INGREDIENTS

Serves 8

1½ pounds lean ground beef or lamb

1 cup uncooked rice

1 small yellow onion, peeled and finely chopped

3 cloves garlic, peeled and minced

2 teaspoons dried parsley

½ tablespoon dried oregano

1 egg

All-purpose flour

2 cups tomato juice or tomato-vegetable juice

1 14-ounce can diced tomatoes

Optional: Water, as needed

2 tablespoons extra-virgin olive oil

Salt and freshly ground black pepper, to taste

1. Make the meatballs by mixing the ground beef or lamb together with the rice, onion, garlic, parsley, oregano, and egg; shape into small meatballs and roll each one in flour.

2. Add the tomato or tomato-vegetable juice and can of diced tomatoes to the pressure cooker. Carefully add the meatballs. If necessary, pour in enough water to completely cover the meatballs, making sure not to take the liquid above the fill line. Add the oil.

3. Lock the lid into place and bring to low pressure; maintain pressure for 10 minutes. Remove from heat and allow pressure to release naturally for 10 minutes. Quick-release any remaining pressure and remove the lid. Taste for seasoning and add salt and pepper if needed.

MEDITERRANEAN BRAISED LAMB SHANKS

Serve over creamy polenta.

INGREDIENTS
Serves 4

2 tablespoons flour

1 teaspoon salt

½ teaspoon ground black pepper

4 large lamb shanks, trimmed (3 pounds)

1 tablespoon olive oil

1 red onion, peeled and chopped

1 carrot, peeled and chopped

2 stalks celery, chopped

½ cup red wine

2 garlic cloves, thinly sliced

2 red bell peppers, seeded and cut into thick 1" strips

3 zucchini, thickly sliced into 1" rounds

1 eggplant, cut into 1" dice

5 fresh roma tomatoes, halved (or one 28-ounce can whole stewed tomatoes)

1 tablespoon tomato paste

½ cup vegetable stock

1 bunch fresh basil, torn

1. Put the flour, salt, black pepper, and lamb in a large plastic bag and shake to coat. Heat olive oil in an uncovered pressure cooker over medium heat. Brown the shanks on all sides and set aside. Add the onion, carrot, and celery and sauté until softened (about 5 minutes).

2. Deglaze the pressure cooker with the wine and let the liquid almost completely evaporate. Return the shanks to the cooker, along with the rest of the ingredients. Close and lock the lid.

3. Turn the heat up to high and when the cooker reaches pressure, lower the heat to the minimum needed to maintain pressure. Cook for 40–45 minutes at high pressure.

4. When time is up, open the pressure cooker by releasing pressure.

5. Remove the shanks and vegetables to a serving platter using a slotted spoon; cover with foil and keep warm. Skim any fat from the cooker.

6. Return the pressure cooker to medium-high heat and simmer uncovered for 10–15 minutes or until the sauce is reduced to desired thickness.

7. Pour over shanks and serve.

MOROCCAN LAMB TAGINE

For a traditional Moroccan flavor, you can serve this dish with a cardamom-infused basmati rice. Just make your rice in the usual way, and throw in a few crushed cardamom pods.

INGREDIENTS

Serves 6

1 teaspoon cinnamon powder

1 teaspoon ginger powder

1 teaspoon turmeric powder

1 teaspoon cumin powder

2 cloves garlic, crushed

3 tablespoons olive oil, divided

3-pound lamb shoulder, cut into 1" pieces

10 ounces dried plums

2 onions, roughly sliced

1 cup vegetable stock

1 bay leaf

1 cinnamon stick

3 tablespoons honey

1 teaspoon salt

1 teaspoon pepper

½ cup sliced almonds, toasted

1 tablespoon sesame seeds

1. Mix the cinnamon, ginger, turmeric, cumin, and garlic with 2 tablespoons of olive oil to make a paste; cover the lamb with this paste and set aside. Place the dried plums in a bowl and cover with boiling water. Set aside.

2. Heat 1 tablespoon olive oil in an uncovered pressure cooker over medium heat. Add onions and cook until softened (about 3 minutes). Remove onions and set aside. Add the meat and brown on all sides (about 10 minutes). Deglaze the pressure cooker with the vegetable stock, scraping the bottom well and incorporating any brown bits into the rest of the sauce. Return onions to the pan and add the bay leaf and cinnamon stick. Close and lock the lid.

3. Turn the heat up to high and when the cooker reaches pressure, lower the heat to the minimum needed to maintain pressure. Cook for 25 minutes at high pressure.

4. Open with the natural-release method—move the pressure cooker to a cool burner and wait for the pressure to come down on its own (about 15 minutes). For electric pressure cookers, disengage the "keep warm" mode or unplug the cooker and open when the pressure indicator has gone down (20–30 minutes).

5. Remove and discard the bay leaf and cinnamon stick. Keeping the pressure cooker on medium heat, add honey, salt, pepper, and drained dried plums. Simmer, uncovered, until the liquid is reduced (about 5 minutes).

6. Sprinkle with toasted almonds and sesame seeds and serve.

Meat Switcharoo

You can make this same dish with chicken or beef by adjusting the cooking times accordingly, but it should not be made with pork. The majority of Moroccans are Muslim and adhere to a Halal diet, which forbids consuming pork.

HAM AND BARLEY SKILLET DINNER

You can substitute brown rice for the pearl barley. Follow the same cooking instructions given in Step 2, but leave the lid ajar over the rice for 20 minutes instead of 10.

INGREDIENTS
Serves 8

4 tablespoons butter

1 cup pearl barley, rinsed and drained

1 teaspoon salt

4 cups water or chicken broth

1 tablespoon oil

2 teaspoons fresh ginger, peeled and grated

2 cloves garlic, peeled and minced

1 large green bell pepper, seeded and diced

1 large red bell pepper, seeded and diced

1 stalk celery, sliced

1 5-ounce can sliced water chestnuts, drained

8 ounces fresh mushrooms, cleaned and sliced

8 green onions, chopped and whites and greens separated

½ pound bean sprouts, rinsed and well drained

1 pound cooked ham, diced

1 tablespoon toasted sesame oil

Soy sauce, to taste

1. Melt the butter in the pressure cooker over medium-high heat. Stir in the barley and salt. Add the water.

2. Lock the lid into place and bring to high pressure; maintain pressure for 4 minutes. Reduce to low pressure; maintain low pressure for 20 minutes.

3. Remove from heat and allow pressure to release naturally for 10 minutes. Quick-release any remaining pressure.

4. Unlock the lid, but leave the pressure cooker covered with the lid slightly ajar for 10 minutes.

5. If necessary, drain or place the pan over low heat for a few minutes to remove any excess moisture.

6. Bring the oil to temperature in a large, deep nonstick skillet or wok over medium-high heat. Add the ginger and garlic; sauté for 30 seconds.

7. Add the peppers, celery, water chestnuts, mushrooms, and the whites of the green onions; sauté an additional 2 minutes, stirring frequently.

8. Stir in the bean sprouts, barley, and ham; stir-fry for 3 minutes or until the ingredients are hot and most of the liquid given off by the vegetables has evaporated.

9. Stir in the onion greens. Stir in the toasted sesame oil. Taste for seasoning and add soy sauce to taste.

HAM AND POTATO CASSEROLE

This is an assemble-it-on-the-plate casserole. Serve it with warm, buttered dinner rolls. The ham hocks will add a salty back note to the sauce, but have salt and pepper at the table for those who wish to add it.

INGREDIENTS

Serves 4

4 smoked ham hocks

1 tablespoon gin

1 medium sweet onion, peeled and quartered

2 stalks celery, tops only

1 large carrot, peeled and quartered

1 cup chicken broth

3 cups water

4 large red potatoes, scrubbed and quartered

4 Belgian endives, rinsed, drained, and cut in half lengthwise

¾ cup heavy cream

1. Add the ham hocks, gin, onion, celery tops, carrot, broth, and water to the pressure cooker.

2. Lock the lid into place and bring to low pressure; maintain pressure for 30 minutes. Remove from the heat and allow pressure to release naturally. Remove the lid.

3. Transfer the ham hocks to a serving platter; keep warm. Strain the pan juices. Discard the cooked vegetables.

4. Skim off any fat from the top of the strained juices and discard. Pour the strained, defatted juices back into the pressure cooker.

5. Add the potatoes to the pressure cooker, cut-sides down. Lock the lid into place and bring to low pressure; maintain pressure for 7 minutes.

6. Quick-release the pressure and remove the lid. Adjust heat to maintain a low simmer and add the endives.

7. Loosely cover the pan and simmer for 4 minutes to steam the endives. Transfer the endives and potatoes to the serving platter with the ham hocks; keep warm.

8. Stir the cream into the pan juices remaining in the pressure cooker. Bring to a boil over medium-high heat; boil hard for 5 minutes.

9. To assemble, place a ham hock, 4 potato quarters, and 2 endive pieces on each plate. Generously spoon the sauce over the potatoes and endives. Serve.

HAM AND SCALLOPED POTATOES

You can easily increase the number of servings to 8 by adding a thinly sliced sweet onion and a sliced bell pepper to the potatoes.

INGREDIENTS
Serves 6

1 cup chicken broth

6 medium potatoes, peeled and cut into ½-inch slices

¼ teaspoon salt

⅛ teaspoon freshly ground white or black pepper

1 tablespoon fresh chives, chopped

½ cup milk

2 tablespoons butter, softened

2 tablespoons all-purpose flour

½ cup sour cream

1 pound cooked ham, diced

4 ounces medium or sharp Cheddar cheese, grated

Optional: Sweet paprika

1. Add the broth, potatoes, salt, pepper, and chives to the pressure cooker. Lock the lid into place and bring to high pressure; maintain pressure for 5 minutes.

2. Remove the pressure cooker from the heat, quick-release the pressure, and remove the lid.

3. Treat a 9" × 13" ovenproof casserole dish with nonstick spray. Use a slotted spoon to transfer the potatoes to the casserole dish. Preheat the oven to 350°F.

4. Place the uncovered pressure cooker over medium-high heat. Stir the milk into any broth left in the pressure cooker and bring to a boil.

5. Add the butter and flour to a small bowl; mash into a paste, then stir in 1–2 tablespoons boiling liquid from the pressure cooker.

6. Whisk the butter-flour mixture into the liquid in the pressure cooker; boil and stir for a minute and then continue to cook and stir until the mixture begins to thicken.

7. Remove from heat and stir in the sour cream. Pour over the potatoes in the casserole dish.

8. Evenly sprinkle the ham over the potatoes. Top with cheese. If desired, evenly sprinkle paprika to taste over the cheese.

9. Bake for 15 minutes or until the cheese is melted and bubbly.

Cheese-Lover's Scalloped Potatoes

To make this dish even cheesier, melt 4 ounces of cubed cream cheese into the sauce before you add the sour cream and increase the amount of Cheddar cheese used to top the scalloped potatoes to 8 ounces. If desired, sprinkle 2 tablespoons or more grated Parmigiano-Reggiano cheese over the Cheddar cheese.

MAPLE-GLAZED HAM WITH RAISINS

Why buy expensive honey-baked ham when you can make your own in minutes? Make this for dinner, Sunday brunch, or just to have around for delicious ham sandwiches.

INGREDIENTS
Serves 6

1 (2-pound) ready-to-eat ham

1 large onion, peeled and sliced

⅛ teaspoon ground cloves

¼ teaspoon ground ginger

½ teaspoon ground cinnamon

1 cup water

2 tablespoons raw sugar

½ cup raisins

1 small pineapple, peeled, cored, and chopped (or one 14-ounce can pineapple chunks, drained)

½ cup apple butter

¼ cup maple syrup

1 tablespoon balsamic vinegar

1. Add the ham and onion to the pressure cooker. Stir together the cloves, ginger, cinnamon, water, sugar, and raisins. Pour over the ham. Close and lock the lid.

2. Turn the heat up to high and when the cooker reaches pressure, lower the heat to the minimum needed to maintain pressure. Cook for 15–18 minutes at high pressure.

3. Open with the natural-release method—move the pressure cooker to a cool burner and wait for the pressure to come down on its own (about 15 minutes). For electric pressure cookers, disengage the "keep warm" mode or unplug the cooker and open when the pressure indicator has gone down (20–30 minutes).

4. Move the ham to a serving platter and keep warm while you finish the sauce.

5. Skim and remove any fat from the pan juices in the pressure cooker. Put the pan over medium heat; simmer to reduce the pan juices to about 1 cup. Stir in the pineapple chunks, apple butter, maple syrup, and vinegar.

6. Taste for seasoning and adjust if necessary, adding additional maple syrup if you want a sweeter sauce or more vinegar if you need to cut the sweetness.

7. Serve separately to spoon or pour over ham slices.

STUFFED HAM STEAKS

The instant potato flakes serve as a thickener for the stuffing. Because the veggies are already in the ham steaks, you can serve Stuffed Ham Steaks with a tossed salad and have a complete lunch. For dinner, consider adding a sweet potato dish and biscuits or warm homemade bread.

INGREDIENTS

Serves 4

1½ cups fresh spinach or collard greens, chopped

1 medium onion, peeled and diced

1 stalk celery, finely diced

Pinch dry red pepper flakes, crushed

⅓ cup instant mashed potato flakes

2 1-inch–thick ham steaks

1 cup chicken broth

½ cup water

1 large red or green bell pepper, seeded and diced

2 tablespoons butter, softened

2 tablespoons all-purpose flour

1. Add the spinach or collard greens, onion, celery, red pepper flakes, and potato flakes to a bowl and mix together.

2. If necessary, trim ham steaks so they'll fit onto the rack of the pressure cooker.

3. Pour the broth and water into pressure cooker. Add the diced bell pepper. Place one ham steak on rack.

4. Spread the spinach or collard greens mixture evenly over the ham steak. Place the other ham steak on top of the mixture. Place the rack in the pressure cooker.

5. Lock the lid into place and bring to high pressure; maintain pressure for 5 minutes.

6. Remove from heat and allow pressure to release naturally. Remove lid. Transfer ham to a heated serving platter and keep warm.

7. Add enough water or broth to the pressure cooker to bring the remaining pan juices to 1 cup.

8. Place the pressure cooker over medium-high heat and bring the pan juices and cooked bell pepper mixture to a boil.

9. Mash the butter and flour into a paste, then thin it with some of the boiling pan juices. Whisk the thinned butter-flour mixture into the pan and boil for 1 minute.

10. Reduce heat and simmer and stir until the mixture thickens into a gravy. Pour over the stuffed ham steaks. Cut into 4 portions and serve.

BRAISED QUAIL

You can also make this dish with any small poultry.

INGREDIENTS
Serves 4

4 whole quails, cleaned and rinsed

1 teaspoon salt

¼ teaspoon pepper

1 tablespoon olive oil

3½ ounces smoked pancetta (or bacon), diced

2 shallots, roughly chopped

1 bunch thyme, chopped (reserve 1 whole sprig for garnish)

1 bunch rosemary, chopped (reserve 1 whole sprig for garnish)

1 bay leaf

¾ cup Spumante, Champagne, or any sparkling white wine

1. Season quail with salt and pepper; set aside.

2. Heat olive oil in an uncovered pressure cooker over medium heat. Add the pancetta, shallots, thyme, rosemary, and bay leaf. When the pancetta begins to sizzle and the shallots have softened, move the contents of the pan to one side and put the quails breast-side down in contact with the pan. Turn and brown all sides, and then position them breast-side up.

3. Pour in the wine, deglazing the pan and scraping up any brown bits that may be stuck to the bottom and incorporating them in the sauce. Reduce the wine by about ⅓, about 3 minutes. Close and lock the lid.

4. Turn the heat up to high and when the cooker reaches pressure, lower the heat to the minimum needed to maintain pressure. Cook for 7–9 minutes at high pressure.

5. When time is up, open the pressure cooker by releasing pressure.

6. Delicately remove the quail from the pressure cooker and set aside. Strain the cooking liquid and put it back in the cooker over medium-high heat to reduce to about half.

7. When the sauce has reduced, place the quails back in the pan, and continuously spoon the sauce over the quail to warm and glaze them, about 2 minutes.

8. Place the quail on the serving platter and spoon remaining sauce over them. Garnish with reserved herb sprigs.

DUCK IN ORANGE SAUCE

Save the rest of the white wine to serve with the meal. Serve over cooked brown rice along with steamed asparagus or broccoli.

INGREDIENTS
Serves 4

4 duck leg thigh sections

1 tablespoon duck fat or vegetable oil

1 stalk celery, diced

1 large carrot, peeled and grated

2 large shallots, peeled and minced

3 cloves garlic, peeled and minced

¼ cup triple sec or Grand Marnier

½ cup dry white wine

⅛ teaspoon dried thyme

1 teaspoon dried parsley

Optional: ⅛ teaspoon sage

Zest and juice of 1 orange

2 tablespoons white wine or sherry vinegar

Salt and freshly ground black pepper, to taste

1. Rinse the duck legs, blot dry, and place in the pressure cooker skin-side down. Fry over medium-high heat for about 7 minutes on each side. Remove and keep warm.

2. Remove and discard all but 1 tablespoon of fat rendered from the duck. Reduce heat to medium and add the celery and carrot; sauté for 2 minutes. Add the shallots; sauté for 2 minutes or until they begin to soften. Stir in the garlic and sauté for 30 seconds.

3. Add the triple sec or Grand Marnier, white wine, thyme, parsley, and sage if using. Add one quarter of the orange zest. Return the browned duck legs to the pressure cooker. Lock the lid into place and bring to high pressure; maintain pressure for 45 minutes.

4. Quick-release the pressure, remove the lid, and transfer the duck legs to a serving platter; keep warm. Use an immersion blender to pureé the vegetables and juices remaining in the pressure cooker. Stir in the remaining orange zest, orange juice, and half the vinegar. Taste for seasoning and add remaining vinegar if desired, and salt and pepper if needed. Pour the sauce over the duck legs. Serve.

RABBIT CACCIATORA

If you catch a wild rabbit, you will need to marinate it in water and vinegar for about 4 hours. You can add aromatics to the marinade, if you like. Supermarket rabbits are much more tender and their meat does not need to marinate before cooking.

INGREDIENTS

Serves 6

1 cup black salt-cured olives (Taggiesche, French, or Kalamata)

Water, as needed

2 tablespoons flour

1 3-pound rabbit, cut into pieces

1 tablespoon olive oil

1 onion, diced

1 carrot, diced

1 celery stalk, diced

1 clove garlic, smashed

½ cup red wine

1 28-ounce can whole tomatoes, drained

1 sprig sage

1 sprig rosemary

¼ teaspoon salt

⅛ teaspoon pepper

1. Fill a measuring cup with salted black olives, then add water to the 1 cup mark. Set aside.

2. Place the flour and rabbit pieces in a large bag and shake to coat. Heat olive oil in an uncovered pressure cooker over high heat. Brown the meat on all sides and remove to a platter. Keep warm. Add the onion, carrot, and celery to the pressure cooker and sauté until softened (about 5 minutes) and add garlic.

3. Remove the cooker from the heat and add wine to the hot pan. Stir and scrape up the browned bits at the bottom of the pan. Add the rabbit, tomatoes, sage, and rosemary. Drain olives, reserving liquid. Set olives aside and add the soaking liquid to the pressure cooker. Close and lock the lid.

4. Turn the heat up to high and when the cooker reaches pressure, lower the heat to the minimum needed to maintain pressure. Cook for 15–20 minutes at high pressure.

5. Open with the natural-release method—move the pressure cooker to a cool burner and wait for the pressure to come down on its own (about 15 minutes). For electric pressure cookers, disengage the "keep warm" mode or unplug the cooker and open when the pressure indicator has gone down (20–30 minutes).

6. Discard the herb sprigs and add the olives. Simmer uncovered for about 5 minutes, or until thickened to desired consistency. Taste before seasoning with salt and pepper.

CHAPTER 13

FISH AND SEAFOOD

CATFISH IN CREOLE SAUCE

Serve over cooked rice. Have hot sauce available at the table for those who want it.

INGREDIENTS
Serves 4

1½ pounds catfish fillets

1 15-ounce can diced tomatoes

2 teaspoons dried minced onion

¼ teaspoon onion powder

1 teaspoon dried minced garlic

¼ teaspoon garlic powder

1 teaspoon hot paprika

¼ teaspoon dried tarragon

1 medium green bell pepper, seeded and diced

1 stalk celery, finely diced

¼ teaspoon sugar

½ cup chili sauce

Salt and freshly ground pepper, to taste

1. Rinse the catfish in cold water and pat dry between paper towels. Cut into bite-sized pieces.

2. Add all ingredients except fish, salt, and pepper to the pressure cooker and stir to mix. Gently stir the fillets into the tomato mixture.

3. Lock the lid into place and bring the pressure cooker to low pressure; maintain pressure for 5 minutes. Quick-release the pressure. Remove the lid. Gently stir and then taste for seasoning. Add salt and pepper to taste if needed. Serve.

COCONUT FISH CURRY

Spicy, coconutty, and filling . . . this curry can be served by itself as a rich little fish stew or on a fluffy pillow of basmati rice. The trickiest part of this dish is collecting all of the ingredients!

INGREDIENTS
Serves 6

1 tablespoon vegetable oil

6 fresh curry leaves or bay leaves

2 onions, sliced into strips

2 cloves garlic, minced

1 tablespoon freshly grated ginger

1 tablespoon ground coriander

2 teaspoons ground cumin

½ teaspoon ground turmeric

1 teaspoon cayenne pepper

½ teaspoon ground fenugreek

2 cups unsweetened coconut milk

2 green chiles, sliced into thin strips

1 medium tomato, chopped

1½ pounds fish steaks or fillets, rinsed and cut into bite-sized pieces (fresh or frozen and thawed)

2 teaspoons salt

Juice of ½ lemon

1. Heat oil in an uncovered pressure cooker over medium heat. Drop in the curry leaves and lightly fry them until golden around the edges (about 1 minute). Add the onions, garlic, and ginger and sauté until the onions are soft. Add coriander, cumin, turmeric, cayenne pepper, and fenugreek and sauté them together with the onions until they have released their aroma (about 2 minutes).

2. Deglaze the pan with the coconut milk, making sure to unstick anything from the bottom and incorporate it in the sauce. Add the chiles, tomato, and fish. Stir delicately to coat the fish well with the mixture.

3. Turn the heat up to high and when the cooker reaches pressure, lower the heat to the minimum needed to maintain pressure. Cook for 4–5 minutes at low pressure (or 2–3 minutes at high pressure).

4. When time is up, open the pressure cooker by releasing pressure.

5. Add salt and lemon juice just before serving.

CREAMED CRAB

The moist cooking environment in the pressure cooker allows the flavors to meld without drying out the crabmeat. Serve this rich sauce over cooked rice, egg noodles, or toast along with a large tossed salad.

INGREDIENTS
Serves 4

4 tablespoons butter

½ stalk celery, finely diced

1 small red onion, peeled and finely diced

1 pound uncooked lump crabmeat

¼ cup chicken broth

½ cup heavy cream

Salt and freshly ground black pepper, to taste

1. Melt the butter in the pressure cooker over medium heat. Add the celery; sauté for 1 minute or until celery begins to soften. Stir in the onion; sauté for 3 minutes. Stir in the crabmeat and broth.

2. Lock the lid into place and bring to low pressure; maintain for 3 minutes. Quick-release the pressure and remove the lid. Carefully stir in the cream. Taste for seasoning and add salt and pepper to taste. Serve.

Creamed Crab Options
You can punch up the flavor of Creamed Crab by adding Old Bay Seasoning to taste during the cooking process or by adding some drops of hot sauce when you stir in the cream. Old Bay Seasoning is a mixture of celery seed or salt, bay leaf, mustard seed, black and red pepper, cinnamon, and ginger.

FISH BURRITOS

This recipe is also great with any fresh or frozen fish fillet such as whitefish or cod.

INGREDIENTS

Serves 4

1 tablespoon olive oil

1 yellow onion, chopped

1 green bell pepper, seeded and diced

1½ cups cooked black beans and ½ cup of the cooking liquid

1 4-ounce can green chilies, drained

1 tablespoon chili powder

2 white fish fillets

4 (10") corn tortillas

½ cup tomato salsa

1 cup shredded Monterey jack cheese

1. Heat olive oil in an uncovered pressure cooker over medium heat. Add onion and stir until softened, about 3 minutes. Add bell pepper, beans, cooking liquid, chilies, and powder to cooker. Mix well.

2. Place fish fillets in steamer basket in the pressure cooker. Close and lock the lid.

3. Turn the heat up to high and when the cooker reaches pressure, lower the heat to the minimum needed to maintain pressure. Cook for 3–4 minutes at high pressure.

4. When time is up, open the pressure cooker by releasing pressure.

5. To prepare, place fish and 1 tablespoon of onion mixture onto each tortilla. Top with salsa and cheese. Roll the filling completely into the tortilla.

6. Serve as is or place burritos on a baking sheet and bake at 350°F for about 10 minutes to melt the cheese and crisp up the tortillas.

FISH EN PAPILLOTE

You can substitute a scant tablespoon of minced red onion for each shallot called for in a recipe. Serve with a tossed salad and dinner rolls.

INGREDIENTS
Serves 6

3 pounds whitefish

6 tablespoons butter, softened

¼ cup fresh lemon juice

3 shallots, peeled and minced

2 cloves garlic, peeled and minced

1 tablespoon dried parsley

¼ teaspoon freshly ground white pepper

3 medium potatoes, peeled and cut into matchsticks

3 large carrots, peeled and cut into matchsticks

2 small zucchini, thinly sliced

Salt, to taste

Water, as needed

1. Thoroughly rinse the fish. Cut away and discard any grayish bands of fat. Cut into 6 portions.

2. In a small bowl, mix together the butter, lemon juice, shallots, garlic, parsley, and white pepper.

3. Cut out 6 pieces of parchment paper to wrap around the fish fillets. Brush the parchment with some of the butter mixture. Lay a fish fillet on each piece of parchment. Equally divide the remaining butter mixture between the fish, brushing it over the tops of the fillets.

4. Layer the potatoes, carrots, and zucchini on top of the fish. Salt each fillet-vegetable packet to taste. Enclose the fish and vegetables in the parchment by wrapping the paper envelope-style over them. Crisscross the packets in the steamer basket for your pressure cooker.

5. Add enough water to the pressure cooker to come up to the bottom of the steamer basket. Lock the lid into place and bring to high pressure; maintain pressure for 5 minutes. Remove from the heat and quick-release the pressure.

6. Remove the steamer basket from the pressure cooker. Using a spatula and tongs, transfer the packets to 6 serving plates. Serve immediately.

GULF GROUPER WITH PEPPERS AND TOMATOES

Grouper is delicious baked, grilled, fried, or steamed, as here. It has light flavor and texture that goes great with seasonings like lemons and capers.

INGREDIENTS
Serves 4

1 tablespoon olive oil

1 small onion, peeled and diced

1 stalk celery, diced

1 green bell pepper, seeded and diced

1 14.5-ounce can diced tomatoes

¼ cup water

1 tablespoon tomato paste

3–4 fresh basil leaves, torn

½ teaspoon chili powder

1½ pounds grouper fillets, rinsed and cut into bite-sized pieces

1 teaspoon salt

¼ teaspoon pepper

1. Heat olive oil in an uncovered pressure cooker over medium heat. Add onion, celery, and green pepper and sauté for 3 minutes. Stir in undrained tomatoes, water, tomato paste, basil, and chili powder. Gently stir the fish pieces into the sauce in the pressure cooker. Close and lock the lid.

2. Turn the heat up to high and when the cooker reaches pressure, lower the heat to the minimum needed to maintain pressure. Cook for 4–5 minutes at low pressure (or 2–3 minutes at high pressure).

3. When time is up, open the pressure cooker by releasing pressure.

4. Stir in salt and pepper and serve.

MEDITERRANEAN STEAMED FISH FILLET

Do you always eat fish with lemon? Try using sweet cherry tomatoes and vinegary capers instead! Salty olives and thyme add excitement to an otherwise ho-hum white fish fillet.

INGREDIENTS
Serves 4

2 cups water

1 pound cherry tomatoes, halved

1 bunch fresh thyme

4 whitefish fillets

1 clove garlic, pressed

2 tablespoons olive oil, divided

1 teaspoon salt

1 cup black salt-cured olives (Taggiesche, French, or Kalamata)

2 tablespoons pickled capers

¼ teaspoon ground black pepper

1. Prepare the pressure cooker by pouring in 1–2 cups of water and adding the trivet or steamer basket. Set aside.

2. Line the bottom of a heat-proof dish with half the cherry tomatoes (to keep the fish fillet from sticking) and add thyme sprigs (reserve a few sprigs for garnish). Place the fish fillets over the cherry tomatoes, sprinkle with remaining tomatoes, garlic, olive oil, and salt.

3. Make a foil sling by folding a long piece of foil into three and lower the uncovered heat-proof dish into the pressure cooker. Close and lock the lid.

4. Turn the heat up to high and when the cooker reaches pressure, lower the heat to the minimum needed to maintain pressure. Cook for 7–8 minutes at low pressure (or 4–5 minutes at high pressure).

5. When time is up, open the pressure cooker by releasing pressure.

6. Distribute fish onto individual plates and top with cherry tomatoes, olives, capers, thyme sprigs, a crackle of pepper, and the remaining olive oil.

Insert Choices

For this recipe, you can use a heat-proof dish, an un-perforated insert, or your steamer basket lined with parchment paper (cut the extra around the edges off so it does not interfere with the inner workings of the pressure cooker or obstruct any of the valves).

MISO RED SNAPPER

To prepare this dish, you'll need a glass pie pan that will fit on the rack inside the pressure cooker.

INGREDIENTS
Serves 4

Water, as needed

1 tablespoon red miso paste

1 tablespoon rice wine

2 teaspoons fermented black beans

2 teaspoons sesame oil

1 teaspoon dark soy sauce

½ teaspoon Asian chili paste

Salt, to taste

2 pounds red snapper fillets

1 2-inch piece fresh ginger

2 cloves garlic, peeled and minced

4 green onions

1. Insert the rack in the pressure cooker. Pour in enough water to fill the pan to just below the top of the rack.

2. In a small bowl, mix the miso, rice wine, black beans, sesame oil, soy sauce, and chili paste. Lightly sprinkle salt over the fish fillets and then rub them on both sides with the miso mixture.

3. Peel the ginger and cut into matchsticks 1 inch long. Place half of them on the bottom of a glass pie plate. Sprinkle half the minced garlic over the ginger.

4. Halve the green onions lengthwise and then cut them into 2-inch-long pieces; place half of them over the ginger and garlic. Place the fish fillets in the pie plate and sprinkle the remaining ginger, garlic, and onions over the top. Place the pie plate on the rack inside the pressure cooker.

5. Lock the lid into place and bring to high pressure; maintain pressure for 3 minutes. Remove from heat and quick-release the pressure. Serve.

ORANGE ROUGHY IN BLACK OLIVE SAUCE

If fresh dill isn't available, sprinkle about ¼ teaspoon dried dill over each fillet when you salt them. Add additional dried dill to taste to the sauce if desired.

INGREDIENTS

Serves 2

⅜ cup dry white wine

⅜ cup water

2 (8-ounce, 1-inch thick) orange roughy fillets

Sea salt, to taste

4 thin slices white onion

6 sprigs fresh dill

3 tablespoons butter, melted

4 teaspoons freshly squeezed lime juice

6 Kalamata or black olives, pitted and chopped

1. Pour the wine and water into the pressure cooker. Place the trivet in the cooker. Rinse the fish and pat dry. Lightly sprinkle with salt. Place 2 slices of onion on the trivet and top each onion with a sprig of dill.

2. Place the fish over the onion and dill, and then put a sprig of dill on top of each fillet and top with the remaining two onion slices. Lock the lid into place and bring to high pressure; maintain pressure for 5 minutes. Remove from the heat and allow pressure to release naturally for 5 minutes. Quick-release any remaining pressure.

3. To make the sauce, whisk together the butter, lime juice, and ½ tablespoon cooking liquid from the fish; stir in the olives. Serve the fish topped with the black olive–butter sauce and garnished with the remaining 2 sprigs of dill.

PAPRIKA CATFISH WITH FRESH TARRAGON

Serve over the rice of your choice.

INGREDIENTS
Serves 4

1 14.5-ounce can diced tomatoes

2 teaspoons dried minced onion

¼ teaspoon onion powder

1 teaspoon dried minced garlic

¼ teaspoon garlic powder

1 teaspoon hot paprika

½ tablespoon chopped fresh tarragon

1 medium green bell pepper, seeded and diced

1 stalk celery, finely diced

1 teaspoon salt

¼ teaspoon pepper

1 pound catfish fillets, rinsed and cut into bite-sized pieces

1. Add all ingredients except fish to the pressure cooker and stir to mix. Once mixed, top with the fish. Close and lock the lid.

2. Turn the heat up to high and when the cooker reaches pressure, lower the heat to the minimum needed to maintain pressure. Cook for 4–5 minutes at low pressure (or 2–3 minutes at high pressure).

3. When time is up, open the pressure cooker by releasing pressure.

4. Gently stir and then taste for seasoning. Add salt and pepper to taste if needed.

Un-Bony Fish
Catfish taste delicious; however, they do have lots of little bones. To avoid bones, use trout, cod, or whitefish fillets instead.

POACHED OCTOPUS

Let the octopus defrost for a day in the refrigerator before using it for this recipe.

INGREDIENTS
Serves 6

2 pounds potatoes (about 6 medium), washed

3 teaspoons salt, divided

Water, as needed

1 octopus (about 2 pounds), cleaned and rinsed

3 cloves garlic, divided

1 bay leaf

2 teaspoons whole peppercorns

½ cup olive oil

4 tablespoons white wine vinegar

1 teaspoon salt

½ teaspoon pepper

1 bunch parsley, chopped

1. Place the potatoes in the pressure cooker with 2 teaspoons salt and enough water to just cover the potatoes halfway.

2. Turn the heat up to high and when the cooker reaches pressure, lower the heat to the minimum needed to maintain pressure. Cook for 10–15 minutes at high pressure.

3. When time is up, open the pressure cooker by releasing pressure.

4. Remove the potatoes with tongs (reserve the cooking water), and peel them as soon as you can handle them. Dice the potatoes in bite-sized pieces.

5. Add the octopus to the potato cooking water in the cooker with more water to cover, if needed. Add one whole garlic clove, the bay leaf, and the peppercorns. Close and lock the lid.

6. Turn the heat up to high and when the cooker reaches pressure, lower the heat to the minimum needed to maintain pressure. Cook for 15–20 minutes at high pressure.

7. When time is up, open the pressure cooker by releasing pressure.

8. While the octopus is cooking, prepare the vinaigrette. Crush the remaining garlic cloves and place in a small jar or plastic container. Add olive oil, vinegar, 1 teaspoon salt, and ground pepper. Close the lid and shake to blend.

9. Check the octopus for tenderness by seeing if a fork will sink easily in the thickest part of the flesh. If not, close the top and bring it to pressure for another minute or two and check again. When the octopus is ready, remove and drain. Chop the head and tentacles into small bite-sized chunks.

10. Right before serving mix the potatoes with the octopus; cover with the vinaigrette and sprinkle with parsley.

RED SNAPPER IN RICE WINE AND MISO

Use a heat-proof dish or un-perforated insert to hold the fish, rather than putting it directly in the pressure cooker—otherwise it could easily fall apart during cooking.

INGREDIENTS
Serves 4

2 cups water

1 tablespoon red miso paste

1 tablespoon rice wine

2 teaspoons fermented black beans

2 teaspoons sesame oil

1 teaspoon dark soy sauce

½ teaspoon Asian chili paste

½ teaspoon sea salt, or to taste

2 pounds red snapper fillets

1 (2") piece fresh ginger, cut into matchsticks

2 cloves garlic, peeled and minced

4 green onions, halved and cut into 2" pieces

1. Prepare the pressure cooker by pouring in 1–2 cups of water and adding the trivet or steamer basket. Set aside.

2. In a small bowl, mix the miso, rice wine, black beans, sesame oil, soy sauce, chili paste, and salt. Cover and rub fish with the mixture. Place half the ginger in a heat-proof dish and top with fish fillets. Sprinkle remaining ginger, garlic, and onions on top.

3. Make a foil sling by folding a long piece of foil into three and lower the uncovered heat-proof dish into the pressure cooker. Close and lock the lid.

4. Turn the heat up to high and when the cooker reaches pressure, lower the heat to the minimum needed to maintain pressure. Cook for 7–8 minutes at low pressure (or 4–5 minutes at high pressure).

5. When time is up, open the pressure cooker by releasing pressure.

6. Distribute fish onto individual plates and top with the pan sauce.

Don't Lose Your Head

In some cultures, it's considered a delicacy to cook and serve the entire fish, including the head. If that is something you enjoy, feel free to use the whole fish in this recipe.

RED WINE–POACHED SALMON

You can prepare this dish without alcohol by substituting raspberry-apple juice for the red wine.

INGREDIENTS

Serves 6

1 medium onion, peeled and quartered

2 cloves garlic, peeled and smashed

1 stalk celery, diced

1 bay leaf

½ teaspoon dried thyme

3½ cups water

2 cups dry red wine

2 tablespoons red wine or balsamic vinegar

½ teaspoon salt

½ teaspoon black peppercorns

1 2½-pound center-cut salmon roast

Optional: Lemon

1. Add all ingredients except the salmon and lemon to the pressure cooker. Lock the lid into place and bring to high pressure; maintain pressure for 10 minutes. Remove from the heat and allow pressure to release naturally for 15 minutes. Quick-release any remaining pressure.

2. Set the trivet in the pressure cooker. Put the pressure cooker over medium-high heat and bring the wine mixture to a high simmer.

3. Wrap the salmon in cheesecloth, leaving long enough ends to extend about 3 inches. Use two sets of tongs to hold on to the 3-inch cheesecloth extensions and place the salmon on the trivet. Lock the lid into place and bring to high pressure; maintain pressure for 6 minutes. Remove from the heat and allow pressure to release naturally for 20 minutes.

4. Quick-release any remaining pressure. Use tongs to hold on to the 3-inch cheesecloth extensions to lift the salmon roast out of the pressure cooker. Set in a metal colander to allow extra moisture to drain away. When the roast is cool enough to handle, unwrap the cheesecloth. Peel away and discard any skin.

5. Transfer the salmon to a serving platter. Garnish with lemon slices or wedges if desired.

SHRIMP, BLACK BEANS, AND RICE

This dish is also great with crabmeat or, for a truly New Orleans–style dish, use crayfish.

INGREDIENTS
Serves 4

1 tablespoon olive oil

1 cup brown rice

1 yellow onion, chopped

3 cloves garlic, minced

3 cups water

1 14-ounce can diced tomatoes drained

1 cup dry black beans, soaked

½ teaspoon cumin

⅛ teaspoon cayenne pepper

8 ounces frozen bay shrimp, thawed and coarsely chopped

1 teaspoon salt

¼ teaspoon pepper

1. Heat olive oil in an uncovered pressure cooker over medium heat. Sauté the rice, onion, and garlic for about 3 minutes. Add water, tomatoes, beans, cumin, cayenne pepper, and shrimp. Close and lock the lid.

2. Turn the heat up to high and when the cooker reaches pressure, lower the heat to the minimum needed to maintain pressure. Cook for 18–20 minutes at high pressure.

3. Open with the natural-release method—move the pressure cooker to a cool burner and wait for the pressure to come down on its own (about 15 minutes). For electric pressure cookers, disengage the "keep warm" mode or unplug the cooker and open when the pressure indicator has gone down (20–30 minutes).

4. Stir in salt and pepper and serve.

STEAMED CLAMS

This is another dish that can be served alone, as an appetizer, or on top of spaghetti.

INGREDIENTS
Serves 6

2 pounds fresh clams, rinsed and purged

1 tablespoon olive oil

1 white onion, chopped

1 clove garlic, smashed

½ cup water

½ cup dry white wine

1. Place clams in the steamer basket.

2. Heat olive oil in an uncovered pressure cooker over medium-high heat. Add onion and garlic and sauté until softened (about 5 minutes). Pour the water and wine into the pressure cooker and add the steamer basket. Close and lock the lid.

3. Turn the heat up to high and when the cooker reaches pressure, lower the heat to the minimum needed to maintain pressure. Cook for 4–6 minutes at high pressure.

4. When time is up, open the pressure cooker by releasing pressure.

5. Empty the cooked clams from the steamer basket into the pressure cooker and mix well. Serve clams with a generous scoop of cooking liquid.

TOMATO-STEWED CALAMARI

If you have fresh parsley and basil available, omit the dried herbs and stir 1 tablespoon of each into the calamari after you quick-release the pressure.

INGREDIENTS
Serves 4

2 tablespoons olive oil

1 small carrot, peeled and grated

1 small stalk celery, finely diced

1 small white onion, peeled and diced

3 cloves garlic, peeled and minced

2½ pounds calamari

1 28-ounce can diced tomatoes

½ cup white wine

⅓ cup water

1 teaspoon dried parsley

1 teaspoon dried basil

Salt and freshly ground black pepper, to taste

1. Bring the oil to temperature in the pressure cooker. Add the carrot and celery; sauté for 2 minutes.

2. Stir in the onion; sauté for 3 minutes or until the onion is transparent. Stir in the garlic; sauté for 30 seconds.

3. Clean and wash the calamari; pat dry. Add to the pressure cooker along with the remaining ingredients.

4. Lock the lid into place and bring to low pressure; maintain pressure for 10 minutes. Quick-release pressure. Serve.

TROUT IN PARSLEY SAUCE

This recipe is a way to use up lettuce that's no longer crisp enough for a salad but isn't totally past its prime. Using the lettuce to steam the fish keeps it firm and adds a bit of extra taste to the poaching liquid.

INGREDIENTS
Serves 4

4 fresh (½-pound) river trout

Salt, to taste

4 cups torn lettuce leaves

1 teaspoon distilled white or white wine vinegar

½ cup water

½ cup fresh flat-leaf parsley, minced

1 shallot, peeled and minced

2 tablespoons mayonnaise

½ teaspoon fresh lemon juice

¼ teaspoon sugar

Pinch salt

2 tablespoons sliced almonds, toasted

1. Rinse the trout inside and out; pat dry. Sprinkle with salt inside and out. Put 3 cups of the lettuce leaves in the bottom of the pressure cooker. Arrange the trout over the top of the lettuce and top the trout with the remaining lettuce. Stir the vinegar into the water and pour into the pressure cooker.

2. Lock the lid into place and bring to high pressure; maintain pressure for 3 minutes. Remove from the heat and allow pressure to release naturally for 3 minutes. Quick-release any remaining pressure.

3. Remove the lid and use a spatula to move the fish to a serving plate. Peel and discard the skin from the fish. Remove and discard the heads if desired.

4. To make the parsley sauce, mix together the parsley, shallot, mayonnaise, lemon juice, sugar, and salt. Evenly divide between the fish, spreading it over them. Sprinkle the toasted almonds over the top of the sauce. Serve.

Parsley Sauce Alternatives

Parsley is a versatile herb that will be a worthwhile addition to any garden. For a reduced-calorie parsley sauce, you can replace the mayonnaise with water or low-fat yogurt. For a richer sauce, substitute melted butter or extra-virgin olive oil for the mayonnaise.

WHITEFISH FILLETS WITH VEGETABLES

Omit the nutmeg and turn this steamed meal into a hot fish and vegetable salad by serving it over salad greens.

INGREDIENTS
Serves 2

1 cup broccoli florets, cut into small pieces

1 large potato, peeled and diced

1 large carrot, peeled and grated

1 small zucchini, grated

4 ounces fresh mushrooms, sliced

¼ teaspoon dried thyme

¼ teaspoon freshly grated lemon zest

½ pound cod, halibut, sole, or other whitefish

½ cup chicken broth or white wine

½ cup fresh lemon juice

1 teaspoon dried parsley

Salt and freshly ground black pepper, to taste

Freshly grated nutmeg

1. Place the steamer basket in the pressure cooker. Add the broccoli florets, potato, carrot, zucchini, and mushroom slices in layers to the basket. Sprinkle the dried thyme and lemon zest over the vegetables.

2. Place the fish fillets over the vegetables. Pour the broth or wine and lemon juice over the fish. Sprinkle the dried parsley, salt, and pepper over the fish and vegetables.

3. Lock the lid in place and bring the pressure cooker to low pressure; maintain the pressure for 5 minutes. Quick-release the pressure. Divide the fish and vegetables between two serving plates. Sprinkle freshly ground nutmeg to taste over each serving.

Whitefish Fillets with Vegetables Salad Dressing

Whisk 1 teaspoon Dijon mustard into ¼ cup strained pan juices and 1 tablespoon fresh lemon juice or white wine vinegar. Slowly whisk in 1–2 tablespoons extra-virgin olive oil. Taste for seasoning, adding more oil if the dressing is too tart or more lemon juice or vinegar if it isn't tart enough. Add salt and freshly ground black pepper to taste.

PART VI

VEGETARIAN ALTERNATIVES

CHAPTER 14

BURGERS, CASSEROLES, AND MORE

"BACON" AND AVOCADO BURGER

There are plenty of tasty vegetarian "bacon" options at your local health food store or a national grocery store chain near you. Use one of these fast-cooking options if you don't have time to make your own.

INGREDIENTS
Serves 4

1 cup dried black beans

8 cups water

2 tablespoons vegetable oil

1 teaspoon salt

1 jalapeño, seeded and minced

3 cloves garlic, minced

½ onion, diced

1 tablespoon chili powder

1 tablespoon cumin

½ cup panko bread crumbs

¼ cup parsley

Salt and pepper, to taste

8–12 pieces of tempeh bacon

1 avocado, sliced

1. Add the beans and 4 cups water to the pressure cooker. Lock the lid into place; bring to high pressure for 1 minute. Remove from the heat and quick-release the pressure.

2. Drain the water, rinse the beans, and add to the pressure cooker again with the remaining 4 cups of water. Let soak for 1 hour.

3. Add 1 tablespoon of the vegetable oil and salt. Lock the lid into place; bring to high pressure and maintain for 12 minutes. Remove from the heat and allow pressure to release naturally. Drain the beans.

4. Pour the beans into a large bowl and add the rest of the ingredients except remaining oil, tempeh bacon, and avocado. Mash the mixture with a potato masher. Form the bean mixture into burger patties. Add the remaining oil to a pan and cook the burgers until they are browned on both sides.

5. Top each of the burgers with tempeh bacon and avocado slices.

BBQ TEMPEH BURGER

It's recommended that you always marinate tempeh or cook tempeh in liquid for optimal results. If you don't, it can easily become too dry to eat.

INGREDIENTS
Serves 4–6

1 cup lentils

1 8-ounce package tempeh, crumbled

4½ cups water

1 tablespoon vegetable oil

1 teaspoon salt, plus more to taste

½ cup flour

½ cup mustard

¼ cup sugar

⅛ cup brown sugar

¼ cup cider vinegar

1 tablespoon chili powder

⅛ teaspoon cayenne pepper

½ teaspoon soy sauce

1 tablespoon butter, melted, or vegan margarine, such as Earth Balance

½ tablespoon liquid smoke

Pepper, to taste

1. Add the lentils, tempeh, water, oil, and salt to the pressure cooker.

2. Lock the lid into place; bring to high pressure and maintain for 7 minutes. Remove from the heat and allow pressure to release naturally. Drain the lentils and tempeh and add to a large mixing bowl.

3. Combine the rest of the ingredients with the lentils and tempeh. Mash the mixture with a potato masher. Form the tempeh mixture into burger patties.

4. Preheat the oven to 350°F. Place the burgers on a greased baking sheet. Bake in the oven for 25–30 minutes, flipping after 15 minutes.

BEET RED BURGER

Beets will give your burger the appearance of rare meat but without all of the fat.

INGREDIENTS
Serves 4

5 beets, quartered

1½ cups water

½ cup onions, chopped

1½ cups walnuts, chopped

2 eggs, beaten, or 4 teaspoons cornstarch combined with 4 tablespoons warm water

2 tablespoons soy sauce

1 cup Cheddar cheese, grated, or vegan Cheddar, such as Daiya Cheddar Style Shreds

⅛ cup flour

2 tablespoons olive oil

Salt and pepper, to taste

1. Add the beets and the water to the pressure cooker. Lock the lid into place; bring to high pressure for 8 minutes. Remove from the heat and quick-release the pressure. Drain the beets and add to a large mixing bowl.

2. Combine the rest of the ingredients with the beets. Mash the mixture with a potato masher. Form the beet mixture into burger patties.

3. Preheat the oven to 350°F. Place the patties on a greased baking sheet and bake in the oven for 25–30 minutes.

BROWN RICE BURGER

Protein and iron are two of the vital nutrients found in brown rice.

INGREDIENTS
Serves 4

1 cup long-grain brown rice

2 cups water

½ cup mushrooms, chopped

½ cup corn, chopped

½ cup carrot, shredded

¼ onion, diced

Salt and pepper, to taste

2 cups bread crumbs

1 tablespoon olive oil

1. Add the rice and water to the pressure cooker.

2. Lock the lid into place; bring to high pressure and maintain for 15 minutes. Remove from the heat and allow pressure to release naturally. Fluff with a fork.

3. In a large bowl, combine the rice, mushrooms, corn, carrot, onion, salt, and pepper. Mash the mixture with a potato masher and form into patties. Dredge each patty with bread crumbs and set aside.

4. Add the olive oil to a pan and fry the burgers over medium heat until they are browned on each side.

BULGUR-NUT BURGER

Try topping this basic burger with avocado slices or traditional toppings, such as lettuce, tomato, and cheese.

INGREDIENTS
Serves 4–6

1 cup bulgur

3 cups vegetable stock

2 tablespoons olive oil

½ cup onion, diced

2 garlic cloves, minced

2 cups canned pinto beans, drained

¾ cup walnuts

½ cup cilantro, chopped

1 teaspoon cumin

¼ teaspoon cayenne pepper

1. Add the bulgur and stock to the pressure cooker.

2. Lock the lid into place; bring to high pressure and maintain for 9 minutes. Remove from the heat and allow pressure to release naturally.

3. In a pan, add 1 tablespoon of the olive oil and sauté the onion until it begins to caramelize. Add the garlic and sauté for 1 minute more. Add the pinto beans and cook until the beans are tender. Add a little water if needed.

4. In a large bowl, combine all of the ingredients except remaining oil. Put the mixture in a food processor and pulse until it is finely chopped. Form the mixture into patties.

5. Add 1 tablespoon of olive oil to a pan and fry the patties until they are browned on both sides.

CHILI CHEESEBURGER

If you are short on time, try using a store-bought vegetarian chili, such as Hormel's vegetarian canned chili.

INGREDIENTS
Serves 6–8

1 cup dried black beans

8 cups water

2 tablespoons vegetable oil

1 teaspoon salt

1 jalapeño, seeded and minced

3 cloves garlic, minced

½ onion, diced

1 tablespoon chili powder

1 tablespoon cumin

½ cup panko bread crumbs

¼ cup parsley

Salt and pepper, to taste

6–8 hamburger buns

6–8 slices American cheese, or vegan Cheddar

2 cups Speedy Chili con "Carne" (Chapter 9)

1. Add the beans and 4 cups water to the pressure cooker. Lock the lid into place; bring to high pressure for 1 minute. Remove from the heat and quick-release the pressure.

2. Drain the water, rinse the beans, and add to the pressure cooker again with the remaining 4 cups of water. Let soak for 1 hour.

3. Add 1 tablespoon of the vegetable oil and salt. Lock the lid into place; bring to high pressure and maintain for 12 minutes. Remove from the heat and allow pressure to release naturally. Drain the beans.

4. Pour the beans into a large bowl and add the rest of the ingredients except remaining oil, buns, cheese, and chili. Mash the mixture with a potato masher. Form the bean mixture into burger patties. Add the remaining oil to a pan and cook the burgers until they are browned on both sides.

5. Place 1 patty on each hamburger bun and top with a slice of cheese. Melt the cheese under a broiler or in the microwave for a few seconds, then top with a scoop of chili.

MEXICAN VEGGIE BURGER

Think "Mexican" when deciding on toppings for this festive burger. Try avocado, pickled jalapeño slices, or even salsa.

INGREDIENTS
Serves 2–4

1 cup dried black beans

8 cups water

2 tablespoons vegetable oil

1 teaspoon salt

½ green bell pepper, chopped

½ onion, diced

3 cloves garlic, minced

1 egg, or 2 teaspoons cornstarch combined with 2 tablespoons warm water

1 tablespoon cumin

1 teaspoon chipotle chili powder

½ cup salsa

½ cup panko bread crumbs

Salt and pepper, to taste

1. Add the beans and 4 cups water to the pressure cooker. Lock the lid into place; bring to high pressure for 1 minute. Remove from the heat and quick-release the pressure.

2. Drain the water, rinse the beans, and add to the pressure cooker again with the remaining 4 cups of water. Let soak for 1 hour.

3. Add 1 tablespoon of the vegetable oil and salt. Lock the lid into place; bring to high pressure and maintain for 12 minutes. Remove from the heat and allow pressure to release naturally. Drain the beans and pour into a large mixing bowl.

4. Add all of the ingredients except remaining oil to the bowl. Mash with a potato masher and form the mixture into patties.

5. Add remaining oil to a pan and cook the burgers until they are brown on both sides.

ONION, MUSHROOM, AND CHEESE-STUFFED BURGER

To make this burger in a hurry, use canned beans instead of dried beans and cook for 1 minute to warm through.

INGREDIENTS
Serves 2–4

1 cup dried black beans

8 cups water

3 tablespoons vegetable oil

1 teaspoon salt

½ onion, diced

2 cups white mushrooms, chopped

2 cloves garlic, minced

¾ cup panko bread crumbs

½ tablespoon cumin

1 teaspoon chili powder

½ teaspoon dried thyme

Salt and pepper, to taste

8 slices Swiss cheese, or vegan mozzarella, such as Daiya Mozzarella Style Shreds

1. Add the beans and 4 cups water to the pressure cooker. Lock the lid into place; bring to high pressure for 1 minute. Remove from the heat and quick-release the pressure.

2. Drain the water, rinse the beans, and add to the pressure cooker again with the remaining 4 cups of water. Let soak for 1 hour.

3. Add 1 tablespoon of the vegetable oil and salt. Lock the lid into place; bring to high pressure and maintain for 12 minutes. Remove from the heat and allow pressure to release naturally. Drain the beans.

4. Pour the beans into a large bowl and add the rest of the ingredients, except the remaining oil and the Swiss cheese. Mash the mixture with a potato masher. Fold a slice of cheese in half and form the patties around the cheese to make a stuffed burger.

5. Add the rest of the oil to the pan and cook the burgers until they are browned on both sides.

PINTO BEAN BURGER

Making homemade burgers can be time consuming for a busy family, even with a pressure cooker. If you're pressed for time, try a frozen burger, such as Boca, instead.

INGREDIENTS
Serves 6–8

1 cup dried pinto beans

8 cups water

2 tablespoons vegetable oil

1 teaspoon salt, plus more to taste

1 onion, diced

1 cup walnuts, chopped

½ cup oats

1 egg, beaten, or 2 teaspoons cornstarch combined with 2 tablespoons warm water

¾ cup ketchup

1 teaspoon garlic powder

1 teaspoon dried basil

1 teaspoon dried parsley

Pepper, to taste

1. Add the beans and 4 cups water to the pressure cooker. Lock the lid into place; bring to high pressure for 1 minute. Remove from the heat and quick-release the pressure.

2. Drain the water, rinse the beans, and add to the pressure cooker again with the remaining 4 cups of water. Let soak for 1 hour.

3. Add 1 tablespoon vegetable oil and 1 teaspoon salt. Lock the lid into place; bring to high pressure and maintain for 11 minutes. Remove from the heat and allow pressure to release naturally. Drain the beans.

4. Combine the rest of the ingredients except remaining oil. Mash the mixture with a potato masher. Form the bean mixture into burger patties. Add the remaining oil to a pan and cook the burgers until they are browned on both sides.

QUINOA BURGER

Quinoa is a lesser-known grain popular with some vegetarians because of its high protein and iron content and fast cooking time.

INGREDIENTS
Serves 2

½ cup quinoa

1 cup water

1 carrot, shredded

½ onion, diced

2 15-ounce cans white beans, drained

1 egg, beaten, or 2 teaspoons cornstarch combined with 2 tablespoons warm water

1 tablespoon cumin

1 teaspoon dried sage or basil

Salt and pepper, to taste

1 tablespoon olive oil

1. Add the quinoa and water to the pressure cooker.

2. Lock the lid into place; bring to high pressure and maintain for 6 minutes. Remove from the heat and allow pressure to release naturally. Fluff with a fork.

3. In a large bowl, combine all the ingredients except olive oil and mash with a potato masher. Form the mixture into patties.

4. Add the olive oil to a pan and cook the burgers until they are browned on each side.

ROASTED VEGETABLE BURGER

Roasting veggies before mixing into the patty mixture will bring out more flavor in the bell pepper, onion, squash, and zucchini.

INGREDIENTS

Serves 2–4

1 cup dried black beans

8 cups water

2 tablespoons vegetable oil

1 teaspoon salt, plus more to taste

½ onion, chopped

½ red bell pepper, chopped

½ cup yellow squash, chopped

½ zucchini, chopped

4 cloves garlic, minced

1 tablespoon extra-virgin olive oil

½ jalapeño, seeded and minced

½ cup panko bread crumbs

Pepper, to taste

1. Add the beans and 4 cups water to the pressure cooker. Lock the lid into place; bring to high pressure for 1 minute. Remove from the heat and quick-release the pressure.

2. Drain the water, rinse the beans, and add to the pressure cooker again with the remaining 4 cups of water. Let soak for 1 hour.

3. Add 1 tablespoon vegetable oil and 1 teaspoon salt. Lock the lid into place; bring to high pressure and maintain for 12 minutes. Remove from the heat and allow pressure to release naturally. Drain the beans and set aside.

4. Preheat the oven to 450°F. Toss the onion, bell pepper, yellow squash, zucchini, and garlic in the olive oil. Place on a baking sheet and cook for 30–35 minutes in the oven, turning once.

5. Pour the beans into a large bowl and add the rest of the ingredients except remaining 1 tablespoon vegetable oil. Mash the mixture with a potato masher. Form the bean mixture into burger patties. Add the remaining oil to a pan and cook the burgers until they are browned on both sides.

SMOKED PORTOBELLO BURGER

Portobello mushrooms caps can be cooked in a pressure cooker, on a stove top, on a grill, or in the oven.

INGREDIENTS
Serves 4

4 large portobello mushroom caps

¼ cup red wine vinegar

2 tablespoons extra-virgin olive oil

1 tablespoon shallots, minced

½ tablespoon soy sauce

Salt and pepper, to taste

1 cup water

1 tablespoon liquid smoke

1. Place the mushrooms in a shallow dish. In a small bowl, mix the red wine vinegar, olive oil, shallots, soy sauce, salt, and pepper. Pour the mixture over the mushrooms and allow them to marinate for about 20 minutes, turning 2–3 times throughout.

2. Pour the water and liquid smoke into the pressure cooker and place the steamer tray inside. Place the mushrooms on top of the steamer tray.

3. Lock the lid into place; bring to high pressure and maintain for 5 minutes. Remove from the heat and allow pressure to release naturally.

Liquid Smoke

Liquid smoke helps give food a true barbecue flavor without the hassle of traditional barbecue cooking. It's often sold in small bottles in the condiment aisle (near steak sauce, ketchup, and mustard), or can be ordered online. Use liquid smoke by combining with a liquid when cooking, or brush directly onto ingredients such as mushrooms or veggie burgers.

SPICY BLACK BEAN BURGER

Black bean burgers are one of the most commonly consumed homemade veggie burgers. Omit the spice from this recipe to use it as a base for your own veggie burger creation.

INGREDIENTS
Serves 2

1 cup dried black beans

8 cups water

2 tablespoons vegetable oil

1 teaspoon salt, plus more to taste

1 jalapeño, seeded and minced

3 cloves garlic, minced

½ onion, diced

1 tablespoon chili powder

1 tablespoon cumin

½ cup panko bread crumbs

¼ cup parsley, chopped

Pepper, to taste

1. Add the beans and 4 cups water to the pressure cooker. Lock the lid into place; bring to high pressure for 1 minute. Remove from the heat and quick-release the pressure.

2. Drain the water, rinse the beans, and add to the pressure cooker again with the remaining 4 cups of water. Let soak for 1 hour.

3. Add 1 tablespoon of the vegetable oil and 1 teaspoon salt. Lock the lid into place; bring to high pressure and maintain for 12 minutes. Remove from the heat and allow pressure to release naturally. Drain the beans.

4. Pour the beans into a large bowl and add the rest of the ingredients except remaining oil. Mash the mixture with a potato masher. Form the bean mixture into burger patties. Add the remaining oil to a pan and cook the burgers until they are browned on both sides.

TROPICAL VEGGIE BURGER

To tone down this flavor-rich burger, feel free to omit one or more of the spices.

INGREDIENTS
Serves 2–4

1 cup red lentils

¼ cup brown rice

5 cups water

2 tablespoons vegetable oil

1 teaspoon salt

1½ tablespoons butter, or vegan margarine, such as Earth Balance

1 onion, chopped

4 teaspoons curry powder

⅓ cup carrots, shredded

2 tablespoons white wine

2 tablespoons hot sauce

½ cup panko bread crumbs

4 cloves garlic, minced

4 teaspoons fresh ginger, minced

½ teaspoon allspice

1 teaspoon cumin

1. Add the lentils, brown rice, water, 1 tablespoon of oil, and salt to the pressure cooker.

2. Lock the lid into place; bring to high pressure and maintain for 7 minutes. Remove from the heat and allow pressure to release naturally. Drain the rice and lentils and set aside.

3. Add the butter to a pan and sauté the onion until it begins to caramelize. Add the curry powder, carrots, and white wine. Sauté for 1 minute longer.

4. Pour the lentils and rice into a large bowl and add the rest of the ingredients except remaining oil. Mash the mixture with a potato masher. Form the bean mixture into burger patties. Add the remaining oil to a pan and cook the burgers until they are browned on both sides.

Serving Suggestions

Typical burger toppings, such as ketchup and mustard, might not be the best condiments for this burger. Try topping it with a grilled pineapple ring or mango salsa.

HOMEMADE SEITAN

When pressed for time, use packaged seitan instead of making it at home.

INGREDIENTS
Yields 1¼ pounds

3½ cups whole wheat flour

3½ cups unbleached white flour

3½ cups cold water

7 cups vegetable stock

1. Place the whole wheat and unbleached flour in a large mixing bowl and stir well to combine. While stirring, gradually pour enough water into the flour to form a sticky dough that can be kneaded. Knead for 15 minutes. Cover the dough with cold water, place in the refrigerator, and keep submerged for at least 30 minutes.

2. Transfer the dough from the bowl to a colander and place it in the sink. Under cold running water, carefully knead the dough, rinsing out the starch and bran. After several minutes of cold water rinsing and kneading, the gluten will start to stick together. Alternate between room temperature water and cold water rinses while continuing to knead the dough until it has a firm, rubbery texture.

3. Add the vegetable stock to the pressure cooker. Pull pieces of gluten into small billiard-sized balls. Drop the gluten into the liquid, one piece at a time, stirring occasionally to prevent sticking.

4. Lock the lid into place; bring to high pressure for 20 minutes. Remove from the heat and quick-release the pressure. Seitan can be refrigerated in the cooking liquid for 3–4 days.

BLACK PEPPER SEITAN AND BROCCOLI

Modeled after the popular Chinese dish, this recipe can be served with white or brown rice.

INGREDIENTS
Serves 4–6

1¾ cups whole wheat flour

1¾ cups unbleached white flour

1¾ cups cold water

3½ cups vegetable stock

2 tablespoons vegetable oil

1 onion, sliced

2 cloves garlic, minced

2 cups broccoli, chopped and blanched

2 tablespoons soy sauce

1 teaspoon black pepper

½ teaspoon sugar

1. Place the whole wheat and unbleached flour in a large mixing bowl and stir well to combine. While stirring, gradually pour enough water into the flour to form a sticky dough that can be kneaded. Knead for 15 minutes. Cover the dough with cold water, place in the refrigerator, and keep submerged for at least 30 minutes.

2. Transfer the dough from the bowl to a colander and place it in the sink. Under cold running water, carefully knead the dough, rinsing out the starch and bran. After several minutes of cold water rinsing and kneading, the gluten will start to stick together. Alternate between room temperature water and cold water rinses while continuing to knead the dough until it has a firm, rubbery texture.

3. Add the stock to the pressure cooker. Pull pieces of gluten into small billiard-sized balls. Drop the gluten into the liquid, one piece at a time, stirring occasionally to prevent sticking.

4. Lock the lid into place; bring to high pressure for 20 minutes. Remove from the heat and quick-release the pressure. Remove the seitan and chop into bite-sized pieces.

5. Add the oil to a wok or large pan and sauté the onion on high heat until browned. Add the garlic, seitan, and broccoli and sauté for 1 minute more. Add the soy sauce, black pepper, and sugar. Mix well and sauté for an additional 30 seconds before serving.

Spice It Up

The herbs and spices in this recipe are kept to a minimum, but you can add more flavor if you'd like. Add 1 teaspoon of cayenne pepper for a little kick, and ½ teaspoon of ginger or Chinese five-spice for added flavor.

BRAISED SEITAN, ONION, AND PEPPER SUBS

Mayonnaise and cheese, or vegan versions of them, make delicious accompaniments to this sub sandwich.

INGREDIENTS
Serves 4–6

1¾ cups whole wheat flour

1¾ cups unbleached white flour

1¾ cups cold water

3½ cups vegetable stock

1 tablespoon olive oil

½ onion, sliced

½ green bell pepper, sliced

½ red bell pepper, sliced

1 jalapeño pepper, minced

1 teaspoon soy sauce

Salt and pepper, to taste

4–6 hoagie buns, or vegan buns

1. Place the whole wheat and unbleached flour in a large mixing bowl and stir well to combine. While stirring, gradually pour enough water into the flour to form a sticky dough that can be kneaded. Knead for 15 minutes. Cover the dough with cold water, place in the refrigerator, and keep submerged for at least 30 minutes.

2. Transfer the dough from the bowl to a colander and place it in the sink. Under cold running water, carefully knead the dough, rinsing out the starch and bran. After several minutes of cold water rinsing and kneading, the gluten will start to stick together. Alternate between room temperature water and cold water rinses while continuing to knead the dough until it has a firm, rubbery texture.

3. Add the stock to the pressure cooker. Pull pieces of gluten into small billiard-sized balls. Drop the gluten into the liquid, one piece at a time, stirring occasionally to prevent sticking.

4. Lock the lid into place; bring to high pressure for 20 minutes. Remove from the heat and quick-release the pressure. Remove the seitan and slice into thin strips.

5. Add the oil to a pan and sauté the onion until it caramelizes. Add the seitan and peppers and sauté for 2–3 minutes more. Stir in the soy sauce, salt, and pepper. Serve on hoagie buns.

INDIAN SEITAN CURRY

The combination of curry and cayenne give this dish one healthy dose of spice.

INGREDIENTS
Serves 4–6

1¾ cups whole wheat flour

1¾ cups unbleached white flour

1¾ cups cold water

3½ cups vegetable stock

2 tablespoons olive oil

½ onion, chopped

2 cloves garlic, minced

1 teaspoon fresh ginger, minced

3 tablespoons curry powder

1 teaspoon paprika

1 teaspoon sugar

½ teaspoon cayenne pepper

1 teaspoon soy sauce

1 14-ounce can coconut milk

Salt and pepper, to taste

1. Place the whole wheat and unbleached flour in a large mixing bowl and stir well to combine. While stirring, gradually pour enough water into the flour to form a sticky dough that can be kneaded. Knead for 15 minutes. Cover the dough with cold water, place in the refrigerator, and keep submerged for at least 30 minutes.

2. Transfer the dough from the bowl to a colander and place it in the sink. Under cold running water, carefully knead the dough, rinsing out the starch and bran. After several minutes of cold water rinsing and kneading, the gluten will start to stick together. Alternate between room temperature water and cold water rinses while continuing to knead the dough until it has a firm, rubbery texture.

3. Add the stock to the pressure cooker. Pull pieces of gluten into small billiard-sized balls. Drop the gluten into the liquid, one piece at a time, stirring occasionally to prevent sticking.

4. Lock the lid into place; bring to high pressure for 20 minutes. Remove from the heat and quick-release the pressure. Remove the seitan and chop into bite-sized pieces.

5. Add the olive oil to a pan and sauté the onion until it is caramelized. Add the garlic and ginger and sauté for 1 minute more. Add the seitan and the rest of the ingredients and allow to simmer for 20–25 minutes.

PHILLY CHEESE SEITAN SANDWICH

The city of brotherly love extends their compassion to animals with this sandwich.

INGREDIENTS
Serves 4

1 13-ounce package tempeh

6 cups water

3 cloves garlic, minced

1 teaspoon fresh ginger, minced

1 cup soy sauce

2 tablespoons olive oil

1 onion, sliced

½ green bell pepper, sliced

Salt and pepper, to taste

4–6 French rolls

4–6 slices Provolone cheese, or vegan mozzarella, such as Daiya Mozzarella Style Shreds

1. Cut the tempeh in half lengthwise, then cut the 2 slabs in half widthwise (as if you were slicing a roll), creating 4 squares that are nearly identical in size. Next, cut the tempeh into smaller strips, about 1" x 3".

2. Add the tempeh, water, garlic, ginger, and soy sauce to the pressure cooker. Lock the lid into place; bring to high pressure for 20 minutes. Remove from the heat and quick-release the pressure. Remove the tempeh.

3. Add the oil to a pan and sauté the onion and green bell pepper until they are caramelized. Add the tempeh, salt, and pepper.

4. Preheat the oven to 450°F. Place the tempeh mixture inside the French rolls and place 1–2 slices of the cheese on each. Place the tempeh sandwiches in the oven and bake for 3–5 minutes, or until the cheese has melted.

SEITAN AND DUMPLINGS

These are down-home dumplings that would make any Southern grandmother proud.

INGREDIENTS
Serves 4–6

1¾ cups whole wheat flour

1¾ cups unbleached white flour

1¾ cups cold water

3½ cups vegetable stock

1¼ cups water, divided

2 cups all-purpose flour

3 tablespoons butter, or vegan margarine, such as Earth Balance

1 teaspoon salt

1. Place the whole wheat and unbleached flour in a large mixing bowl and stir well to combine both types of flour. While stirring, gradually pour enough water into the flour to form a sticky dough that can be kneaded. Knead for 15 minutes. Cover the dough with cold water, place in the refrigerator, and keep submerged for at least 30 minutes.

2. Transfer the dough from the bowl to a colander and place it in the sink. Under cold running water, carefully knead the dough, rinsing out the starch and bran. After several minutes of cold water rinsing and kneading, the gluten will start to stick together. Alternate between room temperature water and cold water rinses while continuing to knead the dough until it has a firm, rubbery texture.

3. Add the stock to the pressure cooker. Pull pieces of gluten into small billiard-sized balls. Drop the gluten into the liquid, one piece at a time, stirring occasionally to prevent sticking.

4. Lock the lid into place; bring to high pressure for 20 minutes. Remove from the heat and quick-release the pressure. With a slotted spoon, remove the seitan and chop into bite-sized pieces. Return the seitan to the pressure cooker. Add 1 cup of water and bring the seitan and stock to a simmer.

5. To make the dumplings, combine the flour, butter, salt, and water in a medium bowl. Form the mixture into a dough. Roll the dough very thin with a rolling pin. Cut into 1" squares and drop the dumplings into the simmering stock. Allow to cook for 15–20 minutes.

SEITAN AU JUS SANDWICH

This sandwich can be considered a vegan version of a roast beef sandwich.

INGREDIENTS
Serves 4–6

1¾ cups whole wheat flour

1¾ cups unbleached white flour

1¾ cups cold water

3½ cups vegetable stock

1 cup Au Jus (Chapter 15)

8–12 slices bread

1. Place the whole wheat and unbleached flour in a large mixing bowl and stir well to combine. While stirring, gradually pour enough water into the flour to form a sticky dough that can be kneaded. Knead for 15 minutes. Cover the dough with cold water, place in the refrigerator, and keep submerged for at least 30 minutes.

2. Transfer the dough from the bowl to a colander and place it in the sink. Under cold running water, carefully knead the dough, rinsing out the starch and bran. After several minutes of cold water rinsing and kneading, the gluten will start to stick together. Alternate between room temperature water and cold water rinses while continuing to knead the dough until it has a firm, rubbery texture.

3. Add the stock to the pressure cooker. Pull pieces of gluten into small billiard-sized balls. Drop the gluten into the liquid, one piece at a time, stirring occasionally to prevent sticking.

4. Lock the lid into place; bring to high pressure for 20 minutes. Remove from the heat and quick-release the pressure. Remove the seitan and thinly slice.

5. In a medium sauté pan, warm the Au Jus sauce, then add the pieces of sliced seitan until warmed.

6. Place five slices of seitan on one piece of bread, top with extra sauce, and cover with an additional piece of bread. Serve any extra Au Jus on the side.

SEITAN SLOPPY JOES

Add to the Sloppy Joes by tossing cheese (or vegan cheese) and diced onions onto this messy, delicious sandwich. Be sure to have extra napkins on hand!

INGREDIENTS
Serves 4–6

1¾ cups whole wheat flour

1¾ cups unbleached white flour

1¾ cups cold water

3½ cups vegetable stock

1 tablespoon olive oil

½ onion, diced

½ teaspoon garlic powder

2 teaspoons brown sugar

1 tablespoon mustard

¾ cup ketchup

1 tablespoon vegan Worcestershire sauce

Salt and pepper, to taste

6–8 hamburger buns

1. Place the whole wheat and unbleached flour in a large mixing bowl and stir well to combine. While stirring, gradually pour enough water into the flour to form a sticky dough that can be kneaded. Knead for 15 minutes. Cover the dough with cold water, place in the refrigerator, and keep submerged for at least 30 minutes.

2. Transfer the dough from the bowl to a colander and place it in the sink. Under cold running water, carefully knead the dough, rinsing out the starch and bran. After several minutes of cold water rinsing and kneading, the gluten will start to stick together. Alternate between room temperature water and cold water rinses while continuing to knead the dough until it has a firm, rubbery texture.

3. Add the stock to the pressure cooker. Pull pieces of gluten into small billiard-sized balls. Drop the gluten into the liquid, one piece at a time, stirring occasionally to prevent sticking.

4. Lock the lid into place; bring to high pressure for 20 minutes. Remove from the heat and quick-release the pressure. Drain off the remaining liquid from the seitan.

5. Slice the seitan very thinly. Add the oil to a pan and sauté the onion until it caramelizes. Add the seitan and the rest of the ingredients except buns. Allow to simmer for 5–8 minutes. Serve on hamburger buns.

Seitan Alternatives
There are many alternatives to homemade seitan when making sloppy joes. Crumbled tofu or tempeh will work, as well as vegetarian beef substitutes, such as Boca Ground Crumbles.

SEITAN WITH SAUERKRAUT AND ONIONS

An ale, or another light beer, is recommended over dark beers in this recipe.

INGREDIENTS
Serves 4–6

1¾ cups whole wheat flour

1¾ cups unbleached white flour

1¾ cups cold water

3½ cups vegetable stock

¼ cup olive oil

3 onions, thinly sliced

2 teaspoons brown sugar

3 cups sauerkraut

2 cloves garlic, minced

2 bay leaves

4 red potatoes, quartered

2 carrots, roughly chopped

1 12-ounce beer of your choice

Salt and pepper, to taste

Optional: Chopped parsley

1. Place the whole wheat and unbleached flour in a large mixing bowl and stir well to combine. While stirring, gradually pour enough water into the flour to form a sticky dough that can be kneaded. Knead for 15 minutes. Cover the dough with cold water, place in the refrigerator, and keep submerged for at least 30 minutes.

2. Transfer the dough from the bowl to a colander and place it in the sink. Under cold running water, carefully knead the dough, rinsing out the starch and bran. After several minutes of cold water rinsing and kneading, the gluten will start to stick together. Alternate between room temperature water and cold water rinses while continuing to knead the dough until it has a firm, rubbery texture.

3. Add the stock to the pressure cooker. Pull pieces of gluten into small billiard-sized balls. Drop the gluten into the liquid, one piece at a time, stirring occasionally to prevent sticking.

4. Lock the lid into place; bring to high pressure for 20 minutes. Remove from the heat and quick-release the pressure. Drain off the remaining liquid from the seitan.

5. Chop the seitan into bite-sized pieces. Add the seitan and all the remaining ingredients to the pressure cooker. Lock the lid into place; bring to high pressure for 10 minutes. Remove from the heat and quick-release the pressure. Serve.

SHREDDED BBQ SEITAN

Bottled barbecue sauce will work just as well in this recipe; just make sure it's vegetarian or vegan.

INGREDIENTS
Serves 4–6

1¾ cups whole wheat flour

1¾ cups unbleached white flour

1¾ cups cold water

3½ cups vegetable stock

1 cup prepared mustard

½ cup sugar

¼ cup brown sugar

¾ cup cider vinegar

2 tablespoons chili powder

¼ tablespoon cayenne pepper

1 teaspoon soy sauce

2 tablespoons butter, or vegan margarine, such as Earth Balance

1 tablespoon liquid smoke

Salt and pepper, to taste

1. Place the whole wheat and unbleached flour in a large mixing bowl and stir well to combine. While stirring, gradually pour enough water into the flour to form a sticky dough that can be kneaded. Knead for 15 minutes. Cover the dough with cold water, place in the refrigerator, and keep submerged for at least 30 minutes.

2. Transfer the dough from the bowl to a colander and place it in the sink. Under cold running water, carefully knead the dough, rinsing out the starch and bran. After several minutes of cold water rinsing and kneading, the gluten will start to stick together. Alternate between room temperature water and cold water rinses while continuing to knead the dough until it has a firm, rubbery texture.

3. Add the stock to the pressure cooker. Pull pieces of gluten into small billiard-sized balls. Drop the gluten into the liquid, one piece at a time, stirring occasionally to prevent sticking.

4. Lock the lid into place; bring to high pressure for 20 minutes. Remove from the heat and quick-release the pressure. Drain off the remaining liquid from the seitan.

5. Add the mustard, sugars, vinegar, chilli powder, cayenne pepper, soy sauce, butter, liquid smoke, salt, and pepper to a medium pot. Shred the seitan by hand or with a knife and add to the barbecue sauce. Let simmer for about 10 minutes. Serve.

SMOKED PORTOBELLO AND SEITAN

If you don't have red wine in the house or don't drink alcohol, substitute extra vegetable stock.

INGREDIENTS

Serves 4–6

1¾ cups whole wheat flour

1¾ cups unbleached white flour

1¾ cups cold water

3½ cups vegetable stock

1 tablespoon olive oil

1 onion, chopped

3 portobello mushroom caps, chopped

1 tablespoon soy sauce

¼ teaspoon liquid smoke

½ cup red wine

2–4 tablespoons flour

Salt and pepper, to taste

2 tablespoons parsley, chopped

1. Place the whole wheat and unbleached flour in a large mixing bowl and stir well to combine. While stirring, gradually pour enough water into the flour to form a sticky dough that can be kneaded. Knead for 15 minutes. Cover the dough with cold water, place in the refrigerator, and keep submerged for at least 30 minutes.

2. Transfer the dough from the bowl to a colander and place it in the sink. Under cold running water, carefully knead the dough, rinsing out the starch and bran. After several minutes of cold water rinsing and kneading, the gluten will start to stick together. Alternate between room temperature water and cold water rinses while continuing to knead the dough until it has a firm, rubbery texture.

3. Add the stock to the pressure cooker. Pull pieces of gluten into small billiard-sized balls. Drop the gluten into the liquid, one piece at a time, stirring occasionally to prevent sticking.

4. Lock the lid into place; bring to high pressure for 20 minutes. Remove from the heat and quick-release the pressure. Remove the seitan and chop into bite-sized pieces.

5. Add the olive oil to a pan and sauté the onion and mushrooms until tender. Add the seitan, soy sauce, liquid smoke, and red wine and allow to simmer 2–3 minutes. Remove the seitan, onions, and mushrooms with a slotted spoon. Gradually add the flour to make a gravy. When the gravy is done, drizzle it over the seitan mixture. Add salt and pepper to taste and garnish with parsley. Serve.

BARBECUE TOFU SANDWICH

Not all bread is vegan, but a lot of it is. If you are making the vegan version of this recipe, be sure to read the label on your hamburger buns.

INGREDIENTS
Serves 6

1 16-ounce package firm tofu, crumbled

1 cup mustard

½ cup sugar

¼ cup brown sugar

¾ cup apple cider vinegar

¼ cup water

2 tablespoons chili powder

½ teaspoon soy sauce

¼ teaspoon cayenne pepper

2 tablespoons butter, melted, or vegan margarine, such as Earth Balance

1 tablespoon liquid smoke

Salt and pepper, to taste

6 hamburger buns

1. Wrap the block of tofu in paper towels and press for 5 minutes by adding weight on top. Whisk the rest of the ingredients except buns in a medium bowl and pour them into the pressure cooker.

2. Crumble the tofu with your hands and mix it into the other ingredients in the pressure cooker. Lock the lid into place; bring to high pressure and maintain for 5 minutes. Remove from the heat and allow pressure to release naturally. Serve on hamburger buns.

BLACKENED TOFU SANDWICH

Preparing blackened tofu on the grill is a delicious alternative to using a pressure cooker on a warm summer day.

INGREDIENTS

Serves 6

1 16-ounce package extra-firm tofu

⅓ cup soy sauce

1 tablespoon apple cider vinegar

1 tablespoon garlic, minced

1 tablespoon paprika

2 teaspoons black pepper

1½ teaspoons salt

1 teaspoon garlic powder

1 teaspoon cayenne pepper

½ teaspoon dried oregano

½ teaspoon dried thyme

2 tablespoons vegetable oil

1 cup water

6 hamburger buns

1. Drain the tofu, pat dry with a towel or paper towel, and then cut into four equal-sized pieces. Place in a 1"-deep dish.

2. Whisk together the soy sauce, vinegar, and garlic, and then pour over the tofu. Let stand for 10 minutes, being sure to turn the tofu often or spoon the excess liquid over the top.

3. To make the blackened seasoning mixture, combine the paprika, pepper, salt, garlic powder, cayenne, oregano, and thyme in a small bowl. Remove the tofu from the soy marinade and dip each side into the blackened seasoning.

4. Add the oil to the pressure cooker and sauté the blackened tofu until brown on each side. Remove the blackened tofu. Place the water in the pressure cooker along with the steamer tray. Place the blackened tofu on top of the steamer tray.

5. Lock the lid into place; bring to high pressure and maintain for 5 minutes. Remove from the heat and allow pressure to release naturally. Serve on the hamburger buns.

COCONUT GREEN CURRY TOFU

Coconut milk can range from thin and water-like to something that is almost solid. Experiment with different types of coconut milk until you find the one you like most.

INGREDIENTS
Serves 4–6

1 16-ounce package extra-firm tofu

2 green chilies, seeded and minced

4 scallions, chopped

2 cloves garlic, minced

1 teaspoon ginger, minced

1 tablespoon soy sauce

½ cup fresh cilantro, chopped

¼ cup fresh parsley, chopped

2 tablespoons water

2 tablespoons vegetable oil

1 13-ounce can coconut milk

Salt and pepper, to taste

4 cups cooked rice

1. Wrap the block of tofu in paper towels and press for 5 minutes by adding weight on top. Remove the paper towels and cut the tofu into ½"-thick pieces.

2. In a food processor, combine the chilies, scallions, garlic, ginger, soy sauce, cilantro, parsley, and water. Blend into a smooth paste, adding extra water if necessary.

3. Add the oil to the pressure cooker and sauté the tofu until it is light brown on all sides. Add the coconut milk and the green chili paste.

4. Lock the lid into place; bring to high pressure and maintain for 5 minutes. Remove from the heat and allow pressure to release naturally. Season with salt and pepper, if necessary. Serve with rice.

GENERAL TSO'S TOFU

The combination of sweet and spicy is what makes this dish a hit at Chinese restaurants across the country.

INGREDIENTS
Serves 2–4

1 16-ounce package extra-firm tofu

2 cups water

2 tablespoons cornstarch

2 cloves garlic, minced

1 teaspoon ginger, minced

⅛ cup sugar

¼ cup soy sauce

⅛ cup white wine vinegar

⅛ cup sherry wine

2 teaspoons cayenne pepper

2 tablespoons vegetable oil

2 cups broccoli, blanched and chopped

4 cups cooked rice

1. Wrap the block of tofu in paper towels and press for 5 minutes by adding weight on top. Remove the paper towels and cut the tofu into ½"-thick pieces.

2. In a small bowl, whisk together 1 cup water, cornstarch, garlic, ginger, sugar, soy sauce, vinegar, wine, and cayenne pepper. Set the sauce aside.

3. Add the oil to the pressure cooker and sauté the tofu until brown on all sides. Add the broccoli and sauté for 1 minute more. Add the General Tso's sauce.

4. Lock the lid into place; bring to high pressure and maintain for 5 minutes. Remove from the heat and allow pressure to release naturally. Serve with rice.

Types of Rice

Options are diverse when choosing a rice or grain to serve with a Chinese or Chinese-inspired tofu dish. Long-grain white rice is most commonly used, but you can also use brown rice, quinoa, or couscous.

KUNG PAO TOFU

Kung Pao Chicken is a traditional Szechuan dish that can be made vegan easily. Just replace the chicken with tofu.

INGREDIENTS
Serves 2–4

1 16-ounce package extra-firm tofu

2 tablespoons white wine

2 tablespoons soy sauce

2 tablespoons sesame oil

2 tablespoons cornstarch, dissolved in 2 tablespoons water

½ tablespoon hot chili paste

1 teaspoon rice wine vinegar

2 teaspoons brown sugar

1 cup water

1 teaspoon olive oil

½ red bell pepper, chopped

1 clove garlic, minced

4 tablespoons peanuts

4 cups cooked rice

1. Wrap the block of tofu in paper towels and press for 5 minutes by adding weight on top. Remove the paper towels and cut the tofu into ½"-thick pieces. Place in a 1"-deep dish.

2. Whisk together the white wine, soy sauce, sesame oil, cornstarch, chili paste, rice wine vinegar, and brown sugar in a small bowl and pour it over the tofu. Let stand for 10 minutes, being sure to turn the tofu often or spoon the excess liquid over the top.

3. Place the water in the pressure cooker along with the steamer tray. Place the marinated tofu on top of the steamer tray. Lock the lid into place; bring to high pressure and maintain for 5 minutes. Remove from the heat and allow pressure to release naturally.

4. Add the oil to a wok or pan and sauté the red bell pepper for 1–2 minutes. Add the marinated tofu and garlic and sauté 1 minute more. Add the sauce and cook for 2–3 minutes more. Garnish with the peanuts and serve with rice.

LEMON TOFU TACOS

Tofu mimics the role of fish in these easy-to-make tacos. Kick up the flavor by adding a touch of cayenne or chipotle pepper to the tofu marinade.

INGREDIENTS
Serves 4

1 16-ounce package extra-firm tofu

2 tablespoons lemon juice

½ tablespoon apple cider vinegar

2 tablespoons soy sauce

2 tablespoons olive oil

1 cup water

8 corn tortillas

1 tomato, diced

½ red onion, thinly sliced

2 teaspoons cilantro, chopped

Salt and pepper, to taste

1. Wrap the block of tofu in paper towels and press for 5 minutes by adding weight on top. Remove the paper towels and cut the tofu into ½"-thick pieces. Place in a 1"-deep dish.

2. Whisk together the lemon juice, apple cider vinegar, soy sauce, and olive oil in a small bowl and pour it over the tofu. Let stand for 10 minutes, being sure to turn the tofu often or spoon the excess liquid over the top.

3. Place the water in the pressure cooker along with the steamer tray. Place the marinated tofu on top of the steamer tray. Lock the lid into place; bring to high pressure and maintain for 5 minutes. Remove from the heat and allow pressure to release naturally.

4. Serve the tofu on warm tortillas with tomato, red onion, and cilantro. Season with salt and pepper, to taste, if necessary.

Corn Versus Flour Tortillas

There is no right or wrong answer as to which is better. It solely depends on your taste. Corn tortillas are more full-flavored than flour and they also have a grainier texture. Which variety you decide to use is up to you!

MARINATED TOFU STEAKS

Tofu has very little flavor on its own and is best when marinated in a flavorful liquid before cooking.

INGREDIENTS
Serves 2–4

1 16-ounce package extra-firm tofu

1 cup soy sauce

1 tablespoon white wine vinegar

1 teaspoon garlic, minced

1 teaspoon ginger, minced

2 tablespoons vegetable oil

1 cup water

1. Drain the tofu, pat dry with a towel or paper towel, and then cut into four equal-sized pieces. Place in a 1"-deep dish. Whisk together the soy sauce, vinegar, garlic, and ginger, and then pour over the tofu. Let stand for 10 minutes, being sure to turn the tofu often or spoon the excess liquid over the top.

2. Add the oil to the pressure cooker and sauté the tofu steaks until brown on each side. Remove the tofu steaks. Place the water in the pressure cooker along with the steamer tray. Place the tofu steaks on top of the steamer tray.

3. Lock the lid into place; bring to high pressure and maintain for 5 minutes. Remove from the heat and allow pressure to release naturally.

PALAK TOFU PANEER

Paneer is a type of cheese, but many versions of this popular recipe use tofu instead.

INGREDIENTS
Serves 2–4

1 16-ounce package extra-firm tofu

2 tablespoons vegetable oil

2 cloves garlic, minced

1 teaspoon ginger, minced

2 teaspoons dried red pepper flakes

½ onion, diced

1 tablespoon cumin

1 teaspoon coriander powder

1 teaspoon sugar

1 teaspoon turmeric

1 cup sour cream or soy sour cream

6 cups fresh spinach

⅛ cup cilantro, chopped

Salt and pepper, to taste

1. Wrap the block of tofu in paper towels and press for 5 minutes by adding weight on top. Remove the paper towels and cut the tofu into ½"-thick pieces.

2. Add the oil to the pressure cooker and sauté the tofu until brown on all sides. Add the garlic, ginger, red pepper flakes, onion, cumin, coriander, sugar, and turmeric. Sauté for 1–2 minutes more.

3. Mix in the sour cream and fresh spinach. Lock the lid into place; bring to high pressure and maintain for 5 minutes. Remove from the heat and allow pressure to release naturally. Garnish with cilantro, adding salt and pepper to taste. Serve with rice.

PANANG CURRY TOFU

Panang is a milder type of red curry and is made from chilies.

INGREDIENTS
Serves 4–6

1 16-ounce package extra-firm tofu

1 13-ounce can coconut milk

1 tablespoon Panang curry paste

2 tablespoons soy sauce

1 tablespoon lime juice

2 tablespoons sugar

2 tablespoons olive oil

¼ onion, sliced

½ carrot, sliced diagonally

¼ red bell pepper, chopped

½ cup fresh basil, chopped

4 cups cooked rice

1. Wrap the block of tofu in paper towels and press for 5 minutes by adding weight on top. Remove the paper towels and cut the tofu into ½"-thick pieces. Place in a 1"-deep dish.

2. In a medium bowl combine the coconut milk, curry paste, soy sauce, lime juice, and sugar.

3. Add the oil to the pressure cooker and sauté the tofu until it is light brown on all sides. Add the onion, carrot, and red bell pepper and sauté for 1–2 minutes more. Add the Panang curry sauce to the pressure cooker.

4. Lock the lid into place; bring to high pressure and maintain for 5 minutes. Remove from the heat and allow pressure to release naturally. Garnish with fresh basil. Serve with rice.

TOFU STIR-FRY WITH VEGETABLES

Mix and match the vegetables in this all-purpose stir fry to make your own creation.

INGREDIENTS
Serves 2–4

1 16-ounce package extra-firm tofu

1 red chili pepper, seeded and minced

2 cloves garlic, minced

1 teaspoon ginger, minced

1 tablespoon olive oil

3 tablespoons soy sauce

¼ cup water

1 tablespoon cornstarch

2 tablespoons vegetable oil

2 carrots, cut diagonally

1 red bell pepper, chopped

½ onion, sliced

2 cups head bok choy, chopped

½ cup yellow squash, chopped

4 cups cooked rice

1. Wrap the block of tofu in paper towels and press for 5 minutes by adding weight on top. Remove the paper towels and cut the tofu into ½"-thick pieces. Place in a 1"-deep dish.

2. In a medium bowl, combine the chili pepper, garlic, ginger, olive oil, soy sauce, water, and cornstarch. Pour it over the tofu. Let stand for 10 minutes, being sure to turn the tofu often or spoon the excess liquid over the top. Reserve the excess marinade for use later in the recipe.

3. Add the vegetable oil to the pressure cooker and sauté the tofu until it is light brown on all sides. Add the carrot, red bell pepper, onion, bok choy, and yellow squash and sauté for 1–2 minutes.

4. Pour the reserved marinade into the pressure cooker. Lock the lid into place; bring to high pressure and maintain for 5 minutes. Remove from the heat and allow pressure to release naturally. Serve with rice.

Cooking with Cornstarch

To help thicken a sauce or stew, use cornstarch. To avoid lumps, combine cornstarch with a small amount of cold water, stir until dissolved, then slowly add it to your dish, stirring over low heat until thickened. If lumps do occur, try vigorous stirring to work them out.

BL"T" SANDWICH

Leave the pork off your fork with this vegan version of the popular BLT sandwich.

INGREDIENTS
Serves 4

1 13-ounce package tempeh

6½ cups water

2 cloves garlic, minced

1 teaspoon fresh ginger, minced

¾ cup soy sauce

1 tablespoon maple syrup

½ teaspoon garlic powder

1 tablespoon liquid smoke

2 tablespoons vegetable oil

8 slices bread, toasted

6–8 lettuce leaves

1 tomato, sliced

1. Cut the tempeh in half lengthwise, then cut the 2 slabs in half widthwise (as if you were slicing a roll), creating 4 squares that are nearly identical in size. Next, cut the tempeh into smaller strips, about 1" x 3".

2. Add the tempeh, 6 cups of water, garlic, ginger, and ½ cup soy sauce to the pressure cooker. Lock the lid into place; bring to high pressure for 20 minutes. Remove from the heat and quick-release the pressure. Remove the tempeh.

3. In a small bowl, mix ½ cup water, ¼ cup soy sauce, maple syrup, garlic powder, and liquid smoke. Place the tempeh in a small casserole dish and pour the marinade on top of it. Allow the tempeh to marinate for about 30 minutes.

4. Add the oil to a pan and sauté the "bacon" until it is brown on both sides.

5. Toast the bread in a toaster or broiler. Assemble the sandwiches using the tempeh "bacon," lettuce, and tomato slices. Serve.

CAROLINA-STYLE BARBECUE TEMPEH

Vinegar-based barbecue sauce, as opposed to tomato-based, is popular across the South.

INGREDIENTS
Serves 4

1 8-ounce package tempeh

6 cups water

2 cloves garlic, minced

1 teaspoon fresh ginger, minced

1 cup soy sauce

½ cup apple cider vinegar

½ cup maple syrup

½ cup olive oil

2 teaspoons chipotle powder

1 teaspoon dried thyme

1 teaspoon paprika

1 teaspoon cumin

Salt and pepper, to taste

4 hamburger buns

1. Cut the tempeh in half lengthwise, then cut the 2 slabs in half widthwise (as if you were slicing a roll), creating 4 squares that are nearly identical in size. Next, cut the tempeh into smaller strips, about 1" x 3".

2. Add the tempeh, water, garlic, ginger, and ½ cup of the soy sauce to the pressure cooker. Lock the lid into place; bring to high pressure for 20 minutes. Remove from the heat and quick-release the pressure. Remove the tempeh.

3. In a medium pot, add the rest of the soy sauce, cider vinegar, syrup, oil, chipotle, thyme, paprika, cumin, salt, and pepper. Bring to a simmer and add the tempeh. Let simmer for 15–20 minutes. Serve on a bun.

FRIED TEMPEH WITH WHITE GRAVY

Fried and fatty foods should be kept to a minimum, but the occasional indulgence probably won't hurt.

INGREDIENTS
Serves 4

1 13-ounce package tempeh

8 cups water

4 cloves garlic, minced

1 teaspoon fresh ginger, minced

¾ cup soy sauce

1 tablespoon plus ½ cup vegetable oil

¼ cup onion, diced

½ cup flour

2 tablespoons nutritional yeast

½ teaspoon sage

Salt and pepper, to taste

6–8 biscuits, or vegan biscuits

1. Cut the tempeh in half lengthwise, then cut the 2 slabs in half widthwise (as if you were slicing a roll), creating 4 squares that are nearly identical in size.

2. Add the tempeh, 6 cups water, 2 cloves garlic, ginger, and ½ cup soy sauce to the pressure cooker. Lock the lid into place; bring to high pressure for 20 minutes. Remove from the heat and quick-release the pressure. Remove the tempeh.

3. In a small frying pan over medium heat, heat 1 tablespoon vegetable oil and fry each piece of tempeh for 3 minutes on each side. Remove from the pan when cooked and set aside.

4. Add the remaining oil to a small pot. Sauté the remaining 2 garlic cloves and the onion for 2–3 minutes. Add ¼ cup soy sauce and slowly stir in the flour to create a roux. Slowly stir in the remaining 2 cups water and bring to a boil, stirring constantly for 2–3 minutes. Remove from heat and add the nutritional yeast, sage, salt, and pepper. Serve on top of the tempeh with biscuits.

GENERAL TSO'S TEMPEH

This recipe is very similar to General Tso's Tofu (see recipe in this chapter), and would also be delicious if made with seitan.

INGREDIENTS
Serves 4

1 13-ounce package tempeh

7 cups water

4 cloves garlic, minced

3 teaspoons fresh ginger, minced

¾ cup soy sauce

¼ cup cornstarch

¼ cup sugar

⅛ cup white wine vinegar

⅛ cup sherry wine

2 tablespoons vegetable oil

2 cups broccoli, blanched and chopped

1. Cut the tempeh in half lengthwise, then cut the 2 slabs in half widthwise (as if you were slicing a roll), creating 4 squares that are nearly identical in size. Next, cut the tempeh into smaller strips, about 1" x 3".

2. Add the tempeh, 6 cups water, 2 cloves garlic, 1 teaspoon ginger, and ½ cup soy sauce to the pressure cooker. Lock the lid into place; bring to high pressure for 20 minutes. Remove from the heat and quick-release the pressure. Remove the tempeh.

3. In a small bowl, combine 1 cup water, ¼ cup soy sauce, 2 cloves garlic, 2 teaspoons ginger, cornstarch, sugar, vinegar, and wine to create the sauce.

4. In a wok or large pan, add the oil and sauté the tempeh and broccoli for 1–2 minutes. Add the sauce and cook until it thickens, 2–3 minutes. Serve with rice.

HOISIN-GLAZED TEMPEH

Hoisin is a strongly flavored, slightly spicy, and slightly sweet Chinese sauce.

INGREDIENTS
Serves 4

1 13-ounce package tempeh

6 cups water

4 cloves garlic, minced

2 teaspoons fresh ginger, minced

¾ cup soy sauce

½ cup hoisin sauce

2 tablespoons fresh lime juice

1 lime, cut into wedges

Salt and pepper, to taste

1. Cut the tempeh in half lengthwise, then cut the 2 slabs in half widthwise (as if you were slicing a roll), creating 4 squares that are nearly identical in size. Next, cut the tempeh into smaller strips, about 1" x 3".

2. Add the tempeh, water, 2 cloves minced garlic, 1 teaspoon ginger, and ½ cup of soy sauce to the pressure cooker. Lock the lid into place; bring to high pressure for 20 minutes. Remove from the heat and quick-release the pressure. Remove the tempeh.

3. Preheat the oven to 450°F. Place the tempeh in a casserole dish. In a medium bowl, mix the ¼ cup soy sauce, hoisin sauce, lime juice, 2 cloves minced garlic, and 1 teaspoon ginger. Pour the mixture onto the tempeh and marinate for 10 minutes.

4. Place the tempeh into the oven for 10 minutes, flipping one time. Garnish with the lime wedges and serve with rice. Taste and season with salt and pepper, if necessary.

LEMON-PEPPER TEMPEH

When fresh herbs are in season, add chopped curly or flat-leaf parsley to this dish before serving.

INGREDIENTS
Serves 4

1 8-ounce package tempeh

6 cups water

6 cloves garlic, minced

1 teaspoon fresh ginger, minced

½ cup soy sauce

¼ cup extra-virgin olive oil

2 tablespoons fresh lemon juice

1 teaspoon black pepper

Salt, to taste

1. Cut the tempeh in half lengthwise, then cut the 2 slabs in half widthwise (as if you were slicing a roll), creating 4 squares that are nearly identical in size. Next, cut the tempeh into smaller strips, about 1" x 3".

2. Add the tempeh, water, 2 cloves garlic, ginger, and soy sauce to the pressure cooker. Lock the lid into place; bring to high pressure for 20 minutes. Remove from the heat and quick-release the pressure. Remove the tempeh.

3. Preheat the oven to 450°F. In a bowl, mix the oil, lemon juice, remaining 4 garlic cloves, black pepper, and salt.

4. Place the tempeh in a casserole dish and pour the marinade over it. Allow the tempeh to marinate for 10 minutes. Place the dish in the oven and bake for about 15 minutes, turning once.

Serving Suggestions
Make this tempeh dish the star of the show and serve as a main course, with a vegetable and grain on the side. Or, place the strips on a hoagie roll topped with mayonnaise or vegan mayonnaise and lettuce to make a tasty sub sandwich.

MOJO TEMPEH CUBAN SANDWICH

Mojo is a Cuban sauce made with garlic, olive oil, and citrus juice.

INGREDIENTS
Serves 4

1 13-ounce package tempeh

6 cups water

3 cloves garlic, minced

1 teaspoon fresh ginger, minced

½ cup soy sauce

2 tablespoons orange juice

1 tablespoon lime juice

1 tablespoon lemon juice

2 tablespoons olive oil

3 tablespoons parsley, chopped

½ teaspoon dried oregano

½ teaspoon salt

¼ teaspoon pepper

4 Cuban rolls

6–8 slices Swiss cheese, or vegan mozzarella, such as Daiya Mozzarella Style Shreds

Optional: 2 cups lettuce, shredded

Optional: 1 tomato, sliced

Optional: Dill pickle slices

1. Cut the tempeh in half lengthwise, then cut the 2 slabs in half widthwise (as if you were slicing a roll), creating 4 squares that are nearly identical in size. Next, cut the tempeh into smaller strips, about 1" x 3".

2. Add the tempeh, water, 2 cloves of garlic, ginger, and soy sauce to the pressure cooker. Lock the lid into place; bring to high pressure for 20 minutes. Remove from the heat and quick-release the pressure. Remove the tempeh.

3. In a small bowl, make the Mojo sauce by mixing the orange juice, lime juice, lemon juice, olive oil, 1 clove garlic, parsley, oregano, salt, and pepper. Let the tempeh marinate in the Mojo sauce for 10 minutes.

4. Preheat the oven to 450°F. Place the marinated tempeh on the Cuban rolls and drizzle a little more Mojo sauce on top of the tempeh. Place 1–2 slices of Swiss cheese on each sandwich. Place the sandwiches in the oven and cook for about 3–5 minutes, or until the cheese has melted.

5. Assemble the rest of the sandwich as desired, by adding lettuce, tomato, pickles, and more Mojo sauce. Press the sandwich before serving.

Traditional Cuban Sandwiches

In the United States, Cuban sandwiches are typically identified by the type of bread (Cuban) and condiments on the sandwich. Common ingredients are pickles, mustard, and cheese.

SPICY TEMPEH FAJITAS

Add a dollop of sour cream, or soy sour cream, and salsa to finish off each of your fajitas.

INGREDIENTS .
Serves 4

1 13-ounce package tempeh

6 cups water

2 cloves garlic, minced

1 teaspoon fresh ginger, minced

½ cup soy sauce

1 tablespoon olive oil

½ onion, sliced

½ green bell pepper, sliced

½ cup mushrooms sliced

1 jalapeño, minced

½ teaspoon chili powder

¼ teaspoon chipotle powder

Salt and pepper, to taste

1 tomato, diced

Optional: Chopped cilantro

1 lime, cut into wedges

8–12 corn tortillas

1. Cut the tempeh in half lengthwise, then cut the 2 slabs in half widthwise (as if you were slicing a roll), creating 4 squares that are nearly identical in size. Next, cut the tempeh into smaller strips, about 1" x 3".

2. Add the tempeh, water, garlic, ginger, and soy sauce to the pressure cooker. Lock the lid into place; bring to high pressure for 20 minutes. Remove from the heat and quick-release the pressure. Remove the tempeh.

3. Add the oil to a pan and sauté the onion, green pepper, mushrooms, and jalapeño until caramelized. Add the tempeh, chili powder, chipotle powder, salt, and pepper. Cook for 2–3 minutes more. Garnish with the tomato, cilantro (if using), and lime. Serve on warmed tortillas.

Tricks of the Trade

It may seem like a surprising addition, but many restaurants add soy sauce to fajitas to give them an extra boost of flavor.

TEMPEH BACON

Save money by making your own tempeh bacon instead of buying it prepackaged in stores.

INGREDIENTS
Serves 8

1 13-ounce package tempeh

6½ cups water

2 cloves garlic, minced

1 teaspoon fresh ginger, minced

¾ cup soy sauce

1 tablespoon maple syrup

½ teaspoon garlic powder

1 tablespoon liquid smoke

2 tablespoons vegetable oil

1. Cut the tempeh in half lengthwise, then cut the 2 slabs in half widthwise (as if you were slicing a roll), creating 4 squares that are nearly identical in size. Next, cut the tempeh into smaller strips, about 1" x 3".

2. Add the tempeh, 6 cups of water, garlic, ginger, and ½ cup soy sauce to the pressure cooker. Lock the lid into place; bring to high pressure for 20 minutes. Remove from the heat and quick-release the pressure. Remove the tempeh.

3. In a small bowl, mix ½ cup water, ¼ cup soy sauce, maple syrup, garlic powder, and liquid smoke. Place the tempeh in a small casserole dish and pour the marinade on top of it. Allow the tempeh to marinate for about 30 minutes.

4. Add the oil to a pan and sauté the "bacon" until it is brown on both sides.

TEMPEH SLIDERS

Sliders are mini sandwiches, perfect as an appetizer or a snack.

INGREDIENTS

Serves 4

1 13-ounce package tempeh

6 cups water

2 cloves garlic, minced

1 teaspoon fresh ginger, minced

½ cup soy sauce

1 tablespoon salt

1 teaspoon black pepper

½ teaspoon garlic powder

½ teaspoon onion powder

¼ teaspoon cumin

⅛ teaspoon cayenne pepper

3 tablespoons olive oil

½ red onion, sliced

6–8 slices American cheese or vegan Cheddar

8 mini hamburger buns

1. Cut the tempeh in half lengthwise, then cut the 2 slabs in half widthwise (as if you were slicing a roll), creating 4 squares that are nearly identical in size.

2. Add the tempeh, water, garlic, ginger, and soy sauce to the pressure cooker. Lock the lid into place; bring to high pressure for 20 minutes. Remove from the heat and quick-release the pressure. Remove the tempeh.

3. In a small bowl, combine the salt, pepper, garlic powder, onion powder, cumin, and cayenne pepper. In a small pan, add 1 tablespoon of the olive oil and sauté the red onion until it has caramelized. Set aside.

4. In a large pan, heat the remaining 2 tablespoons of olive oil and add the tempeh sliders. Season the tempeh with the spice mixture and cook until browned on each side. Melt a slice of cheese on each piece of tempeh and top with the caramelized onion. Serve on a mini hamburger bun.

TEMPEH TAMALES

Be sure to use vegetable shortening in this recipe. Plain shortening can be made from the fat of an animal.

INGREDIENTS
Serves 4

1 13-ounce package tempeh

7½ cups water, divided use

2 cloves garlic, minced

1 teaspoon fresh ginger, minced

½ cup soy sauce

15 corn husks

2 Anaheim chilies

1¼ cups corn tortilla flour

½ cup fine cornmeal

¾ teaspoon baking powder

1 teaspoon salt

½ cup plus 1 tablespoon vegetable shortening

½ white onion, chopped

¾ cup fresh corn

½ red onion, thinly sliced

1 lime, cut into wedges for juicing

1 cup tomatillo salsa

1. Cut the tempeh in half lengthwise, then cut the 2 slabs in half widthwise (as if you were slicing a roll), creating 4 squares that are nearly identical in size. Next, cut the tempeh into smaller strips, about 1" x 3".

2. Add the tempeh, 6 cups water, garlic, ginger, and soy sauce to the pressure cooker. Lock the lid into place; bring to high pressure for 20 minutes. Remove from the heat and quick-release the pressure. Remove the tempeh.

3. Submerge the corn husks in hot water, placing a weight on top of them to keep them submerged. Let soak for 30 minutes and then rinse. Cover with a damp towel and set aside. Roast the chilies on medium-high heat until the skin is charred. Place the chilies in a plastic bag, twist closed, and let sit for 10 minutes. Gently remove the skins, the stem, and the seeds. Chop the pepper flesh and set aside.

4. Whisk together the corn tortilla flour, cornmeal, baking powder, and salt in a large bowl. Slowly pour in 1½ cups water, mix slightly, and then let stand for 5 minutes. Add ½ cup shortening and mix together using a spoon or an electric mixer. Set aside.

5. Heat the remaining tablespoon of shortening over medium heat. Add the white onion and sauté until tender. Add the tempeh, chopped chilies, and the corn and cook for about 6 minutes. Remove from the heat and let cool completely before adding to the corn flour mixture.

6. When ready to assemble, stir the cooled tempeh and vegetables into the corn flour mixture. Place one corn husk at a time on a flat work surface and scoop ¼ cup of the filling into the center. Fold the narrow end up to the center, then fold both sides together to enclose the filling. Tie the tamales closed with strands of corn husk.

7. Stand the tamales up in a large steamer or colander; open-end up. Steam for 35 minutes, or until the filling is firm. To serve, slice open the corn husk (or completely remove the husk) and top the filling with sliced red onions, fresh lime juice, and tomatillo salsa.

PART VII
FOR THE KITCHEN

CHAPTER 15

SAUCES

AU JUS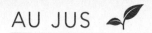

Try Better Than Bouillon, No Beef Base instead of plain vegetable stock in this rich sauce.

INGREDIENTS
Yields 1½ cups

1 tablespoon butter, or vegan margarine, such as Earth Balance

1 shallot, minced

1 tablespoon flour

2 cups faux-beef stock or vegetable stock

1 cup red wine

¼ teaspoon liquid smoke

1 teaspoon salt

1 teaspoon pepper

1. Add the butter to the pressure cooker and sauté the shallot over medium-high heat until golden brown. Stir in the flour to create a roux. Add the stock, red wine, liquid smoke, salt, and pepper to the roux.

2. Lock the lid into place and bring to high pressure. Once the pressure is achieved, turn the heat to low and cook for about 5 minutes. Allow pressure to release naturally.

3. Remove lid and continue to simmer over low heat until the sauce has reduced by half.

Cooking with Wine
Many people think that if you are cooking with wine you can use a lower-quality product than you would if you were drinking it. However, as a general rule, if you wouldn't drink it, you shouldn't cook with it. The flavors will still come through, even cooked.

BASIC MARINARA SAUCE

For a "meaty" marinara, add cooked Boca Ground Crumbles.

INGREDIENTS
Serves 4–6

2 tablespoons olive oil

½ onion, diced

2 cloves garlic, minced

2 14-ounce cans diced tomatoes

½ teaspoons sugar

1 tablespoon tomato paste

⅓ cup water

1 tablespoon fresh lemon juice

2 tablespoons fresh basil, chopped

Salt and pepper, to taste

1. Add the oil to the pressure cooker and sauté the onion until golden brown. Add the garlic and sauté for an additional 30 seconds. Add the tomatoes, sugar, tomato paste, and water.

2. Lock the lid into place and bring to high pressure. Once the pressure is achieved, turn the heat to low and cook for about 5 minutes. Remove from the heat and allow pressure to release naturally.

3. Stir in the lemon juice, basil, and add salt and pepper to taste.

BÉCHAMEL SAUCE

Béchamel is one of the most commonly used "mother sauces," and is the foundation for an Alfredo sauce.

INGREDIENTS
Yields 3 cups

½ cup butter, or vegan margarine, such as Earth Balance

½ cup all-purpose flour

4 cups milk, heated, or unsweetened soymilk

1 teaspoon salt

1 teaspoon pepper

1. Soften the butter over medium heat in the pressure cooker. Add flour and stir to create a roux. Gradually whisk in the warm milk until there are no lumps.

2. Lock the lid into place and bring to high pressure. Once the pressure is achieved, turn the heat to low and allow to cook for about 5 minutes, or until the sauce has thickened. Remove from the heat and allow pressure to release naturally.

3. Season with salt and pepper.

BEURRE BLANC

Try adding a variety of ingredients to this basic beurre blanc—herbs, spices, or even fruit!

INGREDIENTS
Yields 1 cup

2 cups white wine

1 tablespoon shallot, minced

2 cups butter, cold, or vegan margarine, such as Earth Balance

1 teaspoon salt

1. Heat the wine and shallot in the pressure cooker and bring to a simmer. Let the wine reduce to half.

2. While the wine is reducing, begin cutting the butter into medium cubes. Once the wine has reduced, begin whisking the cubes of butter in a few at a time, in order to create an emulsion. Once all the butter has been whisked into the sauce, lock the lid into place and bring to high pressure. When the pressure is achieved, turn the heat to low and cook for about 5 minutes. Quick-release the pressure and remove the lid.

3. Season with salt.

BOLOGNESE SAUCE

This rich meat sauce is the perfect topping for fettuccine. Serve with a tossed salad and crusty, warm garlic bread.

INGREDIENTS
Yields 4 cups

1 tablespoon unsalted butter

1 medium sweet onion, peeled and diced

1 medium carrot, peeled and diced

1 stalk celery with leaves, diced

1 clove garlic, peeled and minced

8 ounces ground round

8 ounces ground pork

8 ounces ground veal

2 tablespoons tomato paste

½ cup dry white wine

1 15-ounce can diced tomatoes

1 bay leaf

½ cup heavy cream

Salt and freshly ground black pepper, to taste

1. Melt the butter in the pressure cooker over medium-high heat. Add the onion, carrot, and celery; sauté for 3 minutes or until the vegetables begin to soften. Add the garlic and ground meat. Fry for about 5 minutes or until the meat loses its pink color, breaking the meat apart as you do so. Drain and discard any rendered fat. Stir in the tomato paste and sauté for 1 minute. Stir in the white wine and boil for about 2 minutes.

2. Stir in the undrained tomatoes. Add the bay leaf. Lock the lid into place and bring to high pressure; maintain pressure for 15 minutes.

3. Remove from heat and quick-release the pressure. Remove the lid. Return the pan to medium-high heat and bring to a boil. Stir in the cream, continuing to cook for about 5 minutes. Taste for seasoning and add salt and pepper as needed.

A Less Expensive Alternative

Omit the ground veal and instead use 12 ounces each of ground round and ground pork. Stir ¾ teaspoon of Minor's Veal Base (*www.soupbase.com*) into the meat when you add the canned tomatoes. The veal base will add some sodium, so taste the sauce before you add any salt, or consider using no-salt-added canned tomatoes.

CASHEW CREAM SAUCE

To make an alcohol-free sauce, double the amount of vegetable stock or water instead of including 1 cup wine.

INGREDIENTS
Yields 2½ cups

1 cup cashews

1 cup white wine

1 cup milk, or unsweetened soymilk

1 cup vegetable stock or water

2 cups béchamel sauce

Salt and pepper, to taste

1. Grind the cashews in a food processor or a coffee grinder. Set aside.

2. Add the white wine to the pressure cooker over medium heat and bring to a simmer. Allow the wine to reduce by half. Stir in the ground cashews, milk, stock, and béchamel sauce.

3. Lock the lid into place and bring to low pressure. Maintain pressure for 5 minutes then allow pressure to release naturally. Remove lid and continue to cook over low heat, until reduced by half.

4. Taste for seasoning, and add salt and pepper if needed.

Uses for Cashew Cream
In many recipes, cashew cream can be used in place of dairy. This savory version would be best suited to replace heavy cream or cheeses, but there are also plain versions of cashew cream that can be used in desserts.

LIGHT MUSHROOM CREAM SAUCE

This is a very rich and strong-flavored sauce that is best used on homemade pasta or rich egg pasta.

INGREDIENTS
Serves 6

1 tablespoon olive oil

2 tablespoons butter, divided

1 pound button mushrooms, roughly sliced

1 bunch parsley, stems and leaves divided and chopped

1 cup vegetable stock

2 ounces dried porcini mushrooms, crumbled

½ teaspoon salt

¼ teaspoon white pepper

1 tablespoon flour

1 cup milk

¼ teaspoon nutmeg

1. Heat olive oil and 1 tablespoon butter in an uncovered pressure cooker over medium heat. Sauté button mushrooms and parsley stems, stirring infrequently until mushrooms are lightly browned. Add the stock, porcini mushrooms, salt, and pepper. Mix well. Close and lock the lid.

2. Turn the heat up to high and when the cooker reaches pressure, lower the heat to the minimum needed to maintain pressure. Cook for 5 minutes at high pressure.

3. When time is up, open the pressure cooker by releasing pressure.

4. Mix in flour, milk, and nutmeg. Purée sauce, using an immersion blender. Simmer sauce on low heat until desired consistency.

5. Sprinkle with parsley leaves before serving.

More Flavor with Less
Combine cheaper button mushrooms with fresh or dried gourmet mushrooms to increase flavor without increasing the cost. If porcini are not available, substitute with cremini, portobello, and even oyster mushrooms!

CHICKEN AND SPINACH CURRY SAUCE

The chicken and spinach create a layer in the pressure cooker that keeps the pasta sauce from burning on the bottom of the pan.

INGREDIENTS
Serves 6

½ cup chicken broth or water

1 pound boneless, skinless chicken, cut into 1-inch pieces

2 10-ounce packages frozen spinach, rinsed of any ice crystals

1½ cups pasta sauce

1 tablespoon mild curry powder

2 tablespoons applesauce

Salt and freshly ground black pepper, to taste

6 cups cooked rice

Optional: Fresh cilantro

1. Add the broth and chicken to the pressure cooker and place the frozen blocks of spinach on top. Mix the pasta sauce together with the curry powder and pour it over the spinach. Do not mix the sauce into the other ingredients.

2. Lock the lid in place. Bring to high pressure over medium heat; maintain the pressure for 5 minutes. Quick-release the pressure. Carefully remove the lid, add the applesauce, and stir well. If the moisture from the spinach thinned the sauce too much, simmer uncovered for 5 minutes or until the sauce is the desired consistency. Taste the sauce and add more curry powder, salt, and pepper if needed. Serve over cooked rice. Garnish with cilantro if desired.

COUNTRY BARBECUE SAUCE

You can use this barbecue sauce as a sauce served on the side, a dipping sauce, or a grilling wet-mop sauce.

INGREDIENTS
Yields approximately 5 cups

4 cups ketchup

½ cup apple cider vinegar

½ cup vegetarian Worcestershire sauce

½ cup light brown sugar, firmly packed

¼ cup molasses

¼ cup prepared mustard

2 tablespoons barbecue seasoning

1 teaspoon freshly ground black pepper

Optional: 1 tablespoon liquid smoke

Optional: 2 tablespoons hot sauce, or to taste

Add all ingredients except optional seasonings to the pressure cooker. Stir to mix. Lock the lid into place. Bring to low pressure; maintain for 20 minutes. Remove from heat and quick-release the pressure. Taste for seasoning and add the desired amount of optional seasoning. Ladle into sterilized glass jars; cover and store in the refrigerator for up to 3 months.

Barbecue Seasoning

Barbecue seasoning is a blend of herbs and spices that can be found in the spice aisle of your local grocery store. To make your own, mix equal parts of brown sugar, ground red pepper, salt, garlic powder, onion powder, paprika, and dried oregano.

KANSAS CITY–STYLE BARBECUE SAUCE

Pan-toasting the smoked paprika before you add the other ingredients will intensify its smoky flavor.

INGREDIENTS
Yields 4 cups

2 tablespoons smoked paprika

3½ cups ketchup

½ cup light brown sugar

¼ cup molasses

¼ cup white distilled or white wine vinegar

¼ teaspoon cayenne pepper

1 tablespoon onion powder

1½ teaspoons celery seed

1 teaspoon celery salt

1½ teaspoons garlic powder

1 teaspoon ground cumin

2 teaspoons mustard powder

1½ teaspoons chili powder

1 teaspoon fresh lemon juice

1 teaspoon freshly ground black pepper

¼ teaspoon ground ginger

¼ teaspoon ground allspice

¼ teaspoon dried thyme

Add the smoked paprika to the pressure cooker. Lightly toast it over medium heat until it begins to release its smoked fragrance. Stir in the remaining ingredients. Lock on the lid and bring to low pressure; maintain pressure for 20 minutes. Quick-release the pressure. Allow sauce to cool and then refrigerate in a covered container for up to a week, or freeze until needed.

MEMPHIS-STYLE BARBECUE SAUCE

Before you shape hamburger to fix on the grill, stir some of this barbecue sauce into the ground meat.

INGREDIENTS
Yields 4 cups

2 cups ketchup

1½ cups distilled white vinegar

¼ cup light brown sugar

2 tablespoons onion powder

¼ cup Worcestershire sauce

¼ cup prepared mustard

1 teaspoon freshly ground black pepper

Salt, to taste

Optional: Cayenne pepper or hot sauce, to taste

Add all ingredients except the salt and cayenne pepper or hot sauce to the pressure cooker. Lock on the lid and bring to low pressure; maintain pressure for 5 minutes. Quick-release the pressure. Stir the sauce and taste for seasoning; add salt and cayenne pepper or hot sauce if desired. Allow sauce to cool and then refrigerate in a covered container for up to a week or freeze until needed.

ESPAGNOLE

Espagnole is one of the "mother sauces," and is used as the foundation for other sauces in this book.

INGREDIENTS
Yields 3 cups

1 small carrot, chopped

1 medium white onion, chopped

¼ cup butter, or vegan margarine, such as Earth Balance

¼ cup flour

4 cups hot vegetable stock, preferably vegan beef flavor

¼ cup canned tomato purée

2 large garlic cloves, chopped

1 celery rib, chopped

½ teaspoon whole black peppercorns

1 bay leaf

1. Sauté the carrot and onion in the butter over medium-high heat in the pressure cooker until golden. Add the flour and whisk to form a roux. Continue to cook, stirring continuously, until the roux is medium brown, about 30 minutes. While whisking, add the hot stock, being sure to prevent lumps. Add the tomato purée, garlic, celery, peppercorns, and bay leaf.

2. Lock the lid into place and bring to high pressure. Once the pressure is achieved, turn the heat to low and cook for about 5 minutes. Remove from the heat and allow pressure to release naturally.

3. Bring the sauce to a simmer; cook, uncovered, until reduced to 3 cups, stirring frequently. Remove the solids from the sauce before serving.

What Is a Roux?

A roux is a blend of equal parts fat, such as butter, margarine, or oil, and flour that is used to thicken sauces. It's cooked over various levels of heat and different lengths of time to achieve either a white, blond, or brown roux.

FRESH TOMATO SAUCE

You can use this sauce immediately, refrigerate it in a covered container for up to a week, or freeze it for 6 months.

INGREDIENTS
Yields 4 cups

2 tablespoons olive oil

2 cloves garlic, peeled and minced

2½ pounds fresh, vine-ripened tomatoes

1 teaspoon dried parsley

1 teaspoon dried basil

1 tablespoon balsamic vinegar

½ teaspoon granulated cane sugar

Salt, to taste

Freshly ground black pepper, to taste

1. Add the oil to the pressure cooker and bring to temperature over medium heat. Add the garlic; sauté for 30 seconds.

2. Peel and dice the tomatoes. Add them to the pressure cooker along with any juice from the tomatoes. Add the remaining ingredients.

3. Lock the lid in place and bring to low pressure; maintain for 10 minutes. Remove from the heat and allow pressure to release naturally.

4. Remove the lid and stir the sauce. If you prefer a thicker sauce, return to the heat and simmer uncovered for 10 minutes or until it reaches the desired thickness.

Balancing the Acidity

When tasting your tomato sauce and thinking "what else do I need to add?" many cooks reach for additional salt, but that might not be the ingredient you need. To balance out the acidity, the taste you may be trying to omit, try adding sugar or even grated carrot to the sauce.

GARDEN MARINARA SAUCE

Serve warmed sauce over pasta, rice, or vegetables.

INGREDIENTS
Serves 4–6

2 tablespoons olive oil

1 large sweet onion, diced

1 small red bell pepper, diced

1 large carrot, peeled and grated

4 cloves garlic, minced

1 tablespoon dried parsley

½ teaspoon dried ground fennel

1 teaspoon dried basil

1 bay leaf

Pinch dried red pepper flakes

¼ teaspoon salt

1 14½-ounce can diced tomatoes in sauce

½ cup vegetable stock

1. Add the oil to the pressure cooker and bring to temperature over medium-high heat. Add the onion, bell pepper, and carrot; sauté for 3 minutes. Stir in the garlic and sauté an additional 30 seconds. Stir in the remaining ingredients.

2. Lock the lid into place. Bring the pressure cooker to low pressure; maintain for 10 minutes.

3. Quick-release the pressure. Remove the lid. Stir the sauce. Remove and discard the bay leaf. If desired, use an immersion blender to purée the sauce.

PLUM SAUCE

Plum sauce is often served with egg rolls, but you can also use it as a glaze on tofu or vegetables.

INGREDIENTS
Yields 4 cups

8 cups (about 3 pounds) plums, pitted and cut in half

1 small sweet onion, diced

1 cup water

1 teaspoon fresh ginger, peeled and minced

1 clove garlic, minced

¾ cup granulated sugar

½ cup rice vinegar or cider vinegar

1 teaspoon ground coriander

½ teaspoon salt

½ teaspoon cinnamon

¼ teaspoon cayenne pepper

¼ teaspoon ground cloves

1. Add the plums, onion, water, ginger, and garlic to the pressure cooker. Lock the lid into place and bring to low pressure; maintain for 5 minutes. Remove from the heat and quick-release the pressure.

2. Use an immersion blender to pulverize the contents of the pressure cooker before straining it, or press the cooked plum mixture through a sieve.

3. Return the liquefied and strained plum mixture to the pressure cooker and stir in sugar, vinegar, coriander, salt, cinnamon, cayenne pepper, and cloves. Lock the lid into place and bring to low pressure; maintain for 5 minutes. Remove from heat and quick-release the pressure. Remove the lid and check the sauce; it should have the consistency of applesauce. If it isn't yet thick enough, place the uncovered pressure cooker over medium heat and simmer until desired consistency is achieved.

QUICK DEMI-GLACE

Quick *is a relative term in this case. This demi-glace version takes several hours to make rather than more than an entire day of simmering sauces on the stovetop. This version omits the tomatoes, leaving you with the option of whisking in some sautéed tomato paste when a tomato back note is needed.*

INGREDIENTS
Yields 1 cup

1½ pounds veal bones

1½ pounds beef bones

1 pound chicken backs

Water, as needed

1 tablespoon vegetable oil

1 medium white onion, peeled and diced

1 large carrot, peeled and diced

1 celery stalk with leaves, diced

1 tablespoon dried parsley

½ teaspoon dried thyme

½ teaspoon whole black peppercorns

1 bay leaf

1. Trim the bones of any fat, but leave some meat attached to them. Discard any chicken skin and chop the backs into 3-inch pieces.

2. Preheat the broiler. Arrange the veal and beef bones in a roasting pan; place the pan in the oven about 6 inches away from the source of heat. Broil for 15 minutes. Remove the roasting pan from the oven and turn the bones. Add the chopped chicken backs to the pan and return the pan to the oven. Broil for another 15 minutes.

3. Pour off and discard the rendered fat from the roasting pan. Place the pan over two burners on medium-high heat until the pan sizzles. Pour in 2 cups of water and stir it into the bones, scraping up the browned bits on the bottom of the roasting pan. Remove from heat.

4. Add the oil to the pressure cooker and bring to temperature. Stir in the onion, carrot, celery, parsley, thyme, and peppercorns; sauté for 3 minutes. Add the bay leaf. Transfer the broiled bones and water to the pressure cooker. If necessary, add additional hot water so that the water level is an inch above the bones. (Note: The bones and water should not fill the pressure cooker beyond two-thirds full. If you're using a small pressure cooker, you'll need to divide the bones and cook the bones in two batches.)

5. Lock the lid into place and bring to high pressure; maintain for 1½ hours. Remove from the heat and allow pressure to release naturally. Strain the stock into a stockpot. Let rest for 10 minutes and then skim off and discard any fat. Place the stockpot over high heat and bring to a boil. Reduce the heat, but maintain and boil for an hour or until the liquid is dark brown and thick; it should be evaporated to about 1 cup at this point. Chilled demi-glace can be cut into cubes, wrapped in plastic, and stored in the refrigerator for 2 weeks, and can be frozen indefinitely in freezer bags.

QUICK SAUSAGE RAGU

A small pressure pan is best, but not required, for making this recipe. If you purchased a pressure cooker set, you can make the sauce in the small pressure pan, and boil water for the pasta in the larger base. Serve with a rustic pasta like orechiette or potato gnocchi.

INGREDIENTS

Serves 6

8 ounces Italian sausage, removed from casing

1 red onion, chopped

1 clove garlic, pressed

3 sprigs fresh oregano, chopped

¼ teaspoon salt

⅛ teaspoon pepper

1 (14.5-ounce can) chopped tomatoes

1. In the cold pressure cooker add the crumbled Italian sausage and set the heat to low, to slowly melt and render the fat. Stir the sausage to break it up. Add the onion and raise the heat to medium-high. Sauté for 5 minutes or until the onion begins to soften. Add garlic, oregano, salt, pepper and tomatoes. Stir well, and scrape the bottom to remove and incorporate and browned bits that may have stuck there. Close and lock the lid.

2. Turn the heat up to high and when the cooker reaches pressure, lower the heat to the minimum needed to maintain pressure. Cook for 5–6 minutes at high pressure.

3. Open with the natural-release method—move the pressure cooker to a cool burner and wait for the pressure to come down on its own (about 15 minutes). For electric pressure cookers, disengage the "keep warm" mode or unplug the cooker. After 10 minutes, release the rest of the pressure using the valve.

Ragu Don'ts

A ragu is an Italian tomato-based meat sauce. It can contain one or several cuts of meat. This includes beef, pork, veal, goat, lamb, rabbit, boar, or other wild and domesticated meats . . . but never chicken or turkey!

MIXED PEPPER SAUCE

You can also serve this dish as a side dish by doubling the recipe. Do not purée the ingredients at the end, and remove with slotted spoon to a serving dish immediately. Serve this with ricotta-filled pasta, like ravioli.

INGREDIENTS
Serves 6

1 tablespoon plus 1 teaspoon olive oil, divided

2 red peppers, thinly sliced into strips

2 yellow peppers, thinly sliced into strips

1 red onion, thinly sliced into strips

1 green pepper, thinly sliced into strips

1 red onion, thinly sliced

4 Roma-type tomatoes, puréed (or 1 cup canned chopped tomatoes)

1 clove garlic, pressed

1 bunch fresh parsley, chopped

1. Heat olive oil in an uncovered pressure cooker over medium heat. Add peppers and onion. Stir infrequently until one side is lightly browned. Add the tomatoes and their liquid. Close and lock the lid.

2. Turn the heat up to high and when the cooker reaches pressure, lower the heat to the minimum needed to maintain pressure. Cook for 3–5 minutes at high pressure.

3. When time is up, open the pressure cooker by releasing pressure.

4. If using for a sauce, add the garlic and parsley and purée using an immersion blender. If serving as a side dish, remove pepper with a slotted spoon to a serving bowl and add fresh garlic. When the peppers have cooled to room temperature add the remaining olive oil and parsley and mix well.

ROASTED RED PEPPER SAUCE

Save time by using canned or jarred roasted red peppers instead of roasting them yourself.

INGREDIENTS
Serves 4

2 cups roasted red peppers

2 cups vegetable stock

2 tablespoons red wine vinegar

2 tablespoons extra-virgin olive oil

1 teaspoon garlic powder

½ cup fresh basil

Salt and pepper, to taste

1. Purée the red peppers, stock, vinegar, and oil in a food processor or blender. Pour the mixture into the pressure cooker and add the garlic powder.

2. Lock the lid into place and bring to high pressure. Once the pressure is achieved, turn the heat to low and cook for about 5 minutes. Remove from the heat and allow pressure to release naturally.

3. Add the basil and season with salt and pepper, to taste, before serving.

SAUSAGE AND MUSHROOM SAUCE

You can use spicy or sweet Italian sausage in this sauce, whichever you prefer. Or you can compromise and use sweet Italian sausage and add a pinch of dried red pepper flakes to taste.

INGREDIENTS

Yields 5 cups

1 tablespoon olive oil

2 medium sweet onions, peeled and diced

8 ounces ground beef

1 pound Italian sausage

1 red bell pepper, seeded and diced

4 cloves garlic, peeled and minced

1 cup mushrooms, sliced

1 medium carrot, peeled and grated

2½ teaspoons dried oregano

1 teaspoon dried basil

½ teaspoon fennel seed

1 teaspoon granulated cane sugar

1 bay leaf

1 15-ounce can plum tomatoes

2 cups tomato juice

½ cup red wine

¼ cup tomato paste

Salt and freshly ground black pepper, to taste

1. Bring the oil to temperature in the pressure cooker over medium-high heat. Add the onions and sauté for 2 minutes. Add the ground beef; fry for 5 minutes or until it renders its fat and loses its pink color. Drain and discard any fat.

2. Remove the casing from the Italian sausage; break the meat apart and add to the pressure cooker along with the bell pepper, garlic, mushrooms, and carrot. Sauté and stir for 3 minutes. Stir in the oregano, basil, fennel seed, and sugar. Add the bay leaf.

3. Dice or pureé the plum tomatoes and juices in the blender. Stir into the meat mixture in the pressure cooker along with the tomato juice, wine, and tomato paste.

4. Lock the lid into place. Bring to high pressure; maintain for 20 minutes. Remove from the heat and quick-release the pressure.

5. Return to the heat; stir and simmer the sauce uncovered for a few minutes to thicken it. Taste for seasoning and add salt and pepper if needed. Discard bay leaf before serving.

Improvised Vegetable Soup

Create a quick soup for 4 by simmering a cup of Sausage and Mushroom Sauce, 2 cups of beef or chicken broth, and a 12-ounce bag of frozen mixed vegetables over medium heat in a large saucepan until the mixture is brought to temperature. Stir in a cup of cooked macaroni. Add 8 ounces diced fully cooked smoked sausage if you're serving the soup as the main course. Serve with garlic bread and a tossed salad.

SPAGHETTI MEAT SAUCE

Be sure to have freshly grated Parmigiano-Reggiano cheese available to sprinkle over the pasta and sauce.

INGREDIENTS
Serves 6

1 pound lean ground beef

1 large sweet onion, peeled and diced

1 stalk celery, diced

1 medium green bell pepper, seeded and diced

1 clove garlic, peeled and minced

Salt and freshly ground black pepper, to taste

1 cup water

1 8-ounce can tomato sauce

⅛ teaspoon dried red pepper flakes

1 teaspoon dried parsley

½ teaspoon dried oregano

½ teaspoon dried basil

¼ teaspoon dried thyme

2 teaspoons sugar

1 6-ounce can tomato paste

1. Add the ground beef, onion, celery, and green bell pepper to the pressure cooker. Fry for 5 minutes over medium-high heat or until the fat is rendered from the meat. Drain and discard the fat. Stir in the remaining ingredients, except for the tomato paste.

2. Lock the lid into place. Bring the pressure cooker to low pressure; maintain pressure for 10 minutes.

3. Quick-release the pressure. Remove the lid and stir in the tomato paste. Simmer the sauce uncovered for 5 minutes or until desired thickness is reached. Serve hot over spaghetti.

SPICY EGGPLANT SAUCE

This sauce, made in double the quantity, can also be served as a side dish! Serve on any short pasta like farfalle, penne, or fusilli.

INGREDIENTS
Serves 6

1 tablespoon olive oil

¼ teaspoon hot pepper flakes

2 anchovies

1 clove garlic, smashed

2 large eggplants, diced

1 teaspoon salt

¼ teaspoon pepper

⅔ cup water

1 sprig fresh oregano

1. In the cold pressure cooker, add the oil, pepper flakes, anchovies, and garlic. Turn on low heat to infuse the oil with these flavors until the garlic begins to sizzle and the anchovies fall apart.

2. Separate the diced eggplant into two piles. Turn the heat up to medium and add half of the eggplant into the pressure cooker, with the lid off. Add salt and pepper to taste.

3. Stir the eggplant around, lightly browning it on most sides for about 5 minutes. Add the remaining eggplant. Mix everything well and add water and oregano sprig on top. Close and lock the lid.

4. Turn the heat up to high and when the cooker reaches pressure, lower the heat to the minimum needed to maintain pressure. Cook for 3–5 minutes at high pressure.

5. When time is up, open the pressure cooker by releasing pressure.

6. Pour the contents on freshly strained pasta, or if using as a side dish remove the eggplant to a serving dish immediately to stop it from cooking further and falling apart.

Even Heat

Infusing the olive oil with hot pepper flakes at the beginning of the recipe (like the one on this page) helps to evenly distribute the heat through the whole dish—versus little pops of heat whenever your diner happens to bite on a flake.

SPICY PEANUT SAUCE

Use as a dipping sauce for broccoli or spring rolls.

INGREDIENTS
Yields 1½ cups

½ cup smooth peanut butter

2 tablespoons maple syrup

2 cloves garlic, peeled

1" piece ginger, peeled and chopped

¼ cup rice vinegar

¼ cup sesame oil

1 teaspoon cayenne pepper

1 teaspoon cumin

2 teaspoons dried red chili flakes

1 cup water

Salt and pepper, to taste

1. In a large blender, combine all the ingredients except salt and pepper, adding the water a little at a time to control the consistency.

2. Lock the lid into place and bring to high pressure. Once the pressure is achieved, turn the heat to low and cook for about 3 minutes. Remove from the heat and allow pressure to release naturally.

3. Taste for seasoning, and add salt and pepper if needed.

VODKA SAUCE

Cooking with alcohol helps bring out flavors in some foods, including tomatoes.

INGREDIENTS
Serves 4–6

2 tablespoons olive oil

½ onion, diced

2 cloves garlic, minced

1 teaspoon dried red pepper flakes

1 cup vodka

2 14-ounce cans diced tomatoes

2 tablespoons tomato paste

⅓ cup water

1 cup heavy cream, or unsweetened soymilk or unsweetened vegan cream, such as MimicCreme

2 tablespoons fresh parsley, chopped

2 tablespoons fresh basil, chopped

Salt and pepper, to taste

1. Add the olive oil to the pressure cooker; sauté the onion until golden brown. Add the garlic and red pepper flakes, and sauté an additional minute. Add the vodka and simmer for about 10 minutes. Add the diced tomatoes, tomato paste, and water.

2. Lock the lid into place and bring to high pressure. Once the pressure is achieved, turn the heat to low and cook for about 5 minutes. Remove from the heat and allow pressure to release naturally.

3. Stir in the cream and simmer for 2 minutes. Add the parsley and basil. Taste for seasoning, and add salt and pepper if needed.

Does Alcohol Burn Off?

It's a common food myth that while cooking with alcohol, the alcohol will burn off. In fact, many cooking methods will retain a large portion of the alcohol in your dish. If you want keep as little alcohol as possible, you will have to cook it for an extended period of time, at least 2 hours.

WHITE BEAN ALFREDO SAUCE

Using white beans as the base of a creamy sauce reduces the amount of dairy and fat in the recipe, and makes for a much healthier alternative.

INGREDIENTS
Serves 4

1 cup dried cannellini beans

8 cups water

¼ cup butter, or vegan margarine, such as Earth Balance

2 cloves garlic, minced

1 cup milk, or unsweetened soymilk

1 teaspoon lemon juice

1½ teaspoons salt

½ teaspoon black pepper

1. Add the beans and 4 cups of water to the pressure cooker. Lock the lid into place; bring to high pressure for 1 minute. Remove from the heat and quick-release the pressure. Drain beans and set aside.

2. Clean pressure cooker and add butter. Sauté the garlic for 2 minutes, stirring continuously. Add the drained beans and remaining 4 cups of water

3. Lock the lid into place; bring to high pressure and maintain for 15 minutes. Quick-release the pressure.

4. Pour the beans into a blender or food processor in batches and purée. The mixture will be thick.

5. Return to the pressure cooker over low heat and slowly stir in the milk until desired consistency is reached. Add lemon juice, salt, and pepper, and heat until warm. Serve with fresh herbs, such as parsley, if desired.

YELLOW PEPPER COULIS

A coulis is a thick sauce often made from puréed fruit or vegetables.

INGREDIENTS
Yields 1½ cups

2 tablespoons olive oil

4 yellow peppers, seeded and diced

4 shallots, minced

1 cup white wine

1 cup vegetable stock

1 teaspoon salt

½ teaspoon black pepper

1. Add the olive oil to the pressure cooker and sauté the yellow peppers and shallots until they start to turn golden brown. Add the white wine and reduce by half. Add the Vegetable Stock.

2. Lock the lid into place and bring to high pressure. Once the pressure is achieved, turn the heat to low and cook for 5 minutes. Remove from the heat and quick-release the pressure.

3. Season with salt and pepper.

CHAPTER 16

JAMS AND CHUTNEYS

BLACKBERRY JAM

Experiment with the types of berries used to make homemade jam, or try a combination of a few.

INGREDIENTS
Yields 4 cups

4 cups blackberries

4 cups granulated cane sugar

1 cup orange juice

1 teaspoon lemon juice

Pinch salt

1 1¾-ounce package dry pectin

1. Add the blackberries, sugar, orange juice, lemon juice, and salt to the pressure cooker. Stir to combine.

2. Lock on the lid and bring to low pressure. Maintain pressure for 3 minutes. Remove from the heat and allow pressure to release naturally.

3. Remove the lid. Either process in a food mill to separate the pulp from the skins or push the blackberry mixture through a strainer.

4. Return the pulp to the pressure cooker. Place over medium-high heat, stir in the pectin, and bring mixture to a rolling boil, stirring constantly. Continue to boil and stir for 1 minute.

5. Skim off and discard any foam. Ladle into hot, sterilized glass containers or jars, leaving 1" of headspace. Seal the containers or jars. Cool and refrigerate for up to 5 weeks or freeze for up to 8 months. (If you prefer, you can follow the instructions that came with your canning jars and process the preserves for shelf storage.)

BLUEBERRY JAM

You can substitute a 6-ounce bottle of pectin for the dry pectin.

INGREDIENTS
Yields 4 cups

4 cups blueberries

4 cups granulated cane sugar

1 cup orange juice

1 teaspoon orange zest

Pinch freshly ground nutmeg

Pinch salt

1 1¾-ounce package dry pectin

1. Add the blueberries, sugar, orange juice, orange zest, nutmeg, and salt to the pressure cooker. Stir to combine.

2. Lock on the lid and bring to low pressure. Maintain pressure for 3 minutes. Remove from the heat and allow pressure to release naturally.

3. Remove the lid. Either process in a food mill to separate the pulp from the skins or push the blueberry mixture through a strainer.

4. Return the pulp to the pressure cooker. Place over medium-high heat, stir in the pectin, and bring mixture to a rolling boil, stirring constantly. Continue to boil and stir for 1 minute.

5. Skim off and discard any foam. Ladle into hot, sterilized glass containers or jars, leaving 1" of headspace. Seal the containers or jars. Cool and refrigerate for up to 5 weeks or freeze for up to 8 months. (If you prefer, you can follow the instructions that came with your canning jars and process the preserves for shelf storage.)

CARIBBEAN RELISH

Think of this relish as hummus with a Caribbean flair.

INGREDIENTS
Serves 12

1½ cups red or white kidney beans

7 cups water

2 teaspoons vegetable oil

Salt, to taste

2 tablespoons tahini paste

¾ cup crushed pineapple, drained

4 cloves garlic, minced

¼ teaspoon dried cumin

¼ teaspoon ground ginger

¼ teaspoon freshly ground white pepper

½ cup fresh cilantro, minced

1. Add the beans to the pressure cooker and pour 3 cups water over them or enough to cover the beans completely. Cover and let soak overnight. Drain and return to the pressure cooker. Pour 4 cups water over the beans. Add the oil. Lock the lid into place. Bring to high pressure; maintain pressure for 10 minutes. Remove from the heat and allow pressure to release naturally for 10 minutes.

2. Quick-release any remaining pressure. Remove the lid and, if the beans are cooked through, drain them. If additional cooking time is needed, lock the lid into place, return to high pressure, and cook for an additional 2–5 minutes.

3. Add the cooked beans, salt, tahini, pineapple, garlic, cumin, ginger, pepper, and cilantro to a blender or food processor. Pulse until mixed but still chunky. Transfer to a covered container and chill.

Tomato Relish

Peel, seed, and dice 2 large tomatoes. Add to bowl and mix them together with ½ cup thawed frozen corn, ¼ cup extra-virgin olive oil, and 6 diced scallions. Season with salt, freshly ground black pepper, and fresh lime juice to taste.

CORN MAQUE CHOUX

You can use drained canned corn, fresh corn cut from the cob, or thawed frozen corn in this recipe.

INGREDIENTS
Serves 4

3 tablespoons butter

2 small onions, peeled and diced

1 small green bell pepper, seeded and diced

½ cup celery, diced

2 cloves garlic, peeled and minced

4 cups whole kernel corn

2 Roma tomatoes, peeled, seeded, and diced

½ cup cilantro leaves, chopped, plus additional for garnish

⅛ teaspoon cayenne pepper

½ cup tomato juice

Salt, to taste

Freshly ground black pepper, to taste

1. Melt the butter in the pressure cooker over medium heat. Add the onions, bell pepper, and celery; sauté for 3 minutes or until the vegetables are soft. Add the minced garlic and sauté an additional 30 seconds.

2. Stir in the corn, tomatoes, chopped cilantro, cayenne pepper, tomato juice, salt, and pepper. Lock the lid into place and bring to low pressure; maintain pressure for 3 minutes.

3. Remove from heat and quick-release the pressure. Use a slotted spoon to immediately transfer the corn and vegetables to a serving bowl. Taste for seasoning and add additional salt and pepper if needed. Garnish with cilantro and serve.

CRANBERRY-APPLE CHUTNEY

Chutney is an Indian dish that was introduced to the rest of the world by the British.

INGREDIENTS
Serves 16

1 12-ounce bag cranberries

1 cup light brown sugar, packed

1 small sweet onion, peeled and diced

1 jalapeño pepper, seeded and minced

2 tablespoons fresh ginger, peeled and grated

1 clove garlic, minced

1 teaspoon yellow mustard seed

3" cinnamon stick

1 teaspoon lemon juice

¼ teaspoon salt

3 pounds tart cooking apples

Optional: Ground ginger, to taste

Optional: Ground cinnamon, to taste

1. Rinse and pick over the cranberries. Add the cranberries, brown sugar, onion, jalapeño, ginger, garlic, mustard, cinnamon stick, lemon juice, and salt to a 5- to 7-quart pressure cooker. Cook over medium heat until the sugar dissolves, stirring occasionally.

2. Peel and core the apples; cut into strips, 1" in length. Place the apples in a layer over the cranberry mixture in the pressure cooker. Do not stir the apples into the mixture.

3. Lock the lid in place and bring to high pressure. Cook on high pressure for 1 minute. Remove from the heat and quick-release the pressure.

4. Remove the cinnamon stick. Taste for seasoning and add ground ginger and ground cinnamon if desired.

5. Store in a covered container in the refrigerator for up to 2 weeks. Serve heated or chilled.

For Best Results

Placing the apples over the cranberry mixture prevents the cranberries from foaming as they cook, which could clog the pressure cooker vent. Serve this chutney with roast pork or turkey. If you'd like to make cranberry-pear chutney, substitute 3 pounds of peeled and cored ripe Bartlett pears for the apples.

DRIED APRICOT PRESERVES

Never fill the pressure cooker more than half full when making preserves, chutneys, or other fruit dishes.

INGREDIENTS
Yields 7 cups

4 cups dried apricots, chopped

2 cups water

5 black peppercorns

5 cardamom pods

2 3" cinnamon sticks

2 star anise

½ cup lemon juice

4 cups granulated cane sugar

1. Add the apricots to a bowl or to the pressure cooker. Pour in the water, cover, and let the apricots soak for 24 hours.

2. Wrap the peppercorns, cardamom pods, cinnamon sticks, and star anise in cheesecloth and secure with a string. Add to the pressure cooker along with the apricots, soaking water, and lemon juice. Lock the lid into place. Bring to pressure and cook on low pressure for 10 minutes. Remove from the heat and allow pressure to release naturally.

3. Uncover the pressure cooker. Remove and discard the cheesecloth spice bag and stir in the sugar.

4. Return the pressure cooker to the heat and bring to a rapid boil over medium-high heat. Boil covered for 2 minutes and uncovered for 2 minutes or until the apricot mixture reaches the gel point.

5. Skim off and discard any foam. Ladle into hot, sterilized glass containers or jars, leaving ½" of headspace. Seal the containers or jars. Cool and refrigerate for a week or freeze. (If you prefer, you can follow the instructions that came with your canning jars and process the preserves for shelf storage.)

Determining the Gel Point

Test a small amount of preserves by spooning it onto an ice-cold plate. It's reached the gel point when it's as thick as you desire. A softer set is ideal for use in sauces; if you prefer a firm, jam-like consistency, you may need to continue to boil the mixture for up to 20 minutes.

EASY GRAPE JELLY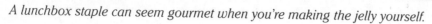

A lunchbox staple can seem gourmet when you're making the jelly yourself.

INGREDIENTS
Yields 5 cups

5 cups grape juice

2 1¾-ounce packages dry pectin

½ cup sugar

1. Add grape juice and pectin to the pressure cooker and bring to medium-high heat. Stir to combine.

2. Lock on the lid and bring to high pressure. Maintain pressure for 1 minute. Remove from the heat and quick-release the pressure.

3. Remove the lid. Slowly stir in the sugar.

4. Skim off and discard any foam. Ladle into hot, sterilized glass containers or jars, leaving 1" of headspace. Seal the containers or jars. Let cool at room temperature for 24 hours then refrigerate for up to 5 weeks or freeze for up to 8 months. (If you prefer, you can follow the instructions that came with your canning jars and process the preserves for shelf storage.)

Choosing Your Juice
For this recipe, avoid using any light or diet juices because they most likely have a higher water content or artificial sweeteners, and will result in less flavor.

FRESH TOMATO CHUTNEY

For a change of pace, you can spread this chutney over Indian chapati bread, flat bread, or pizza crust; top with goat cheese or vegan mozzarella; and bake.

INGREDIENTS
Yields 4 cups

4 pounds ripe tomatoes, peeled

1" piece fresh gingerroot

3 cloves garlic

1¾ cups white sugar

1 cup red wine vinegar

2 onions, diced

¼ cup golden raisins

¾ teaspoon ground cinnamon

½ teaspoon ground coriander

¼ teaspoon ground cloves

¼ teaspoon ground nutmeg

¼ teaspoon ground ginger

1 teaspoon chili powder

1 pinch paprika

1 tablespoon curry paste

1. Purée the peeled tomatoes and fresh ginger in a blender or food processor.

2. Pour the puréed tomato mixture into the pressure cooker. Stir in the remaining ingredients. Stir to mix, lock the lid into place, and cook at low pressure for 10 minutes. Remove from heat and allow pressure to release naturally. Refrigerate in a covered container until ready to use. Serve chilled or at room temperature.

Peeling Fresh Vine-Ripened Tomatoes
Add enough water to a saucepan to cover the tomatoes; bring to a boil over medium-high heat. Use a slotted spoon to submerge the tomatoes in the boiling water for 1 minute, or until their skins begin to crack and peel. Use the slotted spoon to remove the tomatoes from the water and plunge them into ice water. The peelings will slip right off.

GREEN TOMATO CHUTNEY

If you prefer spicy chutney, you can substitute an Anaheim and four small red chili or jalapeño peppers for the red bell peppers.

INGREDIENTS
Yields 5 cups

2 pounds green tomatoes, diced, with stems removed

1 white onion, quartered lengthwise, and thinly sliced

2 red bell peppers, diced

¼ cup dried currants

2 tablespoons fresh ginger, grated

¾ cup dark brown sugar, firmly packed

¾ cup white wine or white distilled vinegar

Pinch sea salt

1. Put all ingredients in the pressure cooker; stir to mix. Lock on the lid and bring to low pressure. Cook on low pressure for 10 minutes. Remove from the heat and allow pressure to release naturally.

2. Cool and refrigerate overnight before serving. Can be stored in a covered container in the refrigerator for 2 months.

MANGO CHUTNEY

This versatile chutney is good with Indian foods, greens or grains, meats and poultry, and even over ice cream.

INGREDIENTS
Yields 2 cups

2 almost ripe mangoes

2 small serrano or jalapeño peppers

1 large clove garlic

2 teaspoons fresh ginger, grated

6 unsweetened dried plums, coarsely chopped

¾ cup dark brown sugar, firmly packed

¾ cup raw cane sugar or turbinado sugar

1 cup white wine vinegar

2 teaspoons mustard powder

Pinch salt

1. Peel mangoes. Remove the pit and cut the fruit into small pieces. Seed and mince the peppers. Peel and mince the garlic. Add the mangoes, peppers, and garlic to the pressure cooker along with the remaining ingredients. Stir to combine.

2. Lock the lid into place. Bring to high pressure and cook for 5 minutes. Remove from the heat and let sit for at least 7 minutes.

3. Quick-release any remaining pressure. Remove the lid, return the pan to the heat, and bring to a boil; boil briskly for 10 minutes or until the mixture is thick. Cover and refrigerate overnight before using. Can be stored covered in the refrigerator for up to 6 weeks.

MINCEMEAT

Use mincemeat as a condiment or in mincemeat pie.

INGREDIENTS
Yields 5 cups

2½ pounds pears

1 tart green apple

1 lemon, juiced and zested

1 orange, juiced and zested

1 cup golden raisins

½ cup dried cranberries or dried currants

½ cup light brown sugar, firmly packed

1 teaspoon ground cinnamon

½ teaspoon ground ginger

¼ teaspoon ground cloves

¼ teaspoon ground nutmeg

Pinch salt

½ cup walnuts or pecans, chopped and toasted

½ cup brandy or cognac

1. Peel, core, and dice the pears and apple. Wash the lemon and orange to remove any waxy coating. Add to the pressure cooker along with lemon zest and juice, orange zest and juice, raisins, cranberries or currants, brown sugar, cinnamon, ginger, cloves, nutmeg, and salt. Stir to combine.

2. Lock the lid into place and bring to high pressure; maintain pressure for 10 minutes. Remove from heat and allow pressure to release naturally.

3. Return to heat and bring to a simmer. Simmer for 10 minutes or until mixture is very thick. Stir in the nuts and brandy or cognac. Continue to simmer for an additional 5 minutes.

4. Ladle into hot, sterilized glass containers or jars, leaving ½" of headspace. Seal the containers or jars. Cool and then refrigerate for a week or freeze. (If you prefer, you can follow the instructions that came with your canning jars and process the preserves for shelf storage.)

Mincemeat Seasoning
Seasoning is an arbitrary thing. You'll want to add some of the spices to the mincemeat before you cook it, but if you prefer to taste for seasoning and then increase the spices according to your taste, use half of the spices during the cooking process, and add more later if desired.

MIXED CITRUS MARMALADE

Jam sugar contains pectin, the soluble dietary fiber extracted from citrus fruits used as a gelling agent for jams, jellies, and marmalades.

INGREDIENTS
Yields 4 cups

1 large orange

1 lime

2 lemons

2 clementines or satsumas

1 pink grapefruit

3 cups water

4 pounds jam sugar

1. Wash the fruit in hot water to remove any wax. Remove the zest from the orange, lime, and lemons; add to the pressure cooker. Quarter all fruit and place in a large (doubled) piece of cheesecloth; twist the cheesecloth to squeeze out the juice into the pressure cooker. Tie the cheesecloth over the fruit and seeds and add it to the pressure cooker along with half of the water. Lock the lid in place and bring the pressure cooker to high pressure; cook on high for 10 minutes. Remove from the heat and allow pressure to release naturally.

2. Remove the lid from the pressure cooker. Place the cooker over medium heat and add the remaining water and sugar. Bring to a boil, stirring continuously until all the sugar has dissolved.

3. While the mixture continues to boil, place the lid back on the cooker (but do not lock it into place). Leave the lid in place for 2 minutes, remove it, and then continue to let the mixture boil for 8 minutes or until the desired gel point is reached.

4. Skim off and discard any foam. Ladle into hot, sterilized glass containers or jars, leaving ½" of head space. Seal the containers or jars. Cool and refrigerate for a week or freeze until needed. (If you prefer, you can follow the instructions that came with your canning jars and process the preserves for shelf storage.)

Sugar Crystals and the Gelling Process
After you've added sugar, putting the lid back on the pressure cooker once the mixture comes to a boil creates steam inside the cooker that will cause any sugar clinging to the sides of the pan to wash down into the mixture. Even one lone sugar crystal can set off a chain reaction that will cause the entire mixture to crystallize rather than remain in its gelled state.

PEACH AND TOASTED ALMOND PRESERVES

Toasting the almonds is an important step that enhances the rich flavor of these preserves.

INGREDIENTS
Yields 4 cups

6 fresh ripe peaches

1 cup water

1 8-ounce package dried apricots, diced

½ cup almonds, toasted

1¼ cups orange juice

¼ cup lemon juice

4½ cups granulated cane sugar

2 whole cloves

1 3" cinnamon stick

Pinch salt

1 1¾-ounce package pectin powder

1. Use a skewer or toothpick to poke several holes in each of the peaches. Place the peaches in the pressure cooker and pour the water over them. Lock the lid on the pressure cooker. Bring to high pressure and maintain for 3 minutes.

2. Quick-release the pressure and remove the lid. Use a slotted spoon to move the peaches to a large bowl of ice water or to a bowl under cold running water. Peel the peaches and then cut them into small pieces, discarding the pits.

3. Add the peaches, apricots, almonds, orange juice, lemon juice, sugar, cloves, cinnamon stick, and salt to water remaining in the pressure cooker. Stir to combine. Lock on the lid and bring to high pressure; maintain pressure for 2 minutes.

4. Remove the pressure cooker from the heat. Quick-release the pressure and remove the lid. Remove the cloves and cinnamon stick; discard. Stir the pectin into the fruit mixture. Return to the heat and bring to a rolling boil over medium-high heat, stirring constantly.

5. Skim off and discard any foam. Ladle into hot, sterilized glass containers or jars, leaving 1" of headspace. Seal the containers or jars. Cool and then refrigerate for up to 5 weeks or freeze for up to 8 months. (If you prefer, you can follow the instructions that came with your canning jars and process the preserves for shelf storage.)

Toasting Nuts
Preheat oven to 350°F. Place nuts on a shallow baking pan. Stirring occasionally, bake for 8 minutes or until the nuts are fragrant and golden brown. You can also toast nuts in a frying pan over medium-high heat. Stir and shake the pan constantly for 5 minutes or until nuts are golden brown.

PEACH JAM

In most states, peach season is during summer. Using in-season fruit will result in the best flavor for homemade jams.

INGREDIENTS
Yields 4 cups

4 cups peaches, peeled and chopped

4 cups granulated sugar

1 teaspoon lemon juice

1 1¾-ounce package dry pectin

1. Add the peaches, sugar, and lemon juice to the pressure cooker. Stir to combine.

2. Lock on the lid and bring to low pressure. Maintain pressure for 3 minutes. Remove from the heat and allow pressure to release naturally.

3. Remove the lid. Place over medium-high heat, stir in the pectin, and bring mixture to a rolling boil, stirring constantly. Continue to boil and stir for 1 minute.

4. Skim off and discard any foam. Ladle into hot, sterilized glass containers or jars, leaving 1" of headspace. Seal the containers or jars. Cool and refrigerate for up to 5 weeks or freeze for up to 8 months. (If you prefer, you can follow the instructions that came with your canning jars and process the preserves for shelf storage.)

RAINBOW BELL PEPPER MARMALADE

Serve Rainbow Bell Pepper Marmalade as a relish for tempeh or seitan, or on top of cheese on crackers.

INGREDIENTS
Yields 2 cups

1 large green bell pepper

1 large red bell pepper

1 large yellow bell pepper

1 large purple or orange bell pepper

1 small yellow, white, or sweet onion

Water, as needed

2 cups granulated cane sugar

Pinch salt

2 tablespoons balsamic vinegar

1. Wash, quarter, and seed the bell peppers; cut them into thin slices or dice them. Peel, quarter, and thinly slice the onion. Add the peppers and onion to the pressure cooker.

2. Add enough water to the pressure cooker to cover the peppers and onion. Bring to a boil over high heat; drain immediately and discard the water.

3. Return the peppers and onion to the pressure cooker. Stir in the sugar, salt, and vinegar. Bring to high pressure and cook for 5 minutes. Remove pan from the heat and let sit for 5 minutes.

4. Quick-release any remaining pressure. Remove the lid and return the pan to the heat. Simmer briskly over medium-high heat for 6 minutes or until the mixture is thickened. Once cooled, store in a covered container in the refrigerator overnight before using.

STRAWBERRY JAM

In addition to the usual uses for fruit spread, this jam is the perfect addition to some plain yogurt or soy yogurt.

INGREDIENTS
Yields 4 cups

4 cups strawberries

3 cups granulated cane sugar

¼ cup fresh lemon juice

1. Rinse and hull the strawberries, then quarter or halve them. Add to the pressure cooker. Stir in the sugar. Set aside for 1 hour or until the strawberries are juicy.

2. Use a potato masher to crush the fruit and mix in the sugar until the sugar is dissolved. Stir in the lemon juice.

3. Lock the lid in place. Bring the cooker to full pressure and cook for 7 minutes. Remove from the heat and allow pressure to release naturally.

4. Remove the lid. Return to heat and bring to a full boil over medium-high heat. Boil for 3 minutes or until jam reaches the desired gel state.

5. Skim off and discard any foam. Ladle into hot, sterilized glass containers or jars, leaving ½" of headspace. Seal the containers or jars. Cool and refrigerate for a week or freeze. (If you prefer, you can follow the instructions that came with your canning jars and process the preserves for shelf storage.)

SWEET ONION RELISH

Use sweet onions like Vidalia, Candy, First Edition, Maui, or Walla Walla for this relish.

INGREDIENTS
Yields 4 cups

4 medium sweet onions

Water, as needed

¾ cup golden raisins

1 cup agave nectar

1 tablespoon cider vinegar

Pinch salt

1. Peel and thinly slice onions. Add onions to the pressure cooker and pour in water to cover. Bring to a boil over high heat; drain immediately and discard water.

2. Return onions to pressure cooker; stir in raisins, agave nectar, vinegar, and salt until agave nectar is evenly distributed throughout onion slices.

3. Lock on lid, bring to high pressure, and cook for 5 minutes. Reduce heat and maintain low pressure for an additional 10 minutes. Remove from heat and allow pressure to release naturally.

4. Remove lid and stir relish. If relish needs thickening, return pan to heat, bring to a gentle boil for 5 minutes. Can be served warm or stored in a covered container in the refrigerator for up to 4 weeks.

THANKSGIVING JAM

This recipe makes enough of this festive jam to last through the entire holiday—with some left over for gifts.

INGREDIENTS
Yields 6 cups

1 pound cranberries

1 pound strawberries, hulled and diced

8 ounces blueberries

4 ounces rhubarb, diced

4 ounces dried black currants or raisins

1 lemon

6 cups granulated cane sugar

¼ cup water

Pinch salt

1. Add the cranberries, strawberries, blueberries, rhubarb, currants or raisins, and lemon zest and juice to the pressure cooker. Stir in the sugar. Set aside for 1 hour, until the fruit is juicy.

2. Stir in the water and salt. Put the cooker over medium-high heat and bring the mixture to a boil. Lock the lid into place and bring the cooker to high pressure. Lower the heat to medium-low or sufficient heat to maintain the pressure for 10 minutes.

3. Remove from the heat and allow pressure to release naturally.

4. Remove the lid and return the pressure cooker to the heat. Bring to a boil. Boil rapidly for 3 minutes or until the gel point is reached. Skim off and discard any foam. Ladle into hot, sterilized glass containers or jars, leaving ½" of head space. Seal the containers or jars. Cool and refrigerate for a week or freeze. (If you prefer, you can follow the instructions that came with your canning jars and process the jam for shelf storage.)

PART VIII
THE FINISH

CHAPTER 17

DESSERTS

BANANA PUDDING CAKE

This is a delicious way to use up ripe bananas. You'll need to use a pressure cooker large enough to hold a 1-quart or 6-cup bundt or angel food cake pan to make this recipe.

INGREDIENTS
Serves 12

1 18¼-ounce package yellow cake mix, or vegan cake mix

1 3½-ounce package instant banana pudding mix, or vegan pudding mix

4 eggs, or 4 ounces silken tofu

4 cups water

¼ cup vegetable oil

3 small ripe bananas, mashed

2 cups powdered sugar, sifted

2 tablespoons milk, or soymilk

1 teaspoon vanilla extract

½ cup walnuts, toasted and chopped

1. Treat a 1-quart or 6-cup bundt or angel food cake pan with nonstick spray. Set aside.

2. Add the cake mix and pudding mix to a large mixing bowl; stir to mix. Make a well in the center and add the eggs and pour in 1 cup water, oil, and mashed bananas.

3. Beat on low speed until blended. Scrape bowl and beat another 4 minutes on medium speed. Pour the batter into the prepared pan. Cover tightly with a piece of heavy-duty aluminum foil.

4. Pour 3 cups water into the pressure cooker and add the rack. Lower the cake pan onto the rack.

5. Lock the lid into place and bring to high pressure; maintain pressure for 35 minutes.

6. Remove the pressure cooker from the heat, quick-release the pressure, and remove the lid.

7. Lift the cake pan out of the pressure cooker and place on a wire rack to cool for 10 minutes, then turn the cake out onto the wire rack to finish cooling.

8. To make the glaze, mix together the powdered sugar, milk, and vanilla in a bowl. Drizzle over the top of the cooled cake. Sprinkle the walnuts over the glaze before the glaze dries.

BASIC YELLOW CAKE

Serve this staple dessert any way you'd like—topped with icing, a dollop of whipped cream or soy whip, or a sprinkling of powdered sugar.

INGREDIENTS
Serves 10–12

1½ cups all-purpose flour

1 teaspoon baking powder

1 cup sugar

½ teaspoon salt

2 eggs, beaten, or 2 mashed bananas

½ cup butter, melted, or vegan margarine, such as Earth Balance

1 teaspoon vanilla extract

1 cup milk, or soymilk

1. In a medium bowl, mix the flour, baking powder, sugar, and salt. In a large bowl, beat the eggs. Add the dry ingredients to the eggs. Slowly stir in the melted butter, vanilla extract, and the milk.

2. Pour the cake mixture into an 8" round pan. Place the cake in the pressure cooker and lock the lid into place. Cook the cake for 30 minutes over a low flame without the weight in place.

3. Remove the pressure cooker from the heat and carefully remove the cake. Serve with whatever topping that you like.

CORNMEAL CAKE

Serve warm with maple syrup or make a maple-infused butter by whisking pats of chilled butter or vegan margarine into heated maple syrup.

INGREDIENTS
Serves 6

2 cups milk or soymilk

¼ cup light brown sugar, packed

1 teaspoon orange zest, grated

½ cup fine yellow cornmeal

2 large eggs or 2 ounces silken tofu

2 tablespoons butter, melted, or vegan margarine, such as Earth Balance

2 tablespoons orange marmalade

1 cup water

1. Bring milk to a simmer over medium heat. Stir in the brown sugar; simmer and stir until the milk is at a low boil. Whisk in the orange zest and cornmeal. Simmer and stir for 2 minutes. Remove from heat. Whisk together the eggs, butter, and orange marmalade. Stir into the cornmeal mixture. Treat a 1-quart soufflé or heatproof glass dish with nonstick spray. Add batter.

2. Pour water into the pressure cooker and add rack. Place soufflé dish on the rack. Lock lid into place and bring to low pressure; maintain pressure for 12 minutes. Remove from heat and allow pressure to release naturally for 10 minutes. Quick-release any remaining pressure and remove the lid. Transfer to a wire rack.

GLAZED LEMON POPPY SEED CAKE

Make this cake ahead of time. The flavor improves if you wrap it in plastic wrap and store it for a day or two before you serve it.

INGREDIENTS
Serves 8

½ cup butter, softened, or vegan margarine, such as Earth Balance

1 cup sugar

2 eggs, separated, or 2 ounces silken tofu

1 teaspoon vanilla

2 lemons

1¼ cups all-purpose flour

1 teaspoon baking soda

1 teaspoon baking powder

¼ teaspoon salt

⅔ cup whole milk, or soymilk

⅓ cup poppy seeds

2 cups water

½ cup powdered sugar, sifted

1. Add the butter and sugar to a mixing bowl; beat until light and fluffy. Beat in the egg yolks, vanilla, grated zest from 1 lemon, and juice from 1 lemon.

2. Mix together the flour, baking soda, baking powder, and salt. Add the flour and milk in 3 batches to the butter mixture, mixing after each addition. Stir in the poppy seeds.

3. Add the egg whites to a chilled bowl. Whisk or beat until stiff. Fold the egg whites into the poppy seed batter.

4. Treat a 4-cup soufflé dish or bundt pan with nonstick spray. Transfer the batter to the pan.

5. Treat a 15" square of heavy-duty aluminum foil with nonstick spray. Place the foil, treated-side down, over the pan; crimp around the edges to seal.

6. Pour the water and place the rack into the pressure cooker. Crisscross long, doubled strips of foil over the rack to create handles to use later to remove the pan.

7. Place the pan on the rack over the foil strips. Lock the lid into place and bring to low pressure; maintain pressure for 40 minutes.

8. Remove from heat and allow pressure to release naturally. Remove the lid. Lift the pan from the pressure cooker and place it on a cooling rack. Remove foil cover.

9. To make the glaze, whisk the juice and grated zest from the remaining lemon together with the powdered sugar. Transfer the cake to a serving platter and drizzle the glaze over the top.

LEMON CHEESECAKE

Serve this rich, popular dessert topped with cherry pie filling or sugared fresh blueberries, raspberries, or strawberries.

INGREDIENTS
Serves 8

12 gingersnaps or vanilla wafers

1½ tablespoons almonds, toasted

½ tablespoon butter, melted, or vegan margarine, such as Earth Balance

2 8-ounce packages cream cheese, room temperature, or vegan cream cheese

½ cup sugar

2 large eggs, or 2 ounces silken tofu

Zest of 1 lemon, grated

1 tablespoon fresh lemon juice

½ teaspoon natural lemon extract

1 teaspoon vanilla

2 cups water

1. Use a pressure cooker with a rack that's large enough to hold a 7" × 3" springform pan. Treat the inside of the pan with nonstick spray.

2. Add the cookies and almonds to a food processor. Pulse to create cookie crumbs and chop the nuts. Add the melted butter and pulse to mix.

3. Transfer the crumb mixture to the springform pan and press down into the pan. Wipe out the food processor bowl.

4. Cut the cream cheese into cubes and add it to the food processor along with the sugar; process until smooth. Add the eggs, lemon zest, lemon juice, lemon extract, and vanilla. Process for 10 seconds.

5. Scrape the bowl and then process for another 10 seconds or until the batter is well mixed and smooth.

6. Place the springform pan in the center of two 16" × 16" pieces of aluminum foil. Crimp the foil to seal the bottom of the pan.

7. Transfer the cheesecake batter into the springform pan. Treat one side of a 10" square of aluminum foil with nonstick spray; lay over the top of the springform pan and crimp around the edges.

8. Bring the bottom foil up the sides so that it can be grasped to raise and lower the pan into and out of the pressure cooker.

9. Pour the water into the pressure cooker. Insert the rack. Set the springform pan holding the cheesecake batter on the rack.

10. Lock the lid into place and bring to high pressure; maintain pressure for 8 minutes. Remove from heat and allow pressure to release naturally. Remove the lid.

11. Lift the covered springform pan out of the pressure cooker and place on a wire rack. Remove the top foil.

12. If any moisture has accumulated on top of the cheesecake, dab it with a piece of paper towel to remove it. Let cool to room temperature and then remove from the springform pan.

MOLTEN FUDGE PUDDING CAKE

Serve warm with a scoop of vanilla bean ice cream or soy ice cream and garnish with fresh fruit or dust with powdered sugar.

INGREDIENTS
Serves 6

4 ounces semisweet chocolate chips

¼ cup cocoa powder

⅛ teaspoon salt

3 tablespoons butter, or vegan margarine, such as Earth Balance

2 large eggs, separated, or 2 ounces silken tofu

¼ cup sugar, plus extra for the pan

1 teaspoon vanilla

½ cup pecans, chopped

¼ cup plus 2 tablespoons all-purpose flour

2 teaspoons instant coffee granules

2 tablespoons coffee liqueur

1 cup water

1. Add the chocolate chips, cocoa, salt, and 2 tablespoons butter to a microwave-safe bowl. Microwave on high for 1 minute; stir well. Microwave in additional 20-second segments if necessary, until the butter and chocolate are melted. Set aside to cool.

2. Add the egg whites to a medium-sized mixing bowl. Whisk or beat with a mixer until the egg whites are foamy. Gradually add ¼ cup of sugar, continuing to whisk or beat until soft peaks form; set aside.

3. Add the egg yolks and vanilla to a mixing bowl; use a whisk or handheld mixer to beat until the yolks are light yellow and begin to stiffen. Stir in the cooled chocolate mixture, pecans, flour, instant coffee, and coffee liqueur.

4. Transfer a third of the beaten egg whites to the chocolate mixture; stir to loosen the batter. Gently fold in the remaining egg whites.

5. Treat the bottom and sides of a 1-quart metal pan with 2 teaspoons of the remaining butter. Add about a tablespoon of sugar to the pan; shake and roll to coat the buttered pan with the sugar.

6. Dump out and discard any extra sugar. Transfer the chocolate batter to the buttered pan.

7. Treat one side of a 15" piece of aluminum foil with the remaining teaspoon of butter. Place the foil butter-side down over the top of the pan; crimp around the edges of the pan to form a seal.

8. Pour the water into the pressure cooker. Place the rack in the cooker. Create handles to use later to remove the pan by crisscrossing long, doubled strips of foil over the rack.

Continued on the next page

9. Place the metal pan in the center of the rack over the foil strips. Lock the lid into place and bring to low pressure; maintain pressure for 20 minutes.

10. Remove pressure cooker from heat, quick-release pressure, and remove the lid. Lift the pan out of the pressure cooker and place on a wire rack. Remove foil cover.

11. Let rest for 10–15 minutes. To serve, either spoon from the pan or run a knife around the edge of the pan, place a serving plate over the metal pan, and invert to transfer the cake.

Vegan Chocolate Chips
Some popular brands of chocolate chips are "accidentally vegan." Check the label of grocery store brands to find a vegan option or order them online.

PEANUT BUTTER AND FUDGE CHEESECAKE

Adults and kids alike love peanut butter and chocolate, so this dessert will be a hit with everyone.

INGREDIENTS
Serves 8

1 cup toasted, unsalted peanuts

½ cup vanilla wafers

1 tablespoon cocoa powder

3 tablespoons butter, melted, or vegan margarine, such as Earth Balance

1 cup peanut butter

2 8-ounce packages cream cheese, softened, or vegan cream cheese

½ cup light brown sugar, packed

½ cup powdered sugar, sifted

2 tablespoons cornstarch

2 large eggs, or 2 ounces silken tofu

¼ cup sour cream, or soy sour cream

1 12-ounce package semisweet chocolate chips

2 cups water

1. Add the peanuts, vanilla wafers, and cocoa to a food processor. Pulse to grind the peanuts and turn the vanilla wafers into crumbs. Add the butter. Pulse to mix.

2. Press into the bottom of a 7" springform pan. Set aside. Wipe out the food processor.

3. Add the peanut butter, cream cheese, and brown sugar to the food processor. Process until smooth.

4. Add the powdered sugar and cornstarch to a small bowl; stir to mix well. Add to the food processor with the eggs and sour cream. Process until smooth.

5. Remove the lid and stir in the chocolate chips. Transfer the batter to the springform pan.

   Wrap the base of the springform pan with heavy-duty aluminum foil. Tear off a 25"-long piece of heavy-duty aluminum foil and treat one side of one 8" end of the foil with nonstick spray. Place the nonstick spray-treated side of the foil over the top of the springform pan and then wrap the remaining foil under and then over the pan again; crimp to seal.

6. Pour the water and place the rack into the pressure cooker. Crisscross long, doubled strips of foil over the rack to create handles to use later to remove the pan.

7. Place the springform pan on the rack over the foil strips. Lock the lid into place and bring to high pressure; maintain pressure for 22 minutes.

8. Remove from heat and allow pressure to release naturally. Remove the lid. Lift the pan from the pressure cooker and place it on a wire rack. Allow to cool slightly. Refrigerate at least 4 hours before serving.

SPICED CHOCOLATE CAKE

Serve with icing, powdered sugar, or ice cream on top.

INGREDIENTS
Serves 10–12

1½ cups all-purpose flour

4 tablespoons cocoa powder

1 teaspoon cinnamon

1 teaspoon cayenne pepper

1 teaspoon sugar

¼ teaspoon salt

1 teaspoon baking powder

2 eggs, beaten, or 2 mashed bananas

4 tablespoons butter, melted, or vegan margarine, such as Earth Balance

1 cup milk, or soymilk

2 cups hot water

1. In a medium bowl, mix the flour, cocoa powder, cinnamon, cayenne, sugar, salt, and baking powder. In a large bowl, beat the eggs. Add the dry ingredients or mash the bananas. Slowly stir in the melted butter and the milk. Pour the cake mixture into an 8" round pan.

2. Add the steaming rack to the pressure cooker and pour in the hot water. Place the cake in the pressure cooker and lock the lid into place. Bring to high pressure, then reduce to low and cook for 30 minutes.

3. Remove the pressure cooker from the heat, quick-release the steam, and carefully remove the cake.

BANANA CREAM CUSTARD

Dark rum bumps up the flavor of this recipe, making it a rich, delicious way to use up ripe bananas. Think of this dessert as like a banana eggnog pudding.

INGREDIENTS
Serves 6

Butter

2 slices bread, crusts removed

2 ripe bananas

2 tablespoons fresh lemon juice

1 cup heavy cream

2 large eggs

½ cup dark brown sugar, packed

1 teaspoon ground nutmeg

2 tablespoons dark rum

1 tablespoon vanilla

1 cup water

1. Butter the inside of a 5-cup casserole dish that will fit inside the pressure cooker on the rack; set aside. Add the bread to a blender or food processor; pulse to create soft bread crumbs. Remove and set aside.

2. Add the bananas and lemon juice to the blender or food processor; pureé while gradually adding in the cream. Add the eggs; pulse to mix.

3. Add the brown sugar, nutmeg, rum, and vanilla; pulse until mixed. Stir in the reserved bread crumbs.

4. Pour the banana mixture into the prepared casserole dish. Cover and wrap tightly in aluminum foil.

5. Pour the water into the pressure cooker. Place the rack in the cooker. Set the foil-covered casserole dish on the rack. Lock the lid into place and bring to low pressure; maintain pressure for 22 minutes. Remove from the heat and allow pressure to release naturally.

6. Transfer the casserole dish to a cooking rack and remove the foil. Serve warm or chilled.

COCONUT CUSTARD

This dessert is delicious as is, but it's also great when combined with other flavors, too. You can serve it topped with some hot fudge or with fresh fruit.

INGREDIENTS
Serves 8

1 cup milk

1 14-ounce can coconut milk

1 10-ounce can sweetened condensed milk

½ teaspoon vanilla

3 eggs

3 egg yolks

2 cups water

1. Add the milk, coconut milk, and sweetened condensed milk to a saucepan. Heat it over medium heat until it's steaming and begins to reach a low boil.

2. Stir in the vanilla. In a separate bowl whisk the eggs together with the egg yolks.

3. Whisk a couple of tablespoons of the milk mixture into the eggs and then stir the eggs into the milk mixture.

4. Reduce heat to low; cook and stir for 4 minutes or until the mixture begins to thicken.

5. Treat a 6-cup soufflé dish with nonstick spray. Pour the heated custard into the treated dish.

6. Cover the dish with a piece of heavy-duty aluminum foil; crimp the edges to form a seal around the dish.

7. Pour the water and place the rack into the pressure cooker. Crisscross long, doubled strips of foil over the rack to create handles to use later to remove the pan.

8. Place the pan on the rack over the foil strips. Lock the lid into place and bring to high pressure; maintain pressure for 30 minutes.

9. Remove from heat and allow pressure to release naturally for 30 minutes. Quick-release any remaining pressure. Remove the lid.

10. Lift the pan from the pressure cooker and place it on a cooling rack. Once the custard has cooled, remove the foil.

11. Use a paper towel to dab any moisture that may have formed on the surface of the custard. Cover the dish with plastic wrap and refrigerate until ready to serve.

LEMON CUSTARD

You can also prepare the lemon custard by fixing it in a 5-cup heatproof casserole dish that will fit on the rack inside the pressure cooker. Increase the pressure time to 20 minutes. Serve these custards dusted with powdered sugar or topped with fresh or cooked fruit.

INGREDIENTS

Serves 6

½ cup sugar

1 tablespoon cornstarch

2 large eggs

2 egg yolks

1½ cups milk

1 cup heavy cream

2 medium lemons

2 cups water

1. Add the sugar and cornstarch to a bowl. Stir to combine well. Whisk in the eggs and egg yolks. Stir in the milk and cream. Grate the zest from one of the lemons and add it to the batter along with the juice from both lemons (about ¼ cup). Evenly divide between six ½-cup custard cups. Tightly cover the top of each custard cup with aluminum foil to prevent any water from getting into the cups.

2. Set the rack in the bottom of the pressure cooker and pour in the water. Place the custard cups on the rack, stacking them if you need to.

3. Lock the lid into place and bring to high pressure; maintain pressure for 12 minutes. Remove the pressure cooker from the heat, quick-release the pressure, and remove the lid.

4. Carefully lift the custard cups from the pressure cooker and place them on a wire rack. Remove the foil.

5. Let custard cool to room temperature. Once cooled, cover each cup with plastic wrap and chill overnight in refrigerator.

CHOCOLATE-BERRY BREAD PUDDING

You can somewhat cut the fat in Chocolate-Berry Bread Pudding by replacing the milk and cream with skim or 2% milk, but add one more egg to the batter if you do.

INGREDIENTS
Serves 6

6 slices day-old challah or brioche, or vegan white bread

½ cup raspberry preserves

½ cup dried strawberries or prunes, diced

½ cup hazelnuts, chopped

½ cup cocoa powder

½ cup sugar

Pinch salt

2 tablespoons butter, melted, or vegan margarine, such as Earth Balance

3 large eggs, or 2 mashed bananas

2 cups whole milk, or 2 cups soymilk

2 cups heavy cream, or 2 cups soymilk

1 tablespoon vanilla

1 cup water

1. If the crusts on the bread are dark, remove them. If using fresh bread, lightly toast it. Spread raspberry preserves over the bread. Treat a 5-cup heatproof soufflé dish with nonstick spray.

2. Tear the bread into chunks. Layer half the bread in the bottom of the soufflé dish. Sprinkle with dried fruit and chopped hazelnuts. Add remaining bread with preserves.

3. Whisk the cocoa, sugar, and salt together. Add butter and eggs; whisk to mix. Whisk in milk, cream, and vanilla. Pour half the cocoa mixture over the bread. Tap down the dish and wait several minutes for the bread to absorb the liquid. Pour in remaining cocoa mixture.

4. Tear off 2 large pieces of heavy-duty aluminum foil. Lay one piece of the foil over the top of the dish, crimping it slightly around the edges, and wrap it around the dish, folding it and tucking it under. Set the dish in the middle of the remaining piece of foil; bring it up and over the top of the dish and crimp to seal.

5. Pour water into the pressure cooker and add the rack. Crisscross 2 long doubled pieces of foil over the rack to help you lift the dish out of the pressure cooker later. Place the covered soufflé dish over the crossed foil strips on the rack.

6. Lock lid into place and bring to high pressure; maintain for 15 minutes. Remove from heat and allow pressure to release naturally.

7. Remove the dish from the pressure cooker, remove the foil, and place on a rack until ready to serve or until it's cool enough to cover and refrigerate.

CREAMY COCONUT RICE PUDDING

Garnish this pudding with a sprinkling of ground cinnamon and serve with a dollop of whipped cream or soy whip.

INGREDIENTS

Serves 6

1½ cups Arborio rice, rinsed and drained

2 cups whole milk or soymilk

1 14-ounce can coconut milk

1 cup water

½ cup sugar

2 teaspoons ground cinnamon

½ teaspoon salt

1½ teaspoons vanilla

1 cup dried cherries, dried strawberries, or golden raisins

1. Add the rice, milk, coconut milk, water, sugar, cinnamon, and salt to the pressure cooker. Cook and stir to dissolve the sugar over medium-high heat and bring to a boil. Lock the lid into place and bring to low pressure; maintain for 15 minutes.

2. Turn off the heat, quick-release the pressure, and remove the lid. Stir in the vanilla and dried fruit. Replace the cover, but do not lock into place. Let stand for 15 minutes. Stir and serve.

DATE PUDDING ☙

This is a rich, decadent dessert in the tradition of an English sticky toffee pudding.

INGREDIENTS
Serves 8

2½ cups dates, pitted and snipped

1½ teaspoons baking soda

1⅔ cups boiling water

2 cups dark brown sugar, packed

½ cup butter, softened, or vegan margarine, such as Earth Balance

3 large eggs, or 3 ounces firm tofu

2 teaspoons vanilla

3½ cups all-purpose or cake flour

4 teaspoons baking powder

Pinch salt

2 cups water

1. Add the dates to a mixing bowl and toss them together with the baking soda. Pour the boiling water over the dates. Set aside.

2. Add the brown sugar and butter to a food processor. Process to cream them together, and then continue to process while you add the eggs and vanilla.

3. Use a spatula to scrape the brown sugar mixture into the bowl with the dates. Stir to mix.

4. Add the flour, baking powder, and salt to a bowl; stir to mix. Fold into the date and brown sugar mixture.

5. Wrap the base of a 7" or 8" springform pan with heavy-duty aluminum foil. Treat the pan with nonstick spray.

6. Press the batter into the springform pan. Tear off a 25"-long piece of heavy-duty aluminum foil and treat one side of one 8" end of the foil with nonstick spray. Place the treated side of the foil over the top of the springform pan and then wrap the remaining foil under and then over the pan again; crimp to seal.

7. Pour the water and place the rack into the pressure cooker. Crisscross long, doubled strips of foil over the rack to create handles to use later to remove the pan.

8. Place the springform pan on the rack over the foil strips. Lock the lid into place and bring to low pressure; maintain pressure for 50 minutes.

9. Remove from heat and allow pressure to release naturally. Remove the lid. Lift the pan from the pressure cooker and place it on a cooling rack.

PIÑA COLADA BREAD PUDDING

If desired, you can add 1 tablespoon butter and 2 tablespoons brown sugar to the juice drained from the pineapple. Simmer and stir over medium-low heat until it thickens, and then serve over the bread pudding.

INGREDIENTS
Serves 8

1 16-ounce can cream of coconut

1 cup heavy cream, or soymilk

3 large eggs, or 3 ounces silken tofu

½ cup butter, melted, or vegan margarine, such as Earth Balance

¾ cup sugar

1½ teaspoons rum flavoring

¼ teaspoon ground nutmeg

1 20-ounce can pineapple chunks, drained

1¼ cups coconut

8 cups French bread, torn into 2" cubes

1½ cups water

1. Add the cream of coconut, cream, eggs, butter, sugar, rum flavoring, and nutmeg to a large bowl. Whisk to mix thoroughly. Stir in the drained pineapple and coconut. Fold in the bread cubes.

2. Treat a 5-cup soufflé dish with nonstick spray. Transfer the bread pudding mixture into the dish. Pour in the water and place the rack into the pressure cooker.

3. Crisscross long, doubled strips of foil over the rack to create handles to use later to remove the pan.

4. Treat one side of a 15"-square piece of heavy-duty aluminum foil with nonstick spray. Lay the foil, treated-side down, over the soufflé dish and crimp the edges to seal.

5. Tear off another piece of heavy-duty foil to completely wrap the soufflé dish to ensure the seal. Place over the crisscrossed pieces of foil.

6. Lock the lid into place and bring to high pressure; maintain pressure for 12 minutes. Remove pressure cooker from heat, quick-release pressure, and remove lid.

7. Remove pan from the pressure cooker, uncover, and place on a wire rack to cool. Serve warm, at room temperature, or chilled.

PLUM PUDDING WITH BRANDY SAUCE

This traditional steamed Christmas pudding can be made up to a month in advance if you refrigerate it in a brandy-soaked cheesecloth in a covered container. If made ahead, steam it or heat it gently in the microwave before serving it with the brandy sauce.

INGREDIENTS
Serves 10

1 cup prunes, snipped

1 cup dried currants

1 cup dried cranberries

1 cup raisins

1 cup candied lemon peel, minced

½ cup dark rum

1 cup butter, partially frozen, or vegan margarine, such as Earth Balance

1½ cups all-purpose flour

1 cup dried bread crumbs

½ cup pecans, chopped

1 tablespoon candied ginger, minced

1 teaspoon baking soda

½ teaspoon salt

1 teaspoon ground cinnamon

¼ teaspoon ground nutmeg

¼ teaspoon ground cloves

3 eggs, or 3 ounces silken tofu

2 cups light brown sugar, packed

3 cups water

1 cup heavy cream, or soymilk

¼ cup brandy

1. Add the prunes, currants, cranberries, raisins, candied lemon peel, and rum to a bowl. Stir to mix. Cover and let stand at room temperature for 8 hours.

2. Partially freeze ¾ cup butter. Add the flour, bread crumbs, pecans, ginger, baking soda, salt, cinnamon, nutmeg, and cloves to a large mixing bowl. Stir to mix.

3. Grate the butter into the flour mixture. Add the marinated fruit. Toss grated butter and fruit into flour mixture. Add eggs and 1 cup brown sugar to a separate bowl; whisk to mix. Pour into the flour mixture. Combine the mixtures together.

4. Wrap the base of a 7" or 8" springform pan with aluminum foil.

5. Transfer the batter to the springform pan, pressing it down into the pan to eliminate any air pockets.

6. Tear off a 25"-long piece of aluminum foil and treat one side of one 8" end of the foil with nonstick spray. Place the nonstick spray-treated side over the top of the pan and then wrap the remaining foil under and over the pan again; crimp to seal.

7. Pour the water and place the rack into the pressure cooker. Crisscross long doubled strips of foil over the rack to create handles to use later to remove the pan.

8. Place springform pan on rack, over foil strips. Lock lid into place and bring to high pressure; maintain for 1 hour.

9. Remove from heat and allow pressure to release naturally. Remove lid. Lift pan from the pressure cooker and cool. Remove foil cover.

10. Let rest and cool for 15 minutes, then run a knife around the edge of the pudding to loosen it from the sides of the pan. Unmold the pudding and transfer it to a plate.

11. For the brandy sauce, add remaining cup of brown sugar, cream, and ¼ cup butter to a saucepan placed over medium-high heat. Simmer and stir until sugar dissolves; stir in brandy. Simmer and stir for 10 minutes. Serve over the warm pudding.

TAPIOCA PUDDING

Add another dimension to this dish by combining it with other flavors. You can stir in some toasted pecans, chocolate chips, or coconut.

INGREDIENTS
Serves 4

½ cup small pearl tapioca

1¾ cups water

⅓ cup sugar

1 tablespoon butter, or vegan margarine, such as Earth Balance

2 large eggs or 2 ounces firm tofu

⅛ teaspoon salt

1½ cups milk, or soymilk

1 cup heavy cream, or soymilk

1 teaspoon vanilla

1. Combine the tapioca and ¾ cup water in a small bowl; cover and let soak overnight.

2. Add the sugar, butter, eggs, and salt to a bowl; beat until smooth. Stir in the milk, cream, and vanilla. Drain the tapioca and stir into the milk mixture.

3. Treat a 1-quart stainless steel bowl with nonstick spray. Pour the tapioca mixture into the bowl. Cover the bowl tightly with heavy-duty aluminum foil.

4. Pour the remaining cup of water into the pressure cooker and add the rack. Crisscross long, doubled strips of foil over the rack to create handles to use later to remove the pan. Center the covered pan holding the tapioca mixture on the foil strips on the rack.

5. Lock the lid into place and bring to low pressure; maintain pressure for 12 minutes. Remove the pressure cooker from the heat, quick-release the pressure, and remove the lid.

6. Lift the pudding out of the pressure cooker. Let rest for 15 minutes and then remove the foil cover. Stir. Taste for flavor and add more vanilla if desired. Chill until ready to serve.

APPLE BUTTER 🌿

Serve on toast or as a sandwich spread.

INGREDIENTS
Yields about 2 cups

1 cup apple juice or cider

12 medium apples (about 3 pounds)

1½ teaspoons ground cinnamon

½ teaspoon ground allspice

⅛ teaspoon ground cloves

1½ cups sugar

Optional: 1 or 2 drops oil of cinnamon

1. Add the apple juice or cider to the pressure cooker. Wash, peel, core, and dice the apples. Lock the lid into place, bring to high pressure, and immediately remove from heat; let the pressure release naturally for 10 minutes. Quick-release any remaining pressure.

2. Press cooled apples through a fine sieve or food mill, or process in a food processor or blender. Return apples and liquids to pressure cooker, add the cinnamon, allspice, cloves, sugar, and oil of cinnamon, if using.

3. Return the pan to medium heat and bring to a simmer. Simmer uncovered and stir until the sugar is dissolved. Reduce heat, simmer, and stir for 1 hour. Note that it's important that you frequently stir the apple butter from the bottom of the pan to prevent it from burning.

BASIC UNSWEETENED APPLESAUCE

There's no need to core the apples to remove the seeds when you'll be using a food mill to process the cooked apples.

INGREDIENTS
Yields 5 cups

1 cup water

12 medium apples (about 3 pounds)

1. Add the water to the pressure cooker. If using organic apples, rinse and quarter the apples. If not, rinse, peel, and quarter the apples. Add to the pressure cooker.

2. Lock the lid into place, bring to high pressure, and immediately remove from the heat; let the pressure release naturally for 10 minutes. Quick-release any remaining pressure.

3. Once the apples have cooled slightly, pass the apples and cooking liquid through a food mill. If you do not have a food mill, add the apples and cooking liquid in batches to a food processor or blender. Refrigerate covered for up to 10 days or freeze for up to 4 months.

CRANBERRY APPLESAUCE

Make sure that the ingredients don't go above the halfway mark on the pressure cooker.

INGREDIENTS
Serves 8

4 medium tart apples

4 medium sweet apples

1 cup cranberries

Zest and juice from 1 large orange

½ cup dark brown sugar

½ cup granulated cane sugar

1 tablespoon unsalted butter, or vegan margarine, such as Earth Balance

2 teaspoons ground cinnamon

½ teaspoon ground cloves

¼ teaspoon freshly ground black pepper

⅛ teaspoon salt

1 tablespoon fresh lemon juice

1. Peel, core, and grate the apples. Wash the cranberries. Add the cranberries to the pressure cooker and top with grated apples. Add the remaining ingredients.

2. Lock the lid into place and bring to low pressure; maintain pressure for 5 minutes. Remove from heat and allow pressure to release naturally. Remove the lid; lightly mash the apples with a fork. Stir well. Serve warm or chilled.

DRIED FRUIT COMPOTE

If you plan to add sugar to the dried fruit compote, do so before the fruit has cooled so that it can be stirred into the fruit mixture until it dissolves.

INGREDIENTS

Serves 6

1 8-ounce package dried apricots

1 8-ounce package dried peaches

1 cup golden raisins

1½ cups orange juice

1 cinnamon stick

4 whole cloves

Optional: Sugar

1. Cut the dried apricots and peaches into quarters and add them to the pressure cooker along with the raisins, orange juice, cinnamon stick, and cloves. Lock the lid into place and bring to high pressure; maintain pressure for 3 minutes. Remove from heat and allow pressure to release naturally. Remove the lid.

2. Remove the cinnamon stick and cloves. Return to medium heat and simmer for several minutes. Serve warm or allow to cool, then add sugar to taste, if using. Cover and store in the refrigerator until needed, up to 1 week.

FRUIT COMPOTE

Serve as a topping for plain or soy yogurt.

INGREDIENTS

Serves 6

1 cup apple juice

1 cup dry white wine

2 tablespoons sugar

1 cinnamon stick

¼ teaspoon ground nutmeg

Zest of 1 lemon

Zest of 1 orange

3 apples

3 pears

½ cup dried cherries, cranberries, or raisins

1. Add the apple juice and wine to the pressure cooker over medium-high heat. Bring to a boil. Stir in the sugar until dissolved. Add the cinnamon stick, nutmeg, lemon zest, and orange zest. Reduce heat to maintain a simmer.

2. Wash, peel, core, and chop the apples and pears. Add to the pressure cooker. Stir. Lock the lid into place and bring to high pressure; maintain pressure for 1 minute. Remove the pressure cooker from heat, quick-release the pressure, and remove the lid.

3. Use a slotted spoon to transfer the cooked fruit to a serving bowl. Return the pressure cooker to the heat and bring to a boil; boil and stir until reduced to a syrup that will coat the back of a spoon. Stir the dried cherries, cranberries, or raisins in with the cooked fruit in the bowl and pour the syrup over the fruit mixture. Stir to mix. Allow to cool slightly, then cover with plastic wrap and chill overnight in the refrigerator.

LEMON CURD

This tart lemon dish is most commonly spread on toast. It can also be used to fill baked tart shells.

INGREDIENTS
Serves 6

1⅓ cups sugar

3 large eggs

1 egg yolk

¼ cup butter, softened

¼ cup fresh lemon juice

1 teaspoon lemon zest, grated

2 cups water

1. Add the sugar to a blender or food processor. Process to create superfine sugar. Add the eggs, egg yolk, butter, lemon juice, and lemon zest. Process until well-mixed.

2. Prepare a 3-cup heatproof casserole dish that will sit on the rack of the pressure cooker by treating it with nonstick spray or coating the inside with butter. Strain the mixture from the blender or food processor into the dish. Cover tightly with aluminum foil.

3. Pour the water into the pressure cooker and insert the rack. Place the foil-covered casserole dish on the rack. Lock the lid into place and bring to low pressure; maintain pressure for 18 minutes. Remove the pressure cooker from the heat, quick-release the pressure, and remove the lid. Remove the casserole dish and place it on a wire rack.

4. Remove the foil from the casserole dish, being careful not to get any moisture clinging to the foil into the lemon curd. Use a small whisk or a fork to whisk the lemon curd.

5. The lemon curd can be served warm, but it will be somewhat runny. Cool, and then refrigerate covered for at least 4 hours to thicken the curd.

Lemon Brunch Croissant

For each croissant, mix ½ teaspoon powdered sugar into 1 tablespoon cream cheese. Split a croissant and spread the sweetened cream cheese inside. Spoon some lemon curd to taste over the sweetened cream cheese. Fold the top of the croissant over the fillings. Serve.

PEARS POACHED IN WINE

Use Bartlett, Anjou, or Bosc pears. If you prefer, replace the cinnamon stick, ginger, and orange zest with a whole split and scraped vanilla bean.

INGREDIENTS
Serves 4

4 ripe, but still firm pears

2 tablespoons fresh lemon juice

1¼ cups dry wine

½ cup sweet sherry

¼ cup sugar

3" cinnamon stick, halved

¼ teaspoon ground ginger

2 teaspoons orange zest, grated

1. Rinse and peel the pears and cut them in half. Use a spoon or melon baller to remove the cores. Brush the pears with the lemon juice.

2. Combine the wine, sherry, sugar, cinnamon, ginger, and orange zest in the pressure cooker. Bring to a boil; stir to blend and dissolve the sugar. Carefully place the pears cut-side down in the pressure cooker. Lock the lid into place and bring to low pressure; maintain pressure for 3 minutes. Remove the pressure cooker from the heat, quick-release the pressure, and remove the lid.

3. Use a slotted spoon to transfer the pears to a serving bowl or to place them on dessert plates. If desired, return the pressure cooker to medium heat and simmer uncovered for several minutes to thicken the sauce. Remove and discard the cinnamon stick pieces. Spoon the sauce over the pears. Serve.

PORT-POACHED FIGS

Serve the figs on top of soy ice cream—or simply on their own—with the syrup.

INGREDIENTS
Serves 4

3 cups tawny port

1½ cups sugar

1 vanilla bean, split and scraped

½ teaspoon cinnamon

¼ cup orange juice

8 whole black peppercorns

12 dried black mission figs

1. Combine the port, sugar, vanilla pods and seeds, cinnamon, orange juice, and peppercorns in the pressure cooker over high heat. Bring to a boil and reduce the heat. Simmer for 20 minutes.

2. Add the figs. Lock the lid into place and bring to high pressure; maintain pressure for 6 minutes. Remove from the heat and allow pressure to release naturally.

SPECIAL OCCASION CHUNKY APPLESAUCE

To sweeten the applesauce, stir in sugar or maple syrup, to taste, after you remove the lid from the pressure cooker.

INGREDIENTS
Serves 6

8 Granny Smith apples

1 cup apple juice or cider

2 tablespoons fresh lemon juice

¼ cup sugar

⅓ cup light brown sugar, packed

½ teaspoon ground nutmeg

¼ teaspoon ground cinnamon

⅓ cup cinnamon hearts candy

1. Rinse, peel, core, and dice the apples. Add to the pressure cooker with apple juice or cider, lemon juice, sugar, brown sugar, nutmeg, and cinnamon. Stir well. Lock the lid into place and bring to low pressure; maintain for 4 minutes. Remove from heat and allow pressure to release naturally for 10 minutes.

2. Quick-release any remaining pressure. Stir in the candy until it's melted and blended into the sauce, mashing the apples slightly as you do so. Serve warm or chilled. Can be stored for several days in the refrigerator.

SPICED PEACHES 🌱

To make spiced peach butter, after Step 2, process the peaches and liquid in a blender or food processor until smooth and return to the pressure cooker. Simmer and stir over low heat for 30 minutes or until thickened enough to coat the back of a spoon.

INGREDIENTS
Serves 6

2 15-ounce cans sliced peaches in syrup

¼ cup water

1 tablespoon white wine vinegar

⅛ teaspoon ground allspice

1 cinnamon stick

4 whole cloves

½ teaspoon ground ginger

Pinch cayenne pepper

Optional: 1 tablespoon candied ginger, minced

Optional: 3 whole black peppercorns

1. Add all of the ingredients to the pressure cooker. Stir to mix. Lock the lid into place and bring to low pressure; maintain pressure for 3 minutes. Remove the pressure cooker from the heat, quick-release the pressure, and remove the lid.

2. Remove and discard the cinnamon stick, cloves, and peppercorns if used.

3. Return the pressure cooker to medium heat. Simmer and stir for 5 minutes to thicken the syrup.

4. Serve warm or chilled. To store, allow to cool and then refrigerate for up to a week.

STEAMED PEARS

Select firm pears for this dish. The pears taste good warm or chilled. Dust with cinnamon and sugar for some extra spice and sweetness.

INGREDIENTS
Serves 4

4 pears

1 lemon

½ cup water

1. Rinse and dry the pears. Halve them lengthwise. Use a melon baller to remove the core from each half. Cut the lemon in half and rub the cut end of the lemon over the cut ends of the pears or brush the pear halves with fresh lemon juice.

2. Add the water to the pressure cooker. Place the rack in the pressure cooker and place a heatproof plate onto the rack. Arrange the pears on the plate. Lock the lid into place and bring to high pressure; maintain pressure for 4 minutes. Remove the pressure cooker from the heat, quick-release the pressure, and remove the lid. Use a slotted spoon to carefully transfer the pears to a serving plate. Serve warm or allow to cool slightly and then cover the plate and refrigerate until needed.

STUFFED APPLES

You can replace the sugar with maple syrup or brown sugar if desired. Serve as dessert, with a scoop of vanilla ice cream or soy ice cream.

INGREDIENTS
Serves 4

½ cup apple juice

¼ cup golden raisins

¼ cup walnuts, toasted and chopped

2 tablespoons sugar

½ teaspoon grated orange rind

½ teaspoon ground cinnamon

4 cooking apples

4 teaspoons butter, or vegan margarine, such as Earth Balance

1 cup water

1. Put the apple juice in a microwave-safe container; heat for 1 minute on high or until steaming and hot. Pour over the raisins. Soak the raisins for 30 minutes. Drain, reserving the apple juice. Add the nuts, sugar, orange rind, and cinnamon to the raisins and stir to mix.

2. Rinse and dry the apples. Cut off the top fourth of each apple. Peel the cut portion and chop it, then stir the diced apple pieces into the raisin mixture. Hollow out and core the apples by cutting to, but not through, the apple bottoms.

3. Place each apple on a piece of aluminum foil that is large enough to wrap the apple completely. Fill the apple centers with the raisin mixture.

4. Top each with a teaspoon of the butter. Wrap the foil around each apple, folding the foil over at the top and then pinching it firmly together.

5. Pour the water into the pressure cooker. Place the rack in the cooker. Place the apples on the rack. Lock the lid into place and bring to high pressure; maintain pressure for 10 minutes.

6. Remove pressure cooker from heat, quick-release the pressure, and remove the lid. Carefully lift the apples out of the pressure cooker. Unwrap and transfer to serving plates. Serve hot, at room temperature, or chilled.

VANILLA-SPICE PEAR BUTTER

Bartlett pears are light green and are especially prevalent in the Pacific Northwest. Serve on scones or toasted English muffins.

INGREDIENTS
Yields about 2 cups

6 medium Bartlett pears

¼ cup dry white wine

1 tablespoon fresh lemon juice

¾ cup sugar

2 orange slices

1 lemon slice

2 whole cloves

1 vanilla bean, split lengthwise

1 cinnamon stick

¼ teaspoon ground cardamom

Pinch salt

1. Rinse, peel, and core the pears, and cut them into 1" dice. Add the pears, wine, and lemon juice to the pressure cooker. Lock the lid into place and bring to low pressure; maintain pressure for 8 minutes.

2. Remove from heat and allow pressure to release naturally for 10 minutes. Quick-release any remaining pressure and remove the lid. Transfer the fruit and juices to a blender or food processor and purée.

3. Return the purée to the pressure cooker. Add the sugar. Stir and cook over low heat until sugar dissolves. Stir in the remaining ingredients. Increase the heat to medium and boil gently, cooking and stirring for about 30 minutes or until mixture thickens and mounds slightly on a spoon.

4. Remove and discard the orange and lemon slices, cloves, and cinnamon stick. Remove the vanilla pod; use the back of a knife to scrape away any vanilla seeds still clinging to the pod and stir them into the pear butter. Cool and refrigerate covered for up to 10 days or freeze for up to 4 months.